DENIS THE CARTHUSIAN'S WORKS
ON THE EUCHARIST AND THE MASS

Devotio Deliciosa

Denis the Carthusian
on
The Eucharist & the Mass

Edited and translated by
ANDREW M. GREENWELL,
in collaboration with
GERHARD EGER *and* ZACHARY THOMAS

*With an Introduction to his
Life, Times, and Works by*
ELIZABETH G. G. SNELLER

First published in the USA
by Angelico Press 2026
Copyright © 2026

All rights reserved:
No part of this book may be reproduced
or transmitted, in any form or by
any means, without permission

For information, address:
Angelico Press, Ltd.
169 Monitor St.
Brooklyn, NY 11222
www.angelicopress.com

pb: 979-8-89280167-6
cloth: 979-8-89280168-3

Book and cover design
by Michael Schrauzer

To my wife, Betsy

Mulierem fortem quis inveniet?
Procul et de ultimis finibus pretium eius.
Confidit in ea cor viri sui,
et spoliis non indigebit.
—Proverbs 31:10–11

To Fr. Stephen Reid, FSSPX

Tu es sacerdos in aeternum
secundum ordinem Melchisedech.
—Ps. 109:4

*Id quod maioribus nostris sacrum erat,
nobis manet sacrum et grande.*

—BENEDICTUS PP. XVI, Epistola ad
Episcopos ad producendas Litteras
Apostolicas Motu Proprio datas, de Usu
Liturgiae Romanae Instaurationi anni
1970 praecedentis, AAS 99 (2007): 798

CONTENTS

Introduction to the Life, Times, and Works
of Denis the Carthusian
xi

Introduction to the Translation
xvii

Dialogue on the Sacrament
of the Altar and the Celebration of Mass
1

Exposition of the Mass
105

On Frequent Communion
195

Six Sermons
213

DOCTOR ECSTATICUS
An Introduction to the Life, Times, & Works of Denis the Carthusian

ELIZABETH G. G. SNELLER

> *Divinae gratiae humilitas semper est familiaris.*
> Humility is always the companion of divine grace.
> —Denis the Carthusian, *Vices and Virtues*, II, 22

IN 1402, A BOY NAMED DENIS DE LEEUWIS was born in the village of Rijkel. Rijkel is a little hamlet in the County of Hesbaye, in what is modern-day Belgium. Hesbaye, commonly called Hasbania in medieval Latin, sits nestled amidst rolling, fecund little hills near the meandering Maas river in the Province of Limburg. Denis would have spent his boyhood amongst fruit trees and flax fields, surrounded by the simple beauty of the verdant Flemish countryside. The abbey and fortified *oppidum* (town) of Sint-Truiden was but a few miles from Rijkel. The young Denis displayed an enviable discipline, a penchant for prayer, and a profound desire to learn at a very young age. A bright, energetic, and enthusiastic boy, Denis attended day school at Sint-Truiden where he showed above-par aptitude.

In 1415, when Denis was about thirteen years old, he left his family for the abbey boarding school at Zwolle in the Dutch province Overijssel. The school at Zwolle was an institution of immense prestige; it attracted promising young minds from Germany and the Low Countries. It was at Zwolle that Denis began the study of philosophy, which would capture his heart and mind. There, he also had his first contact with *Devotio Moderna* and became deeply familiar with the monastic life. During this time, he would have honed and perfected his Latin and would have begun to develop his writing style. Upon the death of teacher and rector John Cele in 1417, Denis returned home; albeit, not for long.

Denis displayed an affinity for the monastic life and discerned his vocation by the age of eighteen. He felt a strong attraction to the Carthusian order, and he applied for admittance to the monastery at Roermond. He was to be promptly denied entry due to his young age—he had to be at minimum twenty to embark on his journey as a Carthusian brother. However, the Prior[1] at Roermond did not want the young applicant to despair; he strongly advised Denis to cultivate his innate love of learning at the University of Cologne. In the ensuing two years, Denis threw himself into the study of theology and philosophy in Cologne until he matriculated. It was at Cologne that Denis began his study in the *via Thomae*, and Thomas Aquinas would remain his *Doctor ordinarius* throughout his long, prolific career,[2] even though Denis would come to oppose strongly some of Aquinas's most prominent views, such as the difference between *esse* and *essentia*, as early as 1430.[3] This later divergence from Thomistic Scholasticism follows the path taken by many of the Albertist thinkers, led by Heymerich van de Velde,[4] who populated the University of Cologne at the time of Denis's academic pursuits therein.[5]

In 1423 or 1424, Denis matriculated, earning his Master of Arts from Cologne.[6] He entered the charterhouse at Roermond with great expedience and excitement and devoted himself to the way of the Carthusians—a life of quiet thoughtful devotion and as deep an understanding of God as one can hope to achieve through contemplation and prayer. The Carthusian Rule required an existence steeped in silence and cloistered from the bustling secular world. Denis would partake in the conventual night office, the conventual Mass, and occasional recreation with his brothers, but devoted the

---

[1] Though Carthusians are monks, they do not have abbots; rather, each charterhouse is headed by a prior.
[2] Kent Emery Jr., "Cognitive Theory and the Relation Between the Scholastic and Mystical Modes of Theology: Why Denys the Carthusian Outlawed Durandus of Saint-Pourçain," in *Crossing Boundaries at Medieval Universities*, ed. Spencer E. Young (Leiden: Brill, 2011), 145-71.
[3] Ibid. Emery gives a brief sketch of Denis's life, peers, and studies at Cologne before delving deeply into his later stances in this article. It is interesting to note that Denis "incepted under the Master Guillelmus de Breda, with whom many years later he would engage in a bitter dispute about simony."
[4] Alessandro Palazzo, "Denis the Carthusian," in *Encyclopedia of Medieval Philosophy: Philosophy Between 500 and 1500*, ed. Henrik Lagerlund (London: Springer, 2011), 258-60.   [5] Emery, "Cognitive Theory," 145-46.
[6] Emery (ibid.) notes that Denis did not study theology at Cologne in the traditional sense, due to both his quick entry into Roermond and the habit of the secular masters at Cologne to teach philosophy via the *Summae* and commentaries on thirteenth-century thinkers such as Thomas and Albert, in the *viae antiquae*.

rest of his daily hours—those that remained after subtracting that time devoted to the hours of the Divine Office which were said privately by the monks in their cells—to what he considered to be the most important aspects of a life best-spent: "contemplation and action."[7] He divided his days into strict halves—the first half was to be spent in ecstatic, solitary prayer, the second half was to be devoted to his writing and studies. Denis's strict adherence to this most rigid of daily schedules is perhaps why he was the most prolific writer of the Middle Ages, churning out an estimated one-and-a-half times as many works as that most beloved, lauded, and productive Doctor of the Church, St. Augustine.[8] He reserved only three hours *per noctem* for rest. He would live the remainder of his life, save a few ventures outside the comforting confines of Roermond, in this fashion.

Despite the eremitic nature of the Carthusian *Statutes* which govern the monks' lives, Denis was not as isolated from his fellow man as it may initially seem. He engaged in spirited correspondence with many of his fellow late medieval thinkers, especially Nicolas of Cusa of the Cologne School,[9] to whom he dedicated some of his writings.[10] He was an avid and enthusiastic participant in the doctrinal disputes that were sparking the interests and ires of the late medieval academic world—both his personal behavior and his works included and embodied all of the spiritual concepts of the fifteenth century, including the works and philosophies of the scholastics, mysticism, the *Devotio Moderna*, reform, monastic theology, and *sermones ad saeculares*.[11] Due to the great breadth of topics broached by the busy Denis, one might rightfully dub him "the last omnicompetent theologian."[12] He was frequently asked for his opinion on a great variety of topics by individuals and by secular

---

[7] Terrence O'Reilly, Introduction in *The Spiritual Writings of Denis the Carthusian*, trans. Íde Ní Riain (Dublin: Four Courts Press, 2005), ix–xiv.
[8] Sixteenth-century bibliographers gave the number at four-to-one, but this is clearly overstated. Kent Emery Jr., "At the Outer Limits of Authenticity: Denys the Carthusian's Critique of Duns Scotus and His Followers," in *Philosophy and Theology in the Long Middle Ages: A Tribute to Stephen F. Brown*, ed. Kent Emery Jr., Russell Friedman, and Andreas Speer (Leiden: Brill, 2011), 641–71.
[9] Andrea Fiamma, "Nicholas of Cusa and the So-called Cologne School of the 13th and 14th Centuries," in *Archives d'histoire doctrinale et littéraire du Moyen Âge*, 2017/1 (84): 91–128. See this for further reading on Cusanus and his relationship to the Cologne School. [10] Palazzo, "Denis the Carthusian," 258.
[11] Kent Emery Jr., *Monastic, Scholastic and Mystical Theologies from the Later Middle Ages*, Variorum Collected Studies 561 (London: Ashgate, 1996).
[12] Denys Turner, "Why Did Denys the Carthusian Write *Sermones ad saeculares?*" in *Medieval Monastic Preaching*, ed. Carolyn Muessig (Leiden: Brill, 1998), 19–36; 20.

and ecclesiastical authorities. He was aware of the sufferings and maladies, both social and spiritual, that plagued the late medieval world, and this is reflected in his conservatism and deep desire for a return to holier times. After all, the motto of Denis's beloved Carthusian Order is *Stat crux dum volvitur orbis*.[13]

In the over one hundred and eighty works produced by Denis, there are clear influences and unifying themes. He drew his inspiration from the Vulgate, Thomas Aquinas, Aristotle, Albert the Great and the fifteenth century Albertists, and Henry of Ghent.[14] His corpus of works is guided by what he refers to as his three great enthusiasms: Scripture, Thomas Aquinas, and Dionysius the Pseudo-Areopagite.[15] He devised a threefold order of wisdom that a helped him to organize his writings: "natural wisdom naturally acquired," "supernatural wisdom naturally acquired," and "supernatural wisdom supernaturally bestowed."[16] *De Lumine Christianae Theoriae* was his first and most sweeping opus—a work where "he managed to deftly address all of the vital topics of his day, displaying a complete mastery of the doctrines of all the major ancient, Arabic, and Jewish philosophers."[17] Denis composed commentaries on the works of Peter Lombard; Boethius; his favorite, the Pseudo-Dionysius; and John Climacus. He wrote over nine hundred sermons. His commentary on the Vulgate earned papal praise while his many treaties, such as his *Summa Fidei Orthodoxae* and *Compendium Theologicum*, cemented his reputation as a theologian. His most applauded philosophical treatises include *De ente et essentia*, *Compendium philosophicum*, and *De venustate mundi et pulchritudine Dei*. The most recent compilation of his massive body of work spans forty-two hefty quarto volumes.[18]

This remarkable output was achieved within the confines of the hermitage in his Charterhouse, save the precious few excursions he made outside of its walls. This did lead to some conflict with the cenobitic community of Roermond. As an example of this we have an inquiry put forth by the Carthusians in 1446; and we know of

---

[13] "The Cross is steady as the world turns."
[14] Palazzo, "Denis the Carthusian," 258.   [15] O'Reilly, Introduction, x.
[16] Kent Emery Jr., "The Matter and Order of Philosophy According to Denys the Carthusian," in *Was ist Philosophie im Mittelalter? Akten des X. Internationalen Kongresses für Mittelalterliche Philosophie der Société Internationale pour l'Etude de la Philosophie Médiévale, 25. bis 30. August 1997 in Erfurt*, Miscellanea Mediaevalia 26, ed. Jan A. Aertsen and Andreas Speer (Berlin/New York: De Gruyter, 1998), 668.   [17] Palazzo, "Denis the Carthusian," 259.
[18] Forty-four if one includes the two index volumes.

this because of Denis's own response to the complaints made against him.[19] While some of his brothers did not think that his extraordinary devotion to his writing, scholarship, and discourse with secular and private persons demanded elucidation and defending, it seems that others within his order deemed his extreme prolifigacy incompatible with the demands of the Carthusian *Statutes*. Denis maintained that his writing was a necessary work of tremendous piety and discipline that actually bolstered his ability to adhere to the stillness of spirit, silence of voice, and seclusion of body required of him.[20] It may also be that the small Charterhouse could not afford the great expense of the materials Denis required for his academic and literary pursuits.[21] In August of 1451, it is believed that he and his peer Nicolas of Cusa embarked on a mission of Papal Legation across the Low Countries and into the Rhineland. Their mission was one of religious renewal and reform, crucial in those times teetering on the brink of the Renaissance.[22] They also cried for a crusade against the ever-encroaching Turks, to whom Constantinople would fall two short years later. Denis's world was one of great religious crisis, and his dogged adherence to tradition was reflective of the tumult and upheaval occurring in the medieval Church. He left Roermond again in 1465 for a brief sojourn to the Charterhouse at Vught—he had been assigned to aid in its foundation and course. His health, once happily robust, began its slow decline. In the last years of his life, he was wracked with chronic pain, the stone, and sporadic paralysis amongst other corporal ailments; he offered up his suffering to God with stoicism, quiet serenity, and valiant resolve. He died in 1471 at the age of sixty-nine.

For centuries after his death, his writings were essential reading for those who were serious students of philosophy and theology. So vital were they considered, in fact, that a common phrase uttered across academic circles at the time was: "He who reads Denis leaves nothing unread."[23] Given his sound doctrine and his heroically holy life, a case could clearly be made for his official beatification; none has yet come to fruition. He posthumously earned the title of "Doctor Ecstaticus" due to the ecstasies he experienced as a young monk. Hagiography has it that his writing fingers are incorrupt and that his skull emitted a pleasant aroma upon his exhumation in 1608.

---

[19] Denis the Carthusian, *Protestatio ad superiorem suum*, in *Opera omnia*, Tome 1, lxxi–lxxii.
[20] *Protestatio*, lxxii. *Fecit etiam libentius me manere in solitudine.*
[21] Turner, "*Sermones ad saeculares?*" 22.   [22] O'Reilly, Introduction, xi–xii.
[23] *Qui Dionysium legit, nihil non legit.*

BIBLIOGRAPHY AND FURTHER READING

Primary Sources
Doctor Ecstaticus D. Dionysius Cartusianus. *Opera omnia, cura et labore monachorum ordinis Cartusiensis*. 42 vols. in 44. Montreuil/Tournai/Parkminster: Typis Cartusiae S. M. de Pratis, 1896–1935.

Secondary Sources
Emery, Kent, Jr., "At the Outer Limits of Authenticity: Denys the Carthusian's Critique of Duns Scotus and His Followers." In *Philosophy and Theology in the Long Middle Ages: A Tribute to Stephen F. Brown*, edited by Kent Emery, Russell Friedman, Andreas Speer, 641–71. Leiden: Brill, 2011.

———. "Cognitive Theory and the Relation Between the Scholastic and Mystical Modes of Theology: Why Denys the Carthusian Outlawed Durandus of Saint-Pourçain." In *Crossing Boundaries at Medieval Universities*, edited by Spencer E. Young, 145–71. Leiden: Brill, 2011.

———. *Monastic, Scholastic and Mystical Theologies from the Later Middle Ages*. Variorum Collected Studies 561. London: Ashgate, 1996.

———. "The Matter and Order of Philosophy According to Denys the Carthusian." In *Was ist Philosophie im Mittelalter? Akten des X. Internationalen Kongresses für Mittelalterliche Philosophie der Société Internationale pour l'Etude de la Philosophie Médiévale, 25. bis 30. August 1997 in Erfurt*. Miscellanea Mediaevalia 26, edited by Jan A. Aertsen and Andreas Speer, 667–79. Berlin/New York: De Gruyter, 1998.

Fiamma, Andrea. "Nicholas of Cusa and the So-called Cologne School of the 13th and 14th Centuries." In *Archives d'histoire doctrinale et littéraire du Moyen Âge*, 2017/1 (84): 91–128.

Palazzo, Alessandro. "Denis the Carthusian." In *Encyclopedia of Medieval Philosophy: Philosophy Between 500 and 1500*, edited by Henrik Lagerlund, 258–60. London: Springer, 2011.

Turner, Denys. "Why Did Denys the Carthusian Write *Sermones ad Saeculares*?" In *Medieval Monastic Preaching*, edited by Carolyn Muessig, 19–36. Leiden: Brill, 1998.

INTRODUCTION
TO THE TRANSLATION

DENIS THE CARTHUSIAN: HIS WORK

NOT SO LONG AGO, DENIS THE CARTHUsian was a household name in the Catholic world, a theological authority of the highest rank blanketing Europe with more than one hundred and eighty works on myriad topics, all of which drew upon the patrimony of fourteen centuries of Christian wisdom, indeed reaching back further into pagan philosophers and some of their commentators.

Denis himself describes his absorption of the Christian intellectual and spiritual patrimony in preparation for his Scriptural commentaries in his "Protestation" to his religious Superior:

> I thank God from the bottom of my heart that I entered religion so young, being of the age of twenty-one. I have now remained in it by the grace of God forty-six years, during which I have been—God be praised—assiduous in study, and have read many authors: viz., on the *Sentences*, the works of Thomas, Albert, Alexander of Hales, Bonaventura, Peter of Tarentum, Giles, Richard of Middleton, Durandus, and others. And also books by saints: St. Jerome on all the Prophets, and many others of his volumes, Augustine, Ambrose, Gregory, Dionysius the Areopagite my favorite teacher (*doctoris mei electissime*), Origen, Gregory Nazianzen, Cyril, Basil, Chrysostom, the Damascene, Boethius, Anselm, Bernard, Bede, Hugh [of St. Victor], Gerson, William of Paris. Besides this, all the common *Summae* and *Chronicles*, all law as I needed, both canonical and civil, many commentaries on both Testaments, and all of the natural philosophers that I was able to get hold of: Plato, Proclus, Aristotle, Avicenna, Algazel, Anaxagoras, Averroës, Alexander, Alpharabius, Abubather, Evempote, Theophrastus, Themistius, and others. Truly, the more spiritually laborious this exercise and the more full of study and trouble, the more has it seemed to me to be salubrious, or the more fit for the mortification of the flesh and of carnal desires. And it also made me remain all the more willingly in solitude.[1]

---

[1] *Doctoris Ecstatici D. Dionysii Cartusiani Opera Omnia*, vol. 1 (Montreuil, 1896).

The Bollandists described Denis as "a brilliant man of great sanctity, sublime contemplation, copious erudition, marvelous genius, singular memory, and incomparable piety."[2] Pope Eugene IV (1383–1447) is said to have exclaimed upon reading one of his works: *Laetetur mater Ecclesiae, quae talem habet filium!*[3] In the sixteenth century, the prevalence of his theological shadow gave rise to a ditty: *Qui Dionysium legit, nihil non legit.*[4] Given his widespread reputation outside the Carthusian cloisters, he was an exception to the general rule *Cartusia sanctos facit, sed non patefacit.*[5] Everyone seemed to know Denis, though he but rarely ventured out of his Carthusian monastery.

Denis the Carthusian is what you get when you blend the rigorous scholasticism of St. Thomas Aquinas, the spiritual zeal and simplicity of Blessed John Ruusbroec,[6] and the high apophatic mysticism of Dionysius the Areopagite into a man of great genius and greater piety from the small town of Rijkel in the Principality of Liège,[7] then robe him with the rough, white habit of Carthusian silence, discipline, and asceticism, and finally place him in a cell at the Bethlehem Mariae Charterhouse in the town of Roermond in the Duchy of Guelders. He is a polished gem of the Catholic Faith.

As Johan Huizinga describes our Denis in his *The Autumn of the Middle Ages*:

> Denis the Carthusian is the perfect type of the powerful religious enthusiast produced by the waning Middle Ages. His life was incredibly energetic; he combined the ecstasies of the great mystics, the wildest asceticism, the continuous visions and revelations of a spiritual seer with a vast activity as a theological writer and practical spiritual adviser.... It is as if through him the entire stream of medieval theology flows once again.[8]

Although Denis is not formally a Doctor of the Church, he received the traditional title of *Doctor Ecstaticus*,[9] the Ecstatic Doctor—a clear reference to the ecstatic timbre of his writings, the

---

[2] *Acta Sanctorum* (Paris, 1865), vol. 8, XII Martii, 243.
[3] Ibid., 245. May Mother Church rejoice that she has such a son!
[4] He who reads Denis leaves nothing unread.
[5] Chartreuse makes saints, but does not make them known.
[6] Denis calls Ruusbroec his *alter Dionyius*.
[7] Currently, the province of Limburg, Belgium.
[8] Johan Huizinga, *The Autumn of the Middle Ages*, trans. R. J. Payton and Ulrich Mammitzsch (Chicago: University of Chicago Press, 1976), 218.
[9] A popular title Denis shares with the German mystic Meister Eckhart (ca. 1260–ca. 1328) and the Flemish mystic John of Ruusbroec (1293–1381).

heights of acquired and infused contemplative prayer he enjoyed, and the mystical states with which he was gifted. Similarly, although he is not formally a *beatus*, he is informally so regarded by the Bollandists, where a treatment of his life is found in their *Acta Sanctorum*.[10] Moreover, saints of the stature of St. Francis de Sales and St. Alphonsus Liguori refer to our Carthusian polymath as Blessed Denis.[11] "His life," John Cuthbert Hedley the Irish Benedictine bishop observed, "was that of a Saint; and we should wonder that he has not been canonised, were he not a Carthusian...[as] that Order has never shown any initiative in procuring this honour to its sons."[12]

Denis's published work is found in forty-four quarto volumes published by the Carthusians between 1898 and 1901 at Montreuil, between 1902 and 1913 at Tournai, and in 1925 at Parkminster.[13] One estimate puts Denis's output "about 25,000 pages—twice the number of pages written by Augustine of Hippo,"[14] who himself is considered one of the more prolific Catholic authors. St. Dominic is said to have spoken only of God or with God (*nonnisi cum Deo aut de Deo loquebatur*). This, of course, is what one would expect of a peripatetic friar dedicated to preaching. It would be unseemly to expect this of a Carthusian monk who applied himself to silence. We might, however, properly say of Blessed Denis that he *wrote* only of God or with God (*nonnis cum Deo aut de Deo ascribatur*). As one scholar summarized Denis's vast works:

> He wrote commentaries on every book of Scripture, on the *Sentences* of Peter Lombard, on Boethius' *Consolation of Philosophy*, and on all of the writings of Pseudo-Dionysius. He also composed works based closely on the teaching of Thomas Aquinas, a *Summa* of vices and virtues, over 900 model sermons, and scores of philosophical, theological, pastoral, and ecclesiastical treatises. In his writings, he

---

[10] *Acta Sanctorum*, vol. VIII (Paris, 1865), where he is described as "Venerable." He is given the day March 12, since he died on that date.

[11] St. Francis de Sales calls Denis "Blessed" in *Treatise on the Love of God*, trans. John K. Ryan (Stella Niagra: DeSales Resource Center 2010), vol. 1, 38, and St. Alphonsus Liguori calls him the same in his *Sermons for All the Sundays of the Year*, 5th ed. (Dublin: James Duffy, 1860), 128, 193.

[12] "Notices of Books," *The Dublin Review* (London: Burns & Oates 1897), vol. 121, p. 213.

[13] Krijn Pansters, "The Carthusians in the Low Countries: Introduction," *The Carthusian in the Low Countries: Studies in Monastic History and Heritage* (Leuven: Peeters, 2014), 12 and n. 3. Most of Denis's volumes are available online at: onlinebooks.library.upenn.edu/webbin/metabook?id=denisworks.

[14] *Biographical Dictionary of Christian Theologians*, eds. Patrick W. Carey and Joseph T. Lienhard (Westport: Greenwood Press, 2000), 155.

cites hundreds of authors, including many ancient, Jewish, and Arabic philosophers. His massive commentaries on the *Sentences*, wherein he recites and analyzes the arguments of numerous scholastic theologians, present a dialectical history of medieval thought.[15]

In more recent times, along with the irresponsible jettisoning of so much of the Church's dear intellectual, religious, spiritual, and liturgical patrimony, Denis the Carthusian's popularity has certainly waned. As Professor Terence O'Reilly expressed this Dionysian fall *de cognito ad incognitum*:

> Four hundred years ago the name of Denis the Carthusian was one that most educated people knew, and his writings were cited by scholars throughout Europe. But who, beyond the confines of his order, reads him now? Most educated people have never heard of him, and although his works may be found in older libraries, few are the scholars who consult them.[16]

A measure of how far Denis the Carthusian's repute had fallen in the life of the Church may be gleaned by Thomas Merton's use of homey passive-aggressive deprecation in describing the Dionysian patrimony:

> [W]hen one looks into the forty-odd volumes of Denis the Carthusian, one gets the impression that with him writing was something like the basket weaving of the early solitaries—a mechanical action that kept him busy and that had no particular reference to an admiring public. Denis could write a book on any subject, much as a pious housewife might knit a sweater or a pair of socks.[17]

AN ECSTATIC ENCOUNTER

Pace Thomas Merton, a pious housewife weaving baskets or knitting sweaters and socks is not what I thought of when my eyes first fell upon Denis's writings. I encountered Denis the Carthusian when, as a result of an earlier decision to attend a parish that

---

[15] Kent Emery Jr., "Denis the Carthusian," in *A Companion to Philosophy in the Middle Ages*, eds. Jorge J. E. Gracia and Timothy B. Noone (Oxford: Blackwell Publishing, 2002), 243.
[16] Denis the Carthusian, *Spiritual Writings* (Portland: Four Courts Press, 2005), ix.
[17] Thomas Merton, *The Silent Life* (New York: Farrar, Straus and Giroux, 1999), 137–38.

celebrated Mass in the *usus antiquior*, I resolved to read Nicholas Gihr's *The Holy Sacrifice of the Mass: Dogmatically, Liturgically, and Ascetically Explained* to learn about it.[18] In this book, Father Gihr makes repeated references to Denis the Carthusian's many works, but especially his *Exposition on the Mass*, *Sermons on the Sacrament of the Holy Eucharist*, and *Dialogue on the Sacrament of the Altar and the Celebration of Mass*. Indeed, Gihr's first quotation in his Preface is from none other than Denis the Carthusian. "*In hac conscriptione, non fuit intentio movere vel tangere nisi ea quae affectum excitare et devotione possunt proficere, exponendo verba missae devotius quo valebam.*"[19]

Gihr is easy and free in his quotations of the Carthusian, and so among his copious samplings one immediately feels the intensity of this monk's writing. It is as if the words carrying the message Denis wishes to convey are ready to burst, as if they contained new wine poured into inadequate old wineskins. Not only are they pressed to the limit in carrying the impossible burden of describing the mysteries of the Eucharist and the Holy Sacrifice of the Mass, they also shoulder the double duty of describing Denis's own fervent love of, and devotion to, the Eucharist. It would seem that, in writing on the Eucharist, Denis "was caught up into paradise, and heard secret words, which it is not granted to man to utter."[20] And yet to utter them he tried, and, in the silence of his cell, as Denis sat or stood at his scriptorium, his quill was pressed into the service of the impossible. As I perused these excerpts in Gihr's work, I thought to myself *someone has to translate this man into English*. And that thought was the genesis of this translation, which seeks to make available to a greater English-speaking public the writings of Denis the Carthusian on the Holy Eucharist and the Sacrifice of the Mass.

Denis the Carthusian's works on the Mass and the Blessed Sacrament are found in Volume III of his *Opera Minora*, published in 1908. They are four in number: *De Sacramento Altaris et Missae Celebratione Dialogus*, a Dialogue on the Sacrament of the Altar and the Celebration of Mass; *Expositio Missae*, an Exposition

---

[18] Nicholas Gihr, *The Holy Sacrifice of the Mass, Dogmatically, Liturgically, and Ascetically Explained*, 6th ed. (St. Louis: B. Herder, 1902).
[19] "In expounding upon the words of the Mass as devoutly as I was able, I had no intention to ask any questions or to bring up anything except those things which are able to excite the affection and increase devotion."
[20] 2 Cor. 12:4.

of the Mass; *De Sacra Communione Frequentanda*, On the Frequenting of Holy Communion; and *De Sacramento Eucharistiae Sermones Sex*, Six Sermons on the Sacrament of the Eucharist.

DIALOGUE ON THE SACRAMENT OF THE ALTAR AND THE CELEBRATION OF MASS

The *Dialogue on the Sacrament of the Altar and the Celebration of Mass* is the longest of all Denis the Carthusian's works on the Eucharist, and theologically the most rigorous. As suggested by its title, it is a treatise in the form of a dialogue between Truth (who is Jesus Christ) and a Priest regarding the Eucharist and the celebration of Mass.

In some ways, the *Dialogue* is also the most intimate of Denis's works on the Eucharist and Holy Mass. The *Dialogue* is peppered with prayers or meditations. More, the dialogue between Truth and the Priest expresses an intimate spiritual or interior colloquy, which is derived not so much from scholastic tomes, but rather from an intimate conference of hearts. It is a thing of *cor ad cor loquitur*. It is a thing of *abyssus abyssum invocat*. It is not a thing of *videtur quod, sed contra, respondeo dicendum*. Surely, it expresses the thoughts, reflections, and internal struggles of the theologically proficient Denis the Carthusian as he prepared for and offered Mass and took communion. The *Dialogue* is a product of Denis's experience as much as it is a product of scholastic theology and learning. In the *Dialogue*, intellect and heart have kissed.

The Dialogue begins with an expression of fear by the Priest based upon St. Paul's first letter to the Corinthians: "*Whosoever shall eat this bread or drink the chalice of the Lord unworthily, shall be guilty of the body and blood of the Lord.*"[21] It is the fear of the

---

[21] 1 Cor. 11:27. One might note that it is precisely this Scripture verse (1 Cor. 11:27), with which Denis begins his *Dialogue*, that has been excised from the Lectionary of the reformed Mass of Paul VI, as Matthew P. Hazell shows in his book *Index Lectionem: A Comparative Table of Readings for the Ordinary and Extraordinary Forms of the Roman Rite* (Lectionary Study Press, 2016). In the *usus antiquior* the Pauline *monitum* was heard by the congregation at least twice a year, on Maundy Thursday (in the Epistle) and during the Feast of Corpus Christi (in both the Epistle and the communion antiphon), though it might also be heard during a votive Mass of the Most Holy Eucharist or during the traditional Office of Tenebrae, where it would be included in the ninth Lesson for Maundy Thursday. The Pauline *monitum* contained in 1 Cor. 11:27 that is so important to Denis is never heard at all in the *Novus Ordo Missae*; it is, as

Lord that elicits the Priest's plea for enlightenment. Fear of the Lord, after all, is the beginning of wisdom.[22]

Truth—the Angel of Good Counsel, whom we immediately recognize as the Lord Jesus—responds to the prayers of the Priest, and the dialogue begins.[23] A number of subjects are addressed in the *Dialogue* either as a result of Truth's decision to instruct or as a result of Truth's response to questions put to him by the Priest. The topics include the various names of the Sacrament of the Altar and, specifically, why among its various names it is also called the Eucharist. The Eucharist is multidimensional. It is Memorial. It is true spiritual food and drink, and so provides spiritual nutrient to the Christian. It is called the *Viaticum*. It is also referred to as Communion. In addition to these names, the Eucharist is also known as Gift, the rite of Sacrifice, the Sacrament of the Altar, the Host "in that it contains Christ himself and he is offered in it,"[24] and finally Deposit or Pledge.

The notion of the Eucharist as spiritual food and drink is developed during the course of the *Dialogue*, in particular in Article Eight. Here, the Eucharist is analogized—and both compared and contrasted to—the food and drink in the temporal world.

The Real Presence of Christ in his humanity in the Eucharist, and by concomitance also his divinity, is the topic of various articles. In Denis's mind there is no doubt of the equivalence of the God-Man Jesus and of the Eucharist: "And so, in the Sacrament, the whole Christ—God and man—is contained, consumed, and offered."[25] This reality is what makes the Eucharist fundamentally different from the other sacraments, and *par excellence* a *mysterium tremendum et fascinans*. In fact, the heart of Denis's works on the Mass and the Eucharist—the *omphalos*, as it were, of his

---

Dr. Peter Kwasniewski stated, "the omission that haunts the Church," because "many seem to be wholly unaware of the terrifying consequences of approaching the sacred banquet without being in a state of grace, that is to say, receiving the Eucharist in a state of mortal sin... [T]he concept of an unworthy communion has disappeared from the general Catholic consciousness." Yet according to Denis it is the very *fear of an unworthy communion* that is the starting point for a healthy understanding of the Sacrament of the Eucharist and the worthy celebration of, and participation in, the Mass. See Peter Kwasniewski, *The Holy Bread of Eternal Life* (Manchester, NH: Sophia Institute Press, 2020), 181–95.
[22] Prov. 9:10.
[23] This term (μεγάλης βουλής άγγελος, *megalēs boulēs aggelos*), comes from the Septuagint (Isaiah 9:6). Dionysius the Areopagite identifies Jesus as the Angel of Good Counsel in his *Mystical Theology* and the *Celestial Hierarchy*.
[24] *Dialogue*, Article Seven.   [25] *Dialogue*, Article Eleven.

doctrine—can be distilled into two Latin words, precisely those that Bishop Athanasius Schneider chose for the title of one of his books:

Dominus est!
It is the Lord!

From the infinite dignity of the Sacrament of the Altar, the dialogue turns to the dignity of the priestly power which confects it and makes Christ present. This sacerdotal power is the most noble that exists, and—even in the lowliest priest—it exceeds in dignity the jurisdictional power of bishop and even pope.[26]

The exercise of that sacerdotal power demands proper preparation, and so the *Dialogue* turns to how the priest ought to prepare for the celebration of Mass. (Denis's observations are analogously applicable to the laity.) Drawing from the Old Testament priesthood and its strictures, Truth insists that, under the evangelical law, the priesthood is "more spiritual, more perfect, and more godlike than those priests and Levites under the Law."[27] Thus, more must be demanded of the Christian priest than of the Aaronite priest or Levite. Here, Jesus exhibits a manifest ire, more *Dantean* than Dante, invoking biblical images and maledictions against priests who are negligent (or worse) in their practice of the priestly ministry:

> *I will meet them as a bear that is robbed of her whelps,* I will tear up their insides, *I will devour them as a lion;* I will make *them as an oven of fire,* I will drown them in the infernal pits, I will place them in the sulphureous, blazing wells of the underworld, and they will be enclosed in the burning furnaces of Acheron, cast down unto the bottom of a scorching lake. They will not be tormented so much by the intense cold and fierce fires of Gehenna as by the burden and desolation of extreme bitter despair. *The heavens shall reveal* their *iniquities,* and the earth shall rise against them, and their crimes will be made manifest to all. The entirety of the creatures will fight against them for me.[28]

In reading this expression of the wrath of God as recounted by Denis, we can only hope: *Ab ira Tua, libera nos, Domine!*

Truth insists that the dignity of the sacerdotal office demands that the priest live a virtuous, holy, and exemplary life. Not only that, the priest's conduct must be such that he is virtually in a constant state of recollection of his dignity, so that he may be always at the ready to celebrate Mass. His whole life must be priest.

---

[26] *Dialogue*, Article Twelve.   [27] *Dialogue*, Article Thirteen.   [28] Ibid.

In the proximate preparation for Mass, the priest must keep before him the four principal parts of the Sacrifice. These involve the four cardinal questions *Quis? Quid? Cui? Quare?* (Who? What? To whom? Why?) Here in the *Dialogue*, our Lord gives the Priest an *examen* of conscience as to what vices he should avoid and what virtues he should cultivate.

One of the virtues the priest should have is the virtue of devotion. A significant part of the *Dialogue* therefore addresses the issue of devotion. Truth and Priest speak of the matter of devotion, and its definition, its sufficiency, its many kinds and grades, including the supererogatory devotion that a priest must endeavor with God's grace to attain. Also explored in the conversation between our Lord and the Priest is the intimate relationship between devotion and the love of God.

Next, the *Dialogue* turns to the effects and fruits of the Eucharist, which include the increase of charity, the removal and remitting of venial sins, the repair of the wounds inflicted by original sin (*fomes peccati*), the increase of fervor and zeal, and spiritual refreshment. A distinction is made between the Sacrament considered in and of itself and the Sacrament considered with respect to the disposition of the communicant, and the effects on the communicant are explored based upon this distinction.

In an interesting *excursus*, one which sheds light on medieval piety, the *Dialogue* compares the power and efficacy of the Eucharist to the miracles of saints and their relics. Reference is made to such relics as the cloak of St. John the Evangelist—which converted a man named Aristodemus and brought two men back from the dead—or the staff of St. Peter, which had equivalent restorative powers. If the Lord dispenses such prodigies through the bodies and relics of his saints, Truth asks rhetorically, "how could he not give incomparably greater powers to his Flesh which is now glorified with him?"[29]

This provides the segue into an article that encapsulates or recapitulates what has been discussed thus far in the *Dialogue*, and where Christ's Real Presence in the Eucharist is again stressed, and the essential purpose of the Sacrament, whose effects are so salutary and varied—to inflame faith, hope, and especially charity in us—is summarized. In an interesting digression, Denis—relying on the works of others he does not identify—compares the Sacrament to

---

[29] *Dialogue*, Article Twenty-One.

the six steps leading up to the throne of Solomon.[30] These six steps are faith, desire of the heart, reverence of heart, purity, memory of the Lord's Passion, and, lastly, confidence in God. The eleven effects of the Eucharist are then summarized: remission of sins, cure of vices, guard and protection, comfort of heart, spiritual consolation, increase of liberality, augmentation of virtue, encouragement of good works, illumination of mind, peace of heart, spiritual relish, and unity of the mind with God through the perfection of charity.[31]

Then, in a sort of modulation of *genre*, the *Dialogue* shifts from Christ and Priest in dialogue and Christ expounding doctrine— *Christus docens, Sacerdos discens*—to a short paean of praise of the Eucharist, followed by a *fervorino* by the Priest to all the faithful (in which he includes himself), followed by an interior monologue within the Priest,[32] which is a sort of self-examination or self-reflection in preparation of the celebration of Mass,[33] following which the priest begins a mediation-prayer on preparation for the fruitful celebration of Mass.[34] Thereafter, the Priest addresses two lengthy but artfully-crafted prayers to God thanking him for the Eucharist.[35]

The *Dialogue* then resumes its dialogic character,[36] and a number of topics are handled, among them whether the Eucharist is one sacrament or many, the Eucharist's relationship to the other six Sacraments, the words of consecration, and the matter and form of the Eucharist. These sections are theological in nature, and Denis draws upon the opinions of many in expounding on these issues, including Pope Innocent III, Thomas Aquinas, Bonaventure, Henry of Ghent, Albert the Great, Alexander of Hales, and Bernard of Clairvaux. Denis also addresses the theological marvels—mysteries that are above reason—that are part and parcel of the Sacrament, such as how Christ can be locally in many places at once, how transubstantiation takes place, and so forth. As *auxilia fidei*, perhaps, or some sort of pedagogical strategy, the theological mysteries of the Eucharist are compared to Scriptural *mirabilia*—e.g., the wife of Lot turning into a pillar of salt, and Moses's (or rather Aaron's) rod into a serpent—and even to natural marvels such as how the pupils of the eyes can seize so many objects and so many colors.[37]

---

[30] *Dialogue*, Article Twenty-Two; see 1 Kings 10:19.
[31] *Dialogue*, Article Twenty-Two. [32] *Dialogue*, Article Twenty-Three.
[33] Ibid. [34] *Dialogue*, Article Twenty-Four.
[35] *Dialogue*, Articles Twenty-Five and Twenty-Six.
[36] *Dialogue*, Articles Twenty-Seven through Thirty-Two.
[37] See Gen. 19:26; cf. Ex. 7:10.

The Thirty-Third Article in the *Dialogue* is a discussion of Blessed John Ruusbroec's work, *A Mirror of Eternal Blessedness* (*Speculum aeterna salutis*),[38] and the four "Marian" marks required for worthy reception of the Sacrament of the Eucharist: purity, true knowledge of God, humility, and a will free of concupiscence. Further dialogue addresses the particularities or idiosyncrasies of Ruusbroec's expressions, such as God's love being avaricious, and his charity being all-consuming. "The man," Truth states, "has a particular manner of speaking, frequently metaphorical and obscure, and yet he explains himself."[39] But, despite Ruusbroec's peculiar, idiosyncratic expressions, Truth assures us of Ruusbroec's orthodoxy. The dialogue continues with discussions on Ruusbroec's reflections regarding the difference among communicants, differences of devotion, differences in the subtleness of intellect, differences in elevatedness of spirit, differences in the observance of precepts, and differences in spiritual integrity.

The *Dialogue* then closes with a loving allocution to Jesus Christ, "to the praise and glory of his name, who is God, sublime and blessed above every thing."[40] In this rich illocutionary tapestry of thanksgiving, full of Scriptural references, the Priest, as it were, incorporates all the elements of the *Dialogue*, and purposes to give thanks to God for such an outstanding gift as we have in the most Holy Sacrament of the Altar and in the Sacrifice of the Mass.

EXPOSITION OF THE MASS

Denis the Carthusian's *Expositio Missae* is the most accessible of all his works on the Mass and the Blessed Sacrament. Its aim is to guide the reader through the various parts of the Mass in thirty-nine separate articles, somewhat as Msgr. Ronald Knox did in his sermons later published as *The Mass in Slow Motion*.

After a short introduction, the *Exposition of the Mass* begins with a treatment of devotion, defining what this virtue is, what sort of devotion is required for the proper celebration of Mass,

---

[38] See "A Mirror of Eternal Blessedness," in *The Complete Ruusbroec: English Translation with the Original Middle Dutch Text*, trans. Phayre Crowley, Helen Rolfson, André Lefevere, and Kees Schepers, Corpus Christianorum, Scholars Version, vol. 1 (Turnhout: Brepols Publishers, 2014).
[39] *Dialogue*, Article Thirty-Three.   [40] *Dialogue*, Article Thirty-Four.

and how that devotion should be perfected. Drawing from St. Augustine, Denis then addresses the four considerations that a priest—and frankly anyone serving or attending at Mass—should have before him: *Quis? Quid? Cui? Quare?* Who is offering? What is being offered? To whom is it being offered? Why is it being offered?[41] The answers to these questions help Denis identify the vices the participant or celebrant must avoid and the virtues he must strive to gain to celebrate Mass devotedly and to take communion worthily.

After handling the vices a priest must avoid and the virtues a priest should endeavor to have, Denis discusses the parts of the Mass, giving various opinions on how the parts of the Mass might best be distinguished. From there, Denis addresses, article by article, the parts of the Mass of the Catechumens, the first principal division of the Mass—the priest's confession, the Introit, the *Kyrie*, and the *Gloria*, the authorship of which is traditionally ascribed to St. Hilary of Poitier. Denis's treatment of the *Gloria* is masterful, as he parses out the words of this great prayer and explains their theological import. Denis then launches into an exposition of the Collect, the reading of the Epistle, the Gradual, and the Alleluia. Denis handles the reading of the Gospel and the Creed in one article, and then turns his attention to the Mass of the Faithful, the second principal division of the Mass, which is the great oblation, the Sacrifice of the Eucharist.

Here we have reached the heart of Denis's *Exposition of the Mass*. Denis devotes one article each to the Offertory, the Preface, the *Sanctus*, and then briefly doubles back to address the Preface again, by giving in-depth treatment of one particular Preface: the Preface of the Most Holy Trinity. He chooses this particular Preface because it "is very beautiful, and for some persons quite difficult" to understand.[42] In this particular article, Denis elaborates on the Trinitarian doctrine so perfectly yet succinctly expounded in that Preface.

Rightly, Denis reserves the greatest focus in his *Exposition* for the Canon of the Mass, dividing it into twelve parts and devoting nineteen articles—almost half of his *Exposition*—to it. These articles embed written commentary—in effect, almost a sort of gloss—around separate words or phrases of the Canon which Denis lovingly, with great devotion and zeal, caresses, buttresses,

---

[41] This is also handled in Denis's third sermon on the Eucharist.
[42] *Exposition*, Article Seventeen.

and explains with Scripture and other authorities (such as Hilary, Augustine, Albert the Great, Thomas Aquinas, Giles of Rome, Henry of Ghent, Peter of Tarentaise, and Nicholas of Lyra), and his own explanations, elaborations, and sometimes practical reflections and observations. Denis has bequeathed us a masterful treatise on the Canon.

Having handled the Canon, the summit of the Liturgy of the Mass, which itself is the *fons et culmen*, the "source and summit,"[43] of the Christian life and the mission of the Church, Denis quickly brings his *Exposition of the Mass* to a close, with one article each on the Lord's Prayer, Communion, and Thanksgiving.

ON FREQUENTING HOLY COMMUNION

The work *On Frequenting Holy Communion* is in the form of a letter to a correspondent, a confessor to nuns, who requests advice from Denis as to how he ought to advise nuns under his authority regarding frequenting communion. After an introduction, Denis devotes seven relatively short articles to the issue. Although the letter addresses the issue of nuns frequenting communion, the principles that order and guide Denis's response apply to all communicants, though his focus is on those persons with a religious vocation. Denis notes that unconfessed, unrepented mortal sin always precludes one from partaking in communion. In Denis's eyes, mortal sin is a particularly egregious fault in the life of religious, who are supposed to be devoted to perfection; and he excoriates such religious. When addressing the frequency of communion outside of the conditions of mortal sin, the letter is full of sound advice, and it follows the general thrust of Denis's pastoral suggestions contained in his fourth sermon on the Eucharist. That is, Denis notes the opposing principles: the need to preserve reverence for the Sacrament (which serves as an inhibition to frequent communion) and the prompting of charity (which serves as an impetus to frequent communion). These create a sort of antinomy which must be resolved on a case-by-case basis. In any event, the would-be communicant is to be obedient to the directions of his or her spiritual director or confessor.

---

[43] Vatican II, *Lumen Gentium*, n. 11; *Catechism of the Catholic Church* § 1324.

SIX SERMONS ON THE SACRAMENT OF THE EUCHARIST

Denis the Carthusian has bequeathed us six sermons on the Sacrament of the Eucharist. The sermons give a brief overview of Denis's teaching, beginning with the honor due the Eucharist, its institution and dignity, the proper and worthy celebration of Mass and consumption of the Eucharist, its grace and its fruits, impediments to the celebration of Mass and communion, and the frequency of communion. Each Sermon starts with an appropriate quotation of scripture, and then launches into its topic. The sermons summarize and repeat much of what Denis wrote of the Eucharist and the Mass in his *Exposition of the Mass* and in his *Dialogue on the Sacrament of the Altar and the Celebration of Mass*. Denis's teachings are as orthodox as they are consistent.

The sermons, it ought to be noted, were not necessarily ever delivered by Denis. These sermons constitute more of a theological *genre*, to be written and read for the purpose of edification, and not to be preached with the mouth, as the Carthusians had a rule: "For almost all those whom we receive, if it be possible, it is by writing we teach ... and because we cannot do so by mouth, we preach the word of God by hand."[44] Indeed, this appears to be expressly the case with respect to the sixth sermon which purports to be dedicated and transmitted to the nuns Mechtilde, Christina, and Catherine, who displayed mystical phenomena associated with their partaking in the Eucharist, such as ecstasies, raptures, stigmata, and inedia.[45]

The first sermon's topic is the three levels of honor that are due the Sacrament of the Eucharist. It is framed as a sermon for the Feast of Corpus Christi,[46] and focuses on the specific honor given to the Blessed Sacrament through processions. Denis draws upon the Old Testament[47] to suggest three levels or grades of praise due

---

[44] Guigo I, *Consuetudines* 28, 2–4, quoted in Kent Emery Jr., "Denys the Carthusian," *The Carthusians in the Low Countries: Studies in Monastic History and Heritage* (Leuven: Peeters, 2014), 296, n. 96.

[45] *Sixth Sermon*. This assumes these three are contemporaries of Denis, and not a reference to the historical saints of the same name with devotion to the Eucharist, unless, of course, he is invoking them as literary devices.

[46] In his Bull dated August 11, 1264, *Transiturus de hoc mundo*, Pope Urban IV established the Solemnity of Corpus Christi for the universal Church.

[47] See 1 Chr. 15.

the Sacrament, each one of higher sublimity. The first such level involves *the body*. It is the external praise rendered by ringing bells, carrying candles, singing hymns of praise, and other such rituals and liturgical or paraliturgical practices. The second level involves the *human heart*, which must be inflamed by the fire of charity, a charity ignited by meditating upon the mystery played out before the worshipper in the Eucharist. The last and highest level of honor is that of contemplation, which involves the human *spirit*. Fully aware of their nothingness before the sacramental presence of the Incarnate Lord, the abyss of being between the contemplative and the God contemplated makes one realize—as another Carthusian put it—that we are virtually nothing before God, and, moreover, nothing in rebellion.

> My God, I believe that you are present in me, even though I am nothing. Indeed, I am less than nothing, since I have offended you and rebelled against you! I am therefore below nothing.[48]

It is this awareness of our virtual nothingness before God that allows us to forget ourselves, and in forgetting ourselves, allows us to become fully possessed of and by God. "And thus," Denis says, the Eucharistic contemplative "is reduced to nothing, not in the sense of letting go of his natural existence or his proper substance, but because he no longer reflects on himself, no longer seeks himself, nor anything ultimately in himself, or for himself, or because of himself, but all in God, to God, and because of God."[49]

Denis is aware of the danger that can accompany this sort of spiritual experience and the words used to describe this experience. Though these notions are Scriptural—e.g., *I live, now not I, but Christ lives in me*[50]—describing these mystical experiences can give rise to *ersatz* contemplatives (who can adopt the language without ever having the experience), or give rise to vanity (by thinking that an emotional experience is equivalent to this deeply spiritual contemplative state), or can even lead to the theological error of what in the future would be known as Quietism. But the Carthusian Denis absolutely, dogmatically rejects as false any sort

---

[48] « *Mon Dieu, je crois que vous êtes ici présent en moi, moi pauvre néant. Si je n'étais que néant...! Mais je Vous ai offensé, je me suis révolté contre Vous. Je suis donc au-dessous du néant!* » Jean-Baptiste Porion, O. Cart., Écrits Spirituels (Casalibus, 1992), 11. An English translation of this very lovely book is available as *The Prayer of Love and Silence*, by a Carthusian, published by Gracewing.
[49] *First Sermon.*   [50] Gal. 2:20.

of union that would abolish the creaturely difference, or any sort of Buddhist self-annihilation or any Christian analog of it. Finally, Denis warns that achieving the heights of contemplation does not mean we should be unguarded or expect to be free from the tug of sin: King David, Denis reminds us, attained the heights of contemplation in his youth, and yet he slid into the murderous adultery with Bathsheba when almost sixty.

After discussing the three levels of worship, Denis shifts topic to give us a paean of praise for the Eucharist as the Sacrament of Charity. What an amazing gift that God should become Incarnate, redeem us, and then feed us with the medicine of his own Body, Blood, Soul, and Divinity! What thanksgiving should such divine loving condescension draw out of us, and yet we hardhearted humans resist. "Alas, hard heart, vile, ingrateful heart which is not set aflame by such great charity."[51] We can only marvel at the *kenotic* God, the God who in his exinanition gives himself to us in the Eucharist under the veils of bread and wine to be handled and consumed by men. More, do we not realize the mercies received from consuming the Eucharist, such as obtaining the forgiveness of venial sins, the sacramental grace to escape hell, avoid or lessen our stay in purgatory, and attain heaven? The gift of the Eucharist and its effects should draw out of us Eucharistic praise commensurate to that gift and its effects, that is to say, the praise of thanksgiving, a sacrifice of praise.[52] Before such an act of divine condescension, we must also be aware of our own worthiness. We must never unworthily approach and consume the Blessed Sacrament: "Therefore, in order that we may be rendered worthy to approach, reverently encounter, and salubriously receive this most worthy Sacrament of the Eucharist in accordance with the abilities of our smallness, let us cleanse ourselves from any filth of mind and body, and let us proceed prudently and tirelessly towards perfection through the path of regular discipline."[53]

The second sermon addresses the institution and dignity of the Eucharist. Here, Denis addresses the institution of the Eucharist by our Lord Jesus, and the scandal such words—*I am the bread of life. Take and eat. This is my Body. My flesh is meat indeed. My Blood is drink indeed*—gave to the Jews in Palestine (and still give today to the Protestant and Modernist).[54] Indeed, they scandalized even the

---

[51] *First Sermon.*   [52] Heb. 13:15.   [53] *First Sermon.*
[54] John 6:48, 56, 57; 1 Cor. 11:23–24; Matt. 26:26.

great—though "most wicked and accursed" (*sceleratissime ac maledicte*)—Muslim philosopher Averroës (Ibn Rushd), who ridiculed Christians for harboring the idea that the supernal God could be tied to such a mundane thing as bread and wine.[55] In a short excursus, Denis also harangues Averroës: how dare he who held such foolish theological and philosophical ideas ridicule Christians! Some of the manifest Averroistic errors Denis points out include disbelief in the devil, his theory of the unity of the intellect (which advanced the notion that all humans share one intellect), the rejection of a spiritual, eternal soul, and the rejection of the final judgment.

The foolish wickedness of Averroës's ridicule is not only shown to be philosophically and theologically manifestly false, it is belied by the clear virtues of the Church, the New Israel, whose soul is the God who departed the Synagogue when it rejected Christ as God. That the Church's teaching on the Eucharist is true is buttressed by the miracles seen in the Church, by the fulfillment of the prophecies of the Eucharist contained in the Old Testament, by the teaching of the New Testament and the Church, and the fittingness of the Eucharist (as well as the other Sacraments) as a cure for the condition and circumstances of fallen man. The Eucharist, Denis makes clear, is the superlative, the perfect Sacrament because, while the other Sacraments dispense grace through the presence and virtues of Christ, only in the Eucharist is Jesus Christ contained "truly and substantially by essence."[56]

From this excoriation of Averroës and defense of the Sacrament of the Eucharist, Denis addresses the issue of how grace is present in the other Sacraments. He identifies two opinions—one held by Alexander of Hales, St. Bonaventure, William of Paris, Scotus, and others—and another held by St. Albert, St. Thomas Aquinas, and others. Denis sides with Sts. Albert and Thomas.

After this, Denis covers the classic difference between the sacrament as such (*sacramentum tantum*), the reality and the sacrament (*res et sacramentum*), and the reality itself (*res tantum*). In the Eucharist, these are, respectively, the *appearance* of bread and wine and its

---

[55] According to Craig Martin, "although Averroes became a point of reference in debates of the Eucharist," the Eucharist was "an issue left unexplored in the Muslim's writings." Craig Martin, *Subverting Aristotle: Religion, History, and Philosophy in Early Modern Science* (Baltimore: John Hopkins 2014), 162. Be that as it may, it was certainly a medieval commonplace that Averroës ridiculed the Christian doctrine of the Real Presence of Christ in the Eucharist.

[56] *Second Sermon*. The next two quotations are also from this sermon.

offering and consumption, the *very* Body and Blood of Christ, and the ecclesiastical unity, charity, and grace that the Sacrament effects.

The Eucharist, Denis concludes, "contains the dignity of the Body of Christ," as well as his Soul, and therewith the eternal Word of God to which it is hypostatically united. Its dignity is therefore infinite. "It is infinite," Denis says, "because the dignity of the one person of the Word is infinite," with the result that the "the humanity of Christ is most esteemed by God." For this reason, the Eucharist "is of greater dignity than the entire rest of the universe." It is, then, a treasure worth more than all the rest of the cosmos.

Here, again, as in the first sermon, Denis admonishes the reader that the magnificence of the Eucharist places upon the Christian a duty to respect it, and to prepare for it adequately so that it may be approached and consumed with all the proper dignity, reverence, and devotion it deserves. "With great care, therefore, and solicitous preparation should we approach such a Sacrament."

The third sermon covers the fitting preparation for celebrating Mass and participating in communion. It begins by stressing the vast, incomprehensible abyss between sin, especially mortal sin, and Almighty God, an abyss so infinite that God's relationship can be characterized analogously as hatred. Almighty God, Denis avers, "essentially holy and just, hates and detests sin."[57] Mortal sins warrant eternal punishment, yet all sin is abhorrent to God. Given this reality, no one must celebrate Mass or approach the Sacrament to take communion in a state of mortal sin. It just heaps mortal sin upon mortal sin. All must scrutinize their conscience—assuming them to be properly formed—before approaching this august Sacrament.

Denis again discusses the Augustinian commonplace teaching on sacrifice, which distinguishes four things in any sacrifice: *Quis? Quid? Cui? Quare?* (Who is offering? What is being offered? To whom is it being offered? Why is it being offered?) In response to the first of these queries, Denis provides some guidance to the priest, the celebrant, a sort of *examen* of conscience. Turning to the next questions, Denis stresses the infinite value of what is being offered in the Mass and to whom: "Keep in view," he tells the priest, "that as an official and minister of the Church you are about to offer to God the Father his only-begotten Son, you are about to consecrate, handle, and consume the Body and Blood of the Savior, and to pray for the whole Church." Such a reality should be enough to shake any

---

[57] *Third Sermon.* The next three quotations are also from this sermon.

priest out of his tepidity. Finally, in answer to why the sacrifice of the Mass is offered, Denis expounds the theme of the priest as an *alter Christus*: the reason why the priest celebrates Mass, the reason why the priest ought also to offer the Holy Victim on the altar is "for the same reasons Christ offered himself on the Cross to God the Father."

In the remainder of the third sermon, Denis emphasizes how the duties that are incumbent upon the celebrant should be even more rigorously and lovingly pursued by those in religious life, as distinguished from secular priests. In terms of devotion, Denis here lays out the three stages that the celebrant should go through: the purgative way, the illuminative way, and the unitive or perfective way, in some cases resulting in mystical phenomena of swooning, rapture, and ecstasy. The sermon ends with some rustic images intended to encourage progress in the spiritual life: "Do not say: I jump as far with a little stick as with a staff," or "Do not be like the crab, going forward now, and a little later retreating through negligence, carelessness, talkativeness, distraction, and impatience." Not to progress as one strives towards the perfective or unitive way in the offering of Mass is to regress.

The fourth sermon addresses the fruits of the Eucharist. It is perhaps the most technical of all the sermons. Denis places the Eucharist in the middle of salvation history, specifically focusing on the Incarnation of the Word and the marvel of the hypostatic union in Christ—the one mediator, both fully God and fully man. This hypostatic union of God and man makes its appearance in every Mass when the bread and wine are confected into the Body and Blood of our Lord. The graces found in Jesus are precisely those found in the Eucharist. The relationship between the grace of the Sacraments and habitual and sanctifying grace is briefly discussed, Denis observing that there are two opinions in this regard. The first, held by Sts. Albert and Thomas Aquinas, is that there is a real distinction between sacramental grace and habitual or sanctifying grace. The other is that the grace is the same, but that the difference is to be found only in the effect.

From the dignity of the Eucharist, Denis turns to its fittingness. Just as man needs food and drink to live and to flourish in the temporal world, so something analogous to them is required in the spiritual life. That spiritual food is the Eucharist which, as Denis describes in typical Dionysian run-on, litany-like fashion, "delights the heart's palate, increases, repairs, and preserves the power of the soul, recuperates lost devotion, conserves the life of grace in its vigor, maintains the flow of tears, the dew of heavenly showers, and the water of salutary wisdom, lest they be harmed, dried up, or quenched by the fire of concupiscence, the flames of cupidity, or the heat of self-love, nourishes the increase of virtues, inflames charity, and confers such tranquility, exuberance, and happiness on the heart that it overflows, causing a good and cheerful disposition of body."[58]

It is the very identity of the Eucharist and the enfleshed Son of God that makes the Eucharist such a marvelous mystery, one that should elicit awe, but also instill a holy, filial fear of not receiving the Lord worthily. It is sin which impedes. "And briefly, to conclude many things in few words, since nothing can distance, impede, separate us from him except sin, be most solicitous to avoid fault, as far as human frailty allows." This is certainly true for mortal sins, but it is *mutatis mutandis* also true for venial sins. Removing these impediments allows the Sacrament to effect change in the soul, so that—at its most pure—"the apex of the mind is completely absorbed and immersed into that abyss of the Godhead."

The remainder of the sermon describes the interaction of a perfect soul and God in what is the zenith of Eucharistic communion, where a soul experiences the divine in various mystical ways: the illumination of the divine, infused knowledge, the curing of disorders of all kinds, and delights and mystical graces of every kind, including "supernatural anointings, enkindlings, mystical visions, transformations, illuminations, relishings, and raptures." Indeed, the soul undergoes a deepening divinization, a *theosis*. "Then...you will be deifyingly and supernaturally changed into Christ, inasmuch as a predominating love (especially supernaturally infused) transforms the lover into the beloved." These effects are not only seen in women in the world and in the cloister, but also in some men.[59] Doctors and saints also bear witness to these effects.

After a final dig at Averroës,[60] Denis gives a final peroration encouraging his readers: may our love of the Eucharist be like God, *semper maius*, always more.

---

[58] *Fourth Sermon*. The next four quotations are also from this sermon.
[59] In fact, Denis himself was known to experience various mystical states, including ecstasy, visions, and levitation, which is another reason he is given the title *Doctor Ecstaticus*.
[60] "O reprobate and unhappy Averroës; and clearly, if you had ever, even if only once, partaken of the aforementioned effects and fruits of the most glorious Sacrament, you would not have spoken so blasphemously."

The fifth sermon addresses impediments to the Eucharistic grace in greater detail. What is it in the souls of men that blocks the efficacy of the Eucharist, which ought to sanctify everything it touches? All mortal sin blocks its efficacy. But there are also sins that by reason of their linkage to charity, unity, peace, and unanimity are significant impediments to the grace of the Sacrament. Thus, sins such as "hatred, rancor, envy, dissension, division, confusion, discord, cruelty, and bitterness"[61] render a communicant unworthy of the Sacrament.

In addition to these, however, there are also other impediments arising from a life too tied to the flesh and insufficiently practiced in asceticism and self-denial. These turbulent movements of the soul "strongly depress, entangle, and disquiet the soul" and so impede the Eucharistic grace.

Again, Denis returns to the special duty of the professed religious priests who have taken vows to live in accordance with the evangelical counsels and so to perfect themselves in charity. A religious priest who shirks his duties—indeed, who acts against the counsels—is in a specially precarious position; indeed, worse off than if he had remained a secular priest or a layman. *Corruptio optimi pessima.* Without repentance, Denis warns, such a religious can only anticipate hell as a reward.

Denis ends the fourth sermon with a sort of coda, encouraging his readers to work against those sins that impede the grace of the Sacrament. He does so by encouraging an increase in peace, charity, and unity, all of which can be accomplished by edifying one another, by being of like mind, and by rejecting the divisive example of the devil. Ultimately, Denis encourages us to follow a divine order: we must strive to place ourselves *sub ordini divini amoris*, to subject ourselves to the order of divine love. It comes down to the plenary practice of the *primum mandatum*, the Great Commandment: "let us unceasingly and wisely refer all our interior and exterior practices to the most fervent and sincere love of God and neighbor (but especially of God)."

The sixth and final sermon attends to the issue of frequent communion. The sermon, however, begins by discussing the four ways that Jesus especially shows us his love for us. First, Denis points to the Incarnation. In joining the nature of man through a hypostatic or personal union with the only-begotten Son of God,

---

[61] *Fifth Sermon.* The next two quotations are also from this sermon.

who from eternity is divine in nature, mankind was assumed into the Godhead. From the Incarnation, "we recognize the most burning and most powerful love of the Son of God toward our nature and the human race."[62] The second way Jesus Christ has shown us his love is living among us after God became incarnate. Quoting St. John's first chapter, Denis exclaims: *The Word was made flesh, and dwelt among us, and we beheld his glory.* "Oh how lovingly and sweetly, how fruitfully and salubriously, how holily and how exemplarily did he converse among men in all poverty, with most profound humility, with most steadfast patience, with most immovable meekness, and with the fullest charity!" The third manner in which Jesus Christ has shown us his great love is in instituting the Eucharist. In this Eucharist, God himself gives himself in such a way "that he is both the giver and gift, the refresher and the food, the host and guest." The fourth way Jesus Christ showed his great love was in his Passion and death on the Cross, the Sacrifice with the most intimate nexus—indeed, a nexus of identity—with the Eucharistic Sacrifice. It was not enough for Jesus to offer himself once upon the Cross, "but in addition he ordained and decreed that he should be offered daily for our salvation in the sacred and divine ceremony of the Mass."

Denis then turns to the gravamen of the sermon. How frequently ought one of Christ's faithful—whether laity, religious, or priest—communicate? Ultimately, Denis gives no hard and fast rule. But he does give principles to be conscientiously applied.

The first principle is that the Eucharist is the necessary nutriment for the soul. Just like frequent eating and drinking is necessary to the body, so spiritual eating and drinking is essential to spiritual health. Thus, man's need for spiritual food suggests frequent communion.

Two things, however, are required for worthy reception of the Sacrament. First, the communicant must have a subjective desire—one born of love—to unite himself to Christ. Second, the communicant must have reverence for the Sacrament, a reverence born of fear. There is a tension here. The first desire urges frequent communion. But it is opposed by fear of not being sufficiently reverent. Fear, then, suggests less frequent communion. Here, a man must gauge whether by frequent communion he increases in both charity and reverence, or whether to the contrary frequent

---

[62] *Sixth Sermon.* The next five quotations are also from this sermon.

communion breeds the wrong kind of familiarity and therefore a decrease in charity and reverence. In light of this tension, Denis asserts that, as "far as frequency is concerned, it is up to each person's judgment and discretion."

Denis stresses the importance of communion, and even states that the union effected between a soul and God in communion is "in a certain way more fruitful and salubrious" than the enjoyment of Christ in heaven in the beatific vision! It prefigures and is a foretaste of the beatific vision, and, in terms of joy, it anticipates though it does not reach the joy of the blessed. Denis states the reason why the union between God and man in Eucharistic communion while man is *viator*, that is, in pilgrim state, is more fruitful and salubrious: a worthy communion *in via* renders us more meritorious and therefore more worthy to receive even more abundant fruits and glory in *patria*, in the heavenly fatherland. The ability to merit disappears in heaven.

Finally, Denis addresses the issue of abstaining from communion for reasons of false humility, that is, to cover up negligence and tepidity of heart under a hypocritical cover of counterfeit humility and feigned unworthiness. Denis then points out that all things being equal—*ceteris paribus*—charity, and its desire for communion, should beat out fear and humility, and their concern for reverence.

CONCLUSION

Denis the Carthusian is a paradigm of what Pope Pius XII taught in his encyclical on the liturgy, *Mediator Dei*. Pius XII assures us that "no conflict exists ... between the ascetical life and devotion to the liturgy."[63] The ascetical Denis—whose *leitmotif* in his writings on the Mass and the Eucharist is *devotion*—shows that Pian teaching to be indubitably true. Denis is also an exemplar of the principle that "there is an intimate relationship between liturgy and contemplation," and that "it would be as absurd to wish to sacrifice contemplation to liturgy as to wish to sacrifice liturgy to contemplation."[64] Denis reminds us of the *mysterium tremendum et fascinans* that is the

---

[63] Pius XII, *Mediator Dei*, 36.
[64] Jacques and Raïssa Maritain, *Liturgy and Contemplation* (New York: P. J. Kenedy & Sons, 1960), 11.

Sacrament of the Altar, and he refreshes our minds on the importance of *worthy* reception of that Sacrament in communion. Finally, Denis teaches us that what "earlier generations held as sacred"—that is, the traditional Roman liturgy and a special devotion to the Sacrament of the Altar—"remains sacred and great for us too."[65]

Devotion to the traditional Roman liturgy. The Real Presence of Christ—the whole Christ: Body, Blood, Soul, and Divinity—in the Eucharist. The worthy reception of the Blessed Sacrament. The practice of asceticism. An increase in devotion to the Mass and the Eucharist. The contemplation of God. These are as important now as they ever have been, making the renascence of Denis the Carthusian and his writings on the Mass and the Holy Eucharist timely. Denis is a valuable resource in helping us fulfil the Pauline injunction—the *rationabile obsequium*—that is at the heart of all worship of the most high God: "I beseech you, therefore, brethren, by the mercy of God, that you present your bodies a living sacrifice, holy, pleasing unto God, your reasonable service."[66]

A NOTE ON TRANSLATION

Translating Denis the Carthusian is not an easy task, especially for one who is neither a professional Latinist nor a dogmatic theologian. Part of the difficulty can be ascribed to Denis himself. Indeed, Denis sometimes grasps for words, with a penchant for heaping superlatives upon superlatives. Words like *superpulcherrimus, supersplendissimus, superdignissimus, superpraestantissimus, supereffluentissimus, supergloriosissimus, supersuavissimus*—which could be translated as supermostbeautiful, supermostsplendid, supermostworthy, supermosthigh, supermosteffluent, supermostglorious, supermostsweet—pepper his work. His sentences can be extremely long, being veritable litanies of nouns, verbs, or phrases that give various emphases or different shades of the same thought. Sometimes reading Denis is like climbing the steps of a many-storied house (and panting). Other times it is like travelling down a series of rapids. Some of his words are not to be found in any standard Latin dictionary, and if one googles some of these words—as an

---

[65] Benedict XVI, *Letter to the Bishops on the Occasion of the Publication of the Apostolic Letter "Motu Proprio Data"* Summorum Pontificum *on the Use of the Roman Liturgy Prior to the Reform of 1970.*

[66] Rom. 12:1.

example, the word *mysterialissimum*—to see how others may have used them, the only instance of its use in the entirety of the ethersphere is Denis the Carthusian! Additionally, Denis sometimes lapses unconsciously into prayers, so that in one sentence he is addressing his reader (in second person), in another he is giving a narrative (in third person), and yet in another he is speaking to God (in second person). In short, it is not easy to translate a man in the state of Ambrosian sober inebriation (*sobria ebrietas*), a state which the late Stratford Caldecott described as "ecstatic, rapturous, although at the same time measured, ordered, dignified."[67] The very thing that makes Denis difficult to translate, however, is the very thing that renders him so endearing and so particular.

In translating the many verses of Scripture, I have largely turned to the Douay-Rheims, since it so closely follows the Latin scripture upon which Denis relies; however, I have modernized the verbs and pronouns to conform to contemporary English usage. Where Denis appears to be quoting a scripture exactly or near-exactly, the text is in italics. Where Denis appears to be referring to Scripture obliquely or through paraphrase, it is not italicized. Unless otherwise indicated, the footnotes in the text are found in the original 1908 Latin text. If a footnote starts with an L., it is a note relating to the Latin text, either providing the original Latin term or phrase, or providing some commentary on it. If the footnote starts with an E.N. (explanatory note), it is a note that relates to a historical, theological, or other issue.

Because the *Exposition of the Mass* is almost in the form of a gloss on the prayers of the Mass, I have designated the text that Denis interprets in bold italics and have kept it in its original Latin. Where words are in quotation marks or scare quotes, they are so in the original.

In all the works, words in brackets represent additions to the original text. These are added to clarify sentences which might otherwise be difficult to comprehend or unclear. Where the Latin word or phrase has a technical meaning or is otherwise significant or notable or curious, I have placed it in italics in parentheses after the English word.

In his book *Praying the Psalms: A Commentary*, Father Stanley Jaki observed that particularly when translating poems—but it is

---

[67] Stratford Caldecott, "Liturgy and Trinity: Towards an Anthropology of the Liturgy," archive.secondspring.co.uk/articles/scaldecott16.htm.

equally true for Denis the Carthusian's vibrant prosody—"translations are like women; if beautiful not faithful, if faithful not beautiful." To extend, or rather, correct Father Jaki's unfair metaphor further: It may be that, in a translation, every sentence is a woman, and some are both beautiful and faithful, some beautiful and not faithful, some faithful and not beautiful, some neither faithful nor beautiful. If and where I have failed in fidelity, beauty, or both, I will perhaps take refuge in the words of another translator of the *Ecstatic Doctor*, Sister Íde Ní Riain (R.I.P.): "This translation makes no claim to be either a critical edition or a work of scholarship. It is simply a work of love."[68] "Love," St. Peter tells us, "covers a multitude of sins."[69] Perhaps it covers also imperfections in translation, which are all mine. I do, however, want to thank profusely both Zachary Thomas and Gerhard Eger who reviewed this text and made hundreds of recommendations, all to the better. If this work has any merit, if it is both faithful and beautiful—it is attributable to Denis and to Messrs Thomas and Eger. Whatever merit this translation has is not due to me, but is due to the work of these two fine gentlemen and Latinists.

Andrew M. Greenwell
March 12, Feast of Denis the Carthusian
Anno Domini MMXXV
Beate Dionysi, ora pro nobis!

---

[68] Denis the Carthusian, *Spiritual Writings* (Portland: Four Courts Press, 2005), xix.
[69] 1 Pet. 4:8.

DIALOGUE
ON THE SACRAMENT OF THE ALTAR AND THE CELEBRATION OF MASS

INTRODUCTION

PRIEST: *Whosoever shall eat this bread, or drink the chalice of the Lord unworthily, shall be guilty of the body and of the blood of the Lord.* 1 Cor. 11:27.

O divine Apostle, O Vessel of election,[1] taught the Gospel of Christ not by a man nor from men, you thundered forth this terrible warning. We know that you were raptured even to the third heaven, before the throne of glory, even unto the audience chamber of the immense divine majesty, not for a moment, nor for a brief hour, nor a short while, but three entire days, during which you were without sight, neither eating nor drinking.[2] In this rapture, in which you are believed to have clearly seen the sublime God face to face, you learned the wisdom of the law of the Gospel by means of heavenly revelation; and following this, after an opportune time, you proclaimed and wrote these words just mentioned, by which you truly terrified the hearts of all the faithful. For who will dare to confess himself worthy to consume this supersubstantial bread and divine chalice, when that most sacred friend of the Bridegroom, one who was kindred of the Savior by blood, confessed himself unworthy to undo the laces of his sandals?[3] What, then, remains for us except a decree to cease from such most worthy communion, and a resolution to avoid such great danger, and not to come into contact with these truly heavenly mysteries, wondrous, awesome, and incomprehensible to the angelic spirits too, were it not for you saying on the other hand, O eternal Truth, *Amen, amen I say unto you: Except you eat the Flesh of the Son of man, and drink his Blood, you shall not have life in you.*[4] What do I do in such perplexity? What do I choose? If I approach to consume the most immaculate and superlatively excellent Lamb, and receive the cup of his sacred Blood, I fear to be guilty of the Body and Blood of the Lord. But if I abstain, I am afraid of being destitute of the life of grace in the present and the life of glory in the future. My anxieties are all about me, but it is better for me to die than that any of these dangers should befall me.[5]

TRUTH: Why so consumed with sadness?[6] Is there no Counselor given to you? Am I not the Angel of great counsel,[7] the fountain

---

[1] Acts 9:15. [2] Acts 9:9. [3] John 3:29; 1:27. [4] John 6:54.
[5] Dan. 13:22-23. [6] Mich. 4:9. [7] Is. 9:6 (LXX).

of Wisdom,[8] the Word of God in the highest, of which Scripture says, *if any of you want wisdom, let him ask of God?*[9] If the visible sun running in its orbit puts to flight darkness and mists with its light, how much more does the eternal Sun, whose communicability and light is without end, rescue the mind with its radiance and enlightenment from all uncertainty of perplexity, mist of ignorance, and fear of vacillation? Approach, therefore, the throne of grace,[10] approach to be enlightened.[11] *Call upon me in the day of trouble.*[12]

PRIEST: O Lord—who from the beginning most benevolently visited us in your charity and kindness towards us by assuming our nature, and that which you assumed from us you most liberally communicated to us, handing it over and leaving it to us as a remedy, as a manifold help and salvation, and you moreover made us ministers of such a great Sacrament—through that very same most sweet charity and most abundant kindness now deign to teach me, who am anxious and afflicted, what I should do in my aforesaid perplexity, scrupulosity, and fear.

TRUTH: Did not the Apostle himself add right after the words you mentioned: *But let a man prove himself, and so let him eat of that bread, and drink of the chalice?*[13] What is it to prove oneself, except vigilantly to scrutinize and cleanse one's conscience, and to prepare and decorate the bridal chamber of one's heart to receive the King of glory, to present oneself worthy with all one's strength, with considered weighing of one's ability and weakness in proportion to the incomparable excellence of such a Sacrament? However, before I pursue discussion of the manner of your preparation, I wish to instruct you in a deeper way about the most precious dignity of this most profoundly inscrutable Sacrament, and first to speak of its names.

FIRST ARTICLE
On the diverse names of the Sacrament of the Altar.

TRUTH: It belongs to great artists to produce great and eminent effects; and ordinarily the effect corresponds to its cause, and the higher the nature, the more excellent is its power. Did not therefore the Only-Begotten of God, entirely coequal and co-almighty with

---

[8] Ecclus. 1:5. [9] James 1:5. [10] Heb. 4:16. [11] Ps. 33:6.
[12] Ps. 49:15. [13] 1 Cor. 11:28.

the eternal Father, deign to work marvelous things in his assumed humanity? And because in every ordered multitude there is one thing that is first and highest, among all the great marvels which I did in this world, I did this one most excellent, most gracious, and entirely most incomprehensible mystery: I instituted the Sacrament and produced its effect by constituting myself under the sensible species of inanimate things, converting them substantially into my Body and Blood; that is, transubstantiating them by the same infinite and omnipotent power by which in the beginning of time I created all things visible and invisible from nothing. This mystery, this Sacrament, and this work, although in a certain way all one thing, nevertheless was (and is) also a concatenation of many most eminent and wondrous things, when one preexisting thing was changed in an instant to another preexisting thing without corruption or generation of either; and a thing one in number was in many places, though not locally. And I also held myself in my own hands, held myself out to my disciples, and I personally and completely began to be and then ceased to be in their mouths personally and integrally without me going forth or changing. Indeed, I was no less in each of their mouths and in my hand than I was at the table where I sat. And since this sacramental mystery is of such great excellence, of such great power, of so most gracious salubriousness, and also of such sublime and productive effect, it was fitting, in order to make these things known, to call it by many names, although neither these nor any other names can designate completely its dignity, virtues, properties, marvels, and efficacies.

PRIEST: O highest Truth, how deep is this preface to your speech! It gives rise to most difficult questions, which I trust you will answer below. I beg you to continue what you have begun.

TRUTH: This Sacrament is called the Eucharist, memorial, food, viaticum, communion, gift, sacrifice, medicine, and the Sacrament of the Altar.

SECOND ARTICLE
Why this Sacrament is called the Eucharist.

TRUTH: The sacraments of the law of the Gospel which I handed over are rightly called vessels of medicine, because they not only figure, but also contain, and even cause grace, albeit in different ways.

For just as in a genus or multitude there is one thing that belongs *per se* and other things that belong by participation or incompletely, such as fire in the genus of hot things, and the sun in the genus of luminous things, so among the several sacraments one *per se* and fully signifies, contains, and causes grace, namely, this Sacrament, which contains, by virtue of its conversion, the most sacred Body of Christ, in which the grace of his Soul exists by a great overflowing, and also, through natural concomitance, his Soul and Divinity. And so it most truly contains in itself the perfect and complete person of Christ, the eternal Word incarnate, true God and perfect man. Moreover, in Christ's soul there is the plenitude of grace. Yet the other sacraments do not formally contain grace, which is an infused supernatural habit that perfects the intellectual and rational creature. Rather, sacramental grace is in them as in dispositively and instrumentally causal signs, whose being is lacking and incomplete, as shall be elaborated upon in its proper place. Accordingly, this Sacrament is rightly called the Eucharist, that is, "good grace," because on account of the universal eminence and fullness of its graciousness, it is not called merely "eucharistic" or "well-graced," but even Eucharist, that is, "good grace," just as it is said of a dear friend, "You are my love," or as St. Ignatius said: "My love is crucified."[14]

Second, this Sacrament is called the Eucharist because it is bestowed upon you by me, your most gracious Lord, and by my most gracious will. For I, who am in no need of your goods,[15] give abundantly and freely give to all men,[16] and my merits are gifts, so that all flows originally and fountain-like from my pure kindness and merciful will, which sometimes is called grace, namely, uncreated grace, and is called the grace that makes gracious (*gratia gratians*), just as God is frequently called creating nature (*natura naturans*). Nevertheless, by instituting and communicating this Sacrament, and by commanding its frequent reception, I opened and poured out more exuberantly upon you the fountain of all my benevolence, charity, and munificence—indeed, I communicated to you the very Fountain itself with all its opulence, liberality, and grace, namely, my very self, thus reserving nothing of my own that I have not in some way communicated to you. For, just as I was ready to give,

---

[14] E.N. The verbal or adjectival aspect of giving thanks or receiving grace is nominalized into a noun, Eucharist, like the verb love is nominalized to refer to the object of one's love. The example chosen by Denis is taken from St. Ignatius of Antioch's *Epistle to the Romans*, 7.
[15] Ps. 15:2b.   [16] James 1:5.

expose, and offer myself completely for you on the Cross as a ransom, so in this Sacrament I have given myself completely with a most willing, free, and fervent will. I have offered myself to you as food, as a remedy, as abundance and salvation, just as I foretold through Isaiah: *Behold I bring* upon them *as it were a river of peace, and as an overflowing torrent* of the *glory of the Gentiles.*[17]

This will appear to you not only credible, but also reasonable and certain if you deeply consider the immensity of my love, the overflowing generosity of my goodness, and the utterly inexhaustible wealth of my majesty. Contemplate how I share the riches of my glory and the plenitude of my divinity with all in the Church triumphant. What wonder is it, then, if I, who descended from heaven unto earth out of inexpressible charity, assuming humanity to save the human race, should thus have communicated that very assumed nature to you in the Sacrament? Reflect on the nature and characteristic of charity and liberality; consider how promptly you share yourself and your possessions with someone whom you love sincerely and with your whole heart, and how much you do or would do to save him, especially if he cannot otherwise be saved. What then do you think I have undertaken, who am charity in essence according to my divinity, and indeed am intensively unbounded and infinitely generous charity? Even according to my assumed nature I am so much the more exuberantly full of all holy love the more closely I am united to the divine and uncreated charity and the more filled with the beatific enjoyment of uncreated love than any other created mind, even that of the Seraphim. With what inestimable fire of charity do you suppose my soul burns with zeal for the salvation of men, for whose sake it knows itself to be so closely and hypostatically joined to the eternal Word?

PRIEST: Not only reason, but also experience reveals this to be true.

TRUTH: Indeed, let us observe how many people act and suffer from carnal love, and how they communicate themselves and their possessions to each other. This is clearly evident even in married couples living together in good harmony. There is no doubt that spiritual, divine, and infused love is far more vigorous by its nature than carnal love. In addition, it is certain that, as the contemplation of the blessed in heaven is inexpressibly clearer than all the knowledge of wayfarers on earth, so also the love of the blessed is indescribably

---

[17] Is. 66:12a.

more ardent than the love of all wayfarers. But Christ's soul, according to its superior powers relating to the uncreated object, beheld God immeasurably more clearly than all creatures. Hence, he was proportionately more fervent in the actual love of God and of neighbor, and, therefore, he communicated himself, his own possessions, and even his own Body to us in the aforesaid way most munificently.

Third, this Sacrament is called the Eucharist by reason of its effects, because it works in us good and manifold grace, about which grace-filled and salutary effects more will be said below. Yet briefly, the more a person shows himself to be more capacious, that is, purer, worthier, and better disposed to participate in the gifts of this Sacrament, that much more will he draw richer streams of grace from the Savior's fountains.[18]

Fourth, because it is appointed and ordained that it only be given to the grateful. Indeed, it is incidentally harmful for the ungrateful, because he who partakes in this manner *eats and drinks judgment to himself*.[19] Therefore this is the Eucharist of those who are grateful, who are acceptable and pleasing to God through grace.

Fifth, because it causes, preserves, increases, and perfects grace upon grace in men. Moreover, the other sacraments obtain their power and grace from it, and it is the Sacrament of sacraments.

Sixth, this Sacrament is the golden urn containing manna placed within the Holy of Holies.[20] Indeed, the golden urn is Christ's most holy Flesh, which contains the manna, by which one can understand either the divinity itself dwelling in the Body,[21] or the glorious Soul full of all the sweetness of the most blissful enjoyment [of the beatific vision]. Now, the Holy of Holies is the empyrean heaven, the Church triumphant, and the most secret abode of God. In his sweetness, God prepared this Eucharist *for the poor* (that is, the *humble*) of heart, and through it, the Lord bestows *grace and glory*.[22]

THIRD ARTICLE
Why this Sacrament is most aptly called a memorial.

TRUTH: *He has made a remembrance of his wonderful works, being a merciful and gracious Lord*, as you sing in the Psalm.[23] Knowing the forgetfulness of the human mind and its propensity to ingratitude, I

---

[18] Is. 12:3.   [19] 1 Cor. 11:29.   [20] Heb. 9:4.   [21] Col. 2:9.
[22] Ps. 67:11b; Ps. 83:12b.   [23] Ps. 110:4.

instituted at the Last Supper this most hidden Sacrament, indelibly commemorative of myself and all that I did for the salvation of the human race, especially as a memorial of my love for men and my Passion for them. In these two things, my other mysteries are also included, such as the Incarnation—my having come to live in this world, for if I had not become man and lived in this world, I would not have suffered and been offered on the wood [of the Cross].

PRIEST: Your supreme vicar Urban IV talked about this memorial with great devotion in his sermon *On the Eucharist*, saying: O most sweet memorial, to be embraced, loved, glorified, and received with all our prayers, in which signs are made new, and miracles renewed![24]

Therefore, O Christ, this memorial is worthily proportionate and corresponds to that which it represents, namely, your divine mysteries. For there is no more evident and excellent indication of extraordinary, and indeed, of supreme love, than to give oneself.

TRUTH: How much greater, therefore, my love was and is for you; how much more it is to be appreciated that I, your God and Creator, took up, did, and endured so much and so many things for your salvation; how much more excellent and divine is this memorial; and again, how much more splendidly my love is made manifest in it; so much more vehemently should you be enkindled by my love and more heartily give thanks to me whenever you attend the service of the Mass and observe the elevation (which signifies my exaltation on the Cross and the oblation by which I, the high priest and saving Victim, offered myself upon it to God the Father), or when you personally celebrate or receive communion, or even when you are mindful of the other mysteries of my oblation. If it would be regarded as a great thing to be singularly and familiarly loved by an earthly king or great prince, and to receive the distinguished signs and gifts of such love, how incomparably more ought you to consider that the Lord God, your Creator and Savior, loved you entirely freely, came before you in love, and gave and bequeathed to you such a great memorial of his love, namely, himself veiled in the Sacrament, not only once or rarely, but daily and at your pleasure? Contemplate these things deeply, think about them most diligently, remember them regularly, and give thanks constantly with all your strength. Give back to him whatever reverence, worship, and obedience you can muster, with all custody of heart, profound humility, and fervent love, until the end.

---

[24] Cf. Ecclus. 36:6.

FOURTH ARTICLE
In what way this Sacrament is food and drink.

TRUTH: As I said in the Gospel, *My Flesh is meat indeed, and my Blood is drink indeed.*[25] I provide the necessities of life to irrational creatures, as you have read: *Who provides food for the raven when her young ones cry to God, wandering about because they have no meat?* And again: *Who gives to beasts their food?* And I assert in the Gospel: *Behold the birds of the air, for they neither sow... nor gather into barns; and your heavenly father feeds them.*[26] In so doing, I say, I do not neglect rational creatures. Just as I feed bodies, so I also nourish souls with manifold, exquisite, and noble food, namely the supernatural and infused virtues, gifts, spiritual acts and delights attached and formally inherent to them, as well as the ecclesiastical sacraments, most especially my most precious Body and Blood. And because it befits this food and drink to be really united with what is eaten and drunk, my Body and Blood are substantially contained in this Sacrament. Nevertheless, they are not altered by the person who receives them, nor are they changed into him; indeed, rather, they change him into them.[27] And so, just as I nourish the citizens of heaven with the enjoyment of my divinity, so do I now feed wayfarers with the taking of my Body and Blood under the sensible veils of the species. And because this food and drink is of the spiritual soul, it is therefore invisibly present, not in a bodily or dimensional way. And it is taken by faith, not by evident knowledge, because the soul is a wayfarer, and not a contemplator beholding by sight. This food also incorporates one into Christ and his Mystical Body.

Further, since it is food for the soul, this food and drink do spiritually in the soul what bodily nutrients do in the body. Moreover, bodily food and drink are taken lest the natural heat be consumed by radical humor and serve as remedies against the daily affliction

---

[25] John 6:56. [26] Job 38:41; Ps. 146:9a; Matt. 6:26.
[27] E.N. Compare St. Augustine: "I am the food of strong men; grow and you shall feed on me; nor shall you change me, like the food of your flesh into yourself, but you shall be changed into my likeness" (*Confessions*, VII, 10, 18). "[I]n the case of the Eucharist it is a different Bread: it is not we who assimilate it but it assimilates us in itself, so that we become conformed to Jesus Christ, a member of his Body, one with him." Pope Benedict XVI, Homily on the Solemnity of Corpus Christi, June 23, 2011.

of hunger and thirst.[28] So also the most divine Eucharist must be taken lest the vivifying heat of charity be chilled or extinguished by the overflow of sensual affections and humors of concupiscence. It is effective against spiritual hunger resulting from a lack of internal refreshment and strengthening. In the same way that drink also refreshes and causes good digestion, so this Sacrament tempers the ardor of badly inflamed desires and vices and renders the mind capable of rooting out superfluities. It also moderates and allays the vehemence of holy affections for the clear and pleasing presence of the beloved, since the beloved is already truly (albeit invisibly) present. In addition, just as bodily nutrients fill the stomach's emptiness, so the Eucharist fills the heart against the vanity of empty thoughts and unlawful affections, inspiring one to meditate upon and desire what is salutary, so that all time may be spent fruitfully, and man might become, like the Saints, full of days.[29] In brief, just as a bodily nourishment preserves life, fortifies its strength, sustains the body, and causes a man to grow and attain full size, and also causes a good and cheerful disposition of mind and body, so this heavenly food preserves man in the life of grace, strengthens the powers of the soul, and enables him to make progress every day, and so leads him to the perfection of virtue. It gladdens both mind and body in God, in accord with what is written: *My heart and my flesh have rejoiced in the living God.*[30] Finally, just as manna, a figure of this Eucharist, bestowed upon the just and thankful *the sweetness of every taste*,[31] so this mystical refreshment causes a man to delightfully occupy and exercise himself, not only in one virtue, but rather in all the virtues. Thus, with the sweetness of its inward taste, he prays, meditates, abstains, become peaceable, and humbles himself.

PRIEST: Alas! O Lord God, wretched am I, who have so often consumed this divine food and drink, yet nevertheless am still spiritually arid and barren, and excessively petty, and devoid of

---

[28] E.N. Radical humor (*humidum radicale*) and natural heat (*calor naturalis*) refer to a physiological concept stemming ultimately from Galen's writings (AD 129–216). It posited a natural moisture specific to every being. Nutrients were supposed to increase or at least replenish the radical moisture which acts to counter the natural heat (*calor naturalis*) of the body. Without such a countering, the creature ages, gets sick, and eventually dies. However, Denis appears to reverse this relationship in his analogy, suggesting that the Eucharist reduces the radical moisture of concupiscence.

[29] E.N. The expression appears to come from Enoch 58:3: "The righteous will be...in the light of eternal life; there will be no number to the days of their life, and the days of the saints without number."

[30] Ps. 83:3b.   [31] Wis. 16:20b.

spiritual delights. Indeed, I am still unhappily and damnably prone to the irrational movements of the passions.

TRUTH: Whatever might be the case with you, this applies to those who, as the Apostle said, do not discern the Body of the Lord—those who would adorn their body with exquisite clothes, and behave outwardly in an obsequious manner were they to be invited to dinner by the great men of this age and to sit by them at the table, more than they adorn their soul with virtuous acts and internal reverential modesty when they approach the venerable altar, the table of the heavenly King, to receive the Eucharist, adored by the angels. For this reason, they diminish rather than grow. Indeed, this nourishment and remedy does not work in the recipient as bodily medicine or natural agents do, but according to the will of the giver and healer, and according to the preparation and the merits of the recipient.

PRIEST: On the true and salutary preparation for the celebration of Mass and communion, you will, I trust, speak later. Now, if it pleases you, set forth the reasons for the other names of this Sacrament.

FIFTH ARTICLE
On the reasons why this Sacrament is called the Viaticum.

TRUTH: Although my Passion is said to have caused future things to be as if they were already accomplished, this is not to be understood in an absolute sense. But it is true that my Passion was satisfactory for all men, satisfying both for those who believed in it in advance with a formed faith, and for those who now believe that it happened. I mean that it was satisfactory for all men as regards sufficiency, but as regards efficacy, only for those to whom its power or merit is applied in one way or another. Under the Law of the Gospel, it is applied through the ecclesiastical sacraments concurrently with the faith of the one who applies it or of him to whom it is applied. But if this application cannot take place actually, an effective desire for it suffices. Now the sacraments of the evangelical Law contain and effect multiple graces; something which was not the case for the sacraments of the Old Law. Therefore, as a rule, the power of my Passion operates more abundantly in the New Testament than it did formerly in the Old. Nevertheless, I did not restrict my power to the sacraments in such a way that, either now or formerly, I was not able to bestow the sacramental effect and abundant grace on whomever I wished without sacraments. Hence, some men under both the natural law and the written Law were exceptionally holy through a special bestowal of my mercy. Nevertheless, the time of the Gospel is rightly called the time of grace, for grace is given much more lavishly during it than it was before, and to innumerably more people, among which is the whole of sacramental grace, and most especially, the Eucharist, which, among its excellent effects, strengthens and comforts you on the pilgrimage of this exile to continue in the way of salvation, this narrow path in which you face innumerable, great, and weighty obstacles, until you attain the prize of your heavenly calling.

PRIEST: Several questions occur to me at this point, but I perceive that they have been answered in the aforegoing. Indeed, one might ask why, if these things are as you have said, so many who celebrate frequently or almost daily live their lives and go about in such a way, or, if it is not amiss to say it, plainly go backwards; while some simple folk who rarely commune—I have in mind especially some very saintly persons in ancient times who dwelt in the desert, rarely or never receiving this Sacrament—journeyed expeditiously and victoriously to the country of eternal glory. But as I said, the solution is clear from the above, because no defect arises from the Sacrament, but rather from those who receive it unworthily.

TRUTH: Then come forth refreshed, armed, and fortified by this invincible provision to undertake the proposed struggle; receive it with the greatest reverence, spiritually hold within you what you have received, diligently avoiding any injury to it; and when it is present in you, honor and reverence it with the most heartfelt thanksgiving, and recommend yourself to it, lean upon its gracious help, and grow constantly in its excellent effects, so that you might be protected from above and may escape unscathed the many cliffs, obstacles, invasions, difficulties, and temptations in the way of salvation, and may happily attain it at last.

PRIEST: It is so necessary to receive this viaticum with devotion because a long road lies before us,[32] highly dangerous and difficult, on which the flesh rebels, sensuality resists and brings us down; the world entices, the demons bitterly oppose our progress, and there is never any rest. Moreover, I recall Chrysostom's words: As lions

---

[32] Cf. 1 Kings 19:7.

breathing fire, so we leave the Lord's table made terrible to demons.³³ Of course he is speaking about those who receive worthily.

TRUTH: If you receive thus, *a thousand shall fall at your side, and ten thousand at your right hand*,³⁴ you will reduce the flesh and sensuality to servitude to reason, and you will despise the madness and impurity of the world with all your heart. With the strength this food lends you, you will also daily build a great dwelling on the *mount of God*,³⁵ where he is seen face to face for eternity. And the more fervent you are, and the more frequently, purely, and affectively you aspire to God and to this most holy vision, the further you advance and the more ardently you approach him.

PRIEST: I intend now to dispose myself, more than I have been accustomed, to the daily and devout celebration of Mass.

SIXTH ARTICLE
Why this Sacrament is called Communion.

TRUTH: You have read: *We, being many, are one bread, one body, all that partake of one bread* and one chalice.³⁶ Therefore, this Sacrament is called *communion* or *synaxis*;³⁷ and it is a sign of ecclesiastical unity insofar as, by its power and grace, all the faithful who receive it in charity become and are spiritually one with Christ their Head, with his Mystical Body, my holy Church of which they are members,³⁸ and with each other.³⁹ Indeed, through the reception and frequenting of this Sacrament, the communicant is joined to Christ and he likewise to them; and by the indwelling and increase of grace, they abide in each other; nay, further, by advancing in charity, the member is daily made more and more one with the Head. Therefore, he says: *He that eats my flesh, and drinks my blood, abides in me, and I in him.*⁴⁰ This Sacrament also signifies our communion in the glory of the angels, because participation in the Eucharist is a figure, sign, and pledge of future fruition, and by its worthy reception the angels' fall is repaired, and the communicant himself merits the truth of angelic beatitude. Again, by this Sacrament we share in the merits and rewards of all the blessed, who

---

³³ E.N. St. John Chrysostom, Homily 46, 3 on the Gospel of John, PG 59, 260–61.
³⁴ Ps. 90:7.   ³⁵ 1 Kings 19:8b.   ³⁶ 1 Cor. 10:7.
³⁷ E.N. From the Greek σύναξις (*synaxis*) meaning gathering together or communion.
³⁸ Eph. 1:22–23.   ³⁹ Eph. 5:30.   ⁴⁰ John 6:57.

as wayfarers as well as in the heavenly fatherland communicate to one another their manifold grace and glory, by a joinder of charity and spiritual union, as it is written: *I am a partaker with all them that fear you, and that keep your commandments.*[41] Again, because by reception of this Sacrament the faithful are joined by charity, and do unto others what they would reasonably wish done to themselves; hence, through the Sacrament of the Eucharist and its reception, they charitably support one another, and suffer together, and carry out corporal and spiritual works of mercy. Indeed, they communicate in the sufferings of Christ and the Saints, whose persecutions, afflictions, troubles, and injuries they feel as if they were their own. Finally, they share themselves and all they have with those who participate in this Sacrament with them.

PRIEST: From this I gather how truly Augustine spoke when he said: He who receives the mystery of unity and does not hold fast to the bond of peace, receives not a mystery for himself, but testimony against himself. Further he declares that you, Lord Jesus Christ, commended and instituted this Sacrament using materials, namely, bread and wine, in which many things are made into one (as bread is made from many grains and wine from many grapes), just as also the ecclesiastical unity results from many believers united by participation in this Sacrament.[42]

TRUTH: Therefore, you and everyone else who wishes to celebrate or communicate salutarily, should always be *careful to preserve the unity of the spirit in the bond of peace*,[43] and *all should speak the same thing* and all schism or scandals should be absent from you.[44] Let *nothing be done through contention* or through *vain glory*, but let each man prefer his neighbors to himself in holy humility.[45] Let no one conceive, engender, or hold an unreasonable and unjust dislike against another, nor let *man to man reserve anger*, lest he seek a remedy from God in vain.[46] Indeed, you ought to be so strong and fortified in charity and the other virtues that one cannot easily be offended, scandalized, or disturbed by another, nor be suspected of evil by him. Is it not detestable how the ministers of such an excellent Sacrament are still so petty, so weak, so flighty, childish, and passionate? Let them rather be men of virtue, disciples of reason, obedient to heavenly teaching and humble students thereof; and from love of this great Sacrament, or at least from

---

[41] Ps. 118:63.   [42] E.N. St. Augustine, Sermon 272, PL 38, 1248, 1247–48.
[43] Eph. 4:3.   [44] 1 Cor. 1:10.   [45] Phil. 2:3.   [46] Ecclus. 28:3.

fear of their own condemnation, let them bear with one another and honor God *with one mind* and *with one mouth*.⁴⁷

SEVENTH ARTICLE
On the reasons of the other four names of the Sacrament.

TRUTH: It should now be clear to you how correctly the Eucharist is called a gift, and also a benefit, because out of my pure charity and sheer liberality towards men I have bestowed on them such an excellent good, and not from any need of mine, or to gain for myself any advantage, but for their salvation, so that by the gift of life and the benefits of grace, they might be led to the excellent goods of eternal happiness. Although justice demands and wisdom dictates that I refer all to God's honor and glory, I do so without detriment to your benefit and happiness, because your entire salvation is rooted in God, and no one can be blessed except by a final ordination and complete and pure relation to him who is the Alpha and Omega, the beginning and end.⁴⁸ Furthermore, properly speaking a gift is defined as a present made without any anticipation of repayment, an unreturnable giving. Yet what is given with a view to one's advantage or with expectation of return is more of a sale than a gift; and if one seeks a temporal advantage from something spiritual, he commits the sin of simony. Further, by imparting this gift and so communicating myself to you, I have clearly shown the immensity of my charity, the greatness of my opulence and magnificence, and a cheerful spirit of giving. Indeed, if *God loves a cheerful giver*,⁴⁹ how much more is he cheerful in giving? In communicating this gift, I have opened the treasury of my liberality, and I bestowed gifts in accord with supreme magnificence, giving myself entirely—God and Man, Body, Soul, and Divinity—in the Eucharist. Thus I opened my hand and filled every rational animal with the greatest possible blessing;⁵⁰ and what I give as a revealed reality in the heavenly fatherland, I have given here as a veiled reality. Consider the nobility, copiousness, supereffluence, and most brilliant excellence of this gift, because in it is contained all good, and from it are drawn grace and glory, and by it one attains the fulness of happiness. Rightly, therefore, does the Church sing: *O sacrum convivium, in quo Christus sumitur, recolitur memoria*

---
⁴⁷ Rom. 15:6.   ⁴⁸ Rev. 1:8.   ⁴⁹ 2 Cor. 9:7b.   ⁵⁰ Cf. Ps. 144:16.

passionis eius, mens impletur gratia, et futurae gloriae nobis pignus datur![51] Do not be ungrateful to this giver nor unmindful of his charity and munificence, and do not return evil to him for such a good.[52] Do not draw yourself away from him for he seeks nothing but your self, that is, the glorification of your body and soul.

Further, this Sacrament is rightly called a sacrifice because it most worthily represents and commemorates the Passion of Christ and his immolation on the Cross, and it is offered daily by the Church to God the Father for our reconciliation, purification, and salvation. Indeed, I so ardently love you, I had such a generous spirit towards you, that it was not enough for me to give and offer myself for you once; in the infinite fountain and abyss of my wisdom, I devised and established this most mysterious means whereby I might continually be present and given for you, and offered for you, and be consumed by you in a manner acceptable and proportionate to you, under the veils of bread and wine and not in the form of flesh and blood nor in the proper quantity that I subsist in it, although I am received together with it. From the beginning of the world, this Sacrifice was prefigured in the offerings of Abel and in his slaying; then in the sacrifices of the Patriarchs under the natural law; and in the Law of Moses in the various oblations. And in the beginning of the early Church I instituted it at the Last Supper. This in itself is most acceptable to the eternal Father, and it is most efficacious in achieving all that for which it was instituted and offered. In addition, it is a potent medicine against the remnants of vices, against raging concupiscence, against venial and daily sins, and against forgotten mortal sins; and in a singular way it is effective against all wounds of the soul, as we shall expound more clearly below.

Finally, it is called in a special way the Sacrament of the Altar, for it is confected and offered, received and handled on the altar. In it, one thing is seen exteriorly, another thing is signified interiorly, one thing is externally represented, another thing is internally contained. But for now, let this explanation of the reasons for these names suffice. Yet it is sometimes called by other names too. For it is called Victim insofar as it contains Christ himself, and he is

---

[51] E.N. "O sacred banquet, in which Christ is received, the memory of His Passion is renewed, the mind is filled with grace, and a pledge of future glory given to us." It is the antiphon to the Magnificat in Vespers on the Feast of Corpus Christi. It is attributed to St. Thomas Aquinas.

[52] Cf. Jer. 18:20a.

offered in it. It is also called a deposit or pledge of future glory and salvation, because your whole happiness consists in the clear vision and full enjoyment of that which you invisibly receive here under veiled forms.

EIGHTH ARTICLE
Greater elaboration on the above: in what manner Christ is food for rational creatures according to both his natures, and that the Eucharist is the Sacrament of the most lofty and divine love.

TRUTH: It is not fitting for a rational creature to have a principal and supreme head other than God, nor a source of spiritual life other than God's Spirit; hence it follows that God is his food. For that which nourishes and sustains the vital heat in an animal body is that animal's food. And since only the divine goodness sustains and nourishes the living heat—i.e., charity—by which a rational creature lives spiritually, it follows that God's goodness is truly the food of man, in whom vital heat is the sincere and holy love and spiritual friendship by which the faithful cleave to God and adhere to one another, and by which they take care of one another, and provide for and serve each other with promptness, mutually loving and defending each other in all things. For the uncreated goodness so strongly draws and binds its true lovers, that they also inseparably purely adhere to each other and on account of it embrace one another with sincere love.

PRIEST: This I readily grant, since the limited and defective goodness, sweetness, benefit, and beauty of creatures so intensely excites, nourishes, and increases love of them in him who knows them; how much more, then, does the pure and infinite goodness, whose loving kindness knows no end, which is itself essentially unbounded sweetness, most agreeable, and pure unlimited beauty, do so?

TRUTH: Your argument is sound, because the goodness of any creature is nothing other than a small and tenuous vestige, absolutely and infinitely imperfect, of that first fountain of uncreated goodness which overflows into all things. Accordingly, what is the pleasure that arises from created goodness except a vestige of the vestigial divine goodness and eternal pleasure—nay more, a shadow of its shadow? If, therefore, the lowest of its vestiges—namely the pleasures arising from sensible, carnal, and corruptible things—are able to excite, foment, and inflame men to love them so much that their lovers seem to burn or glow, how much more strongly will the superlatively splendid and beautiful goodness of God excite, nourish, and enkindle holy loves and immaculate desires in the hearts of those it has enlightened? With good reason, therefore, is the divine goodness said to be the food and nourishment of vital and spiritual heat just as a woman's beauty is the nourishment and food of impure love; hence, when such is withdrawn from the heart of a lover through forgetfulness or other occupation, the fire of base love is soon extinguished, but when it is brought before the sight or memory, the unclean love revives and is renewed. Much more so does the Godhead's immense beauty and sweetness feed and kindle in its lovers a dignified and becoming love.

Moreover, when you perceive that a certain man is highly virtuous, just, upright, and wise, does not the report of him alone stir up your love, and all the more so the more distinctly you see his virtues? How much more ought the consideration of the infinite perfection of God in every respect inflame you with incomparable love?

In addition, just as our taste experiences and discovers varieties of food and drink that excite and whet its appetite, and just as the good heart finds that all the words and deeds and entire way of life of a good man — especially a heroic and perfect one — provoke, encourage, and enkindle his love for that man, so the hearts of the elect find that the words and deeds of God stir up and enkindle in them the vivifying heat of holy love, and feed them spiritual delights like so many choice spiritual dishes. Therefore, the words and benefits of God are the food of faithful souls and the fodder of divine love. And so the goodness, beauty, sweetness, and munificence of God, as well as his benefits, words, and promises, are an incitement, fodder, and kindling for a pure love of God and of delight and pleasure in the same. Scripture speaks frequently in this mode: *I shall be satisfied when your glory shall appear;*[53] and, *You shall make them drink of the torrent of your pleasure;*[54] and, *How sweet are your words to my palate!*[55] A good man is amiable and sweet to his beloved, because of his very virtue as well as his good words and deeds, yet all these things are good and sweet due only to the barest sprinkling and tenuous partaking of the highest and uncreated goodness and of the primal and, by comparison, abyssal Sweetness.

---

[53] Ps. 16:15. [54] Ps. 35:9. [55] Ps. 118:103.

Further, some benefits are transitory, and the love proceeding from their possession ceases when these benefits cease. Other benefits last as long as this life, such as the benefits of parents to their children, and most of all the benefits of God to his creatures. Therefore, the love arising from it ought to last for our whole lives—indeed, it ought to grow daily and to burn freshly and more strongly from the continuation, renewal, and multiplication of the heavenly Father's benefits, yet in such a way that all is sincerely ordered towards God. For I speak at present of a rightly-ordered, gratuitous love, not warped nor befouled by self-interest or self-pleasure, a love which is properly called charity, which has no venality or bartering as part of it, by which the lover does not intend to acquire anything for himself nor to make the beloved his own possession. Indeed, this love intends and endeavors to obtain for the beloved whatever is in his interest and honor.

Additionally, as an animal body cannot maintain its life without the incorporation of suitable food,[56] so the life of grace cannot exist in the human heart without the incordation and invisceration of the spiritual food that sustains this life.[57] Now incordation is nothing other than a uniting of the spirit or heart, in other words, love insofar as its motive force is concerned. And as the incorporation of food is a true consumption of it, preceded by such preparations as breaking and chewing, so incordation is a true consumption of that spiritual food. And since no one can possess the life of grace nor the life of glory without incordation, that is, union of heart or love, it follows that without the spiritual consuming of God, neither of these lives can subsist. Therefore, I said: *He that eats me, the same also shall live by me*; and, *He that eats this bread shall live forever*; and also: *I am the Bread of Life*.[58] Indeed, I am the Bread of Life insofar as I make others love me spiritually and nourish them by that love. And pay careful attention to this because it is the root proof of the vivifying and ineffable Sacrament, which a well-disposed intellect must needs grasp.

Further, some heretics deny the truth of this Sacrament due to a double error. First, they equated consumption with mastication, when the food is chewed, ground by the teeth, and passed to the

---

[56] L. *incorporatione*: food being incorporated or becoming part of the body.
[57] L. *incordatione et invisceratione*: the spiritual good becomes incorporated into one's heart and one's deepest self (*viscera*), literally, the bowels.
[58] John 6:58, 59, 35.

stomach. Second, because they did not distinguish between bodily and spiritual consumption. Now bodily eating involves stripping a food of its proper form and changing it into the substance of the person eating it. But in spiritual consumption, the opposite is the case, because the more pure and complete the spiritual food that comes to the heart, the more profoundly it unites with and assimilates it to itself and in a certain way changes the heart into itself, as Augustine has the Lord say: You will not transform me into you, you will be transformed into me.[59]

Now as truth is the food of the intellect, so goodness is the food of the will. Also, truth is to the intellect as light is to the senses; and as bodily food strengthens the body when it is incorporated into it, so truth strengthens and refreshes the intellect with certitude when it is totally united to it, for this is true knowledge and understanding.

Again, as food expands and enlarges the body in three dimensions, namely, length, width or breadth, and immensity or height, so truth extends into the length of the present, past, and future, into the breadth of concomitant and circumspected things, and into the depths of the essential and the intimate. Likewise, breadth in the superior affective power is love, which extends even to enemies for God's sake. Its height, magnificence, or goodness is shown by the fact that only the most luminous first truth is the proper food of the intellect, and that only the first, most pure, and purifying goodness is the food of the will. Indeed, the most proper definition of food is that its consumption appeases hunger, delights the eater, repairs loss, and increases, refreshes, and fills the eater. And it is certain that neither the intellect's hunger or desire nor the will's hunger is appeased until the intellect feasts on the first truth and the will tastes the first, sweetest goodness. This truth and goodness alone suffice to fulfill, appease, and satisfy every capacity, hunger, and appetite of your intellect and will, to content and especially to delight and strengthen them. The intellect cannot rest except in the knowledge of the First Cause, nor the affections except in the enjoyment of the First Cause.[60] But knowing and enjoying are the mind's proper acts of comestion; therefore, the mind's bread and nutriment is the first truth and the highest good, of which all other truths and goodnesses

---

[59] Cf. St. Augustine, *Confessions*, VII, 10.
[60] E.N. The editor notes that some manuscripts read that the affections cannot rest except in the First Goodness (*in primae bonitatis*).

are like the outlines of a cheap and insignificant picture. Indeed, if knowledge of the First Truth is taken away from the intellect, and love of the divine goodness from the will, both are spiritually dead. For an intellect that is ignorant of God and an affection that does not love him are living unjustly, since they do not live unto God, nor do they refer or direct themselves and their resources towards his honor and service, from whom they have been given all that they are and possess. Moreover, uncreated Truth and Wisdom is the created intellect's only spouse; other truths are, as it were, footmen and handmaids, with whom it commits impious fornication when it rests in and adheres to them rather than the First Truth. Similarly, the created affection must be directed to the Highest Good by adhering to it above all and as its end, and by referring to it all the goodness it finds dispersed among creatures. Hence, this heavenly Bread should be eaten not only daily, but always without ceasing; and it ought to be held, embraced, and maintained in the mind without interruption. For this reason, it was called not only the daily, but also supersubstantial [bread],[61] and the loss of it spells the extinction of internal and spiritual life. It is not necessary, however, that the soul be always actually focused on the First Truth. Therefore, since the soul was born to eat this Bread, and God does not create anything uselessly or in vain, he was obliged to present this Bread, namely himself, to the soul in an edible and ingestible form.

Additionally, since God is incomparably more merciful and provident towards the children of his grace that any mother towards the children of her womb, and mothers provide food to their children out of natural piety and charity according to the child's capacity and disposition, in the form of milk, mush, or bread; much more does God's inestimable mercy and fatherly providence dispense this supersubstantial Bread to his adopted children according to their capacity. Some of his children have come of age, strong and robust, namely the citizens of heaven, who can eat this Bread in its proper form. He also has small children, who are unable to eat this Bread in its proper, solid form; therefore, he must set before them the same food in another form which is suitable for them. But there is no form more suitable than bread; any other form would conceal it, and the form of flesh would cause revulsion in those desiring to eat it. But the form of bread was most apt for this purpose. Further, in this life, man is unable to bear that heavenly Bread in its clarity

---

[61] Luke 11:3; Matt. 6:11.

and glory. And if man is shown divine things that are beyond him, his strength fails and he loses himself, as is evident in the visions of the Prophets and the raptures of contemplatives. Now every prophetic vision or contemplation in the present life, however clear it seems to us, is more distant from the lustrous knowledge of the Saints in the heavenly fatherland than the darkest night from the splendor of the fairest day. Therefore, that supersubstantial Bread is set before man under the appearance of material bread because bread is the most basic, universal, and convenient food, and nicely signifies the properties of the divine food.

PRIEST: O supreme Truth, you have subtly and devoutly taught us, insofar as our weak mind is able to grasp, how our souls are refreshed by you. Nevertheless, one might object that the Saints and the elect who from the beginning of the world up to the time of the early Church were nourished by this food even in the present life through the contemplation of faith, and love, as also was the case with many holy anchorites dwelling in perpetual solitude. Therefore, it does not appear that the Real Presence of your assumed humanity, i.e., of your Body and Blood in the Sacrament, is necessary, since a figurative presence seems to suffice, especially because your eternal goodness and uncreated truth seem to be the created mind's food or refreshment only as an objective and efficient cause, and not as an intrinsically inherent formal cause. But that is how knowledge and love of the highest truth and goodness feeds and refreshes us. Therefore, if it please you, show us more persuasively that you are truly present in the Sacrament also in your assumed humanity.

TRUTH: I will demonstrate this directly.

NINTH ARTICLE
That on the table of the altar Christ is truly and really present and contained in the form of his assumed humanity.

TRUTH: The only-begotten Son of God, who became man for the sake of men, exercised and assumed in this world three offices for the benefit of mankind, namely, that of priest, advocate, and physician. For a lesser and inferior priest than he would not have been capable to sacramentalize and sanctify the human race and the assembly of the entire Church militant. Similarly, it was not possible for a lesser advocate to plead the case of the entire human race. Again, it was impossible for a lesser physician to cure the injuries, wounds, and diseases of the entire human race. Since, therefore, these three things are accomplished in the Mass, and the exercise of the Mass includes these three offices, it is necessary that the only-begotten Son of God principally undertake, carry out, and fulfill these three things during the Mass.

Indeed, the Mass is the sacramentalization and sanctification of the entire people of God. This cannot be performed principally by a lesser priest, rather it is necessary to call upon Christ, who is truly the high priest. Therefore, it is evident that he must be present in the sacrament by which the people are sanctified, and that the sacramentalization is primarily done by him. And so it is necessary for him to come in his role as a priest, that is, as man and in human form. Further, the priestly office, which is the sanctification of the people, cannot be fulfilled in the Mass except through the sacrifice by which sanctification and grace are obtained for the people. But no sacrificial victim is able to obtain this grace for all the people except that which Christ himself offered on the altar of the Cross, and this sacrificial victim was Christ himself. Therefore, he himself is personally present and is offered to the Father at Mass.

Additionally, a faithful advocate of a cause which he has undertaken to advance is personally present, if possible, whenever the cause itself requires it. Therefore, since in the Mass the cause of the whole Church is pleaded by the priest, as if by a procurator, before the eternal Father, and since Christ is the almighty and most faithful advocate, with the power to manifest his presence everywhere—which is highly fitting and even necessary for the resolution of such a cause, indeed even to a priest acting as procurator—it is evident that he is really present.

Similarly, it is necessary for a faithful and expert physician to come personally to the patients he has undertaken to cure and who cannot be healed by anyone else whenever their infirmity requires it, and to apply unto them ointments and medicines. Therefore, because the entire Church is sick, and every member of the Church is sick—that is, in need of medicine, whether for healing, for preservation in good health, or for protection from ill health— it follows that he must come to cure whenever the Church's treatment is at issue and the cure of the people is sought. Since this is especially done at Mass, it behooves Christ to be there present as physician, so that he may bestow upon the people the ministry of healing and the grace of health. Therefore, he comes with an alabaster box full of all kinds of spiritual ointments, which is his humanity, wholly broken and opened up on the Cross. Or he comes with his Flesh, which is the most efficacious poultice against all spiritual lesions and pains, as the strongest and sweetest antidote against all noxious humors of vices, and with his Blood, which is like a soothing and most sweet syrup, a liquid medicine effective against all infirmities and wounds of the soul. The powers of these two were most especially exhibited in the Lord's Passion itself.

And so the whole Mass is principally an office of Christ, although the priest and ministers perform their ministries. Hence, it is necessary for him to be present at the solemnity of the Mass and to fulfill for them the previously mentioned ministries. Attend to the fact, therefore, that the celebration of the Mass is nothing other than the sanctification of the people through the invocation of the divine name and the sacrifice, and the pleading or the advancing of the cause of the same people before God through prayers and offerings. It is also the administration of spiritual medication or potions to the same people, as if through an antidote and syrup, as well as their refreshment through the bread and *corn of the elect* and by the *wine springing forth virgins*.[62] Indeed, what is the boon of the Lord, or what is his beauty, but these gifts, these ointments, and these unblemished sacrifices?

Furthermore, just as men advance in natural and social love by the common partaking of bodily refreshment, so ought they especially to be led to spiritual love and ecclesiastical unity through the common partaking of this spiritual food. Finally, to clarify this, certain reasons have been introduced earlier: that food must really be united with the one who eats it, and that a full sign of love ought to correspond to the greatness of charity.

Again, since Christ offered his entire complete self for our benefit, progress, and salvation, and since nothing so enkindles a person towards love as the consideration of the death that someone has suffered voluntarily for him, together with the perfect demonstration of prevenient love of another for him, Christ therefore willed to be really offered in the Mass in commemoration of his Passion for us and of his love towards us. Again, since he is the supreme and incomparable sacrifice acceptable to the heavenly Father and of the sweetest fragrance, he willed to be thus personally offered,

---

[62] Zech. 9:17.

so that he might more abundantly help those for whom he once offered himself on the Cross. Finally, since his heart burned like a furnace with the fire of divine love and the zeal for man's salvation, he offered himself completely to everything that would most promote the worship, reverence, praise, and glory of God the Father, as well as be a manifold and gracious help for the human race. All this is completely fulfilled by the fact that he is personally sacrificed in the Mass. Through this, the highest love, mercy, generosity, and beneficence of God towards men are recalled, his benefits are extolled, his promises magnified, the divine majesty is most devoutly praised, glorified, and honored, and thanks are endlessly offered to him. Nor should this be overlooked: that the greatest opportunity for merit is bestowed upon men in the offering of such an incomprehensible Sacrament, since man's understanding is brought into captivity unto the obedience of Christ, through faith in those most marvelous things which are believed of this Sacrament because of the authority of the divine Truth's testimony.[63]

TENTH ARTICLE
A continuation of these matters.

TRUTH: You see that the ruler of a worldly state appoints public advocates to make up for the incapacity of the inexpert, lest such men lose their rights by the lack of expertise. How much more suitably, then, did the Judge and King of all men, the God of the universe, mindful of the foolishness and inadequacy of men, and addressing to the danger of their eternal damnation, establish a public and entirely sufficient advocate for the whole human race,[64] who, as far as justice allows, unceasingly renders aid to the wretched in the court of God the Father? Finally, since there are three intentions and principal acts of divine worship and true religion, namely, the honoring of God, the obtaining of pardon, and the attainment of grace, much would be lacking in the worship of God if, amidst such great transgression and guilt, there were no advocate and priest, like Christ, effective in obtaining forgiveness and grace for all. Hence, until Christ's coming the worship of God was very incomplete, yet the ancient faithful were heard through their faith in the Savior to come.

---

[63] 2 Cor. 10:5.   [64] 1 John 2:1.

Therefore, Christ, out of his manifold love, mercy, and generosity, so ordered things that he is offered daily in innumerable places and by innumerable priests, although it is one sacrifice and sacrament, so that God the Father might be more abundantly honored when in every place this most pure oblation is offered to him.[65] In this service, his goodness, mercy, excellence, and all his perfection, wisdom, and providence are magnificently extolled, and his most excellent works are proclaimed, and he is honored with many acts of worship. Indeed, experience teaches that, although this Sacrament is utterly incomprehensible, nothing so preserves the actual practice of the Christian faith as does the celebration, sacrifice, and communion of this Sacrament. For this reason, the faithful assemble in the church every day, confess in due time, and prepare themselves for communion through confessions, satisfactions, prayers, fasts, and abstinences. Thus, just as sharing a table and appointed hour for bodily refreshment is the main reason that a family of the same household and the children and servants of the same father gather together physically, so the celebration and consumption of this spiritual food is the main reason that the faithful gather together in mind and body in the church and join together in a kind of spiritual friendship.

PRIEST: These things are altogether as you say. I, on the other hand, setting aside lofty matters, desire to be informed how I ought to prepare myself for this celebration, and also how I should behave during the celebration, and finally how after the celebration I ought to keep myself, give thanks, and remain in grace.

TRUTH: You desire well, and I will soon endeavor to satisfy such a holy desire, with but a little preliminary discussion of the dignity of this Sacrament beyond what has already been said, and also of the dignity of the priestly power and order. Thus, you will be able to understand more clearly how virtuous the life of priests ought to be, and how diligently they ought to prepare, keep, and direct themselves.

ELEVENTH ARTICLE
On the dignity of the Sacrament of the Altar.

TRUTH: Consider that nearly everything that has been introduced up to this point pertains to the explanation of the dignity of the

---

[65] Mal. 1:11.

Sacrament of the Eucharist. For although the bread is converted directly into the Body, and wine into the Blood, yet, as I explained to you, by concomitance, after consecration, both under the species of bread as well as wine, the whole Christ is perfectly and integrally contained and offered to the Father. However, just as Christ according to his assumed humanity—but not according to his divine nature—was able to merit, to suffer, and to make satisfaction, so he was able to offer himself. Yet the efficacy and suitability of meriting so infinitely and making satisfaction for all men so fully derived from his immediate and hypostatic, that is, personal, union with his divine nature. And so, in the Sacrament, the whole Christ—God and man—is contained, consumed, and offered.

And you know that Christ, according to his divine nature, is truly equal to God the Father, and therefore of absolutely infinite dignity, excellence, holiness, and majesty. Moreover, according to his human nature so united to the divinity, he is more worthy and dearer to God than the entire remainder of the universe. Indeed, the more God loves a creature, the more he bestows greater and more goods upon it. Therefore, since the eternal Word has communicated his uncreated personal being to the human nature he assumed, including it in the same being in which the eternal Word eternally subsists, it is evident that he communicated and gave to it a greater good than he gave to all the rest of creation taken together and the entirety of the existing universe. In addition, he provided to Christ's soul a habitual grace that is, in a way, infinite, in other words, so great that no created mind is capable of receiving a greater grace. And the same must be said of the virtues and the gifts and their acts, as well as of the gifts and goods of glory conferred upon Christ's soul from the beginning of his creation. These were, as far as his superior powers are concerned, of such excellence that no creature is capable of receiving such gifts in a more abundant fullness. And although the sanctity, blessedness, and glory of the most blessed Virgin are inestimably greater and fuller than the happiness and glory of any Saint in the heavenly fatherland, as was fitting for the true Mother of the true God—a true co-parent with God the Father incomparably and truly ineffably honored, filled, enriched, beatified, and exalted by God ahead of any other servant of God— yet the grace, holiness, perfection, blessedness, and glory of Christ's humanity transcends inexpressibly more the perfection, holiness, and glory of his most worthy Mother than the perfection and blessedness of the God-bearing Virgin does the grace and glory of any other of the blessed.

PRIEST: The consideration of these things terrifies me. Indeed, from what you say it is easy to consider how incomprehensible the dignity of this most venerable Sacrament is. When I reflect upon this and at the same time compare my own indignity, vileness, and complete perversity, is it any wonder if I shudder with horror, because (as I fear) I have so often approached unworthily, and fear lest I should again approach unworthily? And yet these very things I now hear, I have in the past at some point read about—but, alas!— I have not reflected upon them as I ought. Certainly, I acknowledge and confess that you, O Lord Jesus Christ, the only-begotten Son of the eternal Father, are no less glorious, no less resplendent and radiant, no less adored by the holy angels in the hands of the priest, than you are in the bosom and right hand of God the Father. You are no less worthy to be touched and consumed in the Sacrament than you are in the empyreal heaven—indeed, the more graciously you incline to our lowliness, the more you ought to be received with heartfelt thanksgiving and reverence. Ah! My Lord, what shall I say here? Your most loving and excellent Mother, while you were a small baby newly born of her, cradled you in her most pure lap with a kind of reverential fear and immense reverence. She gazed upon you and pressed you to her virginal breasts, not immoderately presuming upon her maternal authority, or the most singular privilege bestowed upon her, or her incomparable sanctity and supreme grace—on the contrary, she did so scarcely daring to touch you. So also your kinsman the great herald and Forerunner, of whom you asserted, among those born of women none greater had been born, shuddered to baptize you—indeed, he confessed himself unworthy to perform the least service for you.[66] Yet I, the vilest transgressor, have so often approached the celebration of your most sacred mysteries so fearlessly, impurely, and coolly. I have handled you so indisposed, I have received you so unworthily, and afterwards remained so ungrateful, unguarded, and so quickly prone to relapse.

TRUTH: You conclude and reflect wisely. It is not necessary for me to expound further on the dignity or eminence of this Sacrament.

PRIEST: No, my Lord. Yet I marvel at this your inestimable charity, condescension, and generosity to us, and yet I do not wish to marvel. For just as greater movements drive out lesser ones, so

---

[66] Matt. 11:11; 3:14; John 1:27.

does greater wonder drive out the lesser. When I consider that you have fashioned the fragile, fallen, and frail race of men for the clear vision and blissful enjoyment of your superessential divinity, it does not appear to me so surprising that you, for a time in this exile, give yourself to them veiled, since you will soon give yourself revealed in the heavenly palace, to be looked upon supernaturally, clearly, face to face, and unceasingly, to be enjoyed most sweetly and sempiternally, to be possessed most securely with hereditary contentedness. Here, in this valley of tears, you give yourself for our support and merit; there, in the heavenly fatherland, for our glorification and reward.

TRUTH: Blessed are those whom the Paraclete, the Holy Spirit, proceeding from me, teaches of the law of God as he now teaches you[67]—provided that both they and you persist in this grace with prompt obedience and with final perseverance. But if you cast God away from yourself, he will cast you off from himself for eternity.[68]

PRIEST: May your boundless grace and your mercy constantly preserve me from both of these rejections.

TWELFTH ARTICLE
On the most excellent dignity of the power and order of the priesthood of the law of the Gospel.

TRUTH: I was made man and came into this world so that I might deify men, and I bestowed upon them precious and abundant gifts of graces,[69] so that through these they might become partakers of the divine nature—not by losing their own nature, nor by abandoning their substance, but by perfecting it in its accidental qualities. And now, to be sure, in this life this deification is begun and incomplete, advancing daily. Later, in the heavenly fatherland, through the most blessed reward, it will be fixed, happy, and perpetual. Thus I first deified in the highest degree my specially chosen and most beloved Mother, from whose most pure blood I assumed human nature. Next, I deified the most holy Forerunner, and after my Passion, the glorious Apostles, whom I filled with the first fruits of the Holy Spirit above all the Saints of the natural and Mosaic laws. I adorned them most excellently, supernaturally, and divinely with the gifts of sanctifying grace (*gratiae gratum faciens*) and grace freely given (*gratiae gratis data*). To them, among other

---

[67] Ps. 93:12; 1 John 2:27.   [68] 1 Chr. 28:9   [69] 2 Pet. 1:4.

things, I also bestowed ecclesiastical powers, among which the priestly power stands out and shines forth. Such is its greatness that even the angelic hosts marvel profoundly at its magnitude.

PRIEST: Certainly, O Supreme Truth, it quickly becomes evident from what has been said that the greater the dignity and excellence of this life-giving, divine, and adorable Sacrament the more sublime and divine is this supernatural power of consecrating, handling, consuming, and providing to others this Sacrament. Its consecration and dispensing has been granted to none of the angelic spirits, nor to any of the most sacred order of Cherubim and Seraphim, but only to priests. Nor do I think that all powers of jurisdiction, papal and episcopal—by which the Supreme Pontiff outshines all the other ministers of the Church—is as great as this priestly power, with which even the lowest priest is adorned.

TRUTH: Gladly do I hear you discussing a subject in such a Catholic manner. For the Supreme Pontiff does not exercise any greater power over my true Body than the lowest priest, but only over my Mystical Body, which is the Church. Far greater and more worthy than all the other acts which the Supreme Pontiff exercises regarding my Mystical Body it is to consecrate my true Body and Blood, to render me, true God and man, present, and to offer it to God the Father for the whole Church, and to so handle, receive, and distribute it.

PRIEST: O how great is the dignity and yet also the vileness of the impious priest, the carnal presbyter! Indeed, the greater his dignity is from your office, the greater is his vileness from his vice. The great Constantine, converted from paganism to you by evident miracles, understood, considered, and dreaded this, if I err not, as he regarded you during his baptism and called priests gods, saying: If I were to see a priest acting shamefully, I would cover him with my cloak, lest he be seen acting in such a way. Your chosen one, Francis, likewise said: If the martyr Lawrence and a poor little priest should meet me, I would allow St. Lawrence to stand alone and I would run to the poor little priest, and with bended knee kiss his hand.

TRUTH: You speak faithfully. For the light of the sun does not exceed the light of the moon or the stars as much as the priestly order and power all civil and secular powers. Nor does the most precious gold or brightest gem surpass vile mud as much as the dignity of the priests of the Gospel surpasses regal and imperial excellence. Finally, just as the soul is far superior to the body, so is spiritual power far more dignified than the earthly.

PRIEST: Alas, that we fall so short of this!

TRUTH: Listen further. Consider how eminently the priest, through his priestly character, which is the power and sacred order of the presbyterate, shines resplendent above the others and represents me. Just as I consecrated my Body and Blood at the Last Supper and offered it to God the Father on the Cross,[70] and by sacrificing myself possessed the office of advocate, priest, and physician—indeed, also reconciler and savior[71]—so the priest, by the power bestowed upon him, consecrates and offers to the eternal Father on the table of the altar my Body and Blood, and indeed he represents my person and that of my Church, mediating between God and the people. Through prayers, sacrifices, and merits, he reconciles the people to God, and he obtains God's gifts for the people, and exercises the cause and the care of the Church. Thus, in his own way, he vicariously exercises the offices of advocate, mediator, priest, physician, and cooperator of the Savior; wherefore, he is also called an angel of the Lord of hosts.[72] Moreover, since the power of consecrating my true Body and absolving and binding the Mystical Body—namely its subjects in the forum of conscience—are in reality one and the same, they are called two powers because of the difference in actions. It is evident how sublime are the properties and appellations given to priests, since they are heavenly key-bearers, cupbearers of the divine Blood, guests of the supreme King, earthly angels, heavenly men, physicians of the soul, reconcilers of the guilty, correctors of the erring, exhibitors of the divine sacraments, and, in a way, fathers and saviors of their neighbors.

Did not Moses once speak to the Levites, not to the priests, saying: *Is it a small thing unto you that the God of Israel* has chosen *you ... and should stand before the congregation of the people* and *burn incense to him*, etc.?[73] If this was a great thing, how incomparably more excellent is it to stand before the people of Christ to sacrifice and offer, not the flesh of bulls and calves, but the only-begotten Son of the eternal Father? King Uzziah was stricken with leprosy because he usurped the priestly office for himself.[74] Likewise, Gideon, the strongest of men, despite being worthy of an angelic apparition, allocution, and instruction, was brought to ruin because he made an ephod and altar for himself,

---

[70] Matt. 26:26–28; Eph. 5:2.   [71] 1 John 2:1.   [72] Mal. 2:7.
[73] Num. 16:9; 2 Chr. 29:11.   [74] 2 Chr. 26:16 et seq.

intruding beyond his worth with respect to that duty.[75] And note well that the entire Levitical and priestly office of the written law related to carnal, material, and irrational offerings and sacrifices, wherein no sanctity existed formally. Now, if the office of these Levites and priests of the law was worthy of such great reverence and dignity, and if those who usurped it were punished, how incomparably superior is the priesthood of the law of the Gospel, which pertains to a sacrifice of unbounded dignity, and has other equally exalted functions, transcending the priesthood under the Law as light does shadow, truth a figure, and the spirit flesh? And again, how greatly they sin who perform the functions of so great a priesthood unworthily, staining it with a degenerate manner of life?

PRIEST: Nothing truer can be said. And if any read this dialogue, I hope they will be somewhat moved to repentance.

TRUTH: The hearts of many are hardened, and the more they are obligated to live spiritually and virtuously, the more severely they are blinded by the just judgment of God, as they do not strive to live in a manner consonant to the demands of their priesthood.

THIRTEENTH ARTICLE
On the preparation for celebration.

TRUTH: You know how often and in what manner commandments were given through Moses regarding those legal ministers of the temple who offered irrational beasts and inanimate materials: *The priests also that come to the Lord, let them be sanctified, lest he strike them*;[76] and again: The priests offer burnt offering and the bread to God, *and therefore they shall be holy* to their God, and they will not defile his name;[77] and also: *A man who has a blemish, he shall not offer*, etc.[78] Indeed, to the same degree that the priesthood of the law of the Gospel and the law of the Gospel itself are more spiritual, more perfect, and more divine than that typic priesthood of the Law and the pedagogical and servile Law itself,[79] the priests and ministers of the altar of the law of the Gospel must be more spiritual, more perfect, and more godlike than those priests and Levites under the Law. They must be on guard lest they defile the name of God, that is, lest they scandalize the people and provoke

---

[75] Judges 6:11 et seq.; 8:27.   [76] Ex. 19:22.   [77] Lev. 21:6.
[78] Lev. 21:17.   [79] Cf. Gal. 3:24.

them to dishonor their Creator, and lest they offer him an abominable worship, and, as much as it depends upon them, insinuate and show him—before whom they themselves dare to stand so irreverently and greatly defiled—not to be worthy of honor.

PRIEST: We read that the priests of the Law were subject to many commandments, especially at the time of their ministry in the temple. God said to them: *You shall not drink wine nor any thing that may make drunk...when you enter into the tabernacle of the testimony,...that you may have knowledge to discern between holy and unholy.*[80] They were also commanded at that time to abstain from their wives, to leave their homes and the cares and occupations of their family affairs, to dwell in the abodes situated around the temple, and to burn incense in the temple, lest the smell of the sacrifices afflict anyone.[81]

TRUTH: You remember well. And although these things were commanded to them literally, they nevertheless have a spiritual meaning and prefigured other things. For instance, the priests and ministers of the Church ought to avoid all carnality, especially the foul and vile vices of taste and touch in which the greatest disgrace lies, and from which in times past even the priests of the Gentiles—or at least some—withdrew themselves completely. Likewise, priests and all those appointed to the sacred orders of the Church should abstain from all superfluous worldly occupations, indeed even domestic and necessary affairs, and focus on divine things with their whole heart, and with both mind and body present themselves eagerly in the temple. They ought to perfume the Church with the sweet odor of a praiseworthy reputation—a reputation of an exemplary, virtuous life—so that in every place there may be a good fragrance to God and the fragrance of life to the faithful leading to eternal salvation, lest the people of God be disturbed or scandalized by the odor of their infamous manner of life and detestable reputation.[82] Therefore, consider now how grave their sins are, how infinite their condemnation, and how intolerable the punishment deserved by those the priests and clerics of the Gospel law who—having forgotten the fear and reverence due God and all modesty—sully, dishonor, and trample upon their priesthood and the name of their God with the vices of gluttony and lust, avarice, setting bad example, worldly cares, ambition, vanity, negligence, and many omissions.

---

[80] Lev. 10:9, 10.   [81] Ex. 30:8.   [82] 2 Cor. 2:14–16.

PRIEST: O Lord, what judgment hangs over these men! And why are we miserable and foolish priests so temerarious, so negligent, and so dissolute?

TRUTH: *I will meet them as a bear that is robbed of her whelps*, I will tear up their insides, *I will devour them as a lion;* I will make *them as an oven of fire*,[83] I will drown them in the infernal pits, I will place them in the sulphureous, blazing wells of the underworld, and they will be enclosed in the burning furnaces of Acheron, cast down unto the bottom of a scorching lake. They will not be tormented so much by the intense cold and fierce fires of Gehenna as by the burden and desolation of extreme bitter despair. *The heavens shall reveal* their *iniquities*,[84] and the earth shall rise against them, and their crimes will be made manifest to all. The entirety of the creatures will fight against them for me.[85]

If you seek to avoid these torments, therefore, prepare yourself fittingly to celebrate Mass as best you can. Take care lest your heart be immoderately weighed down by food and drink or sleep. Do not engorge your belly through that mouth by which you consume my Body and the Blood. Do not defile your tongue through which you utter the most sacred words of the Mass and the Canon with garrulousness, idle words, or (which would be most abominable) detraction, sowing of discord, lies, or stinging, scandalous words. Diligently restrain and guard your heart from all wandering, distraction, and dissolution, especially in divine matters, and also from all illicit affection. Restrain your eyes from incautious staring and gazing everywhere, but especially in the church. Unceasingly consider the presence of the Almighty, and live solicitously in the presence of your supreme and most fearsome Judge. Advance with fear, and walk in an exemplary manner. Occupy yourself fruitfully and in an orderly way, and strive constantly to make progress.

PRIEST: Such a preparation, I confess, is good. Yet when I and those like me have read our preparations, we deem ourselves to be prepared to celebrate Mass, having said the confession.

TRUTH: Is such a verbal preparation sufficient? Can there be a true confession without contrition or compunction? But what kind of contrition or compunction is there in a man who, after confession, soon returns to his former frivolities, negligences, or sins? Is not a virtuous life, a clean conscience, and a fearful and grateful mind required?

---

[83] Hos. 13:8; Ps. 20:10.   [84] Job 20:27.   [85] Cf. Wis. 5:21.

PRIEST: Who can live like this among men? And although such a virtuous manner of life might be possible for those in religious life, it appears impossible, or at least very difficult, for secular priests.

TRUTH: Take heed at what is written: *Incline not my heart to evil words; to make excuses in sins.*[86] Moreover, I will show you how this life is possible even for a secular priest. Certainly, if they applied the same effort and diligence to avoiding the loss of the life of grace and the riches of virtues as they do to preventing the loss of their natural life or temporal goods, they would quickly attain sanctity. Consider, if you were to travel through a field or a forest full of enemies and surrounded by robbers, carrying a treasure precious and dear to you, how you would protect yourself, and how fearfully and circumspectly you would proceed. If you were to walk with so much fear of God and vigilance through the narrow path of happiness, would you not immediately fulfill the foregoing? What is this sluggish sloth, not to say the malice of perversity, that you would be more diligent in guarding bodily life and temporal possessions than your spiritual life and the riches of eternal salvation? Does not what is more carefully guarded seem to be more dearly loved?

PRIEST: To me, this is conclusive. I rejoice that I have been vanquished.

TRUTH: I will explain to you even more clearly how holy the manner of life of priests ought to be, and how they ought to prepare themselves to celebrate Mass.

FOURTEENTH ARTICLE
How virtuous, holy, and exemplary the life of a priest ought to be.

TRUTH: Note that my beloved and elect, the great Dionysius, asserts: No one should dare to lead others by the [priestly] office of salvation unless he has become, in every virtue, godlike,[87] that is, greatly similar to God and extremely virtuous, so that he might be able to communicate and influence others from his own fullness and exuberance. Furthermore, in every sacred order, a man is established as a guide to others in divine matters, but this is especially true in the priesthood. If, therefore, those appointed to lesser sacred orders are required to be godlike in this way, how

---

[86] Ps. 140:4.   [87] *De Eccl. hier.*, c. 3.

much more is it demanded of those in the priesthood? Moreover, that same most enlightened Saint asserts that a person constituted in holy orders who executes and exercises divine things unworthily is, as it were, a mocker and blasphemer of God, behaving as if God were ignorant of what he himself knows inwardly. Hence, he sins mortally in every act of the sacred order.[88]

PRIEST: These words seem stern in times like these, where charity has become so cold.

TRUTH: Did I not command through Moses, *You shall follow justly after that which is just*? And again, *You shall be holy because I, your Lord and God, am holy*? And also in the Gospel, *Be perfect, as your heavenly father is perfect*?[89] I did not command these things only to priests and clerics. If only you might efficaciously consider to what virtuous, sincere, and exemplary life every Christian is bound. He is required to love his enemies, to pray for those who persecute him, to do good to those who hate him, and to crucify his body with its vices and concupiscences. If he calls his neighbor "Fool," is liable to hell, if he offends in one thing he offends in all, and he is obliged to proceed by the narrow way. Who can fulfill all this, unless he is always watchful, fearful, and solicitous before God?[90]

Moreover, it is absolutely certain a person is more bound to virtue and purity the higher his office, order, dignity, or rank. Therefore, according to the measure of the dignity and height of the priestly order, the life of every priest must be proportionately more virtuous, eminent, and perfect, so that he might be freer from every excess of passions and from all pride, anger, indignation, impatience, sloth, and carnality. He ought to be better and more godly than the common good man, by reason of the fact that the priesthood is in a higher state and grade. Thus, he should walk worthily before God, in all meekness, patience, and piety, always ready to forgive.[91] Indeed, he should be so good and virtuous that he cannot be offended, overflowing with the bowels of charity, and always fervently aflame with zeal for divine honor and the salvation of his brethren. In all his Hours and prayers, especially during the celebration of the Mass, he should pray with ardent affection for the common good of the Church, for the living and the dead, for his parents, relatives, those committed to him, his benefactors, and

---

[88] *Epist. VIII ad Demophilum.*
[89] Deut. 16:20; Lev. 11:44, 45; 19:2; Matt. 4:48.
[90] Matt. 5:44; Gal. 5:24; Matt. 5:22; James 2:10; Matt. 7:14; cf. Micah 6:8.
[91] Eph. 4:1–2; Col. 3:12–13.

others for whom he is in any way bound to pray. In every way possible, he should draw his neighbors to God.

Finally, that which the Apostle writes about bishops also applies for the most part to priests—indeed, in large part to every Christian. *It behooves*, he says, *a bishop to be blameless, ... sober, prudent, of good behavior, chaste, given to hospitality, a teacher, not given to wine, not violent ... not quarrelsome, not covetous, not angry, one that rules well his own house.*[92] In these things all bishops and priests ought to stand out above the rest to the same degree as they are more eminent in dignity and office than the people, except insofar as being a teacher and managing one's household well pertains to those in positions of governance.

FIFTEENTH ARTICLE
The entire conduct of priests ought to be a continual and real preparation for the celebration of Mass, and an act of thanksgiving for God's blessings.

TRUTH: The praise and honor of the lips are not sufficient for the Almighty unless they proceed from sincerity and devotion of the mind and are adorned with acts of virtue. Therefore, O priest, if you consider wisely how great is the excellence, holiness, and dignity of this Sacrament, you will at once acknowledge you are unable to dispose your heart sufficiently to receive it, nor adequately give thanks for the communion you have received, even if you were to live a thousand years and dedicate day and night without interruption or rest all your strength to preparing for its celebration and offering gratitude for the reception and bestowal of such a great gift.

What, then, remains but that you do all that is within your power, while recognizing that you have done nothing worthy with respect to the incomparable excellence of the Sacrament? Therefore, since the joining of opposite, dissimilar, and discordant things is not proper, but rather the harmony of those whose will is aligned, whose disposition is proper, and whose form is good, it follows that the Lord and Savior—who is most truly present in this Sacrament—is, in his divinity, essentially and infinitely pure and holy, the source of all virtue, and all the more hateful of iniquity the holier, juster, and wiser he is in himself. It is therefore certain that

---

[92] 1 Tim. 3:2–4.

you are much more fit and worthy to celebrate Mass and receive this heavenly mystery, this worthy Sacrament, the freer you are from all negligence, ingratitude, levity, distraction, irreverence, and sin. Conversely, you know yourself to be that much more unfit and unworthy to celebrate Mass the more you are subject to these evils. Therefore, since you celebrate Mass daily or frequently, it behooves you to be unceasingly solicitous, watchful, and fervent every hour, day, and night, lest any fault be found in you by which you might become unworthy or less worthy to celebrate Mass, or ungrateful or less grateful for such great blessings.

Be ashamed to approach the Holy of Holies with an impure mind, a cold heart without reverence, sanctity, or fervor, or to unite yourself to the Fountain of infinite purity, receive the Only-Begotten of God, and treat your God and Judge without due reverence. Indeed, the more frequently you celebrate Mass, that much more devoutly and with greater fear should you strive do so reverently and lovingly. Therefore, say to yourself regularly in your heart: Behold, today or very soon you will celebrate, or you have celebrated, the propitiation of God. Where is your preparation and your thanksgiving? Where is the progress and fruit of such a great Mystery? Do not offend so great a guest; do not remain so ungrateful of his infinite goodness, charity, condescension, mercy, and generosity.

Oh, if you were invited by an earthly king or a great prelate, how humbly and decently would you approach his table! How carefully would you avoid offending him during that banquet! How gratefully would you acknowledge his favor! Indeed, you would strive all the more afterward to please him, even though the food he provided for you might be of little value. Why, then, are you not more ashamed and more eager to avoid being ungrateful to the *King of ages, immortal, invisible*,[93] the true God, the incarnate Son of God, who daily invites you to his table, receives you, and nourishes you with his Body and Blood? From him you also receive all other food and drink, and whatever you have and are. Therefore, endeavor with all your heart, and with all the powers of your soul, to please this most high Lord, this most gracious Lover, this most liberal Refresher, and the God of your whole salvation more and more each day. Cling to him more fervently and steadfastly to him, obey him more perfectly, and embrace him unceasingly within yourself with the arms of the most sincere charity.

---

[93] 1 Tim. 1:17.

PRIEST: O most sweet God, you have abundantly satisfied my desire by instructing me on the preparation for the celebration of Mass, the attention to be paid to it, and the thanksgiving to be rendered afterwards. Nevertheless, I humbly pray to be more fully informed about the quality of devotion, the actual attention, and the elevation of the mind to be observed during the celebration. I also ask whether it is necessary to have a sensory or sensibly sweet devotion, as I sometimes find myself indisposed and seemingly incapable of such.

TRUTH: I will not cease to instruct you on this. Nevertheless, before that I will briefly touch on the four considerations before the celebration of Mass, which pertain to other matters put forward by some.

SIXTEENTH ARTICLE
On the four things principally to attend to before the celebration of Mass, and also during it.

TRUTH: In every oblation and sacrifice, there are four things to consider, namely, who, what, to whom, and why. Therefore, before you celebrate Mass, attend first to yourself: who and what kind of person you are who are proposing to celebrate. Scour your conscience, and before confession examine how you have behaved in all matters: how much and in what way you have indulged excessively in food, drink, and sleep; in words, in thoughts, in desires, and in deeds; and similarly, in your lack of custody of the senses, in the neglect of the Divine Office, in engaging in vain suspicions or in rash judgments. Consider whether you have scandalized or illicitly offended anyone, whether you have duly checked the movements of your passions, whether you have proceeded in accordance with the demands of your vocation, whether you have spent time fruitfully, what goods you have omitted and how much. Reflect on how you have avoided habitual and daily sins since your last confession and former celebration of Mass; with what scrutiny, contrition, and compunction you have confessed every day. Ask yourself whether you conducted yourself charitably, peacefully, and humbly around others; whether you have restrained yourself from all levity, laughter, jesting, and foolish play; whether you have had any disordered movement of the body or impulse, especially through your own fault, imagination, sight, or touch; whether you have completely abstained from all vanity, pretense, duplicity, hypocrisy, and all inordinate consideration of your own advantage and honor. Before you go to sleep and before you go to confession, examine yourself regarding these and similar things. Grieve, groan, weep, and beg for forgiveness. Confess purely, make satisfaction, and amend your ways.

Second, reflect upon what you offer, that is, the truth and dignity of this sacrifice, the holiness of the Eucharist, and that you handle, offer, and consume Christ himself, God and man. Much has already been said about this. Hence, in consideration of your own deficiency and fault, and also of the dignity and the holiness of this Sacrament, approach with the deepest humility, compunction, reverence, and fear, yet principally with ardent charity, born of the contemplation of all the goodness, charity, passion, and blessings of the Savior. Reflect upon what Christ is: humble, meek, patient, pure, holy, charitable, just, and perfect to an utmost degree. If, then, you find yourself still disturbed by movements of pride, anger, impatience, impurity, or injustice, how will you dare to approach? What concord does light have with darkness? Christ with Belial?[94] What concord do the angry, proud, impatient, unjust, passionate, or envious have with the most humble, meek, patient, just, perfect, and affectionate Son of God? First, therefore, examine, amend, and reform yourself in the manner mentioned.

Third, think about to whom you offer, namely, to God the Father almighty and eternal. From the contemplation of his goodness, love, mercy, munificence, and blessings, you ought to be vehemently enkindled with love, and from the consideration of his majesty and justice, you ought yourself to be filled with all humility and reverential fear. Hence, before and during the celebration of Mass you should regard, admire, and honor the goodness, charity, liberality, and mercy of God the Father towards men.

Fourth, take heed why it is you offer, namely, because of the general reasons expressed in the Canon itself: first, for the general good of the whole Church, and the persons there mentioned; then for the living and the dead, as contained in the memorials; and for special causes and persons, for whom the celebrant prays and celebrates with particular intent. Since these reasons are of different kinds and so many, the priest must take care to celebrate and implore with all concern, attention, and humility for them and their fulfillment. Above, let him endeavor to please God so profoundly,

---

[94] Cf. 2 Cor. 6:14–15.

adhere to him so intimately, and serve him so fervently and perfectly, that he may merit to be most mercifully heard.

In addition, some assert that there are six things to be considered before the celebration of Mass. First is the discernment of reason with respect to truth, so that one might consider what it is he will receive, namely, that he, a poor, defective, and weak man, will receive Christ, God and man. Second is the devotion of mind with respect to God's sanctity, that one might consider that the one whom he consumes is the Holy of Holies, and so he ought to be moved with all devotion towards him. Third is the reverence of heart with respect to his majesty, so that one dares not approach and consume so great a Lord without great reverence. Fourth is love and desire with respect to his goodness, by which one should be attracted and inflamed, and by no means should he celebrate with sluggishness or boredom. Fifth is affectionate and humble prayer with respect to the divine clemency, from which consideration one must fervently call upon the Most High for all the previously-mentioned reasons, for forgiveness, grace, and glory, and for all the effects of this Sacrament. Sixth is great attentiveness from the consideration of the immense nobility and majesty of him before whom one must stand with the greatest attention. A seventh consideration may also be added, namely, great fear from the consideration of divine justice, lest by unworthy conduct one eat and drink judgment upon oneself.[95] But all these things can be reduced to the aforementioned four—indeed, to one of them, that is, to the consideration of the second, which is to take heed to what is about to be received: the dignity, sanctity, goodness, mercy, majesty, and justice of him who is received in this Sacrament. And although these things should always be pondered, they must especially be considered as the hour of celebration approaches.

SEVENTEENTH ARTICLE
What is devotion, and on the devotion requisite and sufficient for the celebration of Mass.

TRUTH: You can recognize from elsewhere what devotion is. Indeed, it is an act of worship,[96] namely, a certain promptitude or ready affection of the will towards the things of God, that is, to the execution

---
[95] 1 Cor. 11:29.
[96] L. *latria* here and elsewhere in this article translated as worship.

of the acts and works of the divine cult. For devotion is an act of worship, which is a moral virtue that is employed in the cult and ceremony of God. And so the acts of worship are: devotion, vow, prayer, praise of God, celebration of Mass, the offering of tithes and first fruits and other gifts offered to God, and other ceremonial acts which display submission to God, such as censing, genuflection, prostration, and bowing.

Therefore, if you want to know whether you have true devotion, look within yourself to see whether you detest, abhor, and shun from the sincere affection of your heart, whatever you know to be against the precepts of God and of his vicars your superiors, of whom it is said: *He that hears you, hears me; and he who despises you, despises me.*[97] That is, whether you avoid every mortal sin with due diligence, and you repent, confess, and make satisfaction from your heart regarding any sin which may happen to befall you, and propose to avoid always both that sin as well as every other mortal sin with all your might. Among all the signs of this matter, this is the truest and most secure: that man is in charity and grace and possesses true devotion. Some other signs are less certain, such as a certain sensible fervor, weeping, or zeal in certain acts which of their nature are good—such as willing visiting churches, praying much, giving alms, shedding tears during sermons—when the hearts of those performing such acts are nevertheless interiorly infected with vicious affections and entangled in some mortal vice. Indeed, some men of this kind are avaricious, others ambitious; some are prone to rash judgment, detractions, contentions, or dominant anger, impatience, or similar evils. They neither love their enemies spiritually nor stand before God in rightly ordered charity, such that they would prefer to die and lose all that they have than to sin mortally.[98]

PRIEST: A clear but difficult teaching. And *if*—or rather *because*—these things are so, the definitions or descriptions of those who say that devotion is the fervor of a good will exhibited by certain signs, or that devotion is a certain tenderness of heart by which one is easily moved to tears, do not seem to hold.

---

[97] Luke 10:16.
[98] L. *Caritas ordinata.* Cf. Rufinus, *Summa Decretorum*, Dist. XLII: *Caritas debet esse ordinata, ut post Deum parentes, deindi filii, post domestici ad ultimu extranei diligantur.* "Charity must be ordered, so that after God parents, and then children, after which those in your household, and lastly strangers are to be loved." See also Thomas Aquinas: *Caritas debet esse ordinata.* "Charity must be ordered." *Super Sent.*, lib. 4, d. 15, q. 1, a. 5, qc. 3, arg. 3.

TRUTH: There are different kinds or modes of definition. For some are derived by essential properties, as when it is said, "Man is a rational animal," and "Anger is the appetite of vengeance on account of a slight or offense." Some are derived from the cause, as when it is stated, "Day is the voyaging of the sun above the horizon," because day is caused by the movement of the sun in our hemisphere, although it is not properly the motion or the movement of the sun, but a portion of time. Some are derived from the effect. And so the definition of devotion I assigned earlier is one derived from its essential properties. When it is said, "Devotion is the fervor of good will," it is derived from the cause, because the fervor of a virtuous will—this fervor being an act of charity—is the proximate cause of devotion. Moreover, when it is said, "Devotion is a certain tenderness of heart," it is derived from the effect, because assiduous devotion, especially one sensible in nature, causes a certain softness of heart in a man, by which he easily weeps from devotion. And these two descriptions may thus be maintained, provided that "good will" is understood as the will which is good through the goodness of grace, and not merely through natural goodness of nature or goodness generically, and that "fervor" is understood as the intense affection of charity in the higher part of the soul. For regardless of how lax or imperfect charity may be, yet it is greater and stronger than any cupidity, as you read concerning the words, *The law of your mouth is good to me, above thousands of gold and silver.*[99] Even the smallest charity is greater than the greatest cupidity. For he who loves God out of charity, however imperfectly he may love him, loves him still more than he loves himself and the whole universe. If it were otherwise, he would not love God out of charity and would instead be in mortal sin, since the commandment of charity is to love God with all one's heart.[100] And so, actual love immediately elicited and proceeding from the charity of those beginning in the spiritual life is an intense and powerful affection compared to weaker ones, even if it is lacking when compared to actual love proceeding from the charity of the proficient in the spiritual life and, above all, the perfect.

PRIEST: These things seem to be contradicted by experience. For experience teaches that some carnal and cupidinous men are much more intensely and fervently affected towards carnal and earthly things than some good men are towards God. Indeed, even some

---

[99] Ps. 118:72.   [100] Deut. 6:5; Matt. 22:37.

who live in charity appear sometimes to be more strongly moved by an impulse towards created things than towards the Creator.

TRUTH: Someone is said to be more or less affected towards something in two ways. The first way is *appreciatively*.[101] And whoever loves God in this way, however neglectfully he loves him, nevertheless appreciatively loves him more than he does himself and all created things. Indeed, he loves God more than any lover of the world or of the flesh loves carnal and worldly things. For such a lover, though he be mad, would rather abandon carnal and worldly things than be deprived of his life. Secondly, someone is said to be more or less affected towards something *perceptively*, or with some perceptible and sensible affection, powerful impulse, or fervor. In this way, it is not necessary to be more perceptibly affected towards God, although perfect men commonly are more moved towards God in this way also. In others, however, the affections of charity in the higher affective powers are not generally so perceptible or perceptibly intense as are the affections of the lower appetitive power.

PRIEST: This pleases me greatly. But I pray you to expound more fully for me how the fervor of charity is the proximate cause of devotion, particularly since, according to what has been said earlier, devotion is an act of worship, and it seems to arise immediately from worship. Indeed, again, it appears that it is born immediately from some cognitive apprehension or knowledge, just as love itself is.

TRUTH: This is a useful question, and those are good objections. To arrive at a clear solution, we'll need to take our time. Now, devotion arises immediately and elicitively from worship, just as the other virtuous acts arise from the proper virtues of which they are the proper acts. Moreover, it proceeds immediately and imperially from charity's fervor, because charity moves the other virtues imperatively towards their acts, since it is the most excellent virtue and the end of all the virtues—by charity I mean actual love, that is, the will acting through charity and actual love. Therefore, since

---

[101] L. *appretiative*. Scholastic theologians speak of various levels of love of God, appreciative love of God (*amor appretiative Dei*), meaning a love of esteem, is where one esteems God in preference to everything else, sovereignly appreciative love of God (*amor appretiative summus*) when such appreciative love reaches the highest degree and intensity (and so is properly charity), and intensive love of God (*amor intensive Dei*) which goes beyond the sovereign appreciative love and approaches perfection. From the context, Denis appears to have in mind *amor appretiative summus*.

worship is a subjective part or species of justice, and among the moral virtues is closest to charity, therefore the subject of worship is the will, just as charity and justice. But the will is blind on its own, because in itself it is not able to know; therefore, it needs the direction and illumination of reason and discretion. For this reason, the object of the will is the good insofar as it is understood, that is, apprehended or known by the intellect. Hence, the acts of the virtues existing subjectively in the will proceed immediately from a certain knowledge, not elicitively as they would from their proper virtues, nor do they proceed imperatively as from charity, but directively and causally (*vialiter*), such that knowledge leads those virtues to their acts as if leading them along a road. In this way it produces the acts themselves.

PRIEST: This is a clear and doctrinal answer, which clarifies how devotion and love proceed from worship, charity, and knowledge in different ways. But based on these insights, please explain the main issue, namely, what sort of devotion is necessary and sufficient to celebrate Mass.

TRUTH: Whatever proceeds from charity is meritorious for eternal life and acceptable to God. Therefore, to celebrate Mass meritoriously, it is sufficient and required that the celebrant should be in a state of charity and be moved and proceed to celebrate Mass out of charity. This interior motion should be a certain promptitude of the will for that work of divine worship. For the celebration of Mass is an act so privileged, divine, and eminent that actual devotion is required for it, which includes charity and its act, and a certain contemplation or at least [intellectual] consideration of God. Indeed, when Christ instituted the celebration of this Sacrament, he commanded the Apostles, and through their persons all priests: *As often as you do these things, do them in memory of me*,[102] that is, in loving and devoted memory of my extraordinary love for you, and of my most bitter passion on your behalf.

PRIEST: From this it would seem that the celebrant sins mortally if he utters the words of consecration, or any words of the Mass or the Canon, with notable distraction or without actual devotion.

TRUTH: The affirmative precepts obligate always, but not at every moment. Therefore, though love, attention, and actual devotion are required to celebrate Mass, they are not necessary at every moment of the Mass. Hence, if distraction occurs at any

---

[102] Cf. Luke 22:19; 1 Cor. 11:24–25.

point during the celebration of the Mass as a result of weakness, mortal sin is not immediately incurred. However, the celebrant must attend to what he is doing, lest from lack of custody of the eyes or control of his hearing, or some other culpable way or occasion, he incur distraction and wandering of the mind, and also, lest (God forbid) he dwell unchecked or notably in a distracted state. Otherwise, he might be so unguarded and distracted during Mass that he would sin mortally and lose the charity that he had before or at the start. The priest, therefore, is obligated to have a good, special, and reverent diligence during Mass, so that he celebrates attentively, devoutly, and reverently, and restrains himself from any distraction.

PRIEST: I suppose that devotion is not required to celebrate Mass in the sense that a true celebration of Mass and consecration do take place even if devotion is lacking?

TRUTH: That is correct. Accordingly, devotion and a state of charity are not said to be required because otherwise the celebration of Mass itself would not be meritorious, but because the celebrant himself—by the very fact that he is celebrating without devotion and charity—sins mortally if he is not actually devout and in a state of charity when celebrating Mass.

PRIEST: What is the supererogatory devotion that befits a priest to have when celebrating Mass? And does devotion always arise from love of God?

TRUTH: You ask two important questions, which I will answer for you in the next two articles.

EIGHTEENTH ARTICLE
On the kinds of devotion, and especially on supererogatory devotion, which suits the celebrating priest to have at Mass.

TRUTH: The commonplace is generally true, that if one does not make progress in the way of God, one goes backwards or falls away; and likewise, that he who does not strive to avoid venial sins soon slips into mortal ones. Therefore, one who is stingily content with common devotion rarely experiences or only weakly procures the effect of holy communion of which I shall treat below, obtains little or no fruit from the celebration of Mass, and does not draw the gifts of grace and virtue from the fountain of grace which is the Sacrament of the Eucharist. Indeed, in celebrating Mass he incurs many faults, negligences, distractions, and omissions. It is therefore dangerous and proximate to ruin not to strive towards *things better and nearer to salvation*,[103] and to rest content with common devotion towards so great a mystery. This is especially true considering, as we have noted,[104] that he must shine with an eminence of virtues before the people that corresponds to the higher grade and order in which he has been constituted by his ordination, and so he must assiduously tend towards and strive towards this. For if he does not make this effort, he will not avoid mortal sin for very long, because he cannot remain indefinitely at the lowest level.

Moreover, since devotion springs from charity, three kinds or rather degrees of devotion may be distinguished according to the three degrees of charity. Indeed, it is certain that the more one loves God, the more readily one is moved to worship him. Further, the more the superior part of the soul—namely, the intellect and the will—is perfected and strengthened by the seven gifts of the Holy Spirit, the theological virtues, and everything that is connected with those powers, the more easily and powerfully the inferior, sensitive part and its passions are dominated; and the more they are subject to it, the more strongly and abundantly the acts, affections, and delights of the intellect and will flow over into the inferior powers and the bodily nature, so that the sensitive part does not resist, but rather subserves and cooperates in the mind's elevation to God. Indeed, as you also know from philosophy, just as in the heavens the higher spheres revolve around and push the lower spheres, so the superior affection draws the sensitive after it.

Thus, because there are three degrees of charity and the gift of wisdom, so there are three degrees of devotion. The lowest degree of charity is that of the beginner, the middle that of the proficient, and the third that of the perfect. The lowest degree of charity corresponds to the lowest degree of devotion, the minimum necessary for any man to attain salvation. In this degree each one is prompt, in his own way, to do those things that fall under precept, even as his sensual part strongly—indeed sometimes importunately and wantonly—resists. The second degree of devotion is one which promptly takes up those the things of God, with the passions moderately mitigated and reformed, and the body so subservient to the spirit that devotion's force, charity's affection, spiritual delight, and an intense occupation of the mind flow over noticeably and

---

[103] Heb. 6:9.   [104] See Twelfth Article.

sweetly into the inferior powers.¹⁰⁵ And such devotion can be called sensible, experiential, sweet, and fervent, one in which nature and the inferior part participate in the superior part, agreeing, reveling, subserving, and cooperating with it according to what is written: *For you my soul has thirsted, for you my flesh, O how many ways!*¹⁰⁶ The third degree of devotion is that wherein a man, his sensitive part now reformed and subjugated and his sensitive and cognitive powers recollected, with the whole affection of his heart unencumbered, is borne freely and with great readiness to the things which pertain to the divine worship, and dwells long and delightfully in them, with a delicious overflow of mental consolation into the sensitive powers. Thus the whole man, without any resistance from sensuality—indeed with its attraction and service—is entirely prompt towards acts of worship, executing them with fervent and cheerful affection. Rightly is this devotion called delicious, and even impetuous, since the vehement ardor of his holy devotion is not restrained by reason, but carried freely, eagerly, and lovingly wherever the Spirit of life impels and urges.

The quieting of the passions occurs from various causes. First, directly and very meritoriously, from the progress of the virtues, especially the moral virtues, whose purpose it is to restrain and moderate the movements of passions. Second, from continuous and fervent prayers poured out to God for grace and virtue so as to repress passionate impulses. And the more one is prone to the movements of the passions, whether by natural disposition or by depraved habit, the more earnestly and fervently one ought to pray to the Almighty for their complete extirpation, particularly of those to which one feels more inclined. Third, from the special and gracious prevention and visitation of the Holy Spirit, who sometimes refreshes, anoints, and fills those who are just beginning, weak, and imperfect with sensible affections of devotion, consolation, and spiritual delights. By this, he draws them to interior things, so that they may spurn vain and worldly concerns and turn with their whole heart to God. Fourth, from compunction and heartfelt contrition. The more frequently and bitterly one sorrows and repents of his sins, the more easily and perfectly does he restrain himself from long-lasting disordered movements. Fifth, from heartfelt and constant remembrance of the Lord's Passion, from which a man learns to humble himself, to embrace patience and meekness, and to spurn carnal things. Sixth,

---

¹⁰⁵ Cf. 1 Cor. 9:27.   ¹⁰⁶ Ps. 62:2.

from intense reading of the Scriptures and devotional books, for the greater movements conquer and expel lesser ones.

Therefore, a priest—especially a religious priest who is not to weary himself with common concerns—ought to devote himself with all his strength to the devotion of the proficient in the spiritual life, and by it to the devotion of the perfect, always striving to acquire *the better gifts*.[107]

Moreover, although these two last degrees of devotion are ordinarily accompanied and interwoven with the aforementioned overflowing delights and interior consolations, this is not always the case. Indeed, sometimes these consolations and spiritual delights are withdrawn not only from the proficient, but even from the perfect. This occurs at times by the dispensational and fatherly command of the Most High, so that they may learn to seek solid food and to preserve patience during such deprivation, showing their fidelity to God not by seeking or accepting external solaces, but rather by awaiting with equanimity and fidelity the dispensation of the Beloved, his sweet presence, and his consoling return. Furthermore, by this means they may more humbly recognize their own weakness, deficiency, and imperfection, and flee and aspire to God with greater affection, and, upon recovering consolation, become more cautious. Thus they learn to adhere to and serve their God purely for his own goodness and majesty, not because of the sweetness of his gifts. At times, however, this withdrawal occurs because of one's negligence and faults. Yet men who are truly virtuous and well trained in the divine Scriptures do not overly concern themselves with these consolations, but unceasingly seek to possess true and sincere devotion and grow ever more in it, so that they may become increasingly inclined to and aspire towards everything that concerns the divine worship, to a horror of all vices, to the most sincere affection for all honest goods, to pure, intense, and complete obedience to God by internal and steadfast adherence, and to an absolute and unmixed love for the Divinity free from all self-seeking.

Moreover, devotion is called sweet, sensible, and consoling not only because of the aforementioned overflowing from the higher part of the soul to the lower, but also—indeed even above all else—because of the pure and spiritual delight that remains and rests in the higher part of the soul. For since very virtuous action naturally has a corresponding and connected delight, the higher the

---

[107] 1 Cor. 12:31.

act of worship, charity, and love—as well as the knowledge of the gift of wisdom and the gift of knowledge from which devotion arises—so much the greater is the actual devotion, especially in men who are notably virtuous, the greater spiritual delight remaining attached to the superior affective power, although sometimes it happens otherwise for the aforementioned reasons.

Finally, some divide devotion into rational and sensible devotion—not that devotion subjectively and formally exists in reason, but rather in the will, as does also worship, for which reason it can be called volitional devotion. Nevertheless, it is called rational or intellectual either because it arises from the apprehension of reason and is based upon its judgment rather than upon sensible sweetness, or because reason or intellect is often taken to represent the higher part of the soul, which also includes the will.

And, as it is easy to see, it should also be noted that the aforesaid three degrees of devotion correspond and are proportionate to the three states or degrees of men, that is, of the beginner, the proficient, and the perfect. Likewise, of the animal, rational, and intellectual faculties; of faithful servants, secret friends, and hidden sons; of the purgative, illuminative, and perfective ways; and of the political, purgative, and purified powers of the soul.[108]

NINETEENTH ARTICLE
Whether devotion always arises out of the love of God.

TRUTH: Habitual charity, by which God and neighbor are loved, is one and the same in number in the same lover, yet its acts are distinct. Moreover, devotion, which is the promptitude of the obedient soul to the worship of God, although it principally flows from the love of God—insofar as God, glorious and holy in himself and because of himself is absolutely most worthy of all worship and reverence—nevertheless, it often also proceeds from spiritual and actual love for oneself. This occurs when a man, out of desire for his own salvation, devotes himself to divine worship and,

---

[108] Denis refers to the reason's political power over disordered passions in an unpurged soul, reason's power over the passions in a soul that is in the process of purging itself of the disordered passions, and reason's power in a purged soul where the passions are no longer disordered. Cf. *Summa Theologiae*, Ia, q. 81, art. 3, ad 2; IaIIae, q. 9, art. 2, ad 3; q. 17, art. 7, co.; q. 56, art. 4, ad 3; q. 58, art. 2, co.; and q. 74, art. 1, co.

considering his own weakness, guilt, and insufficiency, flees to the mercy of God through prayer and other acts of worship, and also when he does similarly out of charity and zeal for the salvation of his neighbor, especially for his subjects.

PRIEST: If this devotion proceeds from the consideration of one's own weakness, fault, and need, it seems rather to be tied to pain and sadness than eagerness and joy.

TRUTH: Insofar as it arises from the root of this consideration, what you say is correct, since the consideration of one's own dangers, vices, weaknesses, and miseries directly and by its very nature leads to pain and sadness. However, it is also, by consequence, a cause of cheerfulness, consolation, and joy, inasmuch as a man, fleeing to God and imploring his mercy, rejoices in the Lord both through the consideration of divine kindness as well as through hope and confidence in obtaining his forgiveness, grace, and glory. He likewise gives him thanks for having spared him thus far.

PRIEST: Does this devotion also have sorrow attached to it insofar as it proceeds from the love of God? It would seem not, because the apprehension of so great a good does not appear to give rise to sorrow. Hence it is written: *I remembered God, and was delighted.*[109]

TRUTH: But it is also written: *I languish with love;*[110] and also: *I am wounded by love.*[111] Hence, pallor and emaciation are signs of love. And so I say that the consideration of God and his properties and attributes, namely of the divine goodness, wisdom, mercy, and justice, directly and in itself is a cause of joy and a reason for spiritual rejoicing, since joy is the expansion of the soul in the apprehension of the good, and delight itself arises from the union of the power of the soul with the fitting object. Now, God is the most fitting object, and the intellect and will, by which you are united to him, are the highest powers of the soul. Yet indirectly, secondarily, accidentally, the consideration of such an infinite and superlatively loveable good gives rise to sorrow, embarrassment, pain, fear, wounding, and languor, inasmuch as God is apprehended as still absent rather than present, as yet not attained nor seen face to face, and as one who observes and knows all your evils. He is also seen as a terrible judge leaving no evil unpunished, for the consideration of God brings to mind your own wickedness, and his sight, presence, and justice cause shame and horror. And insofar as you do not yet enjoy such a great

---

[109] Ps. 76:4. [110] Songs 2:5. [111] Ibid., according to the Septuagint.

good, and you do not yet clearly see as you desire this most desirable and superlatively delightful good, nor do you so reverently and perfectly worship him or have affection towards him as you ought to love him causes sadness in you. Indeed, the intensity of longing from delay induces languor and wounding, as you sing in the Psalm: *My soul has thirsted after the strong living God; when shall I come and appear before the face of God? My tears have been my bread day and night, etc.*[112] And again: *Woe is me, that my sojourning is prolonged!*[113] Meanwhile, since the acts of worship are directly related to God and are of the highest dignity, great consolation and joy commonly and directly lie in them. For this reason, the Apostle James advises and exhorts: *Is any of you sad? Let him pray. Is he cheerful in mind? Let him sing.*[114] And the writer of the Psalms also said: *My lips shall greatly rejoice when I shall sing to you;*[115] and again, *I cried to him with my mouth: and I extolled him with my tongue.*[116]

PRIEST: O adored Truth, you have most kindly instructed me concerning these matters, and you have graciously informed me how I should conduct myself before, during, and after the celebration of Mass. Now, I wish to be more fully taught the effects of the most excellent Sacrament. To be sure, you have already mentioned some of them,[117] yet I beg to be instructed more extensively about such a great matter.

TWENTIETH ARTICLE
On the effects of the Sacrament.

TRUTH: I spoke briefly about how the Eucharist, such as it is, does for the soul of the communicant everything that bodily food does for the human body.[118] You now ask me to explain this more fully. Many have written about this subject, assigning a great number of effects to this Sacrament; but basically all are in agreement, and we can speak of a handful of principal effects.

Therefore, just as bodily food is only given to and beneficial to the living, the hungry, and the needy, so this Sacrament, which is food for the soul, should be given only to those who are spiritually alive and who desire it. Further, whether this Sacrament is considered from the point of view of the *sacramentum tantum* which,

---

[112] Ps. 41:3–4.   [113] Ps. 119:5.   [114] James 5:13.   [115] Ps. 70:23.
[116] Ps. 65:17.   [117] Fourth, Sixth, and Ninth Articles.   [118] Fourth Article.

in one manner of speaking, is the Lord's Body, or from the point of view of the *res tantum*, which is charity or the act or enkindling of charity, it has the efficacy and power to remove and remit venial sins. For as food for the soul it restores what the soul loses every day through the heat of natural concupiscence and the other wounds—or *fomes*[119]—inflicted by original sin, namely ignorance, malice or inclination to evil, and weakness, just as bodily food restores the natural heat the body loses each day. Now the soul's loss from these wounds and *fomes* comes from daily venial sins, or the loss of that fervor of charity or of the vigor of the other virtues that results from those venial sins. Therefore, it is proper that such venial sins are remitted and effaced by this Sacrament. Again, since the *res sacramenti* is charity and its exercise is in the celebration of Mass and the taking of communion, and *charity covers a multitude of venial sins*,[120] and its blazing consumes venial sins as fire consumes stubble, it follows that in both respects it takes away venial sin, and does so more or less both with respect to the fault and the punishment, depending on how worthily and fervently we celebrate Mass and receive communion. For mortal sins must be remitted together, not one at a time, as regards guilt and punishment, since they cannot be removed without the infusion of charity and grace, which cannot coexist with mortal sin; but one venial sin can be forgiven without another, in both respects.[121]

PRIEST: If this Sacrament is the most powerful and most noble of all the Sacraments, why does it not take away all venial sins as far as both guilt and punishment are concerned, since Baptism removes not only all venial sins, but also all mortal sins, in both respects?[122]

TRUTH: This Sacrament is both a Sacrament and a Sacrifice, a Sacrament insofar as it is received under sensible forms; and a Sacrifice insofar as it is offered to God the Father. Moreover, insofar as it is a Sacrament, it has two effects: one effect is spiritual refreshment, which comes from the Sacrament's power, and for which it

---

[119] E.N. *Fomes*, literally kindling, tinder, or spark, is used to refer to man's inclination or tendency to sin which persists in him after the fall; it is synonymous with the term concupiscence.

[120] 1 Pet. 4:8.

[121] E.N. One venial sin can be forgiven both as to guilt and any associated temporal punishment, and yet another venial sin remains both as to guilt and temporal punishment.

[122] E.N. Baptism removes both the guilt and temporal punishments associated with both venial sins as well as mortal sins.

was directly instituted; the other is the remission of the guilt and punishment for venial sins, which comes from a certain concomitance, from the fact that the refreshment occurs by the spiritual conjunction and increase of charity, by which fault and punishment are taken away according to the measure of devotion and fervor of the celebrant and communicant. Insofar as it is a Sacrifice, it has the power of satisfaction. But as far as satisfaction goes, the affection of the offerer is more important than the quantity of the oblation. For this reason, the poor widow who offered two mites is said to have given more than the others.[123] Therefore, although this oblation, as far as its magnitude and virtue is concerned, is a suitable satisfaction for all fault and punishment (for the other sacraments also receive their efficacy from it), nevertheless it makes satisfaction for those for whom it is offered and for those who offer it according to the quantity of their disposition and devotion, and not according to the quantity of its own efficacy.

PRIEST: Does this Sacrament, inasmuch as it is a Sacrament or Sacrifice, also take away mortal sins that are unconfessed but forgotten mortal sins, as well as their punishments?

TRUTH: The power and efficacy of this Sacrament may be considered in two ways. First, according to itself: in this respect it is fitting for it to take away any sins from any wayfarers, since it contains the plenitude of all merit and he who is the fount and cause of all remission and grace. Second, it can be considered in relation to the communicant, who, if he has an impediment to participation in the merit, virtue, and grace of this Sacrament, namely, mortal sin, not only does not obtain remission, but adds further sins; but this arises not from a defect or inefficaciousness in the Sacrament, but from the shame of his iniquity. For he who has no spiritual life cannot be spiritually fed; nor can one who is in the state of mortal sin, whether by intention or in conscience, be spiritually joined to Christ by participating in the power and grace of this Sacrament.

Nevertheless, this Sacrament can cause the remission of mortal sin in two ways. One way is by reception, not in act, but in wish, desire, or purpose. The other way is by actual reception by someone who is in mortal sin but not conscious of it, or has not confessed it out of forgetfulness, or, if he has confessed, was not sufficiently contrite. Approaching the Sacrament devoutly and reverently, such a person will obtain the grace of charity, which will perfect his

---

[123] Mark 12:42–43.

contrition and the remission of his sins and will diminish some of its punishment. However, as noted,[124] before celebrating or taking communion one is obliged to examine his conscience carefully. Therefore, if anyone by a neglectful or superficial attitude should forget to confess a mortal sin, he will not obtain the remission of this sin, insofar as he would have had true contrition for it, at least in general, if not in particular, had he done as he was obliged and it came to his memory. And thus, this Sacrament washes away sins of which a man is not conscious after a diligent examination of conscience, as in the prayer, *From my secret ones cleanse me, O Lord*;[125] or as brought about by contrition in the manner previously mentioned.

PRIEST: Since the virtue of this Sacrament is so great, it seems surprising that those who receive it, especially those celebrating it in a state of charity, do not grow more in grace, nor are they more protected from vice.

TRUTH: The body is preserved from future death in two ways: first, nature strengthens it against internal corruption by means of food and medicine, and secondly, it uses weapons to defend itself against exterior assaults and woundings. In both ways, this Sacrament, for its part, preserves man from the death of sin. For, like spiritual food and medicine, its grace joins a person to Christ and strengthens the spiritual life; again, insofar as it is a sign of the Lord's Passion by which the demons were defeated, so does it repel, weaken, and overcome them and their attacks, and also diminishes the *fomes* of sin by increasing charity and grace. All of this occurs, unless one throws up a barrier against it through negligence, indisposition, distraction, or irreverence. Moreover, he who approaches and receives with due preparation, care, and purity, grows, makes progress, and is strengthened and preserved in a wonderful way. And (as one person has said) like a lion breathing flame, he leaves the table of the altar having become terrible to demons.[126] All this is knowable by genuine and certain experience, and those who live in this way know it experientially.

PRIEST: Does this Sacrament or the celebration of Mass profit only the celebrant and recipient, or also the assistants and the rest of the faithful?

TRUTH: I have already told you that this Sacrament, as such, benefits the one consuming it, but as a Sacrifice it is beneficial to

---

[124] Thirteenth Article. [125] Ps. 18:13.
[126] E.N. St. John Chrysostom, Homily 46.

all for whom it is offered as long as they do not raise an obstacle against it. Indeed, in this way it benefits the living and the dead, and everyone for whom one prays or offers Mass.

PRIEST: Do venial sins hinder the effect of this Sacrament?

TRUTH: If one has the requisite contrition for past mortal sins, and suitable contrition for venial sins, the effects of this Sacrament will not be hindered. If the priest is diligent during Mass, yet experiences distraction out of human weakness, but immediately turns away from it when he becomes aware of it, he is not much hindered from receiving the effects of this Sacrament, except that during the distraction he does not feel the actual refreshment, union, or consolation of this Sacrament. Moreover, if one is truly devout, trained, and diligent, then as soon as he notices his distraction, negligence, or similar venial fault, he turns back to God with a more intense affection and with heartfelt displeasure, detestation, and disdain for such a grave fault; in this way, the fault occasionally works together in him for good.[127]

PRIEST: If you please, continue speaking about the effects of this Sacrament.

TRUTH: Four things can be considered with regard to the effect of this Sacrament. First, it contains within it him who, just as he bestowed the life of grace on the world when he came visibly into it, so also works the life of grace when he comes sacramentally into man, as he said: *He that eats me, the same also shall live by me.*[128] Second, what is represented by this Sacrament is the Passion of Christ: hence the effect that the Passion of Christ caused in the world, this Sacrament causes in man. Therefore, when you approach the terrible chalice, approach as if you were about to drink from Christ's side. Third, it is given as food and drink. Therefore, all the effects which physical food and drink have for bodily life, this Sacrament has for spiritual life. Fourth, it is bestowed under the species of bread and wine: which are made from many things gathered into one, as bread is made from many grains and wine from many clusters. And thus it causes the ecclesiastical and mystical unity of the faithful by increasing charity and grace, and by infusing sacramental grace. For this reason, it is called the Sacrament of affection, the sign of unity, the bond of charity. Further,

---

[127] E.N. The fault is the *occasion* for God bringing good out of it (greater devotion and affection and displeasure at one's own weakness and fault).
[128] John 6:58b.

the effect of this Sacrament is the attainment of the glory of eternal life, because it contains Christ, from whom it has its effect, and also that by which it has its effect, namely its use and appearance. Now Christ opened for us the gates of his heavenly kingdom by his Passion. Likewise, the spiritual refreshment and unity designated by the species of bread and wine is imperfectly possessed in this life, but perfectly in the heavenly fatherland; and thus, he gives us the power to attain glory, though he leads us there not immediately, but at the opportune time.

Know also that the frequenting and offering of this Sacrament afford the Blessed the glory of accidental reward, inasmuch as they rejoice in all the good accomplished in the Church militant. But with respect to the essential reward, they do not grow.[129] You should also know that the effect of any Sacrament is judged based on a similarity to the effect of the sacramental matter: so cleansing of the old life and interior washing from sins is accomplished by Baptism, designated and figured through the cleansing of water. Since the matter in this Sacrament is food and drink, namely, bread and wine, the effect of this Sacrament must be understood by comparison to the effect that food and drink have upon the body, as has been explained.

TWENTY-FIRST ARTICLE
Continuing the subject, namely on the most excellent effects and fruits of this Sacrament.

TRUTH: One thing is said to come from another in three ways. First, by natural operation, as fire causes warming. Second, by merit or desert, as when we say: Your sins have done these things to you. Third, by hidden power, either divine or supernatural. Now Christ's Flesh cannot be food for the mind, nor the Blood be drink for the soul by natural operation; nor by the mode of merit, such that merit really and subjectively exists in the flesh, since only an intellectual substance can be the subject of merit. Therefore, they

---

[129] E.N. Man's essential reward or glory arises out of the soul's perfect union with God in the beatific vision. Accidental glory, on the other hand, is the enjoyment of everything that arises from, but is not identified with essential glory, and so is apart from this divine union, e.g., the so-called *aureola* of virgins and martyrs, the enjoyment of communion of the saints and angels, and the glory of the risen body.

refresh the mind by a supernatural and divine power, the same by which the other Sacraments are said to operate as a result of God's institution and good pleasure. So as the power of the Holy Spirit is present in the water to effect an interior cleansing, so the divine power is present in the bodily and exterior eating of the sacramental species to work the Eucharist's interior refreshment of which it is a figure and sign. But if one were to say that this exterior refreshment, or Christ's Flesh, is most powerful on account of God's wisdom and power, of which it is a sort of a garment, he would not depart from pure faith. For if St. John the Evangelist's garment gained such power by touching the sacred body of John that two men were raised from the dead when touched by it through the hand of the still unbelieving Aristodemus, what must pious faith think about this powerful garment of the Almighty?[130] If St. Peter's staff, from the touch of the Apostle Peter, gained such power that by its touch it raised the dead companion of Blessed Martial of Limoges,[131] and St. Maternus, and a third person,[132] and even unto the present retains such power that it continues to cast out demons from possessed bodies and compels them to speak—what then is to be supposed of the most sacred Body of Christ? If Christ the Lord dispenses so many of his powers through Saints' bodies, indeed even through their dried hair, and (what is more marvelous yet) by their dust and their sepulchers, how could he not give incomparably greater powers to his Flesh which is now glorified with him? Moreover, if the fringe of his garment had the power of healing any sick person—for that matter, the shadow of the prince of the Apostles shared this very quality—what power and eminence did he bestow on his Body, united not only to his most sacred Soul, but also to his very Divinity, when by the same divine power he nourishes, strengthens, and perfects your souls?[133] Moreover, if he gave the flesh and fat of the serpent, from which

---

[130] E.N. This refers to an apocryphal story related in the Acts of John, a second century Gnostic text, wherein Aristodemus was the chief priest of Artemis who challenged the Apostle John to drink a poison drink, who tests the poison upon two criminals who die. John drinks with impunity, and then gives his cloak to Aristodemus to place over the dead criminals who are resuscitated. Aristodemus then converts and requests baptism from John.

[131] E.N. This refers to St. Martial of Limoges, to whom, legend relates, St. Peter gave his staff, and by which he revived a fellow companion priest named Austriclinianus.

[132] E.N. St. Maternus of Cologne who is said to have obtained St. Peter's staff and used it to bring back to life his companion St. Eucherius.

[133] Matt. 14:36; Acts 5:15.

antivenom is made, the power of expelling and driving away poison that extinguishes the life of the body, how much must we believe he gave much more power to his Flesh to cure every poison of sin, which extinguishes the life of the soul? Further, if, as some hold, precious and powerful stones have innumerable and wonderful virtues from the scant amount of quintessence that is in them,[134] how much more excellent powers and sacramental effects does the Flesh of Christ have from the presence of the supereminent divine essence? Again, if he conveyed upon the blood of certain beasts such powers [of healing],[135] what of his own Blood? Again, if he gave the herbage of peony and jasper the power to drive away visions and demons, and the words of certain exorcisms the power of warding off demons, and by them other wonderful things are done which are contained in the books of the magical art, how could the eternal Word, by whom all things were made,[136] not embellish the Flesh assumed by him with all the powers of his glory, which, in this regard, are appropriate and expedient for your salvation?

Hence, from these and other innumerable examples, which we omit partly to avoid prolixity and partly because we have not sufficient means to know or to enumerate them all, it is clear how generously and magnificently we are to regard the power of the most excellent Sacrament and of the Body of the Lord. Indeed, in this Sacrament, the form of bread and wine clearly signify that Christ himself is the supersubstantial, daily, solid, delightful, and ever satisfying refreshment of your souls. The form of bread and wine also shows the communion and indistinction of holy love, and also the inseparable society of the Saints. The efficacy of this Sacrament, therefore, is two-fold, because to the extent it is a Sacrifice, it has the effect of reconciliation; insofar as it is a Sacrament, it has the effect of sanctifying. Therefore, the necessity and fruitfulness of the presence of this Sacrament is the medication or treatment of the universal Church, and its reconciliation to the Father, and also the Church's sanctification and spiritual refreshment. Hence, the Mass is the offering of the most fragrant sacrifice, by whose odor of sweetness the whole world is reconciled and its stench washed

---

[134] E.N. In the medieval times men believed that there was a fifth and highest element or essence (quintessence) that comprised the celestial bodies, and that some precious stones harbored this quintessence.

[135] E.N. The blood of some animals was believed to have curative powers. See, e.g., the *Speculum Naturale* of Vincent of Beauvais.

[136] John 1:3.

away. The celebration of this Sacrament, insofar as its power and sufficiency is concerned, is also how the whole world is sanctified. It is also the inauguration of the most opulent, luxurious, and delicious convivial banquet, at which men are splendidly refreshed alongside the holy angels. The Mass is also the pleading of your case by protracted supplication and oblation. Finally, it is medical treatment for the whole body of the Church, and the prescription of the highest medicine, and the work of your reconciliation.

These are the ways, therefore, in which one must celebrate the solemnities of Masses, and attend them with all reverence and filial fear, and pursue this great mystery and business of your reconciliation, and the pleading of all your causes, and the medicine of all the universe, lest these awesome things be unprofitable for you, and lest, on account of your lack of devotion and ingratitude, you should be severely judged and damned. Therefore, in the celebration and reception of this Sacrament, you must take note of God's omnipotence in so many great and wonderful wondrous deeds, and his Providence regarding your internal refreshment and the procurement of your salvation, and his great abundance of goodness by which he makes such a generous communication of himself and his gifts, and finally, his love for you, and his zeal for your salvation, and also his beneficence towards you.

TWENTY-SECOND ARTICLE
On Christ's modes under the Sacrament and its effects, and a summary of what others say upon the subject of the aforegoing.

TRUTH: Based on the aforesaid, ponder how Christ our Lord is contained under the sacramental species as it were in a marvelous mansion and glorious dwelling, and in a banquet hall of delicious refreshment, and in a mysterious atrium of spiritual sacrifice and oblation, and in a bond of friendliest union between God and man.

Indeed, in this Sacrament the whole Christ, true God and perfect man, is most certainly contained, and infallibly found; and it works a great number of incomprehensible things. He is there, as it were, in a delightful banquet hall, because in this Sacrament, *all* spiritual *sweetness* and *the sweetness of every taste* are tasted by the worthily disposed.[137] Christ, the most generous host, invites all

---
[137] Wis. 16:20.

men to this banquet—indeed, he bids them to come.[138] He does not threaten those who approach, and he promises and bestows the precious gifts of grace and glory on those who worthily come. There, he offers himself as food, in a sign of abundant love and the future heavenly feast, in which the blessed enjoyment of his Godhead will be the ultimate and eternal refreshment. Finally, in this Sacrament as if in an atrium of immolation,[139] Christ is sacrificed daily as the supremely acceptable and truly pacifying sacrifice, leading from peace of the heart to the peace of eternity; as a holocaust wholly aflame with the fire of the charity with which he readily offered himself to God the Father in all of his conduct, ever seeking and securing the Father's honor; and as a victim for sin, designated for an eternal sacrifice; and the lamb which was daily offered morning and evening.[140] Finally, Christ exists in this Sacrament in a bond of the friendliest union. For all things that pertain to this Sacrament enkindle charity; and it is communicated to you out of his great charity. There his benefits are recalled, his promises commemorated, and his love towards you and his passion for you are devoutly commended.

Further, this food should be consumed with a special vigor of the three theological virtues, that is, with a certain and clear faith in all that the Church teaches about this most worthy Sacrament; with hope of the immense divine liberality, namely, that God, who gives himself to you in this way, is ready to confer upon you his gracious help and all the effects and abundant glory of this great Sacrament. Therefore, with great confidence and heartfelt gratitude, with all humility and steadfastness, let us beseech the Most High for all the effects of this great Sacrament. Let us also receive this Sacrament with fervent charity, fraternal love, unrestrained affection, internal eagerness, and with the enkindling and increase of holy dilection. It should also be received with bitter compunction arising from consideration of our Lord's Passion, with contrition for our own faults, with unceasing and careful custody of heart, and with spiritual relish, which will doubtlessly be abundantly

---

[138] John 6:54-59.
[139] E.N. This expression appears unique to Denis. As used here, the Latin *atrium* is perhaps a synecdoche referring to that part of the house where the burning hearth exists, or the temple of the holocaust (as in *atrium vestae*), so it might be translated as "temple of immolation." It also has connotations of the inner chamber of the heart (*atrium*), and so "heart of immolation."
[140] Ex. 29:38-39; Num. 28:3-4.

experienced by whoever has prepared himself for holy communion in accordance with the previous instructions.

Now what we have said so far is essentially the same as that which some devoutly write about this Sacrament, saying that as the throne of Solomon was mounted by six steps, so we must approach to receive the Sacrament of the Altar by six distinct and upwardly-leading steps.[141] The first step is faith, which is necessary in this great Sacrament, inasmuch as the things taught regarding this Sacrament transcend all sense, reason, and understanding. It is not expedient to inquire too curiously into this matter nor to ponder morosely how Christ can be contained in this Sacrament, as the Church teaches; but with a mind firmly founded in the faith of Holy Church, on the basis of the reasons given for our belief and on divine illumination, and with the most certain presupposition that all things which the Church teaches about this Sacrament are true, you ought to wonder greatly, contemplate wisely, embrace lovingly, and venerate with all your strength and thanksgiving such incomprehensible goodness, charity, munificence, mercy, and providence displayed towards you poor, weak, and unworthy men. The second step is the heart's desire for this great mystery, because it is to be approached from fervent love, with a heart spiritually eager for this great good. Indeed, desire opens the heart to receive what is desired, and if one approaches with sincere desire, the effect and the fruit of this Sacrament is more abundantly bestowed. Therefore, we must approach this noble and majestic Sacrament not out of arid custom, nor with tedium or dread, nor with laziness or lukewarmness, but with the preparation described above. Hence, the third step is reverence of heart conceived from the consideration of the sublimity of this Sacrament, as explained. The fourth step is purity, because this supercelestial gift—which is the very Giver himself, the God and Creator of the heavens—can be received only with a pure mind. The fifth step is mindfulness of our Lord's Passion, of which this Sacrament is an enkindling memorial. We must therefore ponder every day what and how much the Son of God endured. The recollection of these things leads to compassion, imitation, thanksgiving, admiration, love, and contemplation. The sixth step is to cast oneself upon God, and this means to trust with all one's mind in his kindness, to commit oneself confidently to his most beneficent providence, and to undertake indefatigably those things which are

---

[141] E.N. 1 Kings 10:19.

within one's ability, and so to rest lovingly in God. Of course, these steps can be otherwise and more aptly named: diligent examination of conscience, full contrition, perfect confession, etc.

Finally, these people enumerate the effects of this Sacrament like so: first is the remission of sins; second, the cure of the heart from the remnants of the vices; third, custody or protection; fourth, strengthening of the heart; fifth, spiritual consolation; sixth, an increase of liberality; seventh, increase of virtue; eighth, enlivening, quickening, and zeal for doing good; ninth, illumination of the mind; tenth, peace of heart; eleventh, spiritual relish; twelfth, uniting and unity of mind with God through charity and perfection. These can be reduced to a smaller number. For what else is strengthening, if not the progress of grace and the increase of virtue? Likewise increase of liberality is contained under increase of virtue; and spiritual relish, peace of heart, and spiritual joy coincide, although they are distinguished.[142]

TWENTY-THIRD ARTICLE
Praise of this Sacrament encouraging one to celebrate and commune.

PRIEST: Deplorable is our perversity, ingratitude, folly, negligence, torpor, and acedia, that we are not more moved to celebrate such a superlatively noble Sacrament and to holy Communion, that we abstain so easily, that we so little prepare ourselves. Alas, alas! *Man when he was in honor did not understand.*[143] We shun the heavenly manna because we do not experience the aforesaid fruits and healthful effects; and this because we approach the God of majesty and glory unprepared, without due reverence, and without chaste fear. We do not consider the marvels of God's law;[144] we do not contemplate the loftiness of the plan of the superlatively excellent and sweet Trinity regarding the means of salvation of the human race. Nor do we consider the most rational and beautiful connection of the things we believe. Every one of them, taken by itself, sounds astonishing, and to the children of this age and the wisemen of this world appears incredible. Yet when all are gathered together, and all the tenets of our holy faith are justly weighed, and the connection, consonance, and

---

[142] E.N. The Latin editor notes in the margins: Other [manuscripts read]: "coincide, and cannot be distinguished."
[143] Ps. 48:13.   [144] Cf. Ps. 118:18.

sublimity of the articles of faith are spiritually attended to, nothing is truer, nothing more profound, nothing more rational, or rather superrational than contemplation of the Christian faith.[145]

It is therefore necessary to come *to a lofty heart*,[146] and to be enlightened from above, because all that we believe is completely above man's capacity, rests on supernatural foundations, and is confirmed by supernatural arguments. When this happens, it will be permitted to say—indeed, we will say it out of the fullness of faith and out of astonishment at the exceeding credibility of the articles of faith: *Your testimonies are become exceedingly credible.*[147] O most worthy Sacrament, from the beginning of the world typically presignified by the sacrifices of the natural law, prefigured in the offerings of the Patriarchs, foreannounced by the Prophets, instituted and consumed by the incarnate God himself, carried on by the glorious Apostles, continued by the innumerable Saints of the evangelical law, and declared by innumerable miracles! You are the truly pacifying Victim, continual sacrifice, clean and acceptable oblation, burning holocaust; most efficacious medicine, inexhaustible bread, salvific refreshment of souls, our reconciliation, viaticum leading to glory, expeller of demons, honor of angels; most generous gift, most high object of contemplation, most opulent treasure of the Church, incomprehensible good; end and consummation of the written law, origin of the worship of Holy Church. You are the Sacrament of sacraments, the Sacrifice of sacrifices, remedy of remedies; you must be desired supremely, loved most fervently, celebrated most reverently, worshipped always most devoutly, adored most fearfully, showered with praises, and you are most worthy of all thanksgiving. You are the memorial most sweet, the surety of human salvation, the pledge of eternal inheritance, the loveable prelude to future happiness; you are the dowry of the Bride, the betrothal of the devout mind, the most sweet and indissoluble bond of the Church triumphant and militant, and their shared and most delicious object, hidden and believed in this life, exposed and seen in the next.

Let my soul take heed; let every priest ponder; let every Christian consider how much grace has been granted to you, how much glory has been conveyed, that you can not only converse with Christ

---

[145] E.N. Perhaps a reference to the so-called *analogia fidei* (Rom. 12:6) or *nexus mysteriorum*. "By 'analogy of faith' we mean the coherence of the truths of faith among themselves and within the whole plan of Revelation." CCC § 114.
[146] Ps. 63:7.   [147] Ps. 92:5.

in prayer, not only address your Creator by praying and praising him, not only reach out towards him in the heavenly fatherland with holy hope to obtain support, but can also have him so truly and marvelously present in this life, in this exile; that you have the power to consecrate his Body and Blood, and so to have him, as it were at will, wholly present; to handle the humanized eternal Word with your hands, to receive and hold him in your mouth, and to keep him spiritually within you always.

O faithful mind, O Christian soul, if you are truly the bride of the heavenly Spouse, if you love your Creator, if you are grateful to your Savior, if you truly desire to honor the Lord of absolutely infinite dignity and glory, do not be negligent: adorn without delay the bridal chamber of your heart with all humility, compunction, meekness, purity, with all guardedness and fervor, with every virtue, gift, progress, and heavenly longing; and in this way run to meet him, prostrate yourself before him, and please your God, your Bridegroom, Creator, Savior, and Judge; embrace him with the arms of charity, kiss him with the mouth of your heart, receive him with the utmost reverence, strive to hold him unceasingly within you; exhort him, praise him, and fervently intercede for the entire Church, for the living and the dead, for your parents and relatives, for those committed to your care, and for your benefactors, and do not cease to remain thankful. Do not accept the paltry consolations of other things, do not listen to gossip, do not seek in food and drink something more than necessity requires; abhor negligence and torpor as if they were infernal poisons; do not desist from speaking to gazing at, and making yourself available to God; be constant in psalmody and mediation, be unceasingly aware of God's presence. O priest of the Most High, mark your dignity: see how excellent, salutary, and meritorious it is to be a mediator between God and men, to stand as a bridesman between the heavenly Bridegroom and his bride, the Church; to be the faithful's procurator, advocate, and spiritual physician; to induce the people who assist at Mass to devotion, lamentation, weeping, fervor, and to obtain heavenly gifts for them. Do not hold yourself cheap; put off the old man, hold the animal senses at bay, burn with the love of virtue and purity; present yourself as a worthy minister; remain guarded, fearful, solicitous, grateful, proficient, and unceasingly focused on divine things.

O Only-Begotten of the eternal Father, O Lord Jesus Christ made incarnate and crucified for our sake, who so lovingly, so kindly, so generously bestowed yourself on us, and so graciously and marvelously deigned to be with us, for all your goodness, charity, mercy, and munificence towards us, for all your mysteries and all your benefits, always and efficaciously prepare us for your table, and so make us to receive you now in the Sacrament by faith that after the course of this life we might attain to the blessed vision of you.

TRUTH: The eye of your heart is now enlightened, and your affections enkindled. Persist and grow in them. Begin to address the Lord your God, the Only-Begotten of the Father, daily with loving and holy and vigorously inflaming words, he who shows himself is so incomprehensibly loving, gracious, and generous to you, so that your entire manner of life and all your occupations prepare you to celebrate the Mass.

PRIEST: O eternal Word, almighty utterance, fountain of wisdom, who spoke so wisely, so powerfully, and so graciously when you came into the world in assumed flesh, so that even your adversaries were convinced and compelled to say, *Never did man speak like this man*:[148] teach me to speak so.

TRUTH: Heed the words my elect uttered in their days, and use these and similar words howsoever a fervent devotion shall suggest to you.

TWENTY-FOURTH ARTICLE
An earnest and devout meditation in preparation for the fruitful celebration of Mass.

PRIEST: Only-begotten of the eternal Father, with whom the Father takes immense pleasure,[149] who, by the wise and beneficent plan of the whole superlatively blessed Trinity, for the purpose of restoring the honor and worship due to the divine majesty, and for the salvation of the human race, deigned in your ardent charity and ineffable kindness to descend from the Father's bosom, yea from the heart of your superlatively beloved Begetter, into the womb of the most pure Virgin in the mystery of the Incarnation; sweetest Jesus Christ, O most High, my strength, my refuge, protector of my soul, God of all my salvation,[150] in whom I believe, in whom I hope, whom I love: I approach your throne of grace:[151] open the doorway of your mercy for me; you who promised the crucified

---
[148] John 7:46.   [149] Matt. 17:5.   [150] Cf. Ps. 17:2–3.   [151] Heb. 4:16.

thief entry into paradise:[152] lead me by the most sacred wound of your side into the middle of your breast, and there, from the fountain of your heart, let me drink from the flowing stream of your wisdom. O God of immense mercy: into the bowels of your mercy, in which you have visited us, unceasingly receive, embrace, enclose, and hide me.[153]

O God of infinite excellence, who am I, a vessel of clay, a sinful man, a useless servant, that you should visit me, that you should deign to be consecrated, handled, offered and consumed by me, and through me to work marvels many and great? In times past, you refused Moses, who ardently desired to see you as you are;[154] but now you make yourself present to me, who am so miserable and unworthy, as food and drink, as reconciler and physician, as a guest, spouse, and dweller of the soul. You, immortal and invisible King of all ages,[155] impassible and incomprehensible by your nature, you are my light and my salvation,[156] you are the protector of my life and my mercy,[157] you are my God and Lord, who for my redemption undertook the most bitter and ignominious punishment of the Cross; you are He, and there is no other.

You, O Christ, Word, wisdom, offspring of the Father's mind, sprout of infinite comeliness, whose beauty, graciousness, deliciousness, and most beauteous excellence has no end, eternally begotten from the eternal Father indescribably before all ages, at a time foreordained from on high, and cooperating with the superlatively sweet, wooing paraclete of the Holy Spirit, you enclosed yourself within the tender body of a chosen, holy maiden in an assumed human form, while preserving the immense majesty of your deity, and from her, who remained permanently intact,[158] you deigned to be born and to dwell with men.[159] You, O true glory of God the Father, were regarded as inglorious among the wicked,[160] and so treated by evil men, that you, O Only-Begotten, beautiful above all sons of men,[161] indeed incomparably beautiful above all the minds of angels, had neither comeliness nor sightliness,[162] and appeared as a leper, as a *reproach of men and an outcast of the people*.[163] May this miserable disfiguration, O Jesus, be for me the complete

---

[152] Luke 23:43. [153] Luke 1:78. [154] Ex. 33:13, 18, et seq. [155] 1 Tim. 1:17.
[156] Ps. 26:1. [157] Ps. 58:18.
[158] L. *integerrima permanente*, a reference to Mary's perpetual virginity, the *virgo integerrima*, who remained a virgin *ante partum, in partu, et perpetuo post partum*; here, Denis specifically refers to the virginal and miraculous birth of Christ.
[159] Baruch 3:38. [160] Is. 52:14. [161] Ps. 44:3. [162] Is. 53:2–4. [163] Ps. 21:7.

reformation of my mind and all the passions, an adornment of virtue, and everlasting glory.

From the perfidious Synagogue you came to the Gentiles, and with you thousands of Saints.[164] In your right is the fiery law, which you preached to the Gentiles through the glorious Apostles. You loved all peoples, and for their salvation you offered yourself to God the Father upon the gibbet of the Cross, in an odor of sweetness, a superlatively acceptable Victim. All Saints are in your hand, for you know those you have chosen,[165] and you have mercy upon those you will, and will be merciful to those it pleases you.[166] And those who approach your feet, who faithfully follow your footsteps, will receive your doctrine.[167] For he who wishes to do the will of God the Father, will know by the taste and experience of your heavenly gifts and by internal visitations that your doctrine is from God. For there is no other but you, most righteous God, ascender of heaven, our help, who ascending into heaven and sending the Paraclete, having your habitation above and everlasting arms below, made in your magnificence the clouds to run[168]—that is, the sublime Apostles, the sons of thunder,[169] who spread the light of your doctrine, not merely in the one region of Judaea, but in every place of your mercy, wherever you ordered them to go.[170] You, O Lord, by the Blood of your Cross pouring out from your Body, which I believe is most truly present in this Sacrament, have reconciled us to God, and pacified the things of heaven and the things of earth,[171] and joined both into one,[172] *blotting out the handwriting of the decree that was against us.*[173]

And so that we might constantly remember all of these and your other mysteries fervently and devoutly, you instituted, at that Last Supper, which you desired with desire to have with your disciples,[174] this great Sacrament in which was manifest in the flesh, justified in the Spirit, appeared to the angels, was preached to the Gentiles, is believed in the world, and is taken up in glory,[175] so that we might often recall your love, your Passion, and all your benefits and mysteries, and by recalling them be ignited, and thus ignited, might imitate them, as often as we celebrate the solemnity of the

---

[164] Deut. 33:2–3. [165] John 13:18. [166] Ex. 33:19. [167] John 7:17.
[168] Cf. Deut. 33:26–27.
[169] Mark 3:17. E.N. Commonly, expositors interpreted the image of clouds in the scriptures (e.g., Is. 60:8) as references to the Apostles, e.g., Pope St. Gregory the Great, *Moralia in Job*, XVIII, 26, 36, PL 76, 27.   [170] Job 37:11–13.
[171] Col. 1:20.   [172] Eph. 2:14.   [173] Col. 2:14.   [174] Luke 22:15.
[175] 1 Tim. 3:16.

Mass and partake in the sacred mysteries. I beseech you, O Lord and Savior, by all the goodness, charity, and grace of the superlatively glorious Trinity towards us, by all your virtues, and by all the merits of your most holy Passion and of everything which you did and endured for our salvation, most mercifully dispose, make worthy, preserve, guide, fill with grace, and unceasingly govern us to carry out these divine mysteries.

TWENTY-FIFTH ARTICLE
Another prayer for the same.

PRIEST: O eternal God, Father of mercy, and God of all consolation,[176] who, because you are rich in mercy, because of the measureless charity by which you have loved us, when we were dead through sin you *quickened us together in Christ*[177] (for you did not spare your only Son, but delivered him up for us all[178]); you who renew these your wonderful doings in this Sacrament,[179] in your charity and in the infinite abyss of your mercy towards the whole human race, *show to us*, your unworthy priests, *the light of your mercy*,[180] gracefully anticipate our needs, fill and perfect us with the love of your only-begotten Son, and forgive and take compassion on our improbity. Behold your only-begotten Son, in his immeasurable charity towards us, invites us to his sacred communion and its manifold fruits; yet we, wicked and perverse, flee from him, we excuse and minimize our negligence and laziness, saying that it is dangerous to approach, when, nevertheless, it is extremely fruitful to obey him and to receive this great Sacrament with due preparation. Therefore, we must accuse the indisposition which arises from our negligence and laziness. Illumine fully our heart to carefully consider the purity and reverence with which we ought to receive our Creator and Savior, whose advent our Fathers in times past wished for with such affection in the times of the written [Mosaic] and natural [Noahide] law. Refresh and anoint, feed and strengthen us with all the effects, graces, and heavenly gifts of this most excellent Sacrament.

---

[176] 1 Cor. 1:3.   [177] Eph. 2:4–5.   [178] Rom. 8:32.
[179] L. *innovas*, literally to take and to alter into something new, so the Passion and the Cross of Christ and his bloody Sacrifice is taken and shown as something the same, but also new: an unbloody Sacrifice.   [180] Ecclus. 36:1.

Nevertheless, we confess that we are unable to receive such a pure, heavenly, and divine gift, unless we first purge our souls utterly from vices, from all sensual affections, carnal loves, loquacity, duplicity, and all the vagaries of sin, from unguardedness of the heart and senses, from ingratitude and spiritual torpor. Hence, O Lord, in your immense holiness, grant us truly to know all of our sins, both great and small, to weigh carefully their enormity and gravity, to confess them, weep over them, and chastise ourselves over them completely and entirely, with great contrition and firm purpose of amendment, and thereafter continually to avoid them, as far as human weakness allows, so that by this salubrious Sacrament we may everyday be more closely and more intimately joined to you, and grow to the full spiritual stature of the virtues by its power and grace, and that we may cease from our former faults and vices at all times, and walk in fear before your sight.[181]

O Almighty God, who through your omnipotence work so many wonderful things in this Sacrament, by this same omnipotence strengthen us—who are so imperfect and weak and have such a proclivity towards evil—so powerfully and mercifully with the effects of this great Sacrament that, made steadfast in your grace, we may every day adhere to you more faithfully, serve you more reverently, thank you more wholeheartedly, and be inflamed unceasingly with love of you.

O eternal God, how great is our depravity, our foolishness, yea even our perversity, that we, miserable men, so often and at the slightest opportunity, at so small a temptation, prefer these carnal and fleeting, vain and vile, illicit and forbidden things than incessantly contemplating and fearing, supremely and fervently loving with all our heart, you, our Lord and God, who are so incomparably good and infinitely honorable—we should rather be called impudent dogs than priests! Returning from that heavenly table, we soon become as unserious, dissolute, talkative, and uncaring as we were before; we partake excessively in food, drink, and sleep. Not only do we commit much evil, we also omit so many good deeds. Indeed, sometimes we even engage in things abominable and horrendous and worthy of eternal damnation, we fall into detraction, rash and temerarious judgments, contention, indignation, anger, and impatience. Like faithless traitors, we expel you from our hearts and refuse to be reproved or corrected.

---

[181] Micah 6:8.

Have mercy upon us, O Lord, have mercy, and henceforth let us not be *filled with such great contempt.*[182] Enlighten our interior eyes, lest we slumber in the death of iniquity, lest our cruel enemies say: We *have prevailed against* them, and lest they glory in our excesses,[183] lest we grieve the holy angels, our kindly guardians, and (what is to be avoided above all), lest we gravely offend your presence, most high God! Rather let us diligently beware whatever is offensive to your sanctity and majesty, not only sins, but let us also solicitously avoid occasions of sin, let us always meditate upon salutary things, let us prefer virtuous things, and let us set you unceasingly before the eyes of our heart, and let us glory in adversity *as in all riches.* Make us shrewdly, profoundly, and assiduously to consider how reverently and obediently, purely and gratefully, and with what ardent charity and profound humility all the holy angels and heavenly citizens unceasingly assist and serve you, so that, poor and unworthy as we are, we may endeavor, by their example, with all our effort, reverently, obediently, purely, thankfully, lovingly, fearfully, humbly, everywhere and always to stand before you and serve you, in particular in the celebration of Mass, to the praise and glory of your name.

TWENTY-SIXTH ARTICLE
Second prayer regarding the same matter.

PRIEST: O most blessed Trinity, of your goodness, charity, and mercy towards the human race, on account of your eternal, wise, and superlatively gracious plan regarding the means and reality of our redemption, enlighten our souls to savingly consider how lovingly and mercifully you have acted towards us, and, in proportion to the depth of our faith, make us serve you in a correspondingly deep perfection of the virtues. According to the profundity of Christian wisdom, make us to stand before you steadfast as the sun in wisdom, and do not allow us to vary like the moon,[184] or be troubled by the motions of the passions, or subject to vices. In the presence of your immense light, in the sight of your eternal wisdom, and before the most superlatively holy face of your glory, let us be ashamed to live a base life, to think impure thoughts, to have illicit affections. God forbid that we venerate more the presence

---

[182] Ps. 122:3.   [183] Cf. Ps. 12:4–5.   [184] Cf. Ecclus. 27:12.

of men than of God. Indeed, just as the Father's Only-Begotten *visited and wrought the redemption of his people*[185] so that without inordinate fear and freed from the hands of our enemies we might serve you in holiness and justice unceasingly to the end,[186] so let us ever shake off the devil's yoke, the vile servitude of sin, and all unrighteousness, and thus sincerely adhere to you and submit to you in fear and reverence.[187]

O most glorious Trinity, who created us to enjoy your supernatural beatitude and a clear, delicious, face-to-face vision of you, and who invite us to this noble sacramental repast—a figure of that future repast—how detestable and deplorable is our negligence, nay rather our stupidity and malice, that we neglect such ineffably great, precious, and divine gifts and do not burn *to see the good things of the Lord in the land of the living*,[188] nor do we suitably long for or make haste to contemplate the King of glory in his uncircumscribable and absolutely immense beauty.[189] If a famished pauper were invited to a rich man's luxurious feast by the rich man himself, he would put on his best clothes and go as speedily as possible. And I, a poor, blind, naked, evil man, full of weakness, O Christ, do not burn for, do not prepare myself for, do not with all affection and all humility and veneration run to your table![190]

O Savior, you stand at the door of my mind and knock;[191] by divine and angelic inspirations you rouse, move, and entreat me to let you in and to remove every obstacle to your gracious entrance by instantly fleeing every sin, even a venial one, as if fleeing a snake or dragon, and by ever sighing for you and fervently invoking you,[192] so that thus you might go into the chamber of my soul and dine with me,[193] rejoicing with me at my progress, and supping, as it were, on my virtuous exercises and internal disciplines: yea even changing and converting me into you, to wit, spiritually eating me and incorporating me into you, for your delight is to be with the sons of men who do these things.[194] And so I also sup with you, foretasting those heavenly dishes, nay even eating you in a hearty chewing of love. Moreover, I, unhappy and foolish man, am tardy and remiss in opening up to my great Lord, to such a noble guest; my heart is icy at the idea of sharing a meal with you. But I readily grant audience to a wicked foe who knocks at my heart's

---

[185] Luke 1:68. [186] Luke 1:74–75. [187] Cf. Heb. 12:28. [188] Ps. 26:13.
[189] Cf. Is. 33:17. [190] Cf. Rev. 3:17. [191] Rev. 3:20a. [192] Ecclus. 21:2.
[193] Rev. 3:20b. [194] Cf. Prov. 8:31.

door with his nefarious suggestions, murmurings, and temptations when I foolishly admit vain and frivolous thoughts, depraved desires, vanities, and *unsound falsities*;[195] my soul fornicates with these idols, and I abandon the heavenly Bridegroom to be ravished by demons, copulating with them through forbidden consentings and sundry vices, and thus, base and stupid, when invited to dine in scarlet, I wrap my arms around dung.[196]

Have mercy on me, O Lord, Son of David,[197] and enlighten me so that I may see, so that I might now come to my senses, and that, rejecting all admixture of impurity, I may fervently and unswervingly adhere to you, fountain and lover of all purity, with the utmost care, and may ever draw from your sacraments, as if from pure and living fountains, the waters of salutary wisdom, rivers of graces, and a gushing abundance of spiritual riches.

O bountiful Paraclete, most sweet consoler, most bountiful Holy Spirit, in your immense kindness and munificence, you who are essentially charity and love—the bond and kiss of the Father and the Son—mercifully visit, cleanse, enrich, teach, anoint, enkindle, and unceasingly possess and govern me, an empty, vile, destitute, and supremely unworthy sinner. Prepare, dispose, and elevate me daily to be worthy to celebrate Christ's mysteries and receive sacred communion.

O superlatively worthy Trinity, on account of your eternal internal (*ad intra*) communication and emanation, pour forth and communicate your most merciful and paternal gifts externally (*ad extra*). On account of your superlatively brilliant reciprocal intuition,[198] make us contemplate you now with sincere faith in the reasons for our beliefs, and with the understanding of a purified mind, well-supplied with the gift of wisdom. On account of your ardent and immense reciprocal love, make us fervent lovers of you

---

[195] Ps. 39:5.
[196] Cf. Lam. 4:5. E.N. Denis has *invitatus enutriri in croceis*. This verse is translated in the Douay-Rheims as "they were brought up in scarlet," i.e., as nobility. The reference to the saffron crocus flower might also be a specific reference to the crimson stigma and styles (called threads) of that flower. The saffron spice derived from the crocus was a sign of nobility. In commenting on this verse in his *Commentary on Lamentations*, Denis interprets it as meaning those who are nourished in beautiful and soft garments.
[197] Luke 18:38-42.
[198] L. *intuitionem*. In Scholastic terminology, intuition in this context might be defined as "the act of immediately knowing a present object; vision." Bernard Wuellner, *A Dictionary of Scholastic Philosophy* (Milwaukee: Bruce, 1966) (2nd ed.), 153.

without interpolation,[199] and make us love you more ardently every day. On account of your reciprocal complacency,[200] make us always pleasing to you and more pleasing every day. We ask this through Christ and all his merits. Amen.

TWENTY-SEVENTH ARTICLE
How the Eucharist is a sacrament; and whether it is one sacrament or many.

PRIEST: Because a sacrament is a sign of a sacred thing, and does not contain grace formally, but rather figuratively, or even in a certain sense causally, it seems that the true Body of Christ and his real Blood do not constitute a sacrament, since in Christ's Body his most holy Soul, nay the whole Christ, is the fountain of all grace and virtue. Further, it seems that they are not one sacrament, since they have different matters, as stated in the Post-communion prayer:[201] *We beseech you, O Lord, that the sacraments we consume might purify us.*

TRUTH: In this Sacrament there is something which is a sacrament alone,[202] that is, a sign of a sacred thing, namely, the species or accidental forms of bread and wine, which remain without a subject, the bread being converted and transubstantiated into the Body of Christ, and likewise the wine transubstantiated into the Blood of Christ. These species are a sign of the true Body and Blood of Christ. There is also contained in this Sacrament something that is both reality and sign,[203] that is, the very Body and Blood of Christ, which are the realities signified by the remaining species, as already stated. Nevertheless, they signify and figure the Mystical Body of Christ itself, which is the Church in the elect, or the ecclesial unity, which is the grace of spiritual nourishment and refreshment caused by this Sacrament.

---

[199] L. *sine interpolatione*. Unadulterated or without the mediation of words, concepts, or the perception of the senses.
[200] L. *complacentiam*, the pleasure that the lover obtains in his love of the beloved. "Love always places (puts) a complacency in the lover in the beloved." — "*Amor semper ponit complacentiam amantis in amato.*" St. Thomas Aquinas, *Super Sent.*, lib. 1, d. 10, q. 1, a. 3, co.
[201] The post-communion prayer partly quoted by Denis is found, among other places, in the Thursday Mass of the Fourth Week of Lent in the Roman Missal.
[202] In other words, the *sacramentum tantum*.
[203] That is, the *sacramentum et res*.

Therefore, the Eucharist is a sacrament, yet in a manner different than Baptism and the other sacraments, because being both a reality and a sign,[204] it contains sanctification, holiness, and grace really and formally, insofar as Christ's Soul and the Person of the eternal Word are with his Body by natural concomitance. We do not encounter grace in the other sacraments in the same way. Rather it exists in them as in a sign or instrumental-ministerial cause concurring and cooperating in some sense by divine ordination and power. Such grace is believed to consist in the use of the matter of those sacraments. Thus, the matter is sanctified, and said to be holy or sanctified, insofar as it is ordered, deputed, and applied to effect true and real holiness and grace in a rational creature, with the divine power working principally, and the sacraments, which contain and effect what they figure, working instrumentally and ministerially each in its particular manner.

PRIEST: A succinct answer. It raises a doubt for me, but before I put it before you, please explain how this Sacrament is said to be both one and many.

TRUTH: A thing can be said to be one in many ways. First, if it cannot be divided into parts in act or potency, as in a point. Second, by reason of continuity, as in a line; which is potentially many, because it is able to be divided into many parts. Third, by unity of substantial form, as in natural beings, or a substantial whole, which by dint of its matter and substantial form is a composite of essential parts. Fourth, by relation to one and the same total effect, as a medicine consisting of several materials is called one, because it is used to effect a perfect cure; in this way certain artificial things[205] and instruments are said to be one thing, such as a house.[206] And in this way this sacrament of Christ's Body and Blood is said to be one, because it is ordered by divine institution to the same complete spiritual refreshment of man, a spiritual refreshment that is signified by the bodily act of nutrition, for which food and drink are required. Therefore, it belongs to the integrity of this Sacrament to have something in the way of food, that is to say, his Body, and something in the way of drink, namely, his Blood. Nevertheless, this Sacrament can also be called sacraments in the

---

[204] L. *res et signum*.
[205] L. *artificialia* refers to those things that are man-made artifices, as distinguished from those things as they appear in nature, or *naturalia*.
[206] E.N. E.g., one may say "one hammer," though the hammer is composed of a head and handle combination.

plural due to the material diversity of its signs, or because of the sacramental distinction of the remaining visible species, and because it is consecrated using distinct matters, namely, bread and wine.

PRIEST: Permit me now to raise the doubt which arose from what you have said.

TRUTH: If we enter the dark abyss of scholastic questions, it would exceed the brief space allotted for this work, and we would defeat our purpose. For our intention in this brief dialogue was to treat and address only things that matter for devotion, not scholastic difficulties or subtle questions. Subtle and inquisitive discussions belong elsewhere. They may be necessary for the defense and explanation of the faith; for most people they do not promote but inhibit devotion.

PRIEST: Mainly I want to ask about a few things that are proposed in the treatise of a certain devout person that is widely read by devout people.[207]

TRUTH: Make it brief.

TWENTY-EIGHTH ARTICLE
Whether the form of the words of this Sacrament contain a created supernatural power in some manner concurrent with the cause of transubstantiation.

PRIEST: In this devout man's treatise on the Sacrament of the Eucharist, this question arises: whether the consecrating priest actively concurs in the effect of consecration or transubstantiation, so that he is a co-operator with God in the act of transubstantiating.[208] He answers: I say no, because transubstantiation is miraculous simply speaking, exceeding any power that has been communicated to creatures. Therefore, a priest does not actively concur in the consecration. Indeed, the doctors' common opinion is that generally the ministers of the sacraments do not cooperate productively with God in effects that are the inward realities (*res*) of the sacraments, because when the ministers do everything that is required according to our Lord's institution, he alone immediately[209] causes the prin-

---

[207] E.N. I have been unable to identify this "certain devout person." I initially thought it might be John of Ruusbroec, but I could not find this subject in his works.
[208] L. *concurrat active*. In other words, acts actively and concurrently or jointly in tandem with the divine power. [209] E.N. I.e., without mediation.

cipal effect and reality (*res*) of the sacrament. From this it follows that the sacraments of the New Law do not effect what they signify or figure by a power intrinsic to the elements, the words, the intention, or the signs, or all of these together.[210] Hence, this difference between the sacraments of the New and Old Law—namely, that the sacraments of the New Law effect the grace they figure, while the sacraments of the Old Law do not—means precisely this: that the sacraments of the New Law are instrumental, dispositive causes of sacramental grace, enabling the subject to receive the effect by means of an external disposition, not from their nature, but by the ordination and determination of God, so that the effects are brought about in the way already stated, by dint of the act itself, and not by the act of the minister performing the work.[211] The opposite is true for the sacraments of the Old Testament: if they conferred any good upon those who received them, this was due to the holy prayers of the one doing or receiving the act, and not by virtue of the act itself. This devout man writes this and many like things which seem contrary to your previous discussion. For you said that in the sacraments of the law of the Gospel grace is contained as in a sign and a ministerial-instrumental cause that concurs and cooperates in some way to produce the sacramental effect.[212]

TRUTH: As you know, regarding this matter the teachers have two opinions, as you have no doubt read. The one I have explained is the truer.

PRIEST: Did not the Apostle Paul point out in his epistles, especially in the epistle to the Hebrews,[213] this distinction between the Law of Christ and the Law of Moses: that the Evangelical Law contains grace, saves, and justifies, but the Law of Moses does not? And here when he refers to the Evangelical Law, he includes its sacraments, for the sacraments contain and cause grace as we have explained.

In fact, that most holy, brilliant, and authoritative Doctor, Thomas, in Book IV of his commentary on the *Sentences*, in the eighth distinction, having stated the above opinion, says: This opinion lessens the dignity of the sacraments of the New Law; therefore, one must believe that there is a certain power from God in the

---

[210] E.N. I.e., neither the matter nor the form of the sacraments nor the intent of the celebrant have, in themselves, the power to effect what the sacrament signifies or figures.
[211] E.N. In other words, by means of the acts themselves (*ex opere operato*), and not as a result of the act of the person celebrating the sacrament (not *ex opere operantis*). [212] Twenty-Seventh Article. [213] Rom. 8:3-4; Hebr. 7:19.

words of consecration, as there is in the other sacramental forms; this power is a quality which does not have complete existence in nature, as in the principal power of some agent acting according to his form, but rather it has an incomplete existence, like the power an instrument has from the intention or the impression of a principal agent,[214] and like the likenesses of color in the air.[215] Further, in the third part of the *Summa*,[216] he says that some have said that the words of consecration do not have a created power to effect transubstantiation, nor do the forms of the other sacraments or the sacraments themselves have power to produce their sacramental effects; this is contrary to what the Saints have said, and lessens the dignity of the sacraments of the New Law. Hence, since the Sacrament of the Eucharist is of greater dignity than the other sacraments, it follows that its form of words has a certain created power to cause the conversion in it, though, as in the other sacraments, this power is instrumental. For since these words are uttered in the person of Christ and by his command, they receive instrumental power from him, just as his other deeds and sayings have a certain saving power instrumentally.

And this position is approved by many Saints. For Augustine says in his tracts on the Gospel of John: What great power the water has, that it touches the body and washes the heart?[217] And Bede: The Lord by the touch of his flesh conveyed regenerative power to the water. Chrysostom wrote the same thing. And Ambrose, in the fourth book of his *De Sacramentis*, says: If the Lord's speech is so powerful that it causes things to exist from nothing, how much more able is it to change them into something else? Thomas also defends this view in the *Summa Contra Gentiles*.[218] In his *De Sacramentis*, William of Paris agrees,[219] and many other eminent doctors

---

[214] E.N. E.g., as a chisel may be said to have power as a result of the handling and intention of a carpenter.
[215] E.N. The color is not in the air completely or by nature, as it might be in paint on a wall, since air is transparent, and yet it is not entirely absent from the air; the air is, as it were, color's conduit.
[216] *Summa Theologiae*, IIIa, q. 78, art. 4, co.
[217] E.N. See St. Augustine's *In Evangelium Ioannis Tractatus*, 80.3 (*Unde ista tanta virtus aquae, ut corpus tangat et cor abluat, nisi faciente verbo*), which is quoted by St. Thomas in his *Commentary on the Sentences. Super Sent.*, lib. 4, d. 1, q. 1, a. 4, qc. 1, co.   [218] *Summa Contra Gentiles*, IV, c. 63.
[219] E.N. William of Auvergne (1180/90–1249), Bishop of Paris, also known as William of Paris, who wrote on a number of theological and philosophical subjects. Perhaps his most famous work is the *Magisterium Divinale*.

affirm it. This view is given even greater weight by the words of the divine Dionysius,[220] who asserts at the end of *De Ecclesiastica hierarchia*: These consummating invocations, that is, the words of the sacraments, have their operative powers from God. Likewise, Ambrose and Eusebius attest: Christ's speech changes creatures, and indeed the consecration of the heavenly word changes bread into the Body of Christ, and wine into his most holy Blood.

In addition, the priest can only cause transubstantiation if he utters words. Therefore, if the words did not have power to transubstantiate, priests would have no spiritual power to confect the Sacrament, nor even Orders, which is a certain power to do this. Moreover, if the priest does not cooperate instrumentally in transubstantiation, the words of the Saints who praise the excellence of the priestly power would not be true. Thus in a sermon ascribed to blessed Bernard,[221] among other things we read: O venerable and excellent power of yours! Surely, after God, there is no power like your power. Perhaps you would like to know what this great power is? I say: to consecrate the Body of Christ and the Blood of the Lord. Witnessing this power of yours, witnessing such a singular privilege, heaven is amazed, the world is astonished, and the angels on high stand in great awe.

Nor does the Damascene's opinion—that transubstantiation is effected by divine power alone—stand in contradiction, because the power of the principal agent does not exclude the power of the instrumental cause. Man, by divine and supernatural power, can be a concurrent cause in a miraculous effect, not out of any lack on the part of the Almighty, but because in his benevolence he lets creatures participate in his powers and share in his operations.

And Alexander,[222] Albert the Great,[223] and others are of the same

---

[220] Pseudo-Dionysius the Areopagite, a Christian philosopher and theologian of the late fifth or early sixth century that was believed (wrongly) to have been the Athenian convert of St. Paul mentioned in Acts 17:34.

[221] E.N. St. Bernard of Clairvaux (1090–1153), Cistercian abbot who founded the monastery of Clairvaux. A doctor of the Church, he is known as the *Doctor Mellifluus* (the Mellifluous or Honey-Sweet Doctor).

[222] E.N. Alexander of Hales (ca. 1185–1245), a Franciscan scholastic philosopher and theologian, also called the *Doctor Irrefragibilis* (the Irrefutable Teacher) and the *Doctor Doctorum* (the Teacher of Teachers).

[223] E.N. St. Albert the Great or Albertus Magnus (ca. 1193–1280) was a famous Dominican friar and bishop. The range of his knowledge—theology, philosophy, science—is remarkable. He is also a Doctor of the Church, and is known as the *Doctor Universalis* (the Universal Doctor) or the *Doctor Expertus* (the Expert Doctor).

mind. Bonaventure[224] refuses to pass judgment on either opinion; nevertheless, he admits that this one is more in harmony with the Saints.

TRUTH: You've made a persuasive case.

PRIEST: The treatise makes further claims about which I should like to be informed.

TRUTH: Mention them briefly.

TWENTY-NINTH ARTICLE

An inquiry into the contents of a treatise by a certain devout person.

PRIEST: Regarding the form for the consecration of the sacred Blood, the devout man writes:

> Regarding the form, there are three opinions. The first is that the essential and necessary form for consecration of the Blood is: *This is the chalice of my Blood*, such that the wine is converted into the Blood when they are uttered. The second opinion is that the following words are included in the form: *of the new and eternal Covenant, the mystery of Faith*. The third opinion is that the consecration requires the remaining words: *Which shall be shed for you and for many for the remission of sins*. The third opinion is less common, and not at all probable. For this reason, St. Thomas, Henry of Ghent,[225] and many others do not even mention it.

Now it seems that his view cannot stand. For Thomas in the fourth section of his *Commentary on the Sentences*, in the eighth distinction,[226] asks whether the form of consecration for the Blood consists in these words alone: *This is the chalice of my Blood*. And having laid out the arguments on both sides, in three questions and solutions of arguments he convincingly concludes that it does not. He asserts that all the remaining words, *of the new and eternal Covenant, mystery of Faith, which shall be shed for you and for many for the remission of sins*, pertain to the form of the consecration,

---

[224] E.N. St. Bonaventure (1221–1274), an Italian Franciscan friar, was head of the Franciscan order, later Bishop of Albano. He wrote on multiple subjects and is known as the Seraphic Doctor (*Doctor Seraphicus*) of the Church.

[225] Henry of Ghent (ca. 1217–1293) was a scholastic philosopher and theologian and was known as the *Doctor Solemnis*, or Solemn Doctor. He was a regent master at the University of Paris, and was heavily involved in the controversy between the mendicant orders and the secular priesthood, taking the side of the latter.

[226] *Super Sent.*, lib. 4, d. 8, q. 2, a. 2.

and gives a reasonable explanation for it.

TRUTH: You need not go any further, because anyone who disagrees can consult the writing of that holy teacher and will find it as you report. It will also become clear later on.

PRIEST: Likewise, in the third part of the *Summa* he discussed the form of consecration for the Blood saying that there are two opinions on the matter.[227] Some have said that the substance of the form is only: *This is the chalice of my Blood*. But this seems incorrect, because the following words are determinations of the predicate, i.e., of the words *my Blood*. Thus they pertain to the integrity of the phrase. Hence, others more soundly argue that all the subsequent words are of the essence of the form up to the words, *As often as you do these things*, etc., which are a matter of custom and therefore not part of the substance of the form. This is why the priest pronounces all these words with the same posture and manner of holding the chalice. Thus far Thomas. Although he reports only two opinions, still in his discussion of the second opinion he includes also the third, which is the one he holds, explains, and approves both here and in the fourth part of his *Commentary on the Sentences*. And although Albert held the first opinion in his *Summa on the Body of Christ*, yet in his commentary on the fourth book of the *Sentences*, he rejects it and follows the latter opinion.

TRUTH: So it is. And this position is in accord with the rite and custom of the Church, which does not elevate the chalice until all those words have been uttered up to *As often as you do these things*, etc.

PRIEST: The same devout man writes in his treatise:

> We must say that all the moral virtues, except justice, are in the sensitive appetite alone, and not in the will as St. Thomas says,[228] and many theologians and philosophers who follow him; or else, if they are principally in the will, as others maintain, it is still necessary for the sensitive appetite to have virtuous habits, by which it gladly and promptly obeys reason.

So says the devout man. One may object that not only Thomas, but the shared opinion of all theologians and philosophers holds that prudence is a moral virtue that is subjectively in the intellect, and not in the sensitive appetite. If, therefore, according to the

---

[227] *Summa Theologiae*, IIIa, q. 78, art. 3, co.
[228] *Summa Theologiae*, IaIIae, q. 56, art. 3.

second opinion, there are in addition to the moral virtues also virtuous habits in the sensitive appetite, one would have to ask whether these are themselves moral virtues; and if they are, why is it necessary to posit further moral virtues in the will? It would also seem necessary to ask whether these two types differ from each other specifically. Again, those who say that the moral virtues are really in the will say that they are in the sensitive appetite only by a certain impression. Again, if the sensitive appetite is able to receive such virtuous habits subjectively, then it is also able to receive moral virtues which pertain to the same object of the virtues.

TRUTH: These points lack the force of the previous ones; though what you object about prudence is true. But with few exceptions this devout man speaks humbly, cautiously, and soberly; therefore, he should be handled gently.

PRIEST: I have not mentioned these things in order to tear him down, but to caution readers. For he also says some objectionable things about types of devotion and their effects. But we can pass them over out of respect.

TRUTH: Yes, let's move on. We have some things to discuss regarding the matter and form of this Sacrament.

THIRTIETH ARTICLE
On the matter of this Sacrament.

TRUTH: The only-begotten Son of God personally instituted the matter and form of this Sacrament at the Last Supper; and he left to his ministers to continue what he had done. Therefore, just as for the consecration of this Sacrament, the form of words which Christ himself used in consecrating and giving it is required, so also for the matter he used to confect and institute it, namely wheaten bread and wine of the vine. And just as it is provable that the wine was mixed with water, since in that land the wines are strong, and he observed and taught the greatest temperance in all things, so the Church mixes a small amount of water in the chalice. This water is absorbed by the wine and is changed into it. Thus nothing is converted into the Blood of Christ except for wine. Nevertheless, the admixture of water takes place for other reasons, figurative and mystical. For both blood and water flowed from the side of Christ on the cross.[229] Further, water signifies the people. Hence mixing it with the wine expresses the union of the people with Christ. Therefore, although consecration can take place with bread and wine, even with other materials mixed in—as long as the true nature of the wheaten bread and the true nature of the grape wine predominate—yet it is fitting both on account of the reverence due to the Sacrament as well for its spiritual signification, that the bread should be beautiful and pure (or at least not much mixed), and not crumbly, broken, or discolored. The same holds for the wine in its own way; therefore, it is not suitable to use new wine that still has sediment; or if one cannot avoid this, it must be allowed to rest so that the dregs settle, and only thus purified should it be brought to the altar.

PRIEST: Some say spelt bread can be confected, and that even verjuice or must can be used.

TRUTH: Must can be used; as to the rest, keep to what I said. It must be confected with unleavened wheat bread, not leavened bread, though consecration will occur in the latter; and some do so, but they sin by not following the custom of the Roman Church, since the Savior himself used unleavened bread. The Jews removed all leavened food from their houses on Thursday evening, the very day the Sacrament was instituted.[230] The Greeks err grievously when they assert that our Lord anticipated eating the paschal lamb by one day, so that the Last Supper occurred on Wednesday.

PRIEST: In some lands neither wheat nor wine is to be found; therefore, it seems that they were not considered when this venerable Sacrament was instituted.

TRUTH: It is not so difficult to import them from other lands.

PRIEST: Since the flesh of the paschal lamb is more like Christ's flesh than bread is, why did he not consecrate in lamb's flesh?

TRUTH: Because it would not be convenient for communal eating and handling, nor would it so clearly designate ecclesiastical unity, nor the purity of Christ's body from the stain of concupiscence and sin, as does wheaten bread.

PRIEST: If you please, let's move on to the Sacrament's form.

---

[229] John 19:34.
[230] Ex. 12:15. E.N. The Jewish Passover required yeast to be absent of the home for seven days.

THIRTY-FIRST ARTICLE
On the form of consecration for the Body and Blood of Christ.

TRUTH: On the form for the consecration of the Body of Christ all are in accord that it is this, *For this is my Body*;[231] although the conjunction "for" is not an essential part of the form, nor did Christ utter it. Thus if it is omitted the consecration still occurs. But to omit it on purpose is blameworthy because it is against the Church's custom, and that highest and most general vicar of Christ, the blessed Peter, added it based on an intimate and secret inspiration of the Holy Spirit for a most reasonable cause: to designate a continuation and ordering to the preceding words and acts.

PRIEST: Does the celebrant utter these words only in the person of Christ, and so only recitatively and materially, or also in his own person, and significatively?[232]

TRUTH: In the person of Christ principally and recitatively; but also in own person, insofar as he is Christ's minister and priest, and significatively, such that they effect what they signify. For Christ commanded priests to do that which he himself did, saying: *Do this in memory of me.*[233]

PRIEST: Teach me about the form of consecration for the wine.

TRUTH: There is not as much agreement among the teachers on the form of consecration for the Blood, as you have already pointed out.[234]

PRIEST: It is astonishing that uncreated Wisdom, who disposes of all things well,[235] has permitted his Church to remain undecided with regard to such a matter, with great teachers having diverse opinions, and disagreeing among themselves, in this matter of salvation.

TRUTH: You ought not to think so, for in matters necessary for salvation, the Church is well provided for. Is she not infallibly enlivened and directed by the infallible Holy Spirit? Therefore, the custom of the true and universal Catholic Church is most authoritative. And the Church has received the form for consecration of

---

[231] Matt. 26:26; Luke 22:19; 1 Cor. 11:24.
[232] E.N. In other words, the priest uses these words not merely narratively (as referring to the past), but also referring to the matter before him on the altar, and hence significatively, that is, effecting what they signify. See *Summa Theologiae*, IIIa, q. 78, art 5, co.
[233] Luke 22:19; 1 Cor. 11:24-25.   [234] Twenty-Ninth Article.   [235] Cf. Wis. 8:1.

Christ's Blood from the apostolic tradition, moved principally by the Holy Spirit, and she does not raise the chalice until all words belonging to the form have been said: From *This is the chalice of my Blood,* including all the determinations mentioned above, up to *As often as you do these things.* Therefore, all the faithful must obey this custom and use that form in its integrity, without hesitation. The Catholic teachers who have differed about this matter have spoken as a matter of opinion, either subject to the Church's correction, or under an implicit condition, abstaining from temerarious and pertinacious assertions.

PRIEST: Your words please me greatly; and I confess frankly that on this matter the holy and excellent Catholic doctor Thomas seems to have written more soundly and reasonably and more to my way of thinking.

TRUTH: Explain his teaching, then, for the reader's instruction.

PRIEST: In Book IV of his *Commentary on the Sentences,*[236] among other things he writes: Some say Christ, whose power over the Sacraments is surpassing, consecrated the Sacrament with divine power without uttering words, and only later expressed the form by which others were to consecrate it. Innocent relates this opinion as a speculation rather than an assertion.[237] Others say Christ uttered those words twice, once to silently consecrate, and a second time to give the others the form. The sounder position is that Christ uttered the words once, both consecrating and passing on the form to others, such that he consecrated by blessing and giving to his disciples.

Moreover, some say nothing belongs to the form of consecration of the Blood except these words: *This is the chalice of my Blood*; so that the forms of consecration for both species are similar. For these words seem to signify the conversion of the wine into the Blood as perfectly as the words *This is my Body* signify the conversion of the bread into Christ's Body. But since conditions linked to a subject or predicate are an integral part of an expression,[238] others argue more convincingly that everything following is part of the

---

[236] *Super Sent.*, lib. 4, d. 8, q. 2, a. 1, qc. 1, ad 1.

[237] Pope Innocent III (1198–1216), who before elevation to the papacy held the opinion, later considered temerarious, that Christ consecrated the bread and wine by a mere blessing of it, without a form of words used by priests in the consecration. See *De Sacro Altaris Mysterio*, IV, vi, PL 217, 859.

[238] E.N. Meaning that the phrase "the chalice of" is appositive, or referential, to both the subject "this," and "my Blood."

form, since it is not a stand-alone expression but a determination of the predicate.[239] For the most part, these words are taken from various places in Scripture, although they are not recorded in their entirety anywhere, because the Evangelists did not want to reveal the sacramental forms publicly. But the interposed words *mystery of faith* are also from Christ, coming to us from the holy Apostles. Again, many words are added to the consecration of the Blood rather than to the consecration of the Body. This is because the Sacrament of the Eucharist is a memorial of our Lord's Passion, but in the consecration of the Body the *subject* of the Passion is represented, while in the consecration of the Blood the *mystery* of the Passion is represented. For Christ's Blood was parted from his Body because of the Passion. Therefore, the conditions of our Lord's Passion are expressed in the words that follow the consecration of the Blood rather than the Body; and although these conditions may not be properties of Christ's Blood as blood, they are its essential properties insofar as it was poured out in the Passion.

These words also express the conditions of Christ's Passion especially as it operates in the sacraments. Now, regarding Christ's Passion as it operates in the sacraments, there are three things to consider. The first is the effect it brings about, which is the remission of sins, referred to in the words: *Which shall be shed for you and for many for the remission of sins*. The second is the means by which this effect is applied to others, namely faith, by means of which it produces its effect on those who have gone before as well as those who follow; and this is referred to in the words *Mystery of Faith*. The mystery is both the Passion itself (which is a mystery of faith, as a sort of secret hidden in the faith of all believers, especially the ancients, for whom it was shrouded in mystery, prefigured in various ways) and the Blood insofar as it is contained in the Sacrament under the species of wine (which is very difficult to believe). In this sense *mystery of faith* is said antonomastically.[240] The third thing is the end to which it draws us, which is the reception of eternal goods, to which Christ leads us by the Blood of his own Passion. His Blood ratifies a New Testament, not one promising

---

[239] E.N. That is, the appositive terms are not independent of the predicate, but an essential part of it.
[240] L. *antonomastice*. The rhetorical device of antonomasia substitutes an epithet or title for the proper name, so that "Mystery of *Faith*" is used antonomastically to refer to the mystery of the *Passion* and the mystery of the Blood contained in the sacrament.

temporal things, as the Old Testament, but eternal rewards. For this reason, these words are said: *of the new and eternal Covenant.* Now, since the end is prior in intention, therefore the words of the form begin with the end, then proceed to the means, in order to show the effect of the Passion. Now a testament is a legal decision regarding the inheritance to be received by the children from the father; therefore, the New Testament properly refers to the promise of the goods which our heavenly Father distributes to us. And this Testament is called *new*: first because of this Sacrament which was instituted for the renewal of the world; second, because of the promise confirmed by Christ's Blood, which removed the old impediment to obtaining the inheritance, and thus Christ's death renewed the promise. The Testament is called *eternal* for other reasons: first, because it concerns eternal goods; second, because this Sacrament contains Christ who is an eternal person; third, because of the eternal predestination that prepared the way for this grace. — Thus far the holy Doctor.

TRUTH: These words are Catholic, and give a wise account of the sacramental forms.

PRIEST: Now teach me about the marvels of this incomprehensible Sacrament.

TRUTH: You distract me from my principal purpose. As I said, my intention in this short work was to treat this matter in a devotional way, avoiding scholastic jargon.[241] Remember what is written, *Seek not the things that are too high for you, and search not into things above your ability: but the things that God has commanded you, think on them always, and in many of his works be not curious.*[242] And also, *As it is not good for a man to eat much honey, so he that is a searcher of majesty, shall be overwhelmed by glory.*[243]

PRIEST: Nevertheless, it is also written: *Your testimonies are wonderful: therefore my soul has sought them.*[244] And does not Scripture bless those who search, for it says, *Blessed are they who search his testimonies: that seek him with their whole heart?*[245] There is, therefore, O highest Truth, a certain temperate inquiry by which one endeavors, according to the capacity of one's intellect, and with reverence, modesty, and fear, to find some reason for what he believes. So by the gift of understanding we can say that an acute mind sees and penetrates the objects of faith, sincerely looking

---

[241] Twenty-Seventh Article.   [242] Ecclus. 3:22.   [243] Prov. 25:27.
[244] Ps. 118:129.   [245] Ps. 118:2.

into the reasons for the things we believe, whether for the purpose of persuading others of the articles of faith, or to respond to the inquiries of unbelievers, as exhorted by the most blessed prince of the Apostles: *Be always prepared to satisfy everyone that asks you a reason of that which is in you* by faith and hope.[246]

TRUTH: Still, how many good men under this pretense began to scrutinize, ponder, discuss, and immerse their minds in these marvels of the Sacrament with a spirit of moderation, who proceeding further and immoderately *failed in their search*,[247] and instead of achieving an enlightened faith went mad! And just as the eyes fixed on the sun are repelled and rendered blind, so their mental powers are obscured and blinded. Therefore, it is not fruitful for solitaries like you to dwell on the wonders of this mystery. Instead, accept the truth of our faith with completely firm certitude, and marvel devoutly, sweetly, and deeply at the inestimable goodness, love, mercy, and munificence of God towards the human race, and his many benefits. Mediating on these things, may a fire of divine love flame up in you, that from the depths of your heart you might say: *What shall I render to the Lord, for all the things he has rendered unto me?*[248] Again: *Bless the Lord, O my soul, and never forget all he has done for you.*[249] And again with the great and devout Isaiah you may say: *I will remember the tender mercies of the Lord, the praise of the Lord for all the things he has bestowed upon us, and for the multitude of his good things... which he has given them according to his kindness.*[250] Take warning from the example of some people, who for a time were wonderfully affected with devotion and sweetness towards this Sacrament, then—at the suggestion of the Enemy—began to pry, to scrutinize, indeed even to speculate incautiously, only to become exhausted and oppressed by the immense weight of the Sacrament.

What did Abbot Copres[251] respond to his brother monks who asked him, "What does this scripture mean: 'The heavens are not pure in God's sight?'"[252] Did he not say, "Brothers that scrutinize heavenly things instead of their sins?" Upon hearing that, each one fled to his cell. Moreover, even a man of such exceptional discretion and preeminent sanctity, Abbot Pastor,[253] did he not fear to speak

---

[246] 1 Pet. 3:15b. [247] Cf. Ps. 63:7. [248] Ps. 115:12. [249] Ps. 102:2. [250] Is. 63:7.
[251] St. Copres (also spelled Kopres or Copris), one of the Desert Fathers.
[252] Cf. Job 15:15.
[253] Abba St. Poemen the Great (ca. 340–450), also known as Abba Pastor, was an Egyptian monk and one of the early Desert Fathers.

about Scripture's deep passages? When a certain very aged man from a faraway place came to him and began to speak of the deep passages of Scripture, the Saint became silent. Afterwards, however, learning of the habit of that holy man, the old man returned saying, "What should I do, Abbot, because the passions still dominate my soul?" The holy man rejoiced and said: "Now you have come for the right reason; now I will open my mouth and fill it with good things." And when he elegantly expounded the means of prevailing over the passions and vices, the old man, greatly edified, responded, "Truly, *this is the way*, and there is no other."[254]

PRIEST: All these things are most wholesomely expressed and provide a useful caution. In accordance with your instruction, I will also guard against excessively curious exploration, and will not attempt to go beyond the boundaries set for me.[255] Yet, if it please you, say something about this topic to satisfy the studiousness — or curiosity — of others, and remedy any superficial ignorance in this matter.[256]

TRUTH: I acknowledge that there may be a certain moderate and praiseworthy examination of the objects of faith, so I will satisfy your pious intentions.

THIRTY-SECOND ARTICLE
The marvels of the Sacrament of the Eucharist are exceedingly credible and convincing to reason.

TRUTH: I have already told you how, taken by themselves and separately, some objects of belief (*credibilia*) appear exceedingly marvelous and even incredible.[257] And yet, when all the things that must be believed (*credenda*) are brought together along with their reasons and proofs and connections, the wonder ceases in large part. And they seem not only believable (*credibilia*), but even reasonable (*rationabilia*), and indeed super-rational and exceedingly reasonable (*superrationabilia ac rationabilissima*). Therefore, who is not amazed that the Body and Blood of Christ are contained in the Sacrament? But only note that the Body and Soul have been assumed into a unity of person with the eternal Word, and tell me whether it would not be more marvelous were this Body not

---

[254] Cf. Is. 30:21. [255] Cf. Prov. 22:28.
[256] E.N. On the distinction between studiousness (*studiositas*) and curiosity (*curiositas*), and their meaning as used by Denis, see *Summa Theologiae*, IIaIIae, q. 166-67. [257] Twenty-Third Article.

found wherever the eternal Word and only-begotten Son of God is, than that it should be in several places at the same time.

PRIEST: I am not surprised by this, because while the eternal Word is true God, equal to the Father, uncircumscribed and everywhere, the Body is a mere creature, and cannot be everywhere the Word is.

TRUTH: Isn't Christ's human nature supposited in the Word, and so not itself a person, since the Word is his person?[258]

PRIEST: That is what we believe.

TRUTH: Is it true that in all other things in which there are several supposita of the same nature, you find a nature outside one suppositum or person, not the other way around?[259]

PRIEST: Indeed, because a nature is communicable, but not a person.

TRUTH: And yet in Christ you see a person outside of nature, namely the Word, where there is not an assumed nature.[260]

PRIEST: I see what you have in mind, and this is a marvelous thing, but I think that this is found in Christ alone. And yet this does not appear to be such a marvel because the nature is not proper to the Word itself through its proper reason or species, but by assumption, and is a sort of habit in him; nevertheless, it is a marvel.

TRUTH: The very fact that this Body was assumed by the eternal Word suggests that it will have many qualities enjoyed by no other body. Indeed, it is becoming for the Almighty to do more marvelous things through, in, and around this Body than in any other bodily substance. Moreover, as we mentioned above,[261] the Only-Begotten of God, out of his ineffable love for you men, became man for your salvation and offered himself for your redemption to God the Father on the cross, and, in accordance with the assumed nature, devoted himself completely to your salvation and to the honor of God the Father. See: could anything more wise, more subtle, and more profound have been conceived than that he would sacrifice

---

[258] E.N. Meaning that the human nature does not have an underlying human subject (*suppositum*) or person, apart from the person of the Divine Word who assumed the human nature.

[259] E.N. In other words, more than one person can share the same nature, but more than one nature cannot be shared by one person.

[260] E.N. Christ has a human nature without a human person, which suggests that one person is sharing two natures, which violates the general rule of nature that more than one nature cannot be shared by one person (i.e., we are dealing with a marvel).

[261] Third and Ninth Articles.

himself in this way for you every day to the eternal Father, to his glory and honor, and to give you bountiful and manifold succor, grace, and salvation?

PRIEST: We mentioned this point earlier, and others like it. Although these things sound sweet to the ears of the faithful, especially of the enlightened, they do not affect carnal and perfidious men so.

TRUTH: Indeed, the carnal man has no taste for the things of God.[262] But follow me now: Does it not seem marvelous to you how the whole world was converted to this superlatively admirable faith, this arduous law, without the violence of arms, without human power, without the magic arts, and without trickery or cunning? That neither the cruelty of tyrants, nor the rage of persecutors, nor the subtlety of philosophers, nor the might of kings and emperors, nor temptations diabolical or human could eradicate it? Indeed, as long as the Christian people lived according to the law of their faith worthily and efficaciously, this faith grew strong even amidst so much resistance, opposition, and hindrance.

PRIEST: This really is a complete marvel, and no doubt innumerable excellent miracles, signs, prodigies, and portents have strengthened believers' faith in this Sacrament. But now use evidence from nature and elsewhere to explain and convince us that this Sacrament contains the Body of Christ—indeed, the whole and complete Christ.

TRUTH: Consider that God's omnipotence and power is entirely intensively and perfectionally infinite; accordingly, there is no effect so admirable, difficult, or eminent that God's omnipotence, or rather infinite power, does not infinitely surpass.

PRIEST: This too we concede. But there are many things which imply a contradiction—as many things believed about this Sacrament are supposed to—that God cannot do, or better that cannot be done by him; and we confess that it is not because of his lack of power, but because the nature of things does not admit it.[263]

TRUTH: Nothing that God wills us to believe involves a contradiction.

PRIEST: One pre-existing thing converted into another pre-existing thing without being corrupted; a thing numerically one being in different places simultaneously; a large body contained in a tiny place; dimensions that inter-penetrate; one and the same substance

---

[262] Cf. I Cor. 2:14.
[263] E.N. In that they involve a self-contradiction of some kind.

resting and moving at the same time; a substance generated and nourished from accidents; and several other things in this Sacrament or about it and its species—do these things involve no contradiction?

TRUTH: The solution of all those things lies in pondering the omnipotence of the superlatively glorious and bountiful God, who is not constrained in any way by the order, course, or law of the world. Not only Scripture, but even right reason declares this fact, despite the foolishness of certain philosophers who believed otherwise. And the Almighty himself demonstrates it by innumerable miraculous and supernatural deeds. Therefore, beyond the natural and usual transformations, he can instantaneously transubstantiate one subsisting thing into another, handling the prime matter without motion or intermediate change.[264] He is also able to bring it about that one and the same thing is in several places at the same time, by either multiplying it or converting or transubstantiating several things into one and the same thing. Moreover, you know that one and the same thing can be simultaneously at rest and in motion *per accidens*.[265] This does not imply the penetration of dimensions, as it implies that a dimension does not have a part outside a part, or that whiteness is subjectively in a thing and yet the thing is not white.[266] So briefly, the almighty and incircumscribable God can bring about infinitely more, greater, and more marvelous things than is comprehensible to the human mind, which is not able to fully comprehend even the smallest things.[267] Cannot our sublime and adorable Creator, who daily creates so many rational souls from nothing, easily turn one body into another? And do you forget how many marvelous things happen all the time in the course of nature? How a piece of wood is swiftly changed into rock?[268] And if you heed the Scriptures, was not Lot's wife instantly turned into a pillar of salt, the staff of Moses

---

[264] E.N. In Aristotelian (and Thomistic) metaphysics "prime matter" (*materia prima*) was the underlying matter (*Urstoff*) which was nothing but potentiality, made into a substance by imposition of a substantial form.

[265] L. *per accidens*. That is, not substantially, but in its externals (accidents).

[266] E.N. Scholastic philosophers held that the penetrability of a body's dimensions is against nature, because nature resists such penetration. God, however, is not so restricted. In other words, a body is confined to itself, and cannot share its part with another nor can its accidental features be inconsistent.

[267] E.N. See St. Thomas Aquinas's *Exposition on the Apostle's Creed*, prologue: "Our manner of knowing is so weak that no philosopher could perfectly investigate the nature of even one little fly."

[268] E.N. Denis is referring to the phenomenon of petrification, specifically, permineralization, where the cellular material of the wood submerged in water is replaced by minerals, and thus becomes rock.

into a serpent, and the serpent into a staff?²⁶⁹ In the same way, St. John the Apostle by his prayers and merits turned staves and stones into the finest gold; which again, by his prayers, returned to their original forms and nature.²⁷⁰ Likewise at the virgin St. Barbara's just curse, the wicked shepherd's sheep were turned into locusts.²⁷¹ Thus every creature, by an obediential potency innate to it, obeys the Creator's will on command.²⁷² According to Avicenna, Algazel, and certain other philosophers,²⁷³ the mere conception or apprehension of an intelligence can produce an effect in these lower things, even one above or beyond nature, since they posited that inferior things were produced by intelligences.²⁷⁴ How much more shall the superlatively worthy Creator's will be done when he apprehends and commands them? Tell me how the smallest part of your eye's pupil receives the species of so many colors and the likenesses of such large things, representing the things themselves with their various figures, sizes, and dispositions. How can the images and representations of so many masses and varieties and multitudes of things be received and exist at the same time in such a small pupil? Likewise, in the rest of creation, who can sufficiently marvel at the mutual dwelling (*cohabitudinem*) of powers and objects? It amazes you that such a large body is contained in such small species; and how can you grasp, though reason dictates it, that the rational soul, simple and unextended (*inextensa*), extends throughout the whole body, or indeed that the superlatively simple God himself, in whom there is no extension, mass, or quantity whatever, extends throughout the entire universe, so that he exists essentially and personally everywhere? If the Almighty could only locate a body in a place in one way, namely, commensuratively and according to a body's proper

---

²⁶⁹ Gen. 19:26; Ex. 4:3-4.
²⁷⁰ E.N. Denis is referring to the miracle related in Jacob de Voragine's *Golden Legend*.
²⁷¹ E.N. This incident is also found in de Voragine's *Golden Legend*.
²⁷² Obediential potency is the openness of every creature to the power of the Creator to effect in it something beyond its ordinary powers, such as a miracle, or such as receipt of the supernatural life of grace. The Latin uses the word *ad nutum*, literally, "at a nod," meaning at the will or at the pleasure of a person.
²⁷³ Avicenna or Ibn Sina (ca. 980-1037) was a Persian Muslim philosopher and polymath, including in particular medicine. He was deeply influenced by Aristotle. Algazel or Al-Ghazali (ca. 1058-1111) was a Muslim philosopher from Persia. His most famous book may be the book called *The Incoherence of the Philosophers*.
²⁷⁴ E.N. See St. Thomas Aquinas, *De potentia*, q. 3, art. 4, where St. Thomas discusses the theories of Avicenna and Algazel, who held that "the first intelligences [created] the second in giving them being by the power of the first cause communicated to them." See also *Summa Theologiae*, Ia, q. 47, art. 1, co.

quantity, your objection would be justified. Likewise, accidents without a subject are a wonder and have a supernatural cause; is not God able to substitute the supporting power (*vim fulcitivam*) that in the course of nature he infuses into every accident through the substance in which it adheres with a supernatural supporting power infused immediately, so that the accident exists and remains in being by divine power? Finally, we see that bread, fish, and the flesh of beasts are converted into human flesh every day by the power of natural heat, as the soul is able to do; is it not possible then for God to do in an instant by himself with his infinite power that which he can and does do through intermediate natural causes, at least in ways that do not derogate from his excellence, as when Christ instantly converted water into wine?[275] What marvel, then, if he—who by secondary natural causes converts food and drink into human flesh and blood—should turn bread and wine instantaneously into his Body and Blood? Even the tempter, knowing that Jesus's power was able to do this immediately, said to him: *If you be the Son of God, command that these stones be made bread.*[276]

Further, why are you so astonished at the penetration of dimensions, when Christ was born of a Virgin who remained ever intact, and rose from a closed tomb, and entered into the disciples through closed doors?[277] This happened often to others by the divine power, as in Acts, where you read that an angel led the Apostles from a locked prison, which remained locked after their departure.[278] And didn't Thomas gain entry through closed doors to the bed chamber of the bridegroom and bride,[279] and Pope St. Alexander into the prison where the most illustrious martyr Hermes was held?[280] And many like stories have been truly recorded. Moreover, the astrologer Albumasar, in the sixth book of his *Greater Introduction*, admits that in the first decan of Virgo, a pure virgin is born on earth,

---

[275] John 2:7–9.   [276] Matt. 4:3.
[277] E.N. In other words remaining a Virgin *in partu*, given the miraculous non-natural childbirth of Jesus where Mary retained her virginity in integrity even during the birth of Jesus suggesting a miraculous "penetration of dimensions" or two bodies moving through each other. Matt. 27:66; 28:2; John 20:19, 26.
[278] Acts 5:18, 23.
[279] E.N. This appears to be a reference to the apocryphal Acts of Thomas. See Acts of Thomas I.11–14, *The New Testament Apocrypha*, ed. and trans. M. R. James (Berkeley: Apocryphile Press, 2004), 369 ff.
[280] E.N. Pope St. Alexander (died 115) who visited Hermes who was chained in prison, as related in early martyrologies. See Michael Lapidge, *The Roman Martyrs: Introduction, Translations, and Commentary* (Oxford: Oxford University Press, 2018), 562 ff.

sitting upon a padded throne, holding wheat in her hand, cradling her newborn at her breast; is it even possible to doubt him?[281]

PRIEST: Upon considering these things, you have indeed sufficiently, even more than sufficiently, achieved your purpose. On this point, I am pleased, and I thank you.

TRUTH: So you are true to your word, content with a moderate inquiry, not exceeding the boundaries of your fathers.[282] But tell me, have you read the small devotional work of that man anointed by heaven, who wrote both devoutly and simply on this matter, such that one could say about him, *Because I have not known learning, I will enter into the powers of the Lord*?[283]

PRIEST: You refer, if I am not mistaken, to the religious father John Ruusbroec.[284] I confess that I have read that treatise, which seemed to me to arouse great devotion in proportion to the simplicity of the style in which it was written.[285]

TRUTH: Then tell us a bit about it, for the reader's edification.

THIRTY-THIRD ARTICLE
Certain words from the treatise of a certain enlightened man are introduced.

PRIEST: The venerable father John Ruusbroec, writing to a certain nun, said: If you desire to receive our Lord's Body in the holy

---

[281] E.N. Albumasar (Abu Ma'shar) (787–886) was a Persian Muslim astrologer. The "Introduction" refers to Albumasar's *Kitāb al-mudkhal al-kabīr*, written around 848 and translated into Latin by John of Seville in 1133 as *Introductorium in Astronomiam*. As Albumasar was drawing from ancient Chaldean sources, he was considered—along with Virgil, the Cumaean Sybil, the Samian Sybil, and others—a pagan "prophet" who foretold Christ's coming. See Laura Ackerman Smoller, *History, Prophecy, and the Stars: The Christian Astrology of Pierre d'Ailly, 1350–1420* (Princeton: Princeton University Press 2017), 50–51, 55.
[282] Thirty-First Article; Prov. 22:28.   [283] Ps. 70:15b–16a.
[284] E.N. Blessed John Ruusbroec (also spelled Ruysbroeck) (ca. 1293–1381). The Carthusians in general, and Denis in particular, were great promoters of this mystic. Denis called Ruusbroec "the Divine Doctor," the *doctor divinus*, and another Denis the Areopagite, an *alter Dionysius*. See Kent Emery Jr., "The Carthusians, Intermediaries for the Teaching of John Ruysbroeck During the Period of Early Reform and in the Counter-Reformation" in *Analecta Cartusiana* (James Hogg, ed.) (1979), vol. 43, 101–2. As Denis states in his work on the gifts of the Holy Spirit, *De donis Spiritus sancti* (*Opera Omnia*, vol.35): [C]ertus sum virum istum a Spiritu Sancto instructam, propterea magna est eius auctoritas apud me (I am certain that this man was instructed by the Holy Spirit, and therefore I hold him as a great authority).
[285] See "A Mirror of Eternal Blessedness," *The Complete Ruusbroec* (Turnhout: Brepols, 2014), 541–93 (trans. André Lefevere).

Sacrament unto God's honor and your salvation, you must have in you the four marks that the most blessed Virgin Mary had in her and practiced when she conceived the Son of God, because she is the greatest teacher of virtue, and the doctor of all holiness. The first of these is purity; the second, true knowledge of God; the third, humility; the fourth, the concupiscibility of a free will.[286] Therefore, probe and consider the face of your conscience, and consider whether you find in it anything displeasing to God; and confess this humbly and plaintively. And by no means neglect to confess an evil of which you are ashamed; accuse yourself as if you were your own worst and deadliest enemy. In this way you will become clean and sincere. Also confess, in few words, your daily, common, and lighter defects from which scarcely anyone is innocent, to disburden and relieve your mind of them. But foster a great contrition and bitterness of heart for all your sins, and a strong intention always to do good works and to abstain from all mortal and venial sins. And above all, always have a great faith and tender hope in God, for these two things are very powerful to remove sins. But avoid lengthy and verbose confessions, because they will trouble you and make your confession scrupulous and erroneous.

The second [mark] is true knowledge of God, which requires a clean conscience. After her Son, the most glorious Virgin Mary had this knowledge of God in a most high manner, greater than all men that have ever been.

He does not discuss the other two marks, at least after he does these two; and it is clear what humility consists in; but what is meant by the concupiscibility of free will I do not know, and desire to learn.

TRUTH: We may understand him to refer to the fervent desire or internal avidity to take communion, which opens the mind to a saving reception of the Beloved. For blessed are they who hunger and thirst for justice, because they shall be satisfied, and blessed they who hunger and thirst for the source of justice, namely our Lord Jesus Christ contained in this Sacrament, because they will be filled with the beatific vision of him.[287]

PRIEST: He goes on:

> When a great and prudent king wishes to travel far away,
> he convokes his lords, holds a feast for them, and commits

---

[286] E.N. Concupiscibility is a term in Thomistic psychology, meaning the tendency of the soul to desire what it perceives as good.   [287] Matt. 5:6.

the rule of his kingdom, his people, and his family to them until his return. So Christ, the King of kings, before departing this world to the Father, arranged for a great last supper, brought his Apostles to it, and committed to them his Sacraments and his people. And because he was to die the next day, he made there his will and testament, leaving it to his Apostles, and through them to all the faithful even until the end of the world. This Testament is his very Self in the Sacrament. And during the supper he was appointed as the first Bishop of all Christianity by the Father, and he celebrated the first Mass, at which he ordained the Apostles to the priesthood, and in his exceeding charity gave himself to us as food and drink for our souls. The love of Christ is greedy and generous; indeed, it is most exceedingly greedy and generous, for he gives us all that he is and has, and likewise receives from us all that we are and have. Nay, even more, he demands from us, so to speak, more than we have the power to pay. His hunger, i.e., his zeal for our salvation, is great beyond measure. He consumes our whole being completely, down to the marrow of our bones. But we encourage him to do so, and the more we encourage him the better we taste to him. And however much he consumes us, he cannot be filled because he has an insatiable appetite. And although we are poor and needy, he does not care, because he desires to leave us nothing. Therefore, he prepares us as his food. First, he uses love to burn away all our sins and defects, and when we are purified and fully roasted, he opens his mouth like a bird of prey who wants to gulp us down whole; for he wants to consume our sinful life and change it into his own life. And that life is full of grace and glory; it is always ready for us, provided we are willing to deny ourselves, and henceforth to avoid sin. If we could see the hearty appetite Christ has for our salvation, we would not be able to contain ourselves from jumping into his mouth.

He often writes like this, and I would have liked him to explain himself more clearly, rather than going on in this vague manner. For how can the love of Christ be greedy and totally consume us?

TRUTH: The man has a particular manner of speaking, frequently metaphorical and obscure, and yet he does explain himself. So he metaphorically calls the love of Christ greedy because as a greedy man draws and acquires others' goods, so Christ draws his faithful to himself and makes them one in himself through charity. And thus he is said to eat them, inasmuch as he converts and transforms them into himself by love's union, and incorporates them to himself so that they are his Mystical Body. He also conforms them to his life, so that they live in a Christlike manner according to the requirements and spirit of divine charity, and according to the purity of the Gospel, constantly seeking not their own,[288] but always the things of Christ, so that each is able to say of himself: *I live, now not I; but Christ lives in me.*[289] And so he consumes them, not destroying their substance or powers, but taking away from them anything that is of their own will or inordinate desire, so that they are fully resigned and self-denying. And when you have been so cleansed and enkindled by the fire of divine love, Christ opens his mouth like a bird of prey, that is, he joins you to him and absorbs you into him with a deep, hearty affection; and desires you to be ever more fervently and intimately inviscerated into him.[290] And so, if you were able to conceive a clear understanding of the inestimable eminence of his charity for your salvation, you would not be able to restrain yourselves from tending towards him with reciprocal love and grateful affection. He demands more than you are able to repay because he commands you to love him with all your heart,[291] which you cannot do perfectly in this life (*in via*), but only in the heavenly fatherland (*in patria*); or else because his benefits and charity to you are so great, that you are not able to repay it with an equivalent exchange.[292]

PRIEST: I believe that the passages in question have been sufficiently clarified. Now, he also writes:

> The first class of communicants is the devout, people who are tender-hearted by nature. When they are touched by God's grace, if they follow the movement of grace and are obedient to it, their affection and delight towards Christ's humanity is so enkindled that they easily spurn and relinquish all worldly things in order to enjoy their Beloved in the measure in which they are touched according to their sensible and sweet affection. And because the way to approach their Lord closest in this life is in the Sacrament, they fall into ecstasy or swoon with desire for it, so that it seems to them they must go mad or perish unless they can approach the Sacrament. But such persons are few, and usually women or maidens of tender complexion.

---

[288] 1 Cor. 10:24; 13:5.   [289] Gal. 2:20.
[290] L. *invisceremini ei*. Literally, put into his viscera, his digestive system to be consumed and become a part of his body.   [291] Matt. 22:37.
[292] L. *vicem condignam*, a condign or strictly just exchange or repayment for a good received.

Nor are they educated or much enlightened: hence, their experience is sensual and based in desire, and is entirely transformed with Christ's humanity; they are unable to understand or perceive how Christ can be consumed spiritually without the Sacrament, because they burn with desire for the human presence of Christ. And no one can counsel them, help them, or calm them down, until they receive the Sacrament. When they have done so, they are pacified, and enjoy their Beloved in quiet, spiritual relish, and overflowing sweetness, until such a time when grace and striving is again renewed in them; and they slip back into their former ecstasy and desire to communicate, as if they had never received the Sacrament before. Their heart yearns and gapes open to communicate and they seem as if they were senseless. They are therefore signified by that ruler who did stop until Christ came down to his house, believing that otherwise his son would surely die.[293] The second and higher class of communicants are people of subtle intellect, and intellectual in their disposition, but susceptible and unsteady by nature. When they receive God's grace, persevering in it, they must often struggle, for their flesh opposes their spirit. Therefore, they choose an interior life and engage in a spiritual struggle before God, and so escape temptations and movements of concupiscence in this way. If these persons then place more confidence in God and his grace than in their own exercises, strength, merits, and efforts, they are elevated in God's light above their rational knowledge. If they remain elevated, and love and long more for what is above reason and incomprehensible than they love what they can grasp with reason, then their faith becomes perfect, and charity becomes truly and deeply rooted in them. So they become free, and they recognize God and the truth and the root of all virtues. Nevertheless, their nature remains lively in their flesh and blood, and in their disordered passions and inclinations. When they feel these moving in them and recognize them, they reject and spurn them and everything else in themselves that is contrary to God and salvation. And abandoning sensuality, they flee internally in spirit into God's presence with faith, devotion, and humble action, like the Apostle Paul, who was tempted in the flesh.[294] And they are like the centurion, who had a sick servant at home,[295] that is, his natural body not yet cleansed; and as the centurion was uncircumcised, so also they are still in some way unreformed; and although they are weak in the flesh and tempted by their nature, yet in their spirit they are filled with faith, devotion, and love.

---

[293] John 4:46–50.   [294] 2 Cor. 12:7.   [295] Luke 7:2.

They also need strong food, that is, the Sacrament, to be able to overcome their passions and temptations; and they must always have this food, as often as their order, or office, or the good custom of those amongst whom they live conveniently permits. The third class are holy people more elevated in spirit, whose powers, acts, and senses are totally interior; and they are like Zacheus, who climbed up into a tree in order to see Jesus.[296] The fourth class are people who are diligent in observances and precepts. The fifth class are those who are curious and self-pleasing, who put on an outward show, and desire to be honored and esteemed; therefore, they are destitute of grace.

Then he writes some sublime things regarding the life of the perfect, which, as far as I can judge are not suitable for simpletons and common persons to read; his manner of speaking is such that he cannot be understood by such men—indeed, it might be an occasion of error for them; therefore, I omit them.

TRUTH: Even learned men were displeased by his manner of speaking and suppose that he had fallen into error— even the heresy of the Free Spirits.[297] In fact, however, he did not so fall or believe what they did, but rather rejected it.

THIRTY-FOURTH ARTICLE
A loving allocution to Christ, dispositive to communion and giving thanks for God's benefits.

PRIEST: O Lord and Savior, Only-Begotten of God the Father and the most holy Virgin Mother, O Creator and Lover, O Savior and Judge of us all, how much we ought to love you! How we ought to worship and fear you! For according to your divine nature you are naturally and limitlessly good, loveable, desirable, beautiful, sweet, omnipotent, wise, rich, holy, happy, perfect, just and merciful, generous, true, alive, invariable, simple, and most highly and incomparably to be loved, worshipped, praised, and feared. Why,

---

[296] Luke 19:2–4.
[297] E.N. The Free Spirits or Brethren of the Free Spirit were a heretical group, similar to the Beghards and Beguines, that flourished in the thirteenth through fifteenth centuries in parts of Europe. The errors held by them were condemned in 1296 by Pope Boniface VIII in the bull *Saepe sanctam Ecclesiam* and by the decree *Ad nostrum qui* at the Council of Vienne (1311–12). See DS 866, 891–99. Both Meister Eckhart and Ruusbroec were accused of holding, or at least approaching, some of their views.

then, do I not always look upon you? Alas! Why do I not avoid everything that may offend your presence and diminish your holy love? O Lord my God, how ready you are to richly communicate, infuse, and give the gifts of your grace, the ardor of your charity, and increase of virtue! You, who so lovingly anticipate my needs, who offer your very self to me, who so opportunely and in a sense importunely invite me to receive you,[298] promising glorious and eternal goods, provided I draw near, and threatening the evil of eternal damnation if I do not. And so every day you are both giver and gift, guest and food, host and refreshment, doctor and medicine, judge and advocate, creator and reconciler.

The angels look on, marveling at so many mysteries, astonished by God's wonders in the Sacrament; but still more astounded at the charity, mercy, and liberality of God towards men. They sorrow at the ingratitude, irreverence, and moral filthiness of the mass of men. They rejoice at the devotion, sincerity, and progress of the virtuous. With most heartfelt affection, the whole Church triumphant gives thanks to the Most High for the mercy, beneficence, charity, and grace of God in the Church militant. And mankind, miserable and shameless, pays it no heed, feels no warmth for it, and does not give thanks with due affection. In times past, under the law, it was not lawful for anyone but the high priest to enter the Holy of Holies;[299] yet you, O Holy of Holies, deign to enter the mouth and the souls of each of your faithful under the Sacrament. O how reverent and full of terror were the Saints of both Testaments when the holy angels and citizens of the heavenly kingdom appeared to them from heaven! And we, our hearts insensitive and cleaving to the earth, having our faith more dormant than awake, so irreverently and unpreparedly run towards you, O Creator and Lord of the angels. Alas! Because the Sun of Wisdom does not rise upon us, and the light of understanding does not enlighten our minds,[300] because we place the obstacles of our carnality and negligence before it, because we wrap ourselves up in the darkness of imaginations, in the disturbances of inquietude, and the movements of the passions. Yet you, O God of immense purity, infinite wisdom, and unbounded majesty, wish to be received with a pure mind—as is only fitting—to be pondered wisely, and to be handled reverently, lovingly, and fearfully.

---

[298] E.N. The Lord not only invites us to partake in the Eucharist, he, in a certain way, even commands us: *Do this in memory of me.*
[299] Heb. 9:7; Lev. 16:2.
[300] Cf. Wis. 5:6.

O Holy of Holies, O Fountain of all good, O most bountiful and most affectionate Benefactor, with what exuberance of devotion, with what fire of divine love, with what thankfulness was your elect David enkindled, burned, and filled when, recalling your goodness and benefits, he danced before the ark of the covenant with all his might in the sight of all his people, heedless of his royal dignity?[301] And what was this ark but an inanimate object, a figure of your humanity? Why, then, do we stand so tepid, do we remain so frigid, are we so remiss in our praises before this incomprehensible, superlatively dignified Sacrament, approaching it without purity, without fervor, and without spiritual joy? Make your face shine upon us, O Lord,[302] imbue our hearts with the clear light of your gift of wisdom, of orthodox faith, and of Gospel law. Transform us, O Lord, in the riches of your glory; elevate us above ourselves and strengthen and preserve us in purity of heart. Like a destitute beggar I come to you, O most merciful fountain and munificent Father:[303] I cast myself down at the threshold of your immense and bountiful munificence; I beg for the bread of life and understanding, I beseech of you the water of saving wisdom,[304] I wish to receive that daily and supersubstantial bread with all the humility, devotion, and sincerity you deserve.[305] As you wish to give yourself, give me the preparation I need to receive you worthily.

Lo and behold, O my soul, the Lord you seek comes unto you! Rejoice and be glad, meet your God with all humility, care, and fervor. Hold on to him and never let him go. Thank him endlessly, so that he remains with you in eternity. Serve him with a perfect heart and a willing mind,[306] with desire to please him and fear to offend him. Abandon and flee all sin and train yourself in all virtue. To the praise and glory of his name, who is God sublime and blessed above every thing. Amen.

END OF THE DIALOGUE ON THE SACRAMENT OF
THE ALTAR AND THE CELEBRATION OF MASS

---

[301] 2 Kings 6:14.   [302] Ps. 118:135.
[303] L. *paterfamilias*, the head of an extended Roman family.
[304] Cf. Ecclus. 15:3.   [305] Luke 11:3; Matt. 6:11.
[306] Mal. 3:1; Zech. 2:10; Songs 3:4; 1 Chr. 28:9.

EXPOSITION
OF THE MASS

INTRODUCTION

He has made a remembrance of his wonderful works, being a merciful and gracious Lord; he has given food to them that fear him. Ps. 110:4–5.

THAT LOVER OF MANKIND, OUR CREATOR and Savior, recognizing that the human mind is prone to forgetfulness and ingratitude for divine benefits, has bequeathed to us such a memorial of his Passion and love that he who can be ungrateful for such love and liberality thereby shows that he is harder than rock and more rigid than iron. Indeed, *before the festival day of the Pasch, having loved his own who were in the world,*[1] and desiring to bequeath his Mystical Body, the Church militant, a most earnest pledge of his ardent love, he instituted the Sacrament of his Body and Blood as a sort of mirror in which everything that he assumed, did, and endured for our salvation would shine out in the light of faith. He therefore said to his disciples, and through them to all priests: *As often as you do these things, do them in memory of me,*[2] so that our hearts might be enkindled with the flame of divine love as often as they receive or recall the pledge of this great love.

But since the consecration of this Sacrament is entrusted to priests alone and it is not lawful for them to perform it except during the course of the Mass, they ought therefore to prepare themselves with every solicitude and fervor to perform such a service worthily and fruitfully, so that, as the Damascene exhorts in his fourth book, they approach it with all fear, a pure conscience, and an unfaltering faith.[3] For as Dionysius explains, it is not right for evil ministers to touch the sacred symbols (that is, the exterior signs or vessels).[4] This means that every time a priest celebrates Mass without true contrition of heart and heartfelt repentance he sins grievously, as St. Thomas shows in the Third Part.[5]

The priest is bound, therefore, to celebrate Mass with great devotion and lively attention. Now devotion is an act of the will proceeding from divine charity. But the will only loves what the intellect

---

[1] John 13:1.
[2] Cf. Luke 22:19; 1 Cor. 11:24–25.
[3] E.N. St. John of Damascus, *De Fide Orthodoxa*, IV, 13, PG 94, 1149–50.
[4] *De Eccl. hier.*, c. 1.
[5] *Summa Theologiae*, IIIa (Supp.), q. 36, art. 5, co.

knows, as Augustine asserts in the tenth book of *On the Trinity*.⁶ To ensure that the priest is able to pronounce the sacred words of the Mass with devotion and affection, that is, with a certain internal sweetness, it is helpful for him to understand the meaning of these words. But their meaning is often quite difficult, especially if one gives them full and profound consideration. It is profitable, therefore, to expound upon them, and to explain how the celebrant's affections should be formed. Anyone who presumes to perform this task by his own power acts utterly in vain. Therefore one must implore the most merciful kindness of him of whom we sing in the Psalm: *Come to him and be enlightened, and your faces shall not be confounded.*⁷ Trusting in his help and unfailing kindness, I undertake this very thing, not following my own thoughts, but the words of the Fathers, to the praise of him who is sublime and blessed above all things.

ARTICLE I
What devotion is.

The Apostle said: *From henceforth let no man be troublesome to me; for I bear the marks of the Lord Jesus in my body.*⁸ Every priest is obliged, by reason of the [sacramental] order that he has received and the duty enjoined upon him, to lead such a life that these words of the Apostle may apply to him and he may be able to say them about his own person. For he ought always to bear about in his body the mortification of the cross,⁹ as the most blessed head of the Apostles advises in his first epistle, saying: *Christ suffered for us, leaving you an example that you should follow his steps.*¹⁰ For this reason, the sacred canons have laid down that priests should promise chastity, so that spurning the allurements of the flesh, they might handle the Virgin's Son with chastest hands, praise him with pure lips, and receive him with unpolluted mouth. Since it has been said that the priest is bound to celebrate Mass with great devotion and actual attention, it is fitting to clarify what devotion is.

Therefore, it should be observed that charity is called the first and last of all the virtues, even though faith precedes it, for faith is the foundation and origin of the entire spiritual edifice. For, as Isaiah testifies, *He that is unfaithful deals unfaithfully;*¹¹ and Habakkuk

---

⁶ E.N. St. Augustine, *De Trinitate*, X, 1. ⁷ Ps. 33:6.
⁸ Gal. 6:17. ⁹ Cf. 2 Cor. 4:10a. ¹⁰ 1 Pet. 2:21. ¹¹ Is. 21:2a.

says: *the just shall live in his faith.*[12] Hence, in the Gospel it is often said: *Your faith has saved you.*[13] Indeed, according to the Apostle, whatever *is not of faith is sin.*[14] How, then, if faith precedes it, is charity the first of all virtues? Now the answer to this is that the effect of virtue is to perfect the actor and to render his work acceptable to God. No action is meritorious for eternal life or accepted by God unless it proceeds from charity in some way, namely elicitively or imperatively, in accordance with the Apostle's assertion, *If I speak with the tongues of men, and of angels, and have not charity, I am become as sounding brass, or a tinkling cymbal.*[15] It is for that reason, therefore, that charity is called the first of all virtues. For charity graciously joins the affection to God, and it leads and orders the operations of all other virtues to the ultimate end, which is the glorious and holy God. For this reason, it is called the last of all the virtues: for it is the queen of virtues and their end; and as God is the beginning and end of all things, so the charity of God can be called the beginning and end of all the virtues. Accordingly, we ought to refer to the love of God whatever we think, whatever we utter, whatever we do. Nevertheless, faith is said to precede charity because it pertains to the intellect, and directs the affection, and it shows the will that which is to be loved. It is clear, therefore, that faith precedes charity according to the way of *generation*; however, charity precedes faith according to the way of *perfection*.

Therefore, love, which is an act of charity, is founded upon the knowledge of faith; and hence it is commonly said that love proceeds from knowledge. For the Psalmist says: *In my meditation a fire shall flame out,*[16] that is, the ardor of divine love in my mind surges forth when I am intent on meditation. But it might be asked how knowledge is said to be the cause of love, since the good of the thing loved is that which induces and excites love in the soul of the lover. The response to this is that knowledge of the good is the cause of love, insofar as it is the way by which the will tends to the love of the good. But the good of the thing, or rather the object itself of the will, is the motivating, and as it were, efficient cause of love. Therefore, where the knowledge is clearer and the goodness of a thing is greater, the way to love is better, and the cause of loving is more intense. Also, the act of loving God itself has delight adjoined to it, as is written: *I remembered God and was*

---

[12] Hab. 2:4b.
[13] Matt. 9:22; Mark 10:52, etc.
[14] Rom. 14:23b.
[15] 1 Cor. 13:1.
[16] Ps. 38:4b.

delighted; and again: *My soul longs and faints for the courts of the Lord*, from which follows: *My heart and my flesh have rejoiced in the living God.*[17] Accordingly, devotion is nothing else than a ready affection of the will to carry out those things which are of God and which concern the divine honor and worship. Devotion, therefore, is caused by love arising from divine contemplation. For from the fact that we love God and rejoice in his love, our affection is inflamed to fulfill those things which are pleasing to God.

Moreover, in our Lord Jesus Christ there exists a double nature and one person; and we are to contemplate and love him according to both natures. But since his divine nature is more excellent and more perfect than his assumed humanity, contemplating Christ according to the divine nature and loving him according to the same nature is more worthy and sublime than contemplating and loving him according to his human nature. For this reason, the Apostle states: *If we have known Christ according to the flesh, yet now we know him so no longer.*[18] Indeed, in all things this holds true: that to the extent the thing known is better and more divine, the more desirable it is to contemplate and the more meritorious and more acceptable it is to God. Hence, knowledge of the most blessed Godhead and contemplation of the most blessed Trinity is supremely and incomparably desirable. And the love arising from such contemplation is of the highest merit, deifying the one who loves.

But the power to attain such perfection belongs to no one unless he endeavors to imitate the manner of Christ's life in this world, following his humility, embracing his patience, emulating his charity, and imitating his obedience. For *he that says he abides in him ought himself also to walk even as he walked.*[19] Indeed, the ray of divine light cannot shine forth in the superior part of the rational soul nor the ardor of divine love burn in the intellectual appetite or will unless the inferior parts of the soul have been cleansed from the onslaught of passions and the filth of sins. Therefore, he who desires to contemplate and love the divinity of Christ should diligently consider him according to his human nature, vigilantly pondering upon and efficaciously imitating the previously mentioned virtues of his life, and loving him fervently according to these considerations. For then that promise of Christ will be fulfilled in him: *He that loves me, shall be loved of my Father: and I will love him, and will manifest myself to him.*[20]

---

[17] Ps. 76:4a; 83:3.   [18] 2 Cor. 5:16b.   [19] 1 John 2:6.   [20] John 14:21.

ARTICLE II

On the devotion which is required for the worthy celebration of Mass and which is sufficient for salvation, though not yet for perfection.

And that I live now in the flesh: I live in the faith of the Son of God, who loved me, and delivered himself for me.[21] Just as the soul in living things is the principle of natural life and of all natural operations and movements, so the grace of God is the principle in the soul of meritorious life and of all good actions in the soul, according to that statement of the Apostle: *By the grace of God, I am what I am.*[22] Now any action proceeding from the grace of God is accepted by God. Therefore, whoever celebrates Mass in a state of grace acts meritoriously and is worthy of eternal life unless by his own negligence and subversion of will he loses that grace on his way to or during the performance of that service. But such a loss of grace does not occur except through mortal sin which extinguishes charity, which is the life of the soul. Now mortal sin is incurred by the transgression of divine precepts. Christ instructed us to celebrate this most divine sacrament in memory of him, that is, in memory of his extraordinary charity for us and his most bitter and most cruel Passion for us, saying, *Whenever you do these things, you do them for the commemoration of me.*[23] For this reason, it is clear that the priest who celebrates without the aforementioned remembrance of Christ transgresses the divine precept, and therefore sins mortally. From this one understands why it is commonly stated that actual devotion is required for the celebration of Mass, and indeed also for the taking of communion, and that this is a precept of necessity, so that he who does not have this remembrance during the celebration of the divine mysteries sins mortally. For to have this remembrance without actual devotion cannot possibly be the case with him who is in a state of grace. For this remembrance, since it is nothing but a recognition of the benefits and the goodness of Christ, enkindles love: but, as has been shown, love leads to devotion.

Therefore, although this devotion of the will suffices for the worthy (that is, meritorious) celebration of Mass, yet it is not perfect, and a priest ought not to be content with it. For he who is content with this simple devotion, often gains little fruit from the

---

[21] Gal. 2:20.   [22] 1 Cor. 15:10a.
[23] 1 Cor. 11:24–25. E.N. These words, of course, are found in the Canon of the Mass.

celebration of Mass; indeed, he often commits many negligences, suffering many distractions and errant thoughts during Mass. Hence, he does not experience the sweetness of the sweetest Sacrament itself, but leaves that most abundant and most opulent table of Christ feeling lean and empty; nor is he enkindled with the fire of great charity, but he remains cold, and dries up within himself.

ARTICLE III
On the perfect and pure devotion which it befits the celebrant to have, because of the great dignity of the Sacrament.

Priests *shall be holy to their God and shall not profane his name: for they offer the burnt offering of the Lord, and the bread of their God, and therefore they shall be holy.*[24] As Dionysius observes, one is called holy because he is free from admixture of stain and because he is free from all contagion of earthly and worldly cupidity and carnal love.[25] But some ask: Who can be like that in this life, wherein *if we say that we have no sin, we deceive ourselves,* wherein, moreover, the just man falls seven times a day?[26] For as Solomon testifies, There *is no just man upon earth, that does good, and sins not.*[27] The answer is that sanctity is ascribed to things according to the requirements and capacity of their state. For the blessed God is essentially and totally holy. But all the blessed in the heavenly fatherland, although they are not holy by essence, yet they are so by participation, and so they are holy in the manner that holy has just been defined: for they have no blemish or stain of inordinate affection, nor are they able to, since they are confirmed in the good. Now this is commonly the case of all good and truly faithful Christians, who lack the filth of mortal sins, because the love of God and the highest good in them preponderates over the love of temporal things, although sometimes they are affected and delighted in transitory things inordinately or more than is just. Moreover, it is characteristic of holy men diligently to endeavor to avoid venial sins, and those which from time to time they are unable to avoid they daily incessantly lament, acknowledge, confess, and make amendment for. Hence, although they fall venially daily, they can rightly be called holy. For the solicitude of holy devotion and the fire

---

[24] Lev. 21:6.
[25] *De Divin. Nom.*, c. 8, 12.
[26] 1 John 1:8; cf. Prov. 24:16a.
[27] Eccl. 7:21.

of divine love in them quickly and completely consumes whatever they venially transgress or omit to do. Indeed, since all things work together in them for good,[28] not only do they sufficiently deplore and correct their imperfection, but also, exploiting the occasion of their venial faults, they daily become more perfect and more holy. This is so because while they are unable to make as much progress as they desire, they profoundly humble themselves, they vehemently despise themselves, and they walk with great care; and they regard as nothing whatever little [good] they have done before, and they strive to be more sincere before God and to live their lives more reverently, so that they can say with the Apostle: *Forgetting the things that are behind, and stretching forth myself to those that are before, I press towards the mark, to the prize of the supernal vocation.*[29]

This, then, is the holiness which the Holy Spirit exhorts priests to possess. For if the previous words, Priests *shall be holy to their God*, etc.,[30] are said regarding the priests of the Old Testament, who handled only figurative and carnal sacrifices and sacraments, how much more is it incumbent upon the priests of the New Law—who consecrate, handle, and consume the most divine Eucharist, which is the end and truth of all the sacrifices of the Old Law—to be holy to their God and not profane his name? For in the way that the faithful are said to sanctify the name of God when they worthily serve him *in holiness and justice*[31] (for thus their lives show that he whom such service pleases is holy), so they profane the name of God when they dishonor it and, in contempt of it, are attached to changeable things, and devote their time to unclean and obscene pleasures. Therefore, the priests of Christ should strive to be holy in this world in order that they might reverently handle and gratefully receive the only Son of God, and retain him in their pure souls, lest they be found ungrateful of such dignity and the love of the Son of God. This is the perfect devotion by which a rational creature should readily surrender himself to the worship of God, so that he might diligently cast off those things which distance him from openness to, and contemplation and veneration of, God, so that he might say: *It is good for me to adhere to my God*; and again: *One thing is necessary.*[32] For then is it most truly said with the Prophet Isaiah: *Your name, and your remembrance are the desire of the soul*; and with the Psalmist: *My soul has stuck close to you.*[33] He will

---

[28] Cf. Rom. 8:28a.   [29] Phil. 3:13–14.   [30] Lev. 21:6.   [31] Cf. Luke 1:74–75.
[32] Ps. 72:28a; Luke 10:42.   [33] Is. 26:8b; Ps. 62:9a.

also experience in a brief time that which Jeremiah truly says: *The Lord is good to them that hope in him, to the soul that seeks him.*[34]

Now although such a life and such a kind of devotion is seen in men living the cloistered life, and especially in hermits, nevertheless secular priests should aspire to it and approach it with all their powers, as far as their state allows for it. For that reason, they are commanded to live continently and abstain *from worldly affairs,*[35] which are greatly distracting to the soul.

Moreover, though a person endeavors to live according to this perfection, and opts to choose such a quiet and pure and fervent devotion, yet he will not always find himself with as much devotion as he might wish. I am not however of the opinion that such a man should abstain from the celebration of Mass or communion, as long as he has done all that is in him, namely, scrutinizing his life and his conscience, confessing sins, imploring grace, and approaching in the hope of divine clemency. For although a person may not have experientially that devotion and its perceptibly sweet affection, which is frequently caused by the flowing over from the superior appetite to the inferior, or from the will to the senses, yet if his reason itself labors to adhere to God and to disavow vices, and his will dominates the movements of the inferior appetite, then true and intellectual devotion is present. And this devotion suffices—indeed, it is also safer, as Matthew of Cracow wrote in a notable *Dialogue on Communion.*[36] This sort of devotion is also a probable sign of God's grace.

ARTICLE IV

On the four things to be considered by the priest before the celebration of Mass.

My sons, be not negligent: the Lord has chosen you to stand before him and to minister before him, and to worship him, and to burn incense to him.[37] These are the words of the most religious king Hezekiah to the Levites. As Augustine states in the tenth book of the *City of*

---

[34] Lam. 3:25.   [35] Cf. 2 Tim. 2:4.
[36] E.N. Matthew of Cracow (ca. 1335-1410) was a German-Polish scholar and priest who wrote several works including one on the celebration of Mass entitled *De celebratione Missae.* Denis is, however, likely referring to Matthew of Cracow's *Dialogus exhortatorius ad frequentem communionem,* or *Dialogue exhorting to frequent communion.*   [37] 2 Chr. 29:11.

God, the outward and visible sacrifice is the sacrament, that is, the sacred sign, of the interior and invisible sacrifice.[38] But the interior sacrifice refers to that by which a rational spirit offers and submits himself to God, in accordance with this: *A sacrifice to God is an afflicted spirit*; and in Ecclesiastes: *It is a wholesome sacrifice to take heed to the commandments.*[39] Now, according to Augustine, in every sacrifice there are four things that are to be considered, namely: the one who offers, the one to whom one offers, what one offers, and why one offers.[40] Before you approach to worship at the altar of God, O priest of Christ, you should think profoundly and intimately, and not superficially or cursorily, of these four things.

Consider yourself first; see how poor and helpless you stand, how ungrateful and unworthy of such great benefits, how irreverently and imperfectly you walk before your God every day. Lament heartily, therefore, and confess and resolve to amend yourself from these and other evils and vices. Secondly, think who it is to whom you offer. For you sacrifice to the eternal and omnipotent God, to the immense God, living and true. Contemplate his goodness and love for us, how he *spared not his own Son, but delivered him up for us all.*[41] Indeed, because of his *exceeding charity by which he loved us*, God the Father *sent* his most beloved Son *into the world, that we might live* and be blessed *by him.*[42] By considering this, your love should be inflamed and your hope strengthened, so that you might fervently and confidently approach the altar. Contemplate the majesty and also the justice of God most high, so that you may conduct yourself in all things with holy fear. For if *the pillars of heaven tremble and dread at his beck*,[43] and if the angelic spirits assist, attend to, and serve God with reverent fear, with how much more solicitude and custody of heart and fear of mind ought we poor ones have to stand before and offer sacrifice to the most high God?

Third, the priest ought to consider what he is offering. Take heed, O celebrant, of the dignity of your sacrifice. Are you not offering the Body and Blood of Christ—indeed the whole Christ, true God and man? The union of dissimilar things is inappropriate. For

---

[38] E.N. St. Augustine, *On the City of God*, X, 5.
[39] Ps. 50:19a; Ecclus 35:2a.
[40] E.N. St. Augustine, *On the Trinity*, IV, 14.
[41] Rom. 8:32a.   [42] Eph. 2:4b; 1 John 4:9.
[43] Job 26:11. E.N. This is also a reference to the apocalyptic and apocryphal Book of Enoch 18:12–13.

what concord has *light with darkness*, and *Christ with Belial*, that is, "him who is without yoke"?[44] What agreement does the son of Venus have with the Son of the Virgin? Finally, what concord do the proud, the angry, the glutton, or the envious have with the meek, and humble, with the loving and sober Son of God? It is therefore not lawful nor profitable for you to celebrate Mass, to handle or to receive Christ, unless you find yourself to be similar to him according to the demands of your state, and if not in effect, yet in affection; namely, that you propose and endeavor with your whole heart to imitate the footsteps of Christ. If you do otherwise, you will *make yourself guilty of his Body and Blood*.[45] For as it is written in the seventh chapter of Leviticus of the priests of the Old Testament, *If any one that is defiled shall eat of the flesh of the sacrifice of peace offerings, which is offered to the Lord, he shall be cut off from his people*.[46] How much more shall the priest of the New Law perish in eternity if he presumes to consecrate and consume the Sacrament of the Body and Blood of the Lord while living carnally and viciously? Hence also Moses said: *The priests also that come to the Lord, let them be sanctified, lest he strike them.*[47] *For the time is*, as Peter the Apostle states, *that judgment should begin at the house of God.*[48]

Fourth, the priest must think why he offers this host. For it is offered for the living and the dead. In addition to the general reason that the Church enjoins upon the priest, the priest may celebrate solemnities of Masses for various persons and causes. Therefore, so that the intention for which he celebrates may merit to be heard, the priest should strive so to live and to be so familiar and dear to the most worthy God, that he may be a suitable mediator between God and his people. Indeed, the priest is the middleman between God and the people because he represents and offers to God those things that are the people's—namely, their prayers, promises, and gifts. He also procures, dispenses, or bestows upon the people those things which pertain to God, namely grace and the sacraments. The priest must therefore be exemplary in all things to the people, and be beloved by, and familiar with, God.

---

[44] E.N. Denis is referring to an etymology of the word Belial, advanced, for example, by St. Jerome in his *Commentary on Judges* (19:22), as meaning "without yoke."
[45] Cf. 1 Cor. 11:27b.   [46] Lev. 7:20.   [47] Ex. 19:22.   [48] 1 Pet. 4:17a.

ARTICLE V
Of the vices which priests ought especially to avoid, as figured in the Old Testament.

The Lord said to Aaron: *A man of your seed who has a blemish, shall not offer bread to his God.*[49] As the Law of Moses was a type of the law of Christ, so all those things which were done in the Old Law represented those things which are done in the law of grace. For *all these things happened to them in figure*, according to the Apostle.[50] Therefore, as the Old Law is a figure of the New Law, so the New Law is a figure of the state of the Blessed in the heavenly fatherland, according to Dionysius in the fourth chapter of his *Ecclesiastical Hierarchy*. Because the Law of Moses was figurative of the New Law, which is further figurative of the future life, the figures of the Old Law are more obscure than the figures of the New Law. For this reason, the Apostle said: *The law having a shadow of the good things to come, did not have the very image of the things.*[51] For it represented the future good obscurely, which the New Law represents more clearly. Hence, the New Law contains an image, that is, a perfect representation, of things or future goods; but a shadow is more obscure than an image. Therefore, the rituals and the state of the law of grace lies midway between the state of the written Law and the future life, as Dionysius teaches. Moreover, the priesthood under the Law existed as a figure of the priesthood of Christ, and by the physical defects on account of which the sons of Aaron were rendered unfit for the priesthood are signified the spiritual defects by which priests are made unworthy to celebrate the mysteries of Christ.

And it was forbidden in the Law that a priest should be blind or lame, should have a large or small or crooked nose, and also that he should have a broken foot or hand, that he should be hunchbacked or lame, and should have a blemished eye, have an unhealing scab or impetigo, and that he not have a hernia.[52]

Analogously, the priest of Christ should not be blind, that is, unlearned. For this reason, it is stated in Hosea: *Because you have rejected knowledge, I will reject you, that you shall not do the office of priesthood to me*; and again: *I desire mercy and not sacrifice, and knowledge of God more than holocausts.*[53] The priest of Christ also

---

[49] Lev. 21:17.   [50] 1 Cor. 10:11a.   [51] Heb. 10:1a.   [52] Lev. 21:18–20.
[53] Hosea 4:6; 6:6.

ought not to be lame, that is, inconstant. For a fool changes like the moon, but the wise man remains like the sun.[54] But he should be constant, so that he might walk the royal way, and neither be exalted by prosperity nor crushed by adversity, as is stated in Job: *Until I die, I will not depart from my innocence*; and again: *although he should kill me, I will trust in him.*[55] Additionally, a priest of the New Law will not have a great or small or crooked nose, that is, a corrupt taste or indiscrete soul; but as the nose discerns odors, so he must discern between good and evil. He ought not to have a broken foot or hand, that is, be slothful or lazy; but banishing tedium, he should handle divine things with great affection and serve them reverently and readily. He ought not be hunchbacked, that is, having the "back" of his mind turned down towards earthly things; nor ought he be obese, that is, carnally wise; nor ought he to have a blemish in his eye, that is, the presumption of holiness in his heart, supposing himself to be something, or attributing to his own powers or merits the goods bestowed upon him by God, so that he might truly say that verse from Daniel in the Mass [during the Offertory]: *In a humble spirit, and a contrite heart, may we be received by you, O Lord.*[56] Therefore, the priest ought not to have unhealing scabs, that is, tenacious adherence to wantonness of the flesh; nor ought he have impetigo, that is, avarice. And he ought not to have a hernia, that is to say, lumbering, carrying the burden of foulness or malice in the heart, even if he does not carry it out in deed. Hence it is stated in the Gospel: *When you offer your gift at the altar, ... go first to be reconciled to your brother*; and again: *Forgive if you have anything against any man.*[57] And the Apostle also: *Let not the sun*, he says, *go down upon your anger.*[58]

These virtues which priests ought to wear are signified by the sacred vestments which they use in the celebration of divine things. It seems we should pass over discussing these vestments and their meaning, because they are fully and beautifully discussed in the *Rationale divinorum officiorum.*[59] But also St. Thomas, in the first part of the second part [of his *Summa Theologiae*] and in the fourth book of his *Commentary on the Sentences*, discusses the sacred vestments of the altar ministers of the New Law.[60]

---

[54] Cf. Ecclus. 27:12.   [55] Job 27:5b; 13:15.
[56] Dan. 3:39b.   [57] Matt. 5:23a, 24a; Mark 11:25a.   [58] Eph. 4:26b.
[59] E.N. A reference to William of Durand's (ca. 1230–1296) encyclopedic work on the liturgy, *Rationale Divinorum Officiorum* (*Rationale for the Divine Offices*).
[60] E.N. *ST* IaIIae, q. 102, art. 5, ad 10; *Super Sent.*, lib. 4, d. 24, 1. 3, a. 3, arg. 1.

ARTICLE VI
On the parts of the Mass.

The Office of the Mass is divided in various ways by different authors. For a gloss on that verse in Timothy, *I desire... first of all, that supplications, prayers, intercessions, and thanksgivings be made for all men*, states that the Mass is divided into these four parts.[61] But Thomas, in the fourth part of his *Commentary on the Sentences*,[62] divides the Mass into three parts, namely: into a beginning, which according to him is called "prayer" (*oratio*) and lasts up to the Epistle; a middle, which is the celebration of Mass itself, lasting up to the post-Communion; and an end, the thanksgiving, which lasts until the end of Mass. He subdivides these parts in the eighth distinction of the aforesaid book, and those who desire to follow this method can find it there.

Finally, others divide the Mass into four parts, of which they call the first part the preparation, the second the consecration, the third the reception, and the fourth the thanksgiving. Now this division seems more convenient and clear, and it differs from the first only in nomenclature: for that part of the Mass which the gloss calls supplication it calls preparation; but the part which according to the gloss is called prayer, it calls consecration; and that part also which according to the gloss is called intercession, it calls reception. Both call the fourth part the thanksgiving.[63] The first part lasts up until the Offertory, the second to the end of the Consecration, the third to the end of Communion, and the fourth to the end of the service.

But to understand these things, it is necessary to know the difference between supplication, prayer, petition, and thanksgiving.[64] Supplication is the invocation of God by the commemoration of something sacred or divine, by whose power and merit we wish to obtain something, such as when we say: "By your Incarnation, deliver us." Therefore, since the first part of the Mass calls to mind the teaching of Christ, the Apostles, and the Evangelists, along with

---

[61] 1 Tim. 2:1.
[62] E.N. *Super Sent.*, lib. 4, dist. 8, in expositio textus.
[63] E.N. In Latin, the pairings are as follows, with the gloss usage given second: 1. *praeparatio* v. *obsecratio*; 2. *consecratio* v. *oratio*; 3. *sumptio* v. *postulatio*; and 4. *gratiarum actio* (both).
[64] E.N. Denis uses his own nomenclature for the fourfold division of the Mass: *obsecratio* (supplication), *petitio* (petition), *postulatio* (request), and *gratiarum actio* (thanksgiving).

divine invocation and praise, the first part of the Mass is called *supplication* (*obsecratio*). The gloss states that supplication regards difficult things, such as the justification of the wicked. Going on, petition (*petitio*) is the invocation of God for the goods of wayfarers in this life, which are ordered to those things which we ultimately desire. In the second part of the Mass, prayer is made for the blessing and consecration of the bread and wine into the Body and Blood of Christ, whose Body, as it exists in the Sacrament, is called the provision for our journey (*viaticum*) and the supreme good by which we are refreshed on the way. Therefore, the second part of the Mass is called *petition* (*petitio*), and also *consecration*, because the petition is ordered to the consecration and ends in it as in its last and principal part. Now intercessions are the invocation of God for the goods of our heavenly fatherland. Since after the consecration we ask for the goods of the fatherland, the third part of the Mass is rightly called the intercession (*postulatio*). Finally, thanksgiving is the consummation of prayer, by which all good is referred to God and the way is prepared for obtaining even greater benefits. And since this is done in the last part of the Mass, the fourth and last part of the Mass is therefore called *thanksgiving* (*gratiarum actio*).

ARTICLE VII
On the washing and confession of the priest, and the kissing of the altar.

Wash yourselves, be clean, take away the evil of your devices.[65] As one reads in Exodus, the Lord commanded through Moses that the priests should wash themselves when they approached to minister in the temple.[66] Therefore, the priest of Christ must wash his hands before celebrating Mass; first, because of the reverence due such a great Sacrament; second, to signify the spiritual washing by which he must cleanse the mind from the stains of vices, according to the verse: *Wash me yet more from my iniquity*; and again: *I will wash my hands among the innocent and will compass your altar, O Lord.*[67] Further, according to Dionysius, the washing of the fingers, or rather, of their extremities, signifies the washing away of the smallest faults.[68] The priest therefore should not only abhor and avoid mortal and the graver venial sins, but even the smallest

---

[65] Is. 1:16.   [66] Ex. 30:18-21.   [67] Ps. 50:4a; 25:6.   [68] *De Eccl. hier.*, c. 3.

sins, so that he might stand before God completely clean, with a recollected and steadfast mind. Hence, as a figure of this, the Lord commanded the Levites to shave off all the hair from their skin.[69] For hairs signify thoughts, which rise in the heart like hairs grow on the body. Therefore, O priest of Christ, before you presume to consecrate, touch, eat, and drink the Body and Blood of Christ, your Creator, Savior, and Judge, shave all the hairs from your body, that is, cast off all superfluous thoughts, and worldly cares, and vain wanderings, and firmly imprint Christ, his Passion, and his benefits on your heart, lest you approach such a great duty unprepared and unworthy; otherwise, a small error in the beginning will be a great one at the end.

Moreover, because it is written: *For I know my iniquity*; and, *I said I will confess against myself my injustice to the Lord* (for *the just* man, as Solomon attests, *is first accuser of himself*; and Joshua said, *My son, give glory to... God and confess* your sin); therefore, the priest cleansed within and without, adorned as another Aaron with sacred vestments, makes a confession before the altar, that he might be the more pure and more ready to celebrate Mass.[70] For who is there in this life so pure that he does not need ever more purification?

Then, having made his confession, he kisses the altar. For the altar signifies Christ or his Cross, according to Ambrose. By kissing the altar, therefore, he demonstrates his ardent love for Christ and the celebration of his mysteries; and his desire to unite and conform himself to Christ's sufferings, knowing that *the servant is not greater than his Lord*, and because *if we suffer with him, we shall also reign with him*.[71] For *all that will live godly in Christ shall suffer persecution*.[72] Therefore, since the priest is Christ's vicar, by his kissing the altar, we can understand the Son of God's love for and immediate union with human nature. Hence, when the priest ascends the altar and kisses it, he ought to say some devout words, whichever appeal most sweetly to affections, and lovingly kiss the altar as if it were Christ, that he might draw from it, as if from the fountain of Christ's breast, grace, that is, let him conceive a firm sense of devotion, saying: "Hail, O most gracious Lord Jesus Christ, full of divinity and grace, mercy is with you, blessed be your Passion and your wounds, and blessed be the Blood from your wounds"; or, "Come, Holy Spirit, etc." or something similar.

---

[69] Num. 8:7.   [70] Ps. 50:5a; 31:b; Prov. 18:17a; Joshua 7:19.
[71] John 13:16a; Rom. 8:17b; 2 Tim. 2:12a.   [72] 2 Tim. 3:12.

Indeed, the greatest solicitude must be taken not to start such a service without fervent and actual devotion. For virtue in the beginning shines forth and continues in what ensues, and (as mentioned earlier), a small error in the beginning becomes great as one progresses. The priest, therefore, ought to make his confession before the altar with the greatest attention, and never out of dry habit, so that the exterior humbling of his body and the beating of his breast might be true signs of his interior humility and mental self-abnegation. He ought also heartily beg others to pray for him, and hope that by the prayers of others help will come to him, piously and humbly believing others better than himself, and more likely to be heard by God than he.

ARTICLE VIII
On the Introit of the Mass.

Give praise to the Lord *our God, all you his servants, ... small and great.*[73] Because the entire service of the Mass is ordered to call to mind God's benefits, according to the Savior's saying, *As often as you do these things, do them for the commemoration of me,*[74] yet for God's benefits we are able to return nothing more worthy than honor and praise, for God *has no need of our goods,*[75] the Mass therefore begins with God's praise. For the *Introit* contains praise of God, and its melody is sung to honor the Most High, so that the hearts of all those present might be excited and kindled to love and holy devotion to God, and so take part with fervor and eager delight in the entire service that follows.

Moreover, the *Introit* is frequently taken from a Psalm, or at least sung with a Psalm verse, for two reasons. First, because the Psalms include everything contained in sacred Scripture in the mode of praise, as Dionysius says in the third chapter of his *On the Ecclesiastical Hierarchy*. Second, because Pope Celestine instituted that the Psalms should be sung antiphonally at the beginning of Mass. But Gregory, in place of the Psalms, ordered the *Introit* sung; but he retained one verse from those Psalms which had been sung antiphonally beforehand, and from which the *Introit* is often taken. One can also add a third reason: As David was the most excellent of the Prophets and thus wrote more excellently and fully of Christ,

---

[73] Rev. 19:5.   [74] Cf. 1 Cor. 11:24–25.   [75] Cf. Ps. 15:2.

his Passion, and his mysteries, therefore his Psalms or prophecies are more extensively used in the celebration of Christ's mystery.

It should be noted, however, that in the *Decretum, de consecratione*, in the first distinction, it is stated that James, the brother of our Lord, that is, Christ's kinsman, and Basil, the bishop of Caesarea, composed the celebration of Mass, that is, they ordained many of the things which are said and done in the Mass, with regard to the ceremonies and prayers.[76] For Christ at the Last Supper, having instituted this Sacrament, celebrated the first Mass; but James the Lesser, on account of his most excellent sanctity, was singled out by the Apostles for this honor: that he would be the first bishop in Jerusalem and the first after Christ to celebrate Mass according to the form set forth by our Lord, and the rest of the Apostles after him, adding the Lord's Prayer after the words of consecration. Then the prince of the Apostles, Peter, added further prayers. Later, however, as Dionysius recounts, the Epistles and the Gospel were added. And so according to the Holy Spirit's disposition, as time passed and the Christian religion grew, we read that diverse things were added by the holy Fathers, especially by that glorious Basil, who shone so wonderfully in the house of God.

Therefore, the *Introit* of the Mass is to be sung or read with great devotion, and the heart's affection is to be very carefully directed towards God. And because the heart's dispersion to other things detracts from this devotion, the priest ought to know before Mass what *Introit* is going to be read, and to know thoroughly in advance everything that he has to say and do, lest preoccupation with such things cause distraction and loss of devotion.

ARTICLE IX
On the Kyrie eleison.

He that loves God shall obtain pardon for his sins by prayer, and shall refrain himself from them, and shall be heard.[77] In every divine service, especially in prayer and in the divine praise, it is incumbent upon us to consider two things, namely, God's mercy and our misery. Now, by God's mercy I mean all those things which refer to his goodness, namely, his charity, liberality, and his patience towards us. By our misery, I mean those things which concern our imperfection, fault,

---

[76] E.N. D. 1, *de cons.*, c. 47.   [77] Ecclus. 3:4.

and weakness. These things, therefore, we ought to ponder intently, insofar as we aspire to contemplate the divine goodness and clemency and approach *with confidence to the throne of grace* in the fullness of faith, knowing most certainly that whatsoever we ask the Father in the name of the Son, he will give to us as long as we perseveringly and indefatigably knock, as that James admonishes, saying: *Let him ask in faith, nothing wavering*.[78] For he will do to us according to our faith.[79] Now it goes without saying how much persevering and trusting prayer pleases our Almighty God. But from the consideration of our misery, let us humble ourselves and be dissatisfied with ourselves, and let us be vile in our own eyes, in the way that David states: *I will be little in my own eyes*.[80] And Paul exhorts us not to please ourselves, just as *Christ did not please himself*.[81] If Christ, then, *who did no sin, neither was guile found in his mouth*,[82] did not please himself, that is, insofar as he was man he did not ascribe any good to himself, why do we who are full of misery and vices please ourselves, despising others and preferring ourselves to them?

Therefore, the most holy Church has fittingly decided that, after the *Introit* in which the praise of God is sung, we should return to ourselves and implore God's mercy, saying KYRIE ELEISON, that is, *Lord have mercy*. And it is said nine times, inasmuch as we confess our imperfection nine times, and are led to the perfection and society of the nine orders of angels. KYRIE ELEISON is also said three times to the Father and three times to the Holy Spirit, and CHRISTE ELEISON is said three times to the Son, because we have offended all three of the Persons by our threefold fault, namely, in thought, word, and deed. Now these words have great power. For when Basil cried out *Kyrie eleison*, heretics were confounded, and the doors of the church were opened by divine power. And also, as we read, blessed Germanus turned five kings to flight by exclaiming these words.

Moreover, let it be known that the Church uses three languages in the Mass, for there are some Greek words in the Mass, such as *Kyrie eleison*, some Hebrew words, such as *Alleluia*, that is, "Praise the Lord," and *Sabbaoth*, that is, "of armies," *Hosanna*, that is, "Save, O Lord, I beseech you," *Amen*, that is, "truly," or "be it so," and some in Latin. For the title on Christ's Cross was written in these three languages. Second, because these three languages are more dignified than others; hence the people who do not use these languages are

---

[78] Heb. 4:16a; cf. John 14:13–14; 16:23; James 1:6.
[79] Cf. Matt. 9:29b. [80] 2 Sam. 6:22a. [81] Rom. 15:1b, 3a. [82] 1 Pet. 2:22.

referred to as barbarians. Third, because of reverence for the superlatively blessed Trinity. Fourth because the number three is perfect: for we place all things above three, according to the Philosopher.[83] Accordingly, these three languages signify all languages. And thus, the Church uses these three languages in the Mass service to insinuate that peoples of every language are saved by faith in Christ, as promised to Abraham in Genesis: *In your seed* (that is, in Christ) *shall all the nations of the earth be blessed;*[84] and in the Psalm: *And in him shall all the tribes of the earth be blessed: all nations shall magnify him;*[85] and in Daniel the Prophet: *All peoples, tribes, and tongues shall serve him.*[86] From all this, the error of Muhammad and the Muslims, who say that all nations can be saved by their law, is made clear.[87] Hence Peter, in the Acts of the Apostles, attests regarding Christ: *There is no other name under heaven given to men, whereby we must be saved, except for the name of Jesus Christ.*[88] This agrees with what our Lord said through Isaiah: *I have given you* (namely, Christ) *to be the light of the Gentiles, that you may be my salvation even to the farthest part of the earth.*[89]

It is also evident from this with what humility and affection and contrition of heart these most sacred words, *Kyrie eleison*, etc., must be said, not cursorily, but meticulously, for, insofar as the priest desires to ask forgiveness for himself for all kinds of sins, the more fervently should he say these words and the more often repeat them: for they are repeated so often precisely so that they might always be more devoutly expressed.

ARTICLE X
On the Angelic Hymn, Gloria in excelsis Deo.

Blessing the Lord, exalt him as much as you can: for he is above all praise.[90] Again, after recognizing her own misery, the Church desires to occupy herself with the contemplation and praise of the Most High. For the more one humbles oneself, the more eminently God comes into one's heart. But no one is fit to praise and glorify

---

[83] E.N. Aristotle, *De caelo*, I, 1, 268a10–19.
[84] Gen. 22:18.   [85] Ps. 71:17b.   [86] Dan. 7:14a.
[87] E.N. Denis's argument is that the Christian Scriptures just quoted make it clear that all nations shall worship God and his Christ; therefore, it follows that the Muslim belief that all nations will adopt Shari'a law is false.
[88] Acts 4:12.   [89] Is. 49:6b.   [90] Ecclus. 43:33.

God unless he regards his imperfection and trusts in the mercy of God by living well. For *to the sinner God has said: Why do you declare my justices?*[91] And so after the *Kyrie eleison*, the Church sings the Angelic Hymn, saying with the angels: GLORIA IN EXCELSIS DEO, ET IN TERRA PAX HOMINIBUS BONAE VOLUNTATIS.[92]

Now what follows, from LAUDAMUS TE up until the end, St. Hilary [of Poitier] is said to have added, or—according to St. Albert [the Great]—Pope Symmachus. But, as Nicholas of Gorran discussed in his *Commentary on Luke*, and is in part declared from the *Gesta Pontificum Romanorum*,[93] St. Hilary added it; while Pope Symmachus instituted that this Hymn should be sung during Mass. St. Albert, however, in his *De Mysteriis*,[94] states that Pope St. Telesphorus, who was the ninth from the blessed Peter, made the addition, not Hilary, and that Telesphorus instituted the hymn to be sung on the night of Christ's Nativity at the first Mass, because it was then that the angels sang the initial part of this hymn.[95] However, Pope Symmachus afterwards ordered it sung on Sundays and feasts that were not sorrowful in nature.

Now glory, as Ambrose states, is clear knowledge with praise.[96] Glory can also be understood as meaning joy, and also majesty or perfection. Therefore, when the words GLORIA IN EXCELSIS DEO are said, they have a double meaning. First let *Glory*, that is, clear knowledge, be to God in the highest, that is, in heaven; or else, *in the highest*, that is, in the angels and the blessed in heaven, namely, so that they might have a clear knowledge of God and praise him together, as we sing in the Psalm: *Praise the Lord from the heavens; praise him in the high places; praise him, all his angels.*[97] Hence, *Glory to God in the highest* is not said in the mode of prayer, since it is always the case, but in the manner of praise or thanksgiving, in accordance with this verse: *Adore him all you angels.*[98] Secondly, it can be understood in this way: Let there be *glory*, that is, joy, *to God on high*, that is, to him who dwells in heaven, or *on high*, that is, in his excellent and sublime effects, as it is written: *The Lord*

---

[91] Ps. 49:16a.   [92] Luke 2:14.
[93] E.N. The *Liber Pontificalis* or *Gesta Pontificum Romanorum* consisted of a chronicle of the lives of the Roman pontiffs from St. Peter to Nicholas I (867).
[94] E.N. This appears to be an error, and is probably a reference to the *De Mysteriis* (or *De Missarum Mysteriis*) by Pope Innocent III.
[95] Luke 2:13-14.
[96] E.N. The definition is Augustinian, not Ambrosian. St. Augustine, *Contra Maximianum Arianum*, II, 13, PL 42, 550.
[97] Ps. 148:1-2.   [98] Ps. 96:b.

shall rejoice in his works; and in Ezechiel: *Blessed be the glory of the Lord in his holy place.*[99] But what the Lord says through Isaiah: *I am the Lord, this is my name: I will not give my glory to another,*[100] does not seem to be said of the glory which is understood as meaning knowledge, for all the blessed in heaven see God face to face; nor does it seem to have been said about glory insofar as it signifies joy, which indeed all the blessed enjoy in the beatitude of God. Therefore, glory is here understood as meaning the divine majesty, for no one can be equal to God.

And the Angelic Hymn continues: ET IN TERRA PAX HOMINIBUS BONAE VOLUNTATIS. For Christ is *our peace, who has made both one,* gathering the Church together from the Jews and the Gentiles, and has reconciled us with God and his holy angels.[101] Moreover, Christ is our peace objectively and causally: because he is the meritorious cause of peace according to his assumed nature; and according to his divinity he is the effective and principal cause of our peace, indeed also the final and objective cause of it, because our peace consists in him as our Ultimate End. Now peace is formally the tranquility or rest of the mind in God: and this is considered to exist in *men of good will* because their highest affection is the honor and glory of God, and so they rest with their mind in God. And because this peace is bestowed upon us by God, therefore the Church praises God for this, saying:

LAUDAMUS TE, that is, we assert that you are worthy of praise. BENEDICIMUS TE, that is, we say good things of you or to you. We bless God and God blesses us, but in very different senses. For the blessing of God, according to Gregory, is the conferral and multiplication of divine gifts. The blessing of God is, therefore, the cause of goodness, grace, and holiness in us; for we pray to be blessed by God, that is, to receive grace and mercy from him. But the blessing by which we bless God is a certain profession by which we ascribe all good things to God, as the fount of goodness, holiness, and grace. Hence blessing has a twofold sense: of consecration and of praise; by the first God blesses us; by the second, we bless God, or praise him in our own minds.

ADORAMUS TE, that is, we honor you with a singular and most excellent worship as the first and the most-high Principle, who alone is in need of no one, depends on no one, can do all things,

---

[99] Ps. 103:31b; Ez. 3:12b. [100] Is. 42:8a.
[101] Eph. 2:14; cf. Rom. 5:10; cf. 2 Cor. 5:19-20.

see all things, and are alone able, of your own power, to render aid and help—indeed, and also to harden and to damn, as we read in Deuteronomy: *I will kill and I will make to live*.[102] Now adoration is worship (*cultus*) and an act of worship (*latriae*) offered to God alone. But latria is the virtue that gives worship and ceremonies to the divine nature; and this virtue is also called religion (*religio*).

GLORIFICAMUS TE. We are said to sanctify or magnify God when we serve him in holiness and equity, and thus demonstrate that he is great and holy. In the same manner we also glorify God when we manifest his name to others; and by this we make him celebrated and glorious in the minds of others. GRATIAS AGIMUS TIBI PROPTER GLORIAM TUAM MAGNAM,[103] that is, because of the excellent knowledge we have of you by the Holy Spirit's revelation, by which we know how many benefits you have bestowed upon us, for which *we always and everywhere are obliged to give you thanks*,[104] though never sufficiently.

The rest of this hymn is clear enough—except for what is sung about the Son towards the end of it: TU SOLUS SANCTUS, TU SOLUS DOMINUS, TU SOLUS ALTISSIMUS, IESU CHRISTE. Here the question arises whether such a statement is true without qualification; and this is the same as asking whether an exclusive expression can be added to a personal term when speaking about God, as when saying: "The Father alone is true God," "Only the Son is most high," "The Spirit alone is unbounded," or something similar. The answer is that, if we understand an exclusive expression as an attribute (*categorematice*), that is, as if it posited the signified reality of the subject in an absolute or unqualified sense, then it cannot be attached to a personal term—nor even an essential term—when speaking about God: for then it would posit aloneness in God.[105] But if it is understood as a quantifier (*syncategorematice*), that is, as implying how the predicate relates to the subject, then it can be attached to an essential term and even a personal term, because then it excludes "one thing" in the neuter gender (*aliud neutraliter*) but not "another" in the masculine (*alium masculine*). Thus when it is stated, "The Son alone is the Holy One," or "is Lord," or "is the Most High," the meaning is that the Son, and no other thing

---

[102] Deut. 32:39a.
[103] E.N. Thus (*gloriam tuam magnam* and not *magnam gloriam tuam*) in the Latin text. This is a feature of the *Gloria* in the Carthusian rite. Archdale King, *Liturgies of the Religious Orders* (London: Longmans, Green, 1955), 41.
[104] Cf. *Preface dialogue*.   [105] E.N. I.e., imply that "the Father is alone."

(*aliud*) than the Son, is the Holy One. Now this is certainly true: For the Father is not a different thing (*aliud*) from the Son, but a different person (*alius*); similarly also the Holy Spirit. However, properly speaking, this word "alone" (*solus*) excludes another in the masculine gender. And therefore, according to Thomas in the *Prima Pars* of his *Summa Theologiae*, such a statement is not to be taken over-literally (*extendenda*), but is to be explained carefully (*exponenda*); when, that is, as an exclusive expression is attached to a personal Subject. Hence, according to him, the Church does not sing in an unqualified sense of the Son, "Thou alone art holy," etc., but immediately adds "Together with the Holy Ghost, in the glory of God the Father," because the three Persons are one Most High, and one Holy One, and one Lord.[106]

Therefore, this angelic song must be sung and read with heartfelt joy and with most sweet devotion, which cannot be done unless the intellect is steadfastly and sincerely affixed in the contemplation of God. For the more divine the words, the more they demand attention and pure elevation of mind. Also, the more affectionate and profound the meaning of the divine word, the more vehemently even a slight distraction of the heart hinders and harms devotion.

---

[106] E.N. In the words of St. Thomas Aquinas, a categorematic term is a term "which ascribes absolutely its meaning to a given *suppositum*." A word that can be used as a subject term or predicate term by itself is categorematic. However, a word that cannot be so used alone, and requires to be paired with a categorematic term, is syncategorematic (it is used co-predicatively or quantifies the categorematic term). Thomas defines this as a term that "imports the order of the predicate to the subject," thus "excluding every other *suppositum* from the predicate." *Summa Theologiae*, Ia, q. 31, art. 3, co. The word "only" (*solus*) can be used categorematically or syncategorematically, and so causes ambiguity. It cannot be used categorematically to refer to God. So *God is alone* or *God the Father is alone* is false. However, if used syncategorematically, it can be true. So, for example, saying "God *alone* is eternal" is true since it does not refer to a person, but to the nature of the Godhead. When "alone" (*solus*) is used masculinely, it refers to the person (Father, Son, Holy Spirit, in Latin are masculine gender) and is improper because other than the subsistent relations which distinguish the persons, the attributes of the persons (such as holiness or eternity) are one and the same. When "alone" is used neutrally, however, it refers to the nature of the Godhead or divinity, and so, in a proper case, is perfectly acceptable. Thus "God the Father alone creates" is false, since God the Son participates in creation. But the *Gloria* clearly does not understand the word *solus* to apply categorematically to Jesus Christ insofar as it attributes holiness, lordship, and loftiness to him and appears grammatically to say so exclusively, for the *Gloria* clearly does not intend it in such a manner. Accordingly, in such situations, Thomas states that the syncategorematic term must not be understood over-literally (*extendenda*), but "piously expounded" (*pie exponenda*) when encountered in Scripture or elsewhere as in the *Gloria*. Ibid., arts. 3, 4.

Finally, although we are to beseech God attentively, yet more attentively should we praise him, all the more so because it is a greater and more worthy act to praise God than merely to beseech him. For both are acts of religion or *latria* but, insofar as the object and end of divine praise is more sublime than the object and end of beseeching prayer, that much more sublime and meritorious is it to praise God than to beseech him. For the object of beseeching prayer is some divine gift, and the end of such prayer is to acquire a gift of God. But the object of divine praise is the very excellence of the divine goodness, and the end is God himself. So such an object and such an end is more sublime than the object and end of prayer. Finally, when we pray, we reflect in some way upon ourselves; but when we praise God, we immerse ourselves in the very excellence of the divine nature, contemplating it purely and nakedly. Further, the blessed in the heavenly fatherland are constantly occupied with God's praises, but they do not pray, even for themselves, especially after the day of judgment, according to John's Gospel: *In that day you shall not ask me anything.*[107]

Again, in the same way that we are obligated to love God more than we do ourselves, so is it more just to occupy oneself with God's praise than to pray for oneself. Indeed, since no one is fit to praise God unless his life is upright in God's eyes, since Scripture attests regarding the wicked: *This people... glorify me with their lips, but their heart is far from me;*[108] therefore, prayer is ordained to divine praise as its end. But the end is more excellent than the things which are ordered to it. It is clear, therefore, that it is more worthy and more divine to praise God than to beseech him, but only provided that the heart is cleansed from the fog of vices and the gloom of works of darkness. For as long as one is oppressed by the passions of anger and pride, and overcome by carnal vices and sloth, it is more useful to spend time in prayer than praise. Whence the Psalmist, recognizing that no one is worthy to praise God unless he is separated from the common way of living and vices, prays thus: *Save us, O Lord, our God: and gather us from among nations, that we may give thanks to your holy name, and may glory in your praise.*[109]

Moreover, the sign of virtue is that its action is conjoined with delight, for if one takes delight while suffering adversity, it is a sign that he is truly patient. Therefore, in proportion as praise of God is more excellent than beseeching prayer, so much the more intense

---

[107] John 16:23a. [108] Is. 29:13; Matt. 15:8. [109] Ps. 105:47.

ought we to delight in praising the Most High than we do in mere prayer. And hence it is written: *My lips shall greatly rejoice, when I shall sing to you*; and again: *My mouth shall praise you with joyful lips.*[110] For this is the height of perfection and the most divine activity of the present life: to delight in the divine praise, to give thanks for the blessedness of the eternal God, and to rejoice mentally in his perfection; for such things proceed from fervent charity towards God. Now to the extent we become capable of this divine love and sincerest of praise, we refuse more and more to take comfort in anything other than God, and we come to hate the delights of the belly and vain speech, and we efficaciously seek and keep when found that one thing which alone is necessary, completely abhorring all torpor of mind, bodily rest, and slackening of spirit.[111]

Now because this Angelic Hymn is a song of joy, it is omitted in sorrowful offices.[112]

ARTICLE XI
On the greeting and prayer of the priest before the Epistle.[113]

To whom shall I have respect, says our Lord, *but to him that is poor and little, and of a contrite spirit, and that trembles at my words?*[114] As has been shown, the service of the Mass presents a most orderly mingling of commemoration of the divine excellence, which we praise, and recognition of our own misery, which moves us to pray. So after the confession at the foot of the altar, in which we profess our misery, begins the *Introit*, which is a song of divine praise, and immediately following is the *Kyrie eleison*, in which we again humble ourselves by declaring our misery. Once this is over, we turn to God's praise, saying: *Glory to God in the highest.* When this is completed, a prayer follows in which we again consider ourselves and implore mercy on account of our misery.

But first the priest greets the people, saying: DOMINUS VOBISCUM, that is, "May he pour upon you the grace of devoutly praying with me and worthily and salubriously hearing these sacred words." These words, taken from the book of Ruth,[115] should be uttered with affection by the priest as the mediator between God and the

---

[110] Ps. 70:23a; 62:6b.   [111] Cf. Luke 10:42.
[112] E.N. For example, in Requiem masses, on Holy Innocents, and at other times.
[113] E.N. That is, the Collect.   [114] Is. 66:2b.   [115] Ruth 2:4.

people, out of the requirement of fraternal charity that priests ought to have in abundance. But the bishop, because he stands in the person of Christ, says: PAX VOBIS, for Christ greeted the Apostles in this way after the Resurrection.[116]

The people are greeted openly seven times with the aforementioned words—except that PAX DOMINI SIT SEMPER VOBISCUM is said once in lieu of DOMINUS VOBISCUM—in order to shut out the seven mortal vices and to be filled with the seven gifts of the Holy Spirit and the acts of the seven principal virtues, of which three—namely, faith, hope, and charity—are called "theological," and the remaining four—namely, prudence, which is in the reason; justice, which is in the will; fortitude, which is in the irascible appetite; and temperance, which is in the concupiscible appetite—are called "cardinal," that is, principal, from the fact that they contain all the other moral virtues, which can be reduced to these four. The theological virtues, however, are more noble than the cardinal virtues. The priest also turns towards the people five times, four of these times openly greeting them, and once merely turning in silence. He does this because of the five appearances of Christ on Easter Sunday, four of which are described in the Gospels. But as to the one he is believed to have made to Peter, one reads neither where or how.[117]

Moreover, after the people have returned the greeting with ET CUM SPIRITU TUO, the priest utters a prayer for the people and himself. Now, according to the *Rationale*, the number of Collects will always be odd in number, namely: either one, because of the unity of the divine nature; or three, because of the mystery of the Trinity; or five, because of the five wounds of Christ; or seven, because that is the number of parts in the Lord's Prayer. Except perhaps for some special reason, no more than this should be said, since Christ did not exceed this number. But when several prayers are uttered, the last one must have some correspondence to the first; and therefore, in the Mass for the living, the Collect for the dead is not added, unless it is said second or third to last.

---

[116] John 20:19, 21, 26.
[117] Mark 16:9; John 20:14; Matt. 28:9; Luke 24:13-31, 36; 1 Cor. 15:5; Luke 24:34. E.N. The four described in the Gospels are to Mary Magdalene (Mark 16:9, John 20:14-17), the "other Mary" (Matt. 28:9), to the two disciples on the road to Emmaus (Luke 24:13-16), and to disciples in the absence of Thomas (John 20:19, 20, 24; Luke 24:36-50). As to the appearance to Peter, the Gospels merely say: "The Lord is risen indeed, and has appeared to Simon" (Luke 24:34; 1 Cor. 15:5).

Furthermore, although every Christian should always and everywhere beseech God reverently, purely, and solicitously, yet the priest at Mass must beseech him all the more ardently and sincerely, given that his reason for praying is greater, his office worthier, and his person closer to Christ, since he is a mediator between God and the people. For as St. Basil says: The divine help should not be implored negligently or with a mind wandering here and there. For, as Christ said, *God is a spirit; and they that adore him, must adore him in spirit and in truth.*[118]

Chrysostom beautifully declaims the great dignity of a rational creature who can address God in prayer at will, saying: "Consider how much happiness is granted to you, how much glory is bestowed upon you to be able to speak to God through prayers, to join in conversation with Christ, to wish for what you desire, and to ask for what you need." And again, he says: "He never denies benefits to those who pray, and in his goodness, he spurs them on so that they do not desist in praying."

According to the Damascene, prayer is also a petition to God for something worthy, or the ascent of the mind to God; hence, he who asks without attention, or who asks for things that ought not to be asked for, does not truly pray. And the person praying should take care that he at least begins his prayer fervently; for then all that follows will have virtue, because, according to Thomas, God attends to the original intention of the person praying.[119] If such intention is lacking at the beginning of prayer, that prayer is neither able to obtain its request nor be meritorious, according to the same author. But I do not understand this to mean that the person praying can merit nothing by continuing his prayer if he was not attentive at the beginning. For if he recognizes his distraction and raises his mind to God, he will make up for his neglect. But this I do believe: that distraction of mind in the beginning of prayer is more dangerous and more noxious than if it occurs during its progress. By the same token, distraction at the end of prayer or divine praise is worse than if it occurs in the middle. Hence Cassian earnestly exhorts us to try to end our prayer and divine praise with fervor, and to humbly ask for forgiveness for any faults of omission and commission. Indeed, this is highly profitable.

Now, although the prayer of a good priest is more efficacious in achieving what it asks than that of a sinful one, yet even the

---

[118] John 4:24.   [119] *Summa Theologiae*, IIaIIae, q. 83, art. 13.

prayer (and the whole celebration) of a sinful priest has power and is efficacious in impetration inasmuch as such a priest prays and acts in the person of the whole Church, as Thomas asserts.[120]

ARTICLE XII
On the Epistle and the Gradual and the Alleluia.

Blessed is the man who finds wisdom, and who is rich in prudence; for wisdom is more precious than all riches.[121] The prayer is followed most fittingly by the Epistle, by which the people are disposed for Christ's sacraments by teaching. This instruction is useful for preserving the grace of God which was conferred by the preceding prayer of the priest. It is also necessary to worthily receive and celebrate the heavenly sacraments of mysteries of Christ. For unless we know the grace and mercy and benefits of God, we cannot be grateful or are unable to receive, venerate, or recall him with loving devotion. For the intellective appetite loves nothing except that which the intellect knows. But he who is ungrateful for the gifts of the Most High deserves to lose those he has received and to be deprived of future ones. Hence the Apostle said: *He who does not know, will not be known.*[122] It is therefore necessary to acknowledge God's benefits, as the Apostle says: *Now we have received not the spirit of this world, but the Spirit that is of God, that we may know the things that are given us from God.*[123] For such knowledge strengthens hope, and stirs up a burning charity.

The Epistle, therefore, signifies the teaching of the Apostles. For epistle comes from ἐπιστέλλω, which means "I send" or "I dispatch." Because just as the Prophets added to and, as it were, sent forth their books in addition to the books of Moses, wherein the law was fully set forth, to offer further explanation of the law and formation to the people, so the Apostles sent certain additional writings after the books of the four Evangelists, in which the New Law is perfectly contained, in order to form the people, settle questions that were being raised, and dispel current and future heresies. And these writings are called the *Epistles*, whose teaching is incomplete in comparison to the evangelical teaching, which flowed immediately from Christ, and is ordered towards it as its end. For understanding

---

[120] Ibid., IIIa, q. 82, art. 6. [121] Prov. 3:13, 15a. [122] 1 Cor. 14:38.
[123] 1 Cor. 2:12b.

the Epistles disposes one to understand the Gospels; accordingly, the Epistle is read before the Gospel. Now when the Epistle is read, let us sit following the example of Mary [the sister of Martha and Lazarus], who, *sitting also at the Lord's feet*, attentively and with an eager mind heard his words: for in such a manner also ought we to hear the reading of the Epistle.[124]

It should be recognized also that of those things that are said at Mass, some are pronounced by the priest, namely, those things by which the people are immediately ordered towards God, such as the prayers and the acts of thanksgiving. Yet some of these things the priest says in secret because they pertain to his office. And those things which have been divinely handed down through the ministry of others, such as the Epistle and the Gospel, are proclaimed by the ministers. But some are said by the whole choir, namely, those things which pertain to disposing the people.

Now from the teaching of the Epistles the faithful should obtain two fruits, namely: progress in the moral life, ascending *from virtue to virtue* by degrees,[125] which is signified by the *Gradual*; and also spiritual joy, according to the Apostle's word: *Rejoice in the Lord always*,[126] which is signified by the *Alleluia*, a Hebrew term meaning "praise the Lord." And this word *Alleluia is* a heavenly, mystical, and potent word, signifying rather than expressing the ineffable exultation of the blessed in heaven. It is repeated because of the twofold garment or glory which the blessed at present partake of in their soul, but which they will one day enjoy in both soul and body.

Sometimes in place of the Epistle there is a reading from the Old Testament, in order to show the harmony of both Testaments. The Apostles' Epistles are read by the subdeacons, but readings taken from the Old Law are read by inferior ministers,[127] not always, but at those times when the figural relation of both laws is being suggested, as in the Ember Day fasts,[128] and when things prefigured in the Old Testament—such as Baptism, Christmas, and the Passion—are celebrated.

In addition, in sorrowful services, a *Tract* is sung instead of the *Alleluia*. The *Tract* represents the misery of the present life by the asperity of its subject matter and the length of its text.

---

[124] Luke 10:42b. [125] E.N. Ps. 83:8. [126] Phil. 4:4.
[127] E.N. E.g., a reader (lector) or acolyte.
[128] E.N. A reference to the fast on the Ember days—Lenty, Penty, Crucy, Lucy, as the mnemonic goes.

ARTICLE XIII
On the Gospel and the Creed.

I am the light of the world, said the only-begotten Son of God.[129] As we have said, the evangelical doctrine—to which the teaching of the Apostles and the Prophets disposes us—is perfect; therefore, following the *Epistle* and those things which signify its effect, comes the *Gospel*.

Now the deacon introduces it with DOMINUS VOBISCUM because Christ said to his disciples whom he sent to preach the Gospel: *Into whatsoever house you enter, first say: Peace be to this house.*[130] Secondly, it is done to indicate that Christ, who is the immediate teacher and author of evangelical truth, is both man and God. Moreover, the Gospel is sung on the left-hand side because Christ, the supreme teacher of the Gospel, did not come *to call the just, but sinners*;[131] secondly, because the Jews remained in their unbelief, while the Gentiles, who are represented by the left hand, believed the Gospel. Now when the Gospel is read, the people stand with their heads bare and sign themselves, because they are not ashamed of Christ's Cross, but glory in it, ready to confess their faith in the Gospel, and even, if need be, to die for it. Hence those persons who without special needs or reason sit or lean on some support during the Gospel are most reprehensible.

Now after the Gospel the Symbol of Faith, namely, the *Creed*, is recited most fittingly: for confession of the Christian faith is a fruit of evangelical instruction. Now the Creed is recited as a sort of aggregation of the articles of the orthodox faith; and it has three forms: the Apostles' Creed, which is silently said in Prime and Compline, so as to suggest that in the early Church the faith suffered persecution and tribulation, and its preachers worked in secret; the other is the Creed of Athanasius, bishop of Alexandria; the third is the Creed of the Fathers, that is, the one published by the three hundred and eight bishops in the Nicene Council against the perfidy of the Arians, who denied the substantial unity of the superlatively most glorious Trinity.

Lastly, the more worthy a virtue, the more meritorious and divine is its act. Since, therefore, the theological virtues, of which faith is one, are most worthy, their acts are of greatest merit; therefore, the actual and devout confession of the Christian faith is so meritorious than it surpasses speech or belief. Therefore, all these Creeds are to be said with greatest attention and diligence, but especially during Mass.

ARTICLE XIV
On the second principal part of the Mass, namely, of the oblation.

Yours, O Lord, is magnificence, and power, and glory, and victory: and to you is praise... yours are riches, for all things are yours, and we have given you what we received from your hand.[132] In the first part of the Mass expounded above, many things are said and done by which both the priest and people are disposed and prepared for the Sacraments of Christ. Now, in this second part of the Mass service, which is called the consecration, the priest and the people are more immediately and directly prepared for the consecration or reception of the Sacrament.

For it is preceded by the *Offertory*, which signifies the spiritual delight of the offerers, for *God loves a cheerful giver*; and also the readiness of the soul to make offering; for an offering sacrificed in this way is very pleasing.[133] Therefore, David says: *I know my God that you prove hearts, and love simplicity, wherefore I also in the simplicity of my heart have joyfully offered all these things.*[134] Then the priest offers the matter to be consecrated to God, saying, IN SPIRITU HUMILITATIS, etc. What comes next, IN NOMINE PATRIS † ET FILII ET SPIRITUS SANCTI, refers to the act which follows, when he sets down the chalice with the sign of the cross. Afterwards, the priest turns to the minister and the people in silence, and says: ORATE, FRATRES, PRO ME, etc. And as the priest represents the person of Christ, so the minister represents the Church, even though he is only one person; and for this reason, the priest addresses him in the plural.

Following this, the priest prays in a low voice, asking God for the effect, the fruit, and the acceptance of the offering presented, and the blessing of the offered matter, as can be seen clearly in the text of the various *Secrets*. Now these prayers are said in silence because they are not said *in the person* of the people; but because they are said *for* the people, they are finished in a louder voice. They are also said in a low voice for this reason: so that they might be uttered with a more recollected and devout mind, or because

---

[132] 1 Chr. 29:11a, 12a, 14b.   [133] 2 Cor. 9:7b.   [134] 1 Chr. 29:17a.

they signify the secret prayers of Christ, as when he would spend the night in prayer to God,[135] or when, having been torn from his disciples, he prayed the Father before his Passion.[136]

Now after the response AMEN is made to the priest, he adds: DOMINUS VOBISCUM. For at this time God's presence and the enlightenment of his grace are all the more necessary inasmuch as the things which remain to be done are more arduous. The priest, therefore, desiring to prepare the people for the divine mysteries by rousing them to divine praise, invites them to praise the Most High in the *Preface*, which begins with the words, VERE DIGNUM ET JUSTUM EST. First he says: SURSUM CORDA. For we cannot praise God sincerely and worthily unless we contemplate divine things, for which it is necessary to relinquish inferior and sensible things and to fix the eye of our mind on the consideration of divine matters. And this is especially required in the Mass service, especially at this point, because this Sacrament is totally divine, spiritual, and hidden. The response to the priest is: DIGNUM ET JUSTUM EST. May our mind and affection agree with our voice; may both the priest and the others there present busy themselves with considering the wisdom, mercy, and benefits of God, especially at this moment, and until the end of the Mass.

Now the priest, agreeing with the choir, repeats the same words, saying: VERE DIGNUM ET JUSTUM EST, AEQUUM ET SALUTARE, NOS TIBI SEMPER ET UBIQUE GRATIAS AGERE. He uses four adjectives which express why we should give thanks to God. For we are bound to give thanks to God: first, because it is fitting; second, because it is just; third, because it is right; fourth, because it is salutary. Now the difference between these four words is suggested by those words which follow: DOMINE SANCTE, PATER OMNIPOTENS, AETERNE DEUS, PER CHRISTUM DOMINUM NOSTRUM. It is fitting to treat each of these at greater length.

ARTICLE XV

On the meaning of the common Preface: Vere dignum et juſtum eſt.

Where were you when ... the morning stars praised me, and all the sons of God made a joyful melody? said the Almighty. Who can declare the order of the heavens, or who can make the harmony of

---

[135] Luke 6:12.   [136] Luke 22:41.

heaven to sleep?[137] This precisely is the perfection of heaven and the angelic life, and the sweetest refreshment and consolation in every affliction of this present dwelling: to busy oneself with, to take delight in, and to be enkindled by the praises of God. This (if I am not mistaken) is what that wise man tasted who said: *My soul shall praise the Lord even to death.*[138] And the divine David: *I will sing,* he said, *to my God as long as I shall be;*[139] and again: *Let my speech be acceptable to him: but I will take delight in the Lord.*[140] Now there are two reasons for praising God, namely, the very goodness of God considered in itself, and the benefits he has bestowed on us. The praise by which we praise the divine goodness in itself and for its own sake may be called glorification. But when we praise God for his benefits, it is called thanksgiving, to which the Apostle exhorts us: *In all things give thanks*; and the Psalmist: *Bless the Lord, O my soul, and never forget all he has done for you.*[141] Hence that illustrious Prophet, the blessed Isaiah, sings with exultant voice: *I will remember the tender mercies of the Lord, the praise of the Lord for all the things that the Lord has bestowed upon us, and for the multitude of his good things... which he has given us according to his kindness.*[142] And John says in Revelation: *We give you thanks, O Lord God Almighty, who are, and who was.*[143]

And so in the Preface, which is so called because it precedes the *Canon* in the manner of a prologue and has to be said before it, the priest, agreeing with the choir, says: VERE DIGNUM ET JUSTUM EST, AEQUUM ET SALUTARE, NOS TIBI SEMPER ET UBIQUE GRATIAS AGERE. There is one reason why it is fitting to give thanks to God, another reason why it is just, another why it is right, and another why it is salutary. These various reasons can be drawn from the four things which follow, namely: DOMINE SANCTE, PATER OMNIPOTENS, AETERNE DEUS, PER CHRISTUM DOMINUM NOSTRUM, which correspond to the aforesaid words. For because God is the holy Lord, it is right for us to give thanks to him; and because he is the Father almighty, it is just to give him thanks; and because he is the eternal God, it is therefore right to do so; and because he redeems us from death by his Son, it is therefore salutary, so it concludes with: *through Christ our Lord.*

Thus it is right for us to give thanks to God because of his universal dominion and government of all things, as we sing in the

---

[137] Job 38:4a, 7, 36. [138] Ecclus. 51:8. [139] Ps. 145:2b. [140] Ps. 103:34.
[141] 1 Thess. 5:18a; Ps. 102:2. [142] Is. 63:7. [143] Rev. 11:17a.

Psalm: *Let us come before his presence with thanksgiving; and make a joyful noise to him with psalms.* And why, unless it be that God is a great Lord, *and a great King above all gods?*[144] For our Lord says through Isaiah: *I the Lord, this is my name: I will not give my glory to another.*[145] Further, it is just for us to give thanks to God because he is our Father, to whom we say every day: *Our Father who art in heaven.* It is just for children to honor their parents; how much more just then to give honor and thanks to the heavenly Father, the almighty and holy Creator? For this reason, our Lord says through Malachi: *If I be a father, where is my honor? And if I be a master, where is my fear?*[146] It is also right for us to give thanks to God for his divine nature and infinite excellence; and that is why it adds: *eternal God.* This is also quite salutary, for ingratitude is the greatest sin. One can also say this in another way: that it is *fitting* for us to give thanks to God because of his majesty; *just*, because of the gifts of nature he has given; *right*, because of the benefits of grace, both general and special; *salutary*, because it is ordered to the promises: for the goods promised and prepared for us in heaven cannot be otherwise received unless we give thanks to God for the benefits we have already received.

Now we should give thanks to God the Father through Christ his Son, not in the sense that we must first and immediately give thanks to the Son and through him to the Father secondarily and mediately; but because we are created and re-created by the Son (for *all things were made by him, and without him was made nothing that was made*),[147] therefore we give thanks to the Father through the Son, inasmuch as we give thanks to the Father by whom and through whom we have received every good of nature and of grace. And we should understand what follows in a similar fashion.

PER QUEM MAJESTATEM TUAM LAUDANT ANGELI, *through whom angels praise your majesty*. In every statement in which one person is said to act or to work through another, the preposition "through (*per*)" signifies some kind of cause or principle. Therefore, since the Son is the cause of the gifts of nature and the benefits of grace in us and in the angels, we give thanks to the Father through the Son, and *through* him the *angels praise the majesty of God*, that is, they together praise his great power. DOMINATIONES, *Dominations*, that is, the angelic spirits who are first in the middle hierarchy, also adore the Father's majesty. POTESTATES, *Powers*

---

[144] Ps. 94:2–3.   [145] Is. 42:8.   [146] Mal. 1:6.   [147] John 1:3.

also, that is, the angels who are the lowest in the middle hierarchy according to Dionysius,[148] TREMUNT, *stand in awe*, that is, they honor with filial reverence and humble admiration and without any fear of punishment: for they do not fear being separated from God, since they have been confirmed in the good. COELI, *the Heavens*, that is, the Thrones, who are the lowest in the supreme hierarchy, COELORUMQUE VIRTUTES, *and the Powers of the heavens*, that is, the angelic spirits who are middle in the second hierarchy according to Dionysius,[149] with whom it is right to consent entirely in this, AC BEATA SERAPHIM, *and the blessed Seraphim*, that is, the angels of the first and highest order of the supreme hierarchy, SOCIA EXSULTATIONE CONCELEBRANT, *unite, exult, and celebrate*, that is, they venerate with shared joy and equal worship.

By the *Heavens* are understood the *heavenly Thrones*, for from the vantage of bodily creatures heaven is in a special sense called the seat (*sedes*) of God, according to that verse of Isaiah: *Heaven is my seat* (*sedes*), *and the earth my footstool*.[150] Thus, among the angelic spirits the *Thrones* are specially called the seats (*sedes*) of God, as it is written: *You have sat on the seat* (*sedes*) *who judges justice*.[151] For thrones in Greek (*throni*) are called seats (*sedes*) in Latin. Also, the angels who belong to the middle order of the second hierarchy, who are called *Powers*, are also called the *Powers of heaven*, as some think, because the motion of the heavenly bodies is caused by them. Nevertheless, by the word *Heavens* in this case can be taken to refer to all the heavenly citizens and spirits, especially those who are not expressly mentioned in the Preface, and yet who can be understood by the terms *Angels* and *Powers*. For all the heavenly spirits are called *Angels*, because all *are ministering spirits, sent to minister for* the elect.[152] They may also all be called *Powers*, according to Dionysius, because of their unfailing vigor and firmness of spirit, by which they are rendered efficacious and powerful in the execution of the divine services which are appropriate to their order.[153]

Therefore, with these blessed spirits, DEPRECAMUR, *we entreat* that our praise and prayer may be heard and received by God, SUPPLICI CONFESSIONE, *in supplicating confession*, that is, not with a presumptuous, but with a humble voice, DICENTES, *saying*: SANCTUS, SANCTUS, SANCTUS.

---

[148] *De Coelest. Hier.*, c. 8.
[149] Ibid.
[150] Is. 66:1a; Acts 7:49a.
[151] Ps. 9:5b.
[152] Heb. 1:14.
[153] *De Coelest. Hier.*, c. 11.

ARTICLE XVI

On the praise and the song of the heavenly spirits: Holy, Holy, Holy.

Bless the Lord, all you his angels: you that are mighty in strength.[154] The sweetly-sounding song which immediately follows the Preface appears to be taken from the words of Isaiah, where one reads of the Seraphim: *And they cried one to another, and said: Holy, holy, holy, the Lord God of hosts, all the earth is full of his glory;*[155] or certainly from that part of Revelation, where it is written: *They rested not day and night, saying: Holy, holy, holy, Lord God Almighty, etc.*[156]

This song, therefore, praises the divinity of our blessed God; and SANCTUS, *Holy* is said three times because in the most simple essence of the Godhead there is a most true trinity of Persons. And so *Holy* is said three times to honor the Trinity, because the whole Trinity is one God and one Lord. Therefore, it continues in the singular: DOMINUS DEUS SABBAOTH, *Lord God of Hosts.*

Moreover, what follows, PLENI SUNT COELI ET TERRA GLORIA TUA, *Heaven and earth are full of your glory*, can be understood in three ways. First, thus: *Heaven*, that is, the heavenly citizens, *and earth*, that is, believers dwelling on earth, *are full of your glory*, that is, clear knowledge of you. Hence the Prophet says: *The earth is filled with the knowledge of the Lord*, namely, according to the needs of its state, and in hope.[157] On the other hand, the blessed in the heavenly fatherland enjoy full, real knowledge of God through sight. Second, thus: *Heaven and earth*, that is, all creatures corporeal and incorporeal, *are full of your glory*, that is, divine majesty, as our Lord says through Jeremiah: *I fill heaven and earth.*[158] For God is in all things by essence, presence, and power. For he is uncircumscribable and truly immense, penetrating all things, containing all things, exceeding the entire universe, as Job puts it: *He is higher than heaven, and what will you do?... The measure of him is longer than the earth, and broader than the sea.*[159] Third, thus: *Heaven and earth are full of your glory*, that is, the divine perfection is reflected in all creatures, visible and invisible. For the wisdom, goodness, and power of the Creator is apparent in all things, in intellectual creatures in the mode of an image, and in inferior creatures in the mode of a vestige. Hence one reads in Ecclesiasticus: *The glory* of God *is in his work.*[160] In this splendor,

---

[154] Ps. 102:20a. [155] Is. 6:3. [156] Rev. 4:8b. [157] Is. 11:9.
[158] Jer. 23:24b. [159] Job 11:8a, 9. [160] Ecclus. 42:15b.

the magnitude of God's glory is reflected. It continues: HOSANNA IN EXCELSIS, *Hosanna in the highest,* that is, Save us, O Lord, so that we might be joined to the company of the Saints in heaven.[161]

Now in what follows, BENEDICTUS QUI VENIT IN NOMINE DOMINI, *Blessed is he who comes in the name of the Lord,* which is the song of the children going out to meet Christ on Palm Sunday, Christ is praised according to this assumed humanity.[162] The blessedness of his human nature is sung about in the Psalm: *You are beautiful above the sons of men: grace is poured abroad in your lips; therefore has God blessed you forever.*[163] And again: *For you have prevented him with blessings of sweetness.*[164] For Christ's humanity was filled eminently with all divine graces, without any previous merits on its part. Here again is repeated: HOSANNA IN EXCELSIS, *Hosanna in the highest.* For we beseech God for the salvation and glorification of our soul and body.

The Preface also, as is clear from the context of the words, is directed to God the Father. For it says: THROUGH CHRIST OUR LORD. Note that there are ten Prefaces, nine of which were ordered by Pope Gelasius; though Pope Pelagius compiled them together, as it were. The tenth, which is about the blessed and glorious Virgin, was written later by Pope Urban. And Pope Sixtus ordered that the *Sanctus* be sung at Mass.

ARTICLE XVII

On understanding the Preface of the superlatively holy Trinity: Qui cum unigenito Filio tuo, *etc.*

Whosoever shall glorify me, him will I glorify, says the Lord; *but they that despise me shall be despised.*[165] Confession is of three kinds. For there is the confession of one's own fault, which is an act of penitence, of which James says: *Confess your sins one to another: and pray one for another, that you may be saved.*[166] There is also a confession of divine praise, of which Christ speaks in the Gospel: *I confess to you, O Father, Lord of heaven and earth.*[167] And this confession is an act of latreutic homage (*latriae*). The third is the confession of beliefs, according to the Apostle: *With the heart we believe unto justice, but with the mouth confession is made unto salvation.*[168]

---

[161] Mark 11:10. [162] Mark 11:10; Matt. 21:9. [163] Ps. 44:3. [164] Ps. 20:4a.
[165] 1 Sam. 2:30b. [166] James 5:16a. [167] Matt. 11:25a. [168] Rom. 10:10.

And this confession is an act of faith. Now an act of faith is meritorious inasmuch as it falls under precept; and the more it is beyond reason and incomprehensible, the more its confession is meritorious. Since, therefore, the article of faith in the most blessed Trinity is not only the first among all articles of the faith, but also the most difficult and incomprehensible, therefore confession of the Trinity—both interiorly, which can be called contemplation, as well as exteriorly, which can be called vocal praise—is the most meritorious of all confessions of faith. And if the soul has been divinely enlightened and taught by the Lord so that it understands with a pure acuity of mind those things which pertain to the faith and praise of the Trinity, then such a confession enkindles a vehement love, and efficaciously excites devotion. Therefore, since the *Preface of the Trinity* is very beautiful, and for some persons quite difficult, it is expedient to focus a little on explaining it, for it cannot be read devoutly, and affectionately, and sweetly unless it is understood.

Now the meaning of this Preface up to that part, *who, together with your only-begotten Son*, is clear from the above.[169] Then, that which is said of the Father, QUI CUM UNIGENITO FILIO TUO ET SPIRITU SANCTO UNUS EST DEUS, UNUS ES DOMINUS, *Who together with your only-begotten Son and the Holy Spirit, are one God, one Lord*, does not contain any difficulty. For nothing in the Godhead makes for a real or personal distinction except a real and subsistent relation, such as paternity, filiation, or procession, according to Boethius's book *On the Trinity*. Though the word "lord" is said in relation to a servant, such a relation does not exist really in God, but only in a creature: for it is not God who has a real relationship with or dependence on creatures, but the contrary. Hence every relation which exists between God and creatures is, on the part of the creatures, real; but on the part of God it is only logical. Therefore, the three persons are *one God*, whom every creature serves at his pleasure. They are also *one God* because in such persons there is one undivided divinity, and the three persons are the one First Cause and one Creator of all things. And so the Father *with the Son* and *with the Holy Spirit* is one God, from whom all things flow and are dependent; and from whom they have whatever goodness they possess. There is also *one Lord*, in

---

[169] E.N. Denis is referring to the introductory part of the *Common Preface* that it is fitting, just, right, and salutary, which the Preface of the Holy Trinity shares in.

whose *dominion all things are placed*;[170] who has done *whatever he has pleased, in heaven* and *on earth*.[171]

What follows, NON IN UNIUS SINGULARITATE PERSONAE, SED IN UNIUS TRINITATE SUBSTANTIAE, *not in the oneness of a single person, but in the trinity of one substance*, is said against heretics. For Arius taught a trinity of substances or natures along with the trinity of persons. For he believed that the Son or the Holy Spirit were not true God, but rather mere creatures. Sabellius, on the other hand, taught the unity of the divine persons and the unity of the divine essence, asserting that the Father, Son, and Holy Spirit are one and the same person. For he did not admit a real and eternal generation or procession in God, holding that God is only called Father because he creates, and Son because of the incarnation, and Holy Spirit because he justifies men by pouring out grace upon them. Now Sabellius asserted that the Father became incarnate; hence, the Sabellians are called Patripassians because they said that the Father became incarnate and suffered. Macedonius, for his part, though believing in the divinity and consubstantiality of the Father and the Son, denied the divinity of the Holy Spirit, claiming that the Holy Spirit is a pure creature, less than and subservient to the Son, as Arius had said. For this reason, the Macedonians are called semi-Arians, because they partially embraced the heresy of Arius. All these exceedingly pernicious and false errors are brought to nothing by the aforesaid words. This is their sense: You, God, the Father, are, with the Son and the Holy Spirit, one God and one Lord, *not in the oneness of a single person*, that is, not so that just as you are one God and Lord with the Son and the Holy Spirit, so you are also one person with them, as if the Father, the Son, and the Holy Spirit were one single person, *but in the trinity of one substance*, that is, such that with the Son and the Holy Spirit you are one God and one Lord so that there is nevertheless a trinity of persons but who share one substance or nature. And so the phrase, *not in the oneness of a single person*, etc., means essentially: not in an identity of persons, but in an identity of essence. The following words declare this:

QUOD ENIM, *for what*, O God the Father, DE TUA GLORIA REVELANTE TE, CREDIMUS, *by your revelation we believe of your glory*, that is, of your essential perfection or excellence, HOC DE FILIO TUO, HOC DE SPIRITU TUO, HOC DE SPIRITU SANCTO,

---

[170] Esther 13:9a.   [171] Ps. 134:6.

SINE DIFFERENTIA DISTINCTIONIS[172] SENTIMUS, *the same do we believe of your Son, the same of the Holy Spirit, without difference or separation*, that is, without the separation or diversity of essence. For as we believe that the Father is eternal, immense, omnipotent, incomprehensible, adorable, superessential, absolutely perfect, and blessed with infinite happiness, so we believe of the Son and also of the Holy Spirit. For whatever absolutely belongs to the Father belongs to each person and is common to the whole Trinity. Hence it continues:

UT IN CONFESSIONE, *so that in confessing*, that is, with knowledge and praise, VERAE SEMPITERNAEQUE DEITATIS, ET IN PERSONIS PROPRIETAS, ET IN ESSENTIA UNITAS, ET IN MAJESTATE ADORETUR AEQUALITAS, *the true and eternal Godhead, in it distinction in persons, unity in essence, and equality in majesty should be adored*, that is, we must confess the true and eternal Godhead itself in such a way, *so that* it may be adored *in the persons*, that is, in adoring it their distinction may be worshipped and believed, that is, that which distinguishes one person from another, namely a real subsisting relation: For the Father is distinguished from the Son by paternity, and the Son from the Father by filiation, and the Holy Spirit from both by passive procession or spiration. It goes on: and the *unity in essence*, namely, is to be adored, for there is one essence in the Godhead; *and in majesty*, that is, in the great power of the divine persons *should be adored*, that is, believed and venerated adoringly, in *equality*. For whatever one person can do, the others can do, since each is called omnipotent; indeed, as the three persons share one nature in the three persons, so also their action is absolutely one, such as their act of understanding, to willing, creating, governing, etc.

It continues: QUAM, *which*, namely, the divine majesty, LAUDANT ANGELI ATQUE ARCHANGELI, CHERUBIM QUOQUE AC SERAPHIM, *the Angels and Archangels, with Cherubim and Seraphim praise*. These four orders—of which two, namely the Angels and Archangels, are the lowest in the last hierarchy, and the other two are the highest in the first hierarchy—are understood to include the five intermediate orders. QUI NON CESSANT, *who do not cease*, that is, they never cease, QUOTIDIE CLAMARE, *to exclaim daily*, that is, to praise with ardent affection, UNA VOCE DICENTES: SANCTUS, SANCTUS, SANCTUS, *with one voice saying,*

---

[172] E.N. Denis gives *distinctionis* instead of the received *discretionis*.

Holy, Holy, Holy. In the heavenly fatherland there is neither day or night, nor is the action of the Blessed measured by time, for it is aeviternal. Yet the angels are said not to rest day and night, but to cry out daily, *Holy, Holy, Holy,* because with an intellectual voice and internal praise they incessantly praise God for a duration or measure which includes all time, and which is called aeviternity, or at least a participated eternity.[173]

ARTICLE XVIII
On the explanation of the first part of the Canon, namely, Te igitur, etc.

Christ, in that he continues forever, has an everlasting priesthood whereby he is able also to save forever them that come to God by him, always living to make intercession for us.[174] As the author of the *Rationale* asserts, what we are trying to express by expounding the *Canon* seems of hardly any importance, because the tongue fails us and the mind is overcome. Nevertheless, what the Spirit of truth deigns to give should not be hidden. The word "Canon" means rule, because it is composed of rules made by Saints, and because by it the Sacrament of the altar is regularly confected. Now the Canon was not composed by one person, but part of it by the Apostle Peter and part by others. It is also said that, after Peter, Pope Gelasius I was principally responsible for arranging the Canon.

Now, the Canon begins: TE IGITUR, CLEMENTISSIME PATER, PER JESUS CHRISTUM, FILIUM TUUM, DOMINUM NOSTRUM, SUPPLICES ROGAMUS AC PETIMUS, *to you, therefore, most merciful Father, we imploringly entreat and beseech, through Jesus Christ, your Son, our Lord*: that is, because it is fitting and just for us to join the angels in giving thanks to you as Father and Lord; therefore, *O most merciful Father, we imploringly*, that is, humbly and with great affection, *entreat and beseech*, that is, we ask with mind and voice, or with body and soul, *you, through Jesus Christ, your Son, our Lord,* UTI ACCEPTA HABEAS, *that you may receive*, that is, that it might be pleasing to you, and not displeasing to you because of our imperfection, ET BENEDICAS, *and you may bless,* that is, that you may imbue them with grace and heavenly power and sanctify them by converting them into the Body and Blood of

---

[173] Rev. 4:8. [174] Heb. 7:24–25.

Christ, HAEC ✠ DONA, HAEC ✠ MUNERA, *these gifts, these presents*, that is, these material things we offer, namely, the bread and wine, which are called *gifts* because they are given us by God, and *presents* because through us they are sacrificed to God; HAEC ✠ SANCTA SACRIFICIA ILLIBATA, *these holy unblemished sacrifices*. These gifts are called *sacrifices* because they are offered to God; and they are also called *holy* in the same way the altar or temple is called holy, namely, because they are ordered towards something sacred, that is, towards the Body and Blood of Christ, into which they will be converted by supernatural transubstantiation. These gifts are also called *unblemished* because they must be literally pure and entire for the signification of, and the reverence due to, such a great sacrament; for the bread ought not be spotted nor the wine mixed, with more than a small amount of water; although the consecration can always take place in wheat bread and wine from the vine as long as their species or natural form remains. Or they are called *unblemished* in the same way they are called holy. These gifts are also called *holy* and *unblemished* because by the utterance of the sacred words and signs of the cross they are modified and as it were improved so that they become matters worthy to be converted into the Body and Blood of Christ. For if the vestments, the temple, and the vessels of the church are blessed and sanctified to be made apt instruments of divine worship, how much more reasonable is it to bless the bread and wine before the consecration to render them apt matter for the exceedingly marvelous and divine transubstantiation? Likewise, the matter of other sacraments is sanctified before their use, out of reverence for the sacrament, such as the water of baptism, the chrism, or the oil of the sick.

It continues: IN PRIMIS QUAE TIBI OFFERIMUS, *which we offer to you in the first place*, that is, *which* first and foremost *we offer to you*, PRO ECCLESIA TUA SANCTA CATHOLICA, *for your holy Catholic Church*, that is, for the whole Christian people. Indeed, the common good is to be preferred to the particular and private good; and therefore holy mother Church, that is, the leaders of our faith, namely, the holy Apostles, ordained that this sacrifice should be offered first and foremost *for* the *Church*, that is, the congregation of the all the faithful, *Catholic*, that is, universal, because it is gathered from every nation of men. The priest may, nevertheless, celebrate Mass for particular reasons and his own good, as devotion suggests or as necessity demands. For the fact that the sacrifice is for the whole Church is an institution of the holy Fathers, whose purpose was to mind the common good; but the priest, out of a special affection and choice, can offer this sacrifice for any pious end, directing his affection and intention to that which he especially desires to obtain from our Lord.

Then follows: QUAM, *which*, namely which Church, DIGNERIS PACIFICARE, *you may deign to grant her peace*, by removing disputes and discords, and by discouraging and casting down enemies of the faith, CUSTODIRE, *to guard*, that is to protect from evil and to preserve in the good, UNIRE, *to unite* by destroying heresies and schisms, ET REGERE, *and to rule*, that is, to direct to the ultimate end and eternal happiness. Now although we pray first and generally for the whole Christian people in the Mass, it is especially necessary to pray for the Supreme Pontiff and the pastor of one's own church, and thereafter for those among the Christian people who shine most illustriously or do good for many, or who defend and expound the faith by their wisdom, of whom is written in Daniel: *They that are learned shall shine as the brightness of the firmament: and they that instruct many to justice, as stars for all eternity.*[175] And therefore the Canon condescends to pray in a special way for such persons. For it adds: UNA CUM, *one*, that is, together with, FAMULO TUO, PAPA NOSTRO, ET ANTISTITE NOSTRO, *your servant, our Pope, and our overseer*, that is, our own bishop, who presides over us spiritually, ET REGE NOSTRO, *and our king*, that is, the Holy Roman emperor, who presides over the civil power, though the Pope boasts the plenitude of both powers; ET OMNIBUS ORTHODOXIS, *and all the orthodox*, that is, those whose faith is glorious or excellent, whose doctrine and life shine brightly in the Church militant. For just as such men do good for many people, so they become harmful to many if they lose grace and live carnally; and therefore, it is especially urgent to pray for them. The Canon goes on: ATQUE CATHOLICAE ET APOSTOLICAE FIDEI CULTORIBUS, *and all those keeping the Catholic and Apostolic faith*: for the Church prays for people who are faithful not only by their faith, but also by their works and in truth. For these, therefore, the priest prays especially, so that God the Father might deign to grant them peace, to guard, to unite, and to rule them.

---

[175] Dan. 12:3.

ARTICLE XIX
On a fuller elucidation of what came before.

Let my prayer be directed as incense in your sight.[176] As Wisdom states, *Every word of God is fire-tried.*[177] And David: *Your word is exceedingly on fire.*[178] So the words of the Canon cited above *blaze and overflow* with the fire of divine love: hence they must be recited with the most ardent affection of mind. Moreover, prayer ought to be ardent and humble, for *the Lord has heard the desire of the poor,*[179] that is, the burning affection of humble souls. For he who prays ardently should be very careful not to trust in or depend on his own merits. On the other hand, he who does not trust in his own merits, but prays humbly, must altogether avoid becoming timid or indolent in his prayers.

The Holy Spirit, who, of course, is the principal author of the Canon, incites us to such prayer when he sets two words at the outset of the Canon, the first of which enkindles love, namely, *Father*, and the other of which gives us confidence of being heard because of the goodness of the addressee, namely, CLEMENTISSIME, *most merciful*. And in order to signify and increase interior humility of heart, the priest bows before the altar when saying these words. He also makes three signs of the cross when he says, *these gifts, these presents, these holy unblemished sacrifices*, to indicate Christ's threefold crucifixion. For he was crucified by the tongues of the Jews which cried out, *Away with him, away with him: crucify him*; again, by the wicked sentence of the judge; thirdly, at the hands of the underlings who fastened him to the wood.[180] Or else they signify the three bitter punishments he endured for us. The first was when his most tender flesh was completely lacerated by scourges; the second, when his most noble head was pierced with the sharpest thorns; the third, when his hands and feet were pierced with hard nails.[181] Others say these signs of the cross are done because of Christ's threefold betrayal; for he was handed over by God the Father, by the traitor Judas, and by the Jews to Pilate.[182]

But it might be asked: since the sacrifice of the New Law is perfect, namely, the true Body and Blood of Christ that is offered for God's Church, how is it that *these gifts, these presents* are offered for

---

[176] Ps. 140:2a. [177] Prov. 30:5a. [178] Ps. 118:140a. [179] Ps. 9:117a.
[180] John 19:15, 16, 18. [181] John 19:1, 2, 18. [182] Rom. 8:32; Luke 22:48; Matt. 27:2.

the Church before the consecration? The answer is that we do not offer the bread and the wine for the Church simply, without qualification, and absolutely, or as the principally-and-finally-intended sacrifice, but in this respect and with this intention: that God's power may convert them into the Body and Blood of Christ, and so we might offer to the heavenly Father a perfect and holy Sacrament, namely, the Body and the Blood of his most beloved Son.

Further, although the celebrant should be as attentive and solicitous as possible during the entire office of the Mass, yet from the beginning of the Canon he ought to maintain a state of complete recollection, with his mind wholly intent on the divine, as far as human frailty can manage and the merciful Spirit deigns to bestow. And in order to deserve such a grace from God in this part of the Mass, he must live so well before and after the celebration that he may be found worthy to be visited, comforted, and enlightened. There is no better preparation for the celebration of Mass than if the priest endeavors to conduct himself through all his life as a worthy minister of so great a Sacrament.

ARTICLE XX

On the second part of the Canon, and how to commemorate those for whom one prays.

The Lord spoke to Moses saying: Thus shall you bless the children of Israel: The Lord bless you, and keep you; the Lord show his face to you, and have mercy on you, and give you peace.[183] As the Apostle states, *For he that loves his neighbor has fulfilled the law.*[184] But he who truly loves another devotes himself to acts of love. Therefore, since the Sacrament of the Altar is instituted for the salvation of the whole Church, we must pray during Mass for the living and the dead, and especially for those who are nearer and dearer to us or who have done us more good. For such persons, therefore, the priest prays, saying: MEMENTO, DOMINE, *Remember, O Lord,* namely, God the Father, to whom all the prayers of the Canon are directed, FAMULORUM FAMULARUMQUE TUARUM, *your servants and handmaids.* And then the priest speaks or thinks within himself the names of those for whom he wants to pray particularly. Now

---

[183] Num. 6:22–26 (I have not indicated missing text in Denis's quote with ellipses).
[184] Rom. 13:8b.

we say to God, *Remember, O Lord*, that is, bring to your mind, not because God can forget, but so that he might be as one remembering by recalling his mercy, lending aid in every tribulation and necessity, and granting the gifts of grace which are being requested from him.

But since the priest's mind should be chiefly focused on the divine and forsake sensible things when reciting the Canon, it seems strange here to commemorate men living in the flesh, since this sort of recollection often impedes contemplation and tends to induce mental wandering. And the answer to this is that the commemoration of the living here is reasonable; however, so that it does not impede devotion or induce distractions, it must be made cautiously, not dwelling on the consideration of persons or the circumstances or things relating to them; rather, when he comes to this commemoration the priest ought to fix the eyes of his heart vehemently on the contemplation of God, thinking about God in ways that most enkindle devotion and charity. In this fervor of mind, he should ardently pray God to hear his prayer for those whom he will name, reflecting only cursorily on these persons, yet praying intently and lovingly for the goods he asks for them.

So the priest can form his affection in this way or similarly: "O God, Father, eternal God, adorable, most sweet, immense, incomprehensible, etc., because of your infinite mercy, because of your paternal charity, because of your immense goodness, because of all your blessedness, because of your superessential perfection and universal sweetness, etc., hear and receive me, giving such and such grace to them for whom I pray to you." And then he silently names them, not unduly lingering when considering them. Or in this way: "O eternal Father, for the sake of your only-begotten Son, Jesus Christ, our Lord, for all his mysteries and benefits, for all those things which he did and endured for our salvation, for the Blessed Virgin Mary, and the prayers and merits of all the Saints, to the praise, glory, and reverence of the superlatively most Blessed Trinity, for all his goodness, charity, mercy, and fullness towards the entire human race, because of his infinite perfection, holiness, and glory, because of all his internal communication and emanation, because of his superlatively most blessed and eternal consistency, because of all his love, mutual insight, complacency, and enjoyment, and on account of every reason of his mutual love: save your universal Church, bring it unity, peace, and reformation in all things; suppress and convert the infidels; have mercy on all my neighbors, those committed to my care, and my benefactors, especially, to this one and that one, and to me give amendment of life and reformation in all things, and all the grace, virtue, and efficacy of this most blessed Sacrament." He should commemorate the dead in like manner, and say this prayer by internal allocution before receiving communion.[185]

Next in the Canon comes the following: ET OMNIUM CIRCUMSTANTIUM, QUORUM TIBI FIDES COGNITA EST, ET NOTA DEVOTIO, *and all gathered here, whose faith and devotion are known to you.* For God alone *searches hearts* and looks into the interior of the soul.[186] Accordingly, the priest prays specially for those who are present at the Mass. But sometimes there is no one standing around, except the one minister; but then the minister represents the person of the Church. Or by *all gathered here* may be understood not only those who are present locally, but also those who are spiritually present, who are pleased with the celebration of the divine mysteries, who are united to Christ through charity, and belong to his Mystical Body.

It continues: PRO QUIBUS TIBI OFFERIMUS, VEL QUI TIBI OFFERUNT HOC SACRIFICIUM LAUDIS, *on whose behalf we offer unto you, or who themselves offer unto you, this sacrifice of praise,* that is, this consecrated matter, in such a way that when the consecration is effected, we offer you a perfect Sacrament and consummate Sacrifice, which is the Body of Christ and his Blood. *Or who themselves offer unto you,* namely, *this sacrifice of praise,* can refer to the priests who are confecting the sacrament (for the priest must pray for himself and for other priests), or to those who are standing around, who offer this sacrifice of praise insofar as they cooperate with the offering priest by a consent of affection and their prayers, or have induced him or helped him to celebrate Mass.

Then the purpose of this offering is made clear: PRO SE, *for themselves,* that is, for his own person, SUISQUE OMNIBUS, *and for all who are theirs,* that is, for all his friends, relatives, or those committed to his care and also for the things which pertain to them, such as temporal goods. For which we must pray that God will preserve them, within reason. And this is explained further in the following words, which are nothing else but an exposition of the aforesaid: PRO REDEMPTIONE ANIMARUM SUARUM, PRO SPE SALUTIS ET

---

[185] E.N. That is, during the *Memento etiam,* later in the Canon.
[186] 1 Chr. 28:9a.

INCOLUMITATIS SUAE, TIBI[187] REDDUNT VOTA SUA AETERNO DEO, VIVO ET VERO; *for the redemption of their souls, for the hope of their salvation and safety, who offer their prayers unto you, the eternal God, the living and the true.* For by the fact that they *offer their prayers unto God,* that is, pour out their desires before him, *for the redemption of their souls,* that is, for the forgiveness of their sins, *for the hope of salvation,* that is, for the attainment of happiness (for here hope refers to the things hoped for), *and for their safety,* that is, bodily health insofar as it is expedient for the soul. Insofar as those standing around do these things, they are said to offer this sacrifice of praise *for themselves and for all who are theirs,* especially when they rely on the power of the Sacrament of the Altar, and not upon their own merits, to obtain these goods from God.

Finally, this Sacrifice is called *a sacrifice of praise* because by it praise is offered to God, insofar as his benefits are called to mind in a most special way at the Mass. Now although every divine Person is eternal God, and all three are but one eternal God, yet eternity is appropriated to the Father, since he alone is from no one, according to St. Hilary in the second book of *On the Trinity*: Eternity is in the Father, likeness in the image, and use in the gift.[188] Indeed, likeness, that is, perfect similitude and beauty, is in the image, that is, in the Son; but the use, that is, the communion of the Father and the Son, is in the gift, that is, in the Holy Spirit, who is the gift of both.

ARTICLE XXI
On the explanation of the third part of the Canon, namely: Communicantes, *etc.*

Let us now praise men of renown, and our fathers in their generation.[189] The priest, taking stock of his imperfection, and perceiving that his own merits are wanting, wishes to be helped by the merits of all the Saints, and yearns to participate in the common prayers and good works of the whole Church, saying in his own person and for those who are standing around him and offering with him, of whom he said, *on whose behalf we offer unto you, or who themselves offer unto you:*

---

[187] E.N. Denis gives "tibi" rather than the received "tibique."
[188] E.N. St. Hilary, *De Trinitate*, II, 1.   [189] Ecclus. 44:1.

COMMUNICANTES, *in communion*, that is, applying to ourselves the prayers and merits of the Saints and those pleasing to you. For all the elect are one Mystical Body, whose head is Christ; and therefore the prayers and merits of one redound to the benefit of others insofar as they are united to Christ. Now this union is accomplished by charity and grace. Therefore, whoever has charity and grace is in communion with all the Saints, that is, he is helped by, and participates in, their merits as Scripture attests: *I am a partaker with all them that fear you.*[190] The merits of the elect are also that much more fully communicated to us the more affectionately we are joined to them and the more generously we venerate them. Therefore, so that he may be more amply aided by the Saints' merits and prayers, the priest makes a special commemoration of them, saying: ET MEMORIAM VENERANTES, *venerating the memory*, that is, proceeding with veneration, or reverently calling to mind, IN PRIMIS, *first of all*, that is, first and foremost, GLORIOSAE SEMPER VIRGINIS MARIAE, GENETRICIS DEI ET DOMINI NOSTRI JESU CHRISTI, *the glorious and ever-Virgin Mary, Mother of God and our Lord Jesus Christ*. For she is the most beloved of God, all beautiful, and most worshipful of all the Saints. SED ET BEATORUM APOSTOLORUM AC MARTYRUM TUORUM PETRI ET PAULI, etc. *But also of your blessed Apostles and martyrs, Peter and Paul*, etc. Confessors are not mentioned here, because the Mass commemorates the mystery of Christ's Passion and Blood, and confessors did not die or shed their blood for Christ; secondly, because at the time the Canon was written, feasts of confessors were not celebrated in the Church. Rather, the Saints in the Canon are those who at that time were most revered by the Roman Pontiff. Now knowing the lives and sufferings of these Saints helps one to commemorate them more devoutly; otherwise, one's commemoration cannot be affective and perfect. And the Canon continues: ET OMNIUM SANCTORUM TUORUM, *and all your Saints*, namely, those whom we have not mentioned to avoid prolixity, though they are worthy of all honor and commemoration, QUORUM MERITIS PRECIBUSQUE CONCEDAS UT IN OMNIBUS, *through their merits and prayers may you grant that in all things*, most especially in this service and this present action, PROTECTIONIS TUAE MUNIAMUR AUXILIO, *we might be defended with the help of your protection*, that is, we might, by your grace, be defended from the snares of the enemy and from the distraction of perverse thoughts.

---

[190] Ps. 118:63a.

Now this commemoration of the Saints is very useful, as Job advises, saying: *Turn to some of the saints.*[191] For we read that Moses, Esdras, and Daniel were mindful of the holy Patriarchs in their prayers, saying to the Lord: *Remember your servants Abraham, Isaac, and Jacob.*[192] And Scripture says of Jeremiah: *This is a lover of his brethren, ... who prays much for the people of Israel.*[193] Hence we know that in the next life the Saints pray for the living, and for those especially who honor their memory.

But it might be asked whether the priest can add Saints to whom he has a particular devotion but who are not mentioned in the Canon. Some say that he can. But this does not seem reasonable. For a rule ought to be applied uniformly to everyone. And since the Canon is a rule, it is therefore not permissible to change it by addition or subtraction. However, Saints not mentioned in the Canon should be invoked before the celebration of Mass, or else in the Mass service itself, in votive collects before the Epistle, as is customary, and at proper times subsequently.[194]

ARTICLE XXII
On the fourth part of the Canon, namely:
Hanc igitur oblationem, *etc.*

Having a great high priest that has passed into the heavens, Jesus the Son of God ... let us go with confidence to the throne of grace.[195] The closer one approaches the words of consecration in the *Canon*, the more divine and devout the words one encounters become, and these must be said with greater relish of heart and warmer affection. In this fourth part of the *Canon*, the priest prays to God so:

HANC IGITUR OBLATIONEM, *therefore, this oblation*, that is, these gifts, these presents, as already stated, QUAESUMUS, DOMINE, UT PLACATUS, *we beseech you, O Lord, that appeased*, that is, forgetful of our evils, ACCIPIAS, *you may receive*, that is, you may take as acceptable and pleasing, not imputing our negligences and malice to us, nor despising our service, but converting this oblation or matter offered to you, into the Body and Blood of Christ, DIESQUE

---

[191] Job 5:1b.   [192] Deut. 9:27a; 2 Esdras 9:7; Dan. 3:35.   [193] 2 Macc. 15:14.
[194] E.N. In certain circumstances priests could say additional votive collects of their choosing, including of favored saints. The exact number of collects one could add was regulated by local rubrics. Each such collect had a matching Secret and Postcommunion.   [195] Heb. 4:14, 16.

NOSTROS, *and our days*, that is, our life and our daily works, IN TUA PACE DISPONAS, *dispose in your peace*, that is, rule in truth, order, and spiritual tranquility, dispelling discord, disturbances, and disputes, ATQUE AB AETERNA DAMNATIONE NOS ERIPI, ET IN ELECTORUM TUORUM JUBEAS GREGE NUMERARI, *and command us to be delivered from eternal damnation, and to be numbered in the flock of your elect*, that is, among the number of the saved, PER CHRISTUM DOMINUM NOSTRUM. AMEN. *Through Christ our Lord. Amen.*

Now it should be noted that in the Canon the offered matter, namely the wine and bread, is sometimes expressed in the plural—such as at the beginning of the Canon, where it says: *these gifts, these presents*, etc.—because of the different natures and accidental forms of the bread and wine. But sometimes it is expressed in the singular—as, when it states, *therefore, this oblation*—because it is ordained to the one perfect sacrament of the Eucharist.

ARTICLE XXIII
On the explanation of the fifth part of the Canon, namely:
Quam oblationem tu, Deus, in omnibus, *etc.*

Jesus, that he might sanctify the people ... suffered outside the gate: through him, therefore, let us offer the sacrifice of praise always to God.[196] In the prayer discussed just above, the priest prayed in general that the oblation might be received by God; here he elaborates, praying in particular for the things he wants to result from God's acceptance, saying:

QUAM OBLATIONEM, *which oblation*, that is, this offered matter, TU, DEUS, *do you, O God*, that is, heavenly Father, IN OMNIBUS, QUAESUMUS, BENE✱DICTAM, ADSCRI✱PTAM, RA✱TAM, RATIONABILEM ACCEPTABILEMQUE FACERE DIGNERIS, *deign, we beseech you, to make in all things blessed, approved, ratified, reasonable, and acceptable*. These five adjectives can be explained in manifold ways; but leaving all these aside, I will give the three explanations which seem better. Consider that in the Sacrament of the Altar there is something which is the sacrament only (*sacramentum tantum*), and something that is the reality and the sacrament (*res et sacramentum*), and also something that is the reality only (*res tantum*). Now a sacrament may be defined as a sign of a sacred thing. Before

---

[196] Heb. 13:12a, 15a.

the consecration, therefore, the bread and wine are a *sacramentum tantum*, because they are merely a sign of a sacred thing, namely of the Body and Blood of Christ into which they will be converted; but after the consecration the *accidents* of the bread and wine are the *sacramentum tantum*, for then the *substances* of the bread and wine do not remain, only their accidents, which take the place of the changed substance for the purposes of representation. Rather the Body and Blood of Christ are the *res et sacramentum*. For they are a sacrament, that is, a sacred sign of the unity of the Mystical Body (that is, the Church), which comes about by charity and the grace of the Holy Spirit, and they are the reality signified by the species of bread and wine. They are, I say, a sacred reality, containing grace in a much more excellent way than the other sacraments. Finally, the effect conferred by this Sacrament on those who worthily receive it, namely, sacramental grace, is the reality only (*res tantum*).

Therefore, the first way to explain the aforesaid words is to say they are about the *sacramentum tantum*, that is, the offered matter, the bread and the wine. For the most sacred words of the Canon give this matter a certain fittingness or spiritual virtue, so that it becomes apt and worthy to be transubstantiated or converted into the most excellent Body and Blood of God's Son. The priest therefore says: *which oblation, do you, O God, deign, we beseech you, to make blessed*, that is, cause to be holy and imbued with a spiritual power, in the same way that a vessel, a church building, and vestments are blessed and sanctified to make them apt instruments for divine service. It goes on: *in all things*, which some say refers to what precedes it, namely *you, O God*, so that it is understood in this sense: *Do you, O God in all things*, that is, do you, O God, who are present and working in all things. For God—since he is boundless and the first principal of all things—penetrates all things, and no created agent can do anything except by virtue of the First Agent, which is the glorious and mighty God. Hence the Apostle says: *For in him we live, and move, and are.*[197] But I think it is better to refer the words *in all things* to the word *blessed*, so that it reads in this sense: *Do you, O God, deign to make this oblation blessed in all things*, that is, so that it should be apt so that all the benefits and fruits of his sacrament may arise from it. For these benefits and fruits, that is, the effects of graces, stem from this oblation insofar as it is converted into the Body and Blood of Christ, which spiritually

---

[197] Acts 17:28a.

nourish, perfect, and repair a worthy recipient of the Sacrament of the Altar. Then follows: *approved*, that is, do you O God, the Father, deign to make this sacrifice *approved* (*adscriptam*), that is, recorded in the book of divine memory, namely, the approval of the divine judgment, the way that good works are said to be written in the book of life, that is, with divine approval, lest, not finding it pleasing, you should disregard our oblation. Or understand it thus: *approved*, that is, regarded among the sacrifices offered worthily and fruitfully to you by others, so that it may please you just as the offerings of the Saints please you. Deign also to make this oblation *ratified*, that is, efficacious, firm, and stable, *reasonable*, that is, suitable, so that it is fit to be converted into the Body and Blood of Christ, and *acceptable*, lest due to indisposition it should displease you, for although the bread can be converted into the Body of Christ without the solemnity of the Mass and these preliminary blessings and prayers, yet it is not fitting to do so; and if it is done in this way, the offering would not be acceptable to God on the part of the person doing the offering.

Secondly, the aforesaid sacred words may be taken with regard to the *res et sacramentum*, namely Christ's Body, or Christ himself, which is the *blessed, approved, ratified, reasonable, and acceptable* victim, so that it can be understood in this sense: *Do you, O God, deign to make this oblation blessed*, that is, deign to convert it into the Flesh and Blood of Christ, which are the blessed Victim, devoid of every stain of fault and adorned with every grace; *approved*, that is, deign to convert it into Christ's Flesh, which is *approved*, that is, inseparably and indelibly united with the Word of the Father in a personal union, and thereby written in a most excellent way in the book of life; *ratified*, that is, deign to convert it into the Flesh and Blood of Christ, which are the ratified Sacrament and the ratified Victim, that is firm and efficacious, lasting even in perpetuity, which no other sacrifice or more perfect sacrament shall follow. The sacrifices and sacraments of the Old Testament did not have this quality, since they ceased at the coming of Christ, when this sacrament was instituted at the Last Supper; *reasonable*, that is, deign to convert it into the Flesh and Blood of Christ, which are the *reasonable* oblation and victim, that is, appropriate and suitable to appease you—indeed, it is *reasonable* that God should be appeased by the oblation of such a worthy Victim; and *acceptable*, that is, deign to convert it into the Body and Blood of our Lord, which are the oblation most highly accepted, gratifying, and pleasing to God. But the Body and the Blood of Christ, as they are consecrated upon the altar, are not two sacraments, but one sacrament in a unity of integrity and perfection, because they are ordered to the same principal effect, that is, the spiritual refreshment of the soul, for which spiritual food and drink, that is, the Body and Blood of Christ, are necessary, as Christ asserts: *For my flesh is meat indeed, and my blood is drink indeed*,[198] not, to be sure, for the belly, but for the mind, which is spiritually nourished, strengthened, perfected, and brought to eternal happiness by this Sacrament.

Thirdly, the aforesaid words can be explained with reference to the *res tantum* in the Sacrament of the Altar, namely, the effect of this Sacrament, or sacramental grace, so that it is understood in this sense: *Deign, O Lord, O God, to make this oblation blessed in all things,* that is, let it be such as to draw your blessing upon us and obtain heavenly grace in all things, *approved,* that is, let it be such as to enroll us in the company of the elect and count us among those who are saved; *ratified,* that is, let it be such that by it we are established in all good in Christ, *reasonable,* that is, let it be such that by it we live lives not in a bestial manner, but reasonably and wisely, and *acceptable,* that is, let it be such that by it we might be pleasing to you.

Now the *Canon* continues: UT NOBIS COR✠PUS ET SAN✠GUIS FIAT, *that it might become for us the Body and Blood,* that is, deign to make this oblation blessed, approved, etc., so that this oblation *might become for us,* that is, for our salvation, for our daily progress, and for the cleansing of our vices and multiplication of all spiritual gifts, *the Body and Blood* DILECTISSIMI FILII TUI, DOMINI NOSTRI, JESU CHRISTI, *of your most beloved Son, our Lord, Jesus Christ.* For the Father loves the Son with an unbounded love, a love not experienced by any created soul. But, O eternal Father, O God of infinite kindness, would that I might be found worthy even for a moment to be moved in affection when I utter these words and be touched by you, so that I might have some small savor and taste of the ardor of charity with which you love your Son and are loved by him. Moreover, realize that God the Father loves Christ, his Only-Begotten, with an intense and infinite love, inasmuch as Christ is God; but insofar as he is man the Father does not love him with an absolutely infinite love, and neither is the Son in this respect infinitely good. Yet still, the Father loves Christ as man more

---

[198] John 6:56.

than the whole universe, visible and invisible, rational, and intellectual. Christ also, inasmuch as he is God, loves the Father with an unbounded love; and we must believe the same of the Holy Spirit. But inasmuch as he is man, his love for the Father is not infinite, but still greater and more ardent than that of all the present and future elect taken together. For the Father bestowed on Christ's manhood a good greater than the whole universe, for he united his humanity to his adorable Son in a personal union, so that the uncreated Son of God and the human nature assumed by the Word are the same person, such that, in the same personal being in which the Word of the Father eternally subsists, the human nature of Christ assumed by the Word always subsists and will subsist without end; and this gift eminently transcends all the gifts ever given to anyone else.

Now three crosses are made over the offered matter while the words *blessed, approved, ratified* are said, in honor of the superlatively holy and adorable Trinity, and also to suggest that the effect of these prayers will be granted to us by the all-blessed Trinity: for it is he who effects this ineffable conversion of the bread into the Body and the wine into the Blood of Christ and lavishes upon us justifying and sacramental grace. Also, two crosses are made at the words, *may become the Body and Blood,* to signify Christ's immolation on the Cross and the shedding of his Blood. Others assign many more reasons, but these are sufficient.

ARTICLE XXIV
What kind of devotion one ought to have in the Canon, especially at this point.

God is a spirit; and they that adore him, must adore him in spirit and in truth.[199] If the Prophet asserts, *Cursed be he that does the work of the Lord negligently,*[200] how much more cursed, indeed, how exceedingly cursed is he who handles this most divine Sacrament, this most heavenly mystery, this most salutary service of the Mass negligently, undevoutly, or irreverently? Assuredly, if the Apostle does not lie, he will be *guilty of the Body and Blood of the Lord.*[201] Just as it is most salutary to celebrate and take communion

---

[199] John 4:24.
[200] Jer. 48:10. E.N. Denis states "negligently," though the Sixto-Clementine Vulgate states "fraudulently."   [201] 1 Cor. 11:27b.

reverently and worthily, so is it most dangerous and also totally damnable to do it irreverently and negligently.

It should be observed, therefore, that according to Hugh of St. Victor and St. Thomas, devotion is of three kinds. The first is attention to the words, so that they are distinctly pronounced; the second, diligent attention to the meaning of the words; the third, when one fixes and locks the eyes of his heart on God. Now these three types of devotion are demanded for the worthy celebration of Mass, especially in the Canon, and most especially in this place and the part which follows, which contain the words of consecration. For the priest must utter the most holy words of the Canon distinctly, he must also attend to the meaning of the words with all his power, and he must direct all his contemplation principally and lovingly to God, recollecting, admiring, loving, praising, and embracing his benefits, banishing every vain image and driving off every distraction. For at the moment of the consecration and sacrifice to the Almighty Father he must stand with fear and reverence, and he should utter the most blessed words with ardent affection and internal relish. For as Basil says regarding that verse in the Psalm, *sing wisely*,[202] just as the bodily taste separates, consumes, and relishes each particle of food, so the mental taste of the intellect ought to distinctly utter and relish every word of the psalmody: how much more the words of the Mass and Canon, so that the priest may say with Jeremiah: *There came into my heart* the word of the Lord *as a burning fire shut up in my bones, and I was wearied, not being able to bear it?*[203]

ARTICLE XXV
On the elucidation of that holy part of the Canon, namely:
Qui pridie quam peteretur, *etc.*

Our *Lord Jesus* Christ, on *the night in which he was betrayed, took bread, and giving thanks, he blessed it.*[204] This part of the Canon is a history, that is, a narrative of an event. Now history is read most attentively, and considered most devoutly, when the very event which has happened is placed before the eyes of the heart, as if it had just happened, and what has come to pass is recalled as if it were now present. Hence, he who desires to meditate on the Passion of Christ

---

[202] Ps. 46:8. E.N. The reference is to the Rule of St. Basil, q. 110, PG 31, 1279–80.
[203] Jer. 20:9.   [204] 1 Cor. 11:23–24a; Matt. 26:26.

with affection and internal compassion should call it to mind as if it were taking place in his presence, using the power of his imagination to form similitudes of the events that took place as if they were present. In order to read this part of the Canon most devoutly, therefore, the priest should imagine the event that occurred, and look upon it as if present, thinking, namely, how Christ, sitting among his Apostles, instituted this most salutary sacrament. And let him say:

QUI, *who*, namely your most beloved Son, O heavenly Father, ACCEPIT PANEM, *took bread*, namely such as was used by the Jews at that time, that is to say, unleavened and wheaten, IN SANCTAS AC VENERABILES MANUS SUAS, *in his holy and venerable hands*, which never stretched out towards iniquity, and were most obedient instruments of the divine will, PRIDIE QUAM PATERETUR, *on the day before he suffered*, that is, the day just before his Passion, namely, Thursday, ET ELEVATIS OCULIS IN CAELUM, AD TE DEUM PATREM SUUM OMNIPOTENTEM, *and with eyes lifted up to heaven, unto you, God, his almighty Father*, demonstrating the magnitude and ardor of his love for your honor and our salvation, TIBI GRATIAS AGENS, *giving thanks to you*, that is, acknowledging that everything he had came from you, and attributing every good to you, BENE ✠ DIXIT, *he blessed* the bread with his divine power, FREGIT, *broke*, that is, divided it — not his consecrated body, of course, since it is indivisible in the sacrament, and preserved perfect and whole under every part of it. Rather, he broke the forms of the consecrated bread, namely, the dimensions or quantity remaining after the consecration, for the accidents of the bread and the wine whose substances are transubstantiated remain and retain their natural actions and qualities; DEDITQUE DISCIPULIS SUIS, DICENS; ACCIPITE ET MANDUCATE EX HOC OMNES: HOC EST ENIM CORPUS MEUM, *and gave it to his disciples, saying: Take this, all of you, and eat of it: for this is my Body*. But what did Christ refer to when he said *of it*? A part of his body? Of course not: for it was received whole by every one of his disciples. What, therefore, does he mean when he says *of it*, except that which is the subject of breaking? For the Body of Christ exists whole and entire in any portion of the converted bread's quantity. Rather, Christ consecrated his own Body under the whole bread, and divided its leftover quantity. And thus the disciples ate of it, namely, of the quantity of the consecrated bread: for each of them received a part of its quantity, and through that part truly partook in the whole Body of Christ.

ARTICLE XXVI
On the subject matter of this treatise.

As it is not good for a man to eat much honey, so he that is a searcher of majesty, shall be overwhelmed by glory.[205] When the soul is intensely occupied in the operation of one power, it is hindered from attending to the acts of its other powers. Accordingly, when the intellect ponders subtle and difficult matters, and strives immoderately or vigorously to understand or examine profound matters, it often renders the affection cold and undevout. But, in expounding upon the words of the Mass as devoutly as I was able, I had no intention to ask any questions or to bring up anything except those things which are able to excite the affection and increase devotion. Hence, though the parts of the Canon treated so far and those which follow raise an immense sea of difficult questions, I decided not to introduce such things in this small book, because it is not profitable to meditate or consider such things during Mass, namely the many wonderful things that take place in this Sacrament. Taking such things on an unshakable faith as being most certain, we should rather contemplate during the Mass service those things which can enkindle the affections, namely: the great charity of God, the great condescension and liberality of Christ, the great goodness, and similar benefits of our King and Savior; how he daily does so many great things for our salvation, that he deigns to be with us in this way, that he does not refuse to join himself to us so intimately, but indeed greatly desires it. Those subtler and more profound considerations of God's marvelous works in this Sacrament do not engender devotion, except perhaps in the greatly practiced, who can ingest solid food.[206]

ARTICLE XXVII
The solution of some useful questions about the present matter.

Every scribe instructed in the kingdom of heaven is like to a man that is a householder, who brings forth out of his treasure new things and old.[207] There can be many inquiries regarding the matter covered so far. The first regards the water which is mixed with the wine, and

---

[205] Prov. 25:27.   [206] Cf. Heb. 10:14a.   [207] Matt. 13:52.

what is to be thought about it. The answer according to Catholic teachers is that the addition of water is not of necessity in this sacrament; for the Blood of Christ can be confected from the wine without added water. Nevertheless, water is mixed with the wine, firstly, because the Church orders it, and second, because of its signification. For water, due to its abundance, signifies the people, regarding which the Psalmist says: *According to your highness, you have multiplied the children of men*; and the wise man [Solomon], who says: *Cast your bread upon the running waters*, that is, a people reduced to beggary and poverty.[208] Accordingly, water is added to the wine to signify that the people are joined to Christ by the Sacrament of Christ's Blood. And again, secondly, because blood and water gushed from the side of Christ wounded by the soldier's spear.[209] Thirdly, as Thomas opines, because Christ probably consecrated wine diluted with water because wines are very strong in the Holy Land and are usually tempered with water.[210] Moreover, according to Innocent, the water is absorbed by the wine, and is changed with the wine into the Blood of Christ; therefore, it must be mixed in very small quantities for safety's sake, because it is not proper to consecrate with cheap or weak wine, any more than it is proper to use spotted bread, because of the honor due this great sacrament.

Further, it can be asked whether Christ consecrated, broke, and gave his own body in the order in which it is narrated in the Canon and in the Gospels. Bypassing various opinions, the answer to this is that the Evangelists do not narrate the underlying events in the order in which they occurred; ultimately Thomas—and many others—concedes this, and those who hold this opinion affirm that when the Evangelists relate history they do not always observe the order in which the events occurred.[211] These people say that Christ consecrated by uttering these words, and he did not repeat them, but confected and determined the form of consecration at the same time. Hence, according to these people, the words of the Canon should be arranged thus: *With his eyes lifted up to heaven*, etc., *he blessed it, saying: This is my Body*; and then he gave it to his disciples.[212] This is the more general position.

Moreover, it might be asked what the word *this* (*hoc*) refers to in the phrase: *For this is my Body*. It cannot refer to the Body of

---

[208] Ps. 11:9; Eccl. 11:1. [209] John 19:34. [210] *Super Sent.*, lib. 4, d. 11, q. 2, a. 4.
[211] *Summa Theologiae*, IIIa, 1. 78, art. 1, q. 1, ad 1.
[212] Matt. 26:26; Mark 14:22; Luke 22:19; 1 Cor. 11:23–24.

Christ because it becomes present only after the recitation of the words; nor does it refer to the bread, because the bread is not the Body of Christ. The answer, according to Innocent, is that the word *this* refers to nothing: for he says that the words of consecration are said by the priest as a recitation, and are thus taken materially. And although this is a subtle and clear argument, yet the doctors generally hold the opposite opinion. So Thomas says that *this* refers to neither the Body of Christ nor the bread, but something contained under the appearances of the sacrament, which was bread before and afterwards becomes the Body of Christ: for the pronoun *this* signifies a substance without any quality, that is, something without any determinate property of its own.[213] Thus the words of consecration are not said only recitatively, but also significatively—indeed also effectively, according to Giles [of Rome]: for they effect what they signify. And this instrumental causality in the consecration of the Body and Blood of Christ is bestowed upon priests by the impression of the priestly character: for this power conferred by God is the priestly character itself. Others simply say that the word *this* signifies the Body of Christ, not present under these forms when these words are uttered, but at the completion of their utterance.

Also, there is the thorny question about the addition of words: for three words or phrases are added which are not reported by any of the Evangelists. In the consecration of the Body, the conjunction *for* (*enim*) is added; also, in the consecration of the Blood, the words *the Mystery of Faith*, and *of the eternal* (*Testament*), which are not to be found in the Gospel. Before the consecration, there is also added, *with eyes lifted up to heaven*, which are found in none of the Evangelists. The answer, according to Dionysius in the last chapter of the *Ecclesiastical Hierarchy*, is that the Evangelists in the Church's infancy did not want to reveal the sacramental forms to the public, to avoid the mockery of the infidels. For the Greeks laughed out loud when they heard that these words were used to consecrate the Body and Blood of Christ. Nevertheless, we must believe that all the words which are required for consecration were uttered by Christ and handed down to the Apostles, and came by way of them to those who followed them. Now this conjunction *for* is not part of the necessary form of the sacrament, but was added by order of the most blessed prince of the Apostles, Peter; hence, anyone who intentionally omitted it would sin grievously. *For* was

---

[213] *Summa Theologiae*, IIIa, q. 78, art. 5, co.

added to designate the continuation of the words of consecration with that which preceded them. And the words *with eyes lifted up to heaven to you, O God, the Father*, are said to have been added by Pope Alexander. For, according to Innocent, it is probable that Christ, who lifted his eyes to the Father at the resuscitation of Lazarus, also did so at the consecration of this incomprehensible sacrament.[214]

Further, it may be asked whether Christ gave his Body to Judas. And the answer according to Dionysius in the *Ecclesiastical Hierarchy* is that he did indeed,[215] and Augustine also supports this view.[216] For one ought not to expose a secret sinner. It is not therefore to be supposed that Christ gave his Body in the dipped morsel, but rather beforehand, to his other disciples, according to Augustine.[217] Hilary, however, holds the opposite. But in such matters we must stand rather with the determination of the most divine and most holy and theological Dionysius, Paul's most loving disciple and a most diligent inquirer into the truth received from the Apostles themselves or, in any case, from apostolic men of his day.

It may further be asked whether Christ received his own Body. And the answer is that as he deigned to be baptized, first doing and then teaching it, so it is believed that he received his own Body before handing it to his Apostles. The following poem speaks of this:

> *The King sits at table*
> *Girded with a group of twelve,*
> *He holds himself in his own hands*
> *He feeds them himself as food.*[218]

Again, it can be asked what kind of Body Christ gave his disciples. Pope Innocent says that many people raise this question, but few understand it. Note that the blessed in the heavenly fatherland are granted seven gifts: three of the soul, and four of the body. The gifts of the soul are fruition, possession, and vision; the gifts of the body are clarity, agility, impassibility, and subtlety.[219] Now it is certain that Christ's soul had the three aforesaid gifts from its creation, for Christ's manhood existed as a perfect *comprehensor* from the instant

---

[214] John 11:41. [215] E.N. *Ecclesiastical Hierarchy*, III, 3, 1, PG 3, 428.
[216] E.N. *Tract. In Ioan.* 62.
[217] E.N. I could not find the Augustinian source, but see *Summa Theologiae*, IIIa, q. 81, art. 1, co.
[218] E.N. This is quoted by St. Thomas in *Summa Theologiae*, IIIa, q. 81, art. 1.
[219] E.N. The endowments of the soul and body are sometimes called dowries. There are various ways of expressing them, as the *Summa* notes. *Summa Theologiae*, IIIa (Supp.), q. 95, art. 5, c.

of his conception. But regarding the corporal gifts there is diversity of opinion. Hugh of St. Victor, the Glorious Doctor, asserted that Christ assumed the four corporal gifts at different times in this life, namely, subtlety in his birth from the Virgin Mother, clarity at his Transfiguration, agility in walking on the sea, and impassibility in the consecration; hence, according to Hugh, Christ gave his disciples an impassible Body. But this position, insofar as impassibility is concerned, cannot stand. For he gave them the Body he had; and if the consecrated Body of Christ had been reserved in a pyx on Good Friday then either Christ would have died in the container or else contradictions would exist in the same object.[220] The answer is, therefore, that Christ gave his disciples the Body he then had, although under the sacramental species Christ has another mode of being, namely, one imperceptible to the senses.

Finally, it might be asked whether the Body and Blood of Christ are one sacrament or two. For it would seem that they are two sacraments since we say in the *Collect: May the sacraments which we have received purify us, O Lord.*[221] But if we say this, then there would not be seven sacraments, but eight. So the answer must be that there is one sacrament, not in a oneness of indivisibility, but of perfection, because they are ordered to the same perfect effect, namely, to the spiritual refreshment of the soul, for which spiritual food and drink are required, just as bodily food and drink are required for bodily refreshment.

ARTICLE XXVIII
The meaning of the seventh part of the Canon, namely:
Simili modo postquam caenatum est, etc.

The blood of Christ, who by the Holy Spirit offered himself unspotted unto God, shall cleanse our conscience from dead works, to serve the living God.[222] This part of the Canon is historical, describing how Christ consecrated his Blood from wine; accordingly, what

---

[220] E.N. Under Hugh's theory of bodily gifts, the Body sacramentally present in the container would remain impassible, which means it would not have suffered death (the separation of the soul), yet the Body of Christ in the sepulcher would be dead because body and soul were separated: hence the contradiction that the same Body would be with soul and without soul.

[221] E.N. The reference is to a Post-Communion prayer in the Roman Missal: *Purificent nos, quaesumus, Domine, sacramenta quae sumpsimus...*

[222] Heb. 9:14.

we said earlier about thinking or forming affections when reciting the preceding part of the Canon, which contains the consecration of the Body of Christ, holds for this part of the Canon as well.

It begins: SIMILI MODO, *in a like manner*, that is, as previously with regard to the bread, POSTQUAM CAENATUM EST, *after supper*, that is, after eating the paschal lamb, not at the end of the meal, as it would appear, since Matthew says: *While they were at supper, Jesus took bread*, and similarly afterwards, *the chalice*.[223] Indeed, as one gathers from the Gospel of John, Christ gave Judas a morsel after the institution of the Sacrament. For John said: *He* (that is, Judas), *therefore, having received the morsel, went out immediately*.[224] And yet Judas received the Body of Christ, as we have argued. Here, therefore, "supper" refers to eating the paschal lamb. Or else it says *after supper* because the meal was over in a manner of speaking, for frequently holy Scripture speaks about a part as if it were the whole.[225] Jesus ACCIPIENS ET HUNC PRAECLARUM CALICEM, *taking also this excellent chalice*, that is, his excellent chalice, which the priest's chalice signifies, or *this*, that is, a chalice similar in type or appearance, called excellent because it was found worthy to be handled by Christ and to be an instrument of this great divine conversion of wine into the Blood of Christ and a vessel of the most precious Blood; IN SANCTAS AC VENERABILES MANUS SUAS, ITEM TIBI GRATIAS AGENS, BENE✠DIXIT, *into his holy and venerable hands, and giving thanks to you, he blessed*—these words have already been expounded—DEDITQUE DISCIPULIS SUIS, DICENS, *and he gave to his disciples, saying*:

ACCIPITE ET BIBITE EX EO, *take and drink from it*, that is, from this chalice containing the Blood, OMNES, *all of you*. Judas, therefore, would appear to have drunk. HIC EST ENIM CALIX SANGUINIS MEI, *for this is the chalice of my Blood*. Here, the container is named to refer to its contents, so it is understood in this sense: This is my Blood presented in the chalice as a drink. And he says, *from the chalice of my blood* rather than *my blood*, because this sacrament is administered to the soul as a spiritual drink; and the word "blood" does not imply a drink, but "chalice" does. It continues: NOVI ET AETERNI TESTAMENTI, *of the new and eternal Testament*, that is, this is the chalice of my Blood by which the new

---

[223] Matt. 26:26–27.   [224] John 13:30.
[225] Matt. 26:27–28; Mark 14:23–24; Luke 22:20; 1 Cor. 11:25. E.N. He is speaking of the rhetorical figure of synecdoche.

and eternal Testament has been confirmed and inaugurated. For a testament is the final distribution or assignment of goods, coming into force upon the death of the testator.[226] Therefore, since Christ by the death and Blood of his Body gave us spiritual and heavenly goods, it is proper to call his faith and law the New Testament, confirmed by the death of Jesus Christ, the mediator between God and man. This Testament is also called new because it began at the Last Supper, and also because it wipes out the oldness of sin and brings in spiritual newness, inasmuch as it *renews our youth like the eagle's*, so that, according to the Apostle, we walk *in newness of life*.[227] This Testament of Christ is also called eternal not because it existed from eternity or from the beginning of the world—except in the divine predestination and mysterious prefiguration—but because it will never fail and no other testament will supplant it as the law of Christ supplanted and voided the Old Testament. It continues: MYSTERIUM FIDEI, *the mystery of faith,* that is, the most secret and hidden mystery in the Christian faith. For the Blood of Christ's existence under the form of wine is a very great secret, incomprehensible to every created intellect; indeed, according to Giles of Rome, even the holy angels are unable to understand it. Therefore, this sacrament of the Blood is a *mystery of faith* and an object of such faith, because faith revolves around this mystery as around an object: for it is by faith alone that we hold and believe that the Body and Blood of Christ is contained under these sensible forms. Then follows: QUI PRO VOBIS, *which for you,* namely the Apostles, ET PRO MULTIS, *and for many,* that is, for all the elect, EFFUNDETUR IN REMISSIONEM PECCATORUM, *shall be shed unto the remission of sins,* both original and actual.[228] Indeed the Blood of Christ was shed for all men insofar as its sufficiency is concerned; but insofar as its efficiency or efficaciousness is concerned, it was shed only for the predestined.

HAEC QUOTIESCUMQUE FECERITIS, IN ME MEMORIAM, *as often as you do these things, you shall do them in remembrance of me.* These words do not pertain to the form of consecration. Rather, with these or similar words Christ conferred upon his Apostles the sacrament of Orders, making them priests, and committed the performance of this mystery to them.

---

[226] Cf. Heb. 9:17.
[227] Ps. 102:5b; Rom. 6:4b.
[228] E.N. Recall that Denis regards this narrative in the Canon as historical.

ARTICLE XXIX
On the solution of some questions regarding what has been stated.

The Father of glory may give unto you the spirit of wisdom . . . in the knowledge of him, . . . so that you may know the hope of his calling.[229] Regarding the form of the consecration of Christ's Blood, doctors have various opinions. For Albert and Henry of Ghent affirm that these words—*For this is my Body*—suffice for the consecration of the Body of Christ; therefore, for the consecration of the Blood it suffices to say, *For this is the chalice of my Blood*. The words that follow, namely, *of the new and eternal Testament* up to *as often as you do these things*, they say are expository of the previous words. This is Albert's opinion in his Summa *On the Body of Christ*; however, he wrote the opposite in his commentary on the fourth book of the *Sentences*.[230] But Thomas and others assert that all these words are the form of consecration for the Blood, up to *as often as you do these things,* because the words *new and eternal testament,* etc., are determinations of the statement *this is the chalice of my blood,* and so they are necessary for the completion of the idea spoken. Whatever may be the truth of the matter, this second position is safer, and accords with the rite of the Church: for the chalice is not raised before these words: *as often as you do these things*. It could even be shown from the words of Pope Innocent that the first opinion is not authoritative. For when Innocent was asked by a certain archbishop why words recorded by none of the Evangelists were included in the formula for consecration of the Blood, in his answer he speaks to this question, suggesting that the added words are part of the form of consecration. Further, the Evangelists wrote not only the words, *This is the chalice of my blood*, but also many more, as explained in the Decretals.[231] And Giles of Rome, expounding on that Decretal of Innocent, came to the same conclusion.

Moreover, Peter of Tarentaise,[232] in his commentary on the fourth book of the *Sentences*, says he believes that the Blood of

---

[229] Eph. 1:17a, 18b.
[230] Dist. 8.
[231] E.N. A reference to Pope Innocent III's response to the inquiry by Archbishop John of Lyons, included in the corpus of canon law under the title *Cum Marthae* (Nov. 29, 1202). See Decretal. III, 41, 6; see also DS 782–83.
[232] E.N. Born Peter of Tarentaise (ca. 1225–1276), this Dominican friar was elected Pope in 1276, and took the name Innocent V, dying less than six months later.

Christ can be consecrated using the words recorded by any of the Evangelists. And it is clear that not every Evangelist wrote all the words of the formula: in fact, none of them wrote them all. Also, the Greeks truly consecrate, yet they do not use all these words. And thus it can be seen that these words are not all essential parts of the form of this consecration.

Also, it can be asked whether the Blood of Christ is contained under the forms of the consecrated bread, and similarly whether the Body of Christ is contained under the forms of the consecrated wine. The answer is that something is contained in this sacrament in two ways, namely: directly, that is, that which results from the conversion of the bread and the wine; and indirectly, or concomitantly, that is, that which is really conjoined to the result of the aforesaid conversion. Therefore, since the substance of the bread is directly converted into the Body of Christ, nothing is contained under the form of consecrated bread except the Body of Christ. But because the rational soul, the Blood, a proper quantity, its own more intrinsic accidents, and the divinity or person of the Word are really conjoined to the Body of Christ, therefore, indirectly or by natural concomitance and consequence, the Blood and the soul of Christ, and all its quantity, and the divinity or person of the Word exist under the appearances of the consecrated bread. And we must believe likewise about the existence of these things and of the Body under the appearances of the consecrated wine or Blood: for the Blood is contained directly under the form of the consecrated wine; but the Body, its quantity and quality, the soul, and the person of the Word are contained concomitantly.

Finally, the previously mentioned words, namely, *as often as you do these things*, are, as Bernard says, brimming with affection. They vehemently enkindle the faithful and true Christian mind and must be uttered by the celebrating priest with great devotion and mental relish. Alas! miserable is the priest who pronounces these words unmindful of the ineffable and extraordinary love and most bitter death of Christ, and runs through them without heartfelt affection. Truly, these words should be pondered, turned over in our minds, and cherished not only during the celebration of Mass, but as often as possible. Indeed, these words of Christ command us to celebrate Mass with actual devotion and diligent remembrance of divine benefits.

ARTICLE XXX
On the effects of this superlatively most worthy Sacrament.

Eat, O friends, and drink, and be inebriated, my dearly beloved.[233] *My flesh is meat indeed: and my blood is drink indeed*, says the Only-Begotten of God the Father.[234] Because this most divine Sacrament is the spiritual sustenance and refreshment of the soul, so whatever bodily food does in the body, this Sacrament of the Body of Christ does to the soul, unless man puts up an obstacle or impediment to grace by approaching unworthily or not keeping proper custody of himself. Therefore, as bodily food preserves and repairs the strength of the body, increases and perfects it in quantity, and also delights the taste, so the Sacrament of the Eucharist preserves virtues and grace in the soul, strengthening the person receiving to do good, and also restoring what has been lost, that is, the lost fervor of charity. It also increases the spiritual quantity of the soul, that is, its progress from virtue to virtue, eventually perfecting it. Moreover, it confers great delight on the internal taste of the person whose soul refuses to be consoled by external, base, and sensible things. Yet this delight, as far as its experiential perception, is not to be desired importunately, but entrusted to the dispensation of divine Wisdom and the immense mercy of Christ.

The first effect of this Sacrament is the bestowal, or perhaps better, the increase of grace. For as Baptism is ordered to the beginning of the spiritual life, which it accomplishes through the infusion of grace, so the Eucharist is directly ordered to the perfection of the spiritual life, which is effected by the increase of grace or greater fervor of charity. And because the increase of grace or fervor of charity consumes venial sins more perfectly as it grows stronger, therefore the second effect of this Sacrament is the remission of venial sins, even as regards to their temporal punishment, not necessarily all of it, but more or less in proportion to the intensity of charity. For although one mortal sin cannot be forgiven without another, one venial sin can be forgiven without another. Further, because grace which is strengthened or charity which is more enkindled detests, at least habitually and in general, all evil, and consequently completes and perfects contrition, accordingly, the third effect of this Sacrament is the remission of forgotten mortal sins, in part as regards their temporal punishment,

---

[233] Songs 5:1b.   [234] John 6:56.

but totally as regards their guilt. Again, because the Passion and the Blood of Jesus Christ opened the gates of the kingdom of heaven for us, therefore the fourth effect of this Sacrament is the attainment of glory or eternal life, inasmuch as by it we are made partakers in the merits of the Savior. For all the sacraments of the New Law, as Hugh of St. Victor says, are a sort of medicinal vessel by which the merits of Christ's Passion are communicated to, applied to, and joined to us.

From all this, it is apparent how fruitful, salubrious, and holy it is to celebrate Mass frequently and gladly, provided that one lives a good life. But in order to be worthy, the priest must live such a life. This is particularly the case for the religious priest, and most of all for those in the solitary life, such as the Carthusians, whose business it is not to hear worldly rumors, not to undertake mundane affairs, not to be anxious about many things, nor to be attached to anything temporal and pertaining to this world, but rather to recollect with a diligent heart, desire with a most ardent affection, and venerate and worship with all one's strength the one thing necessary.[235] And it is much more fruitful and divine for something living in this way to approach the Eucharist with ardent charity than if he abstains out of reverential fear or humility: indeed charity is impatient of separation. But one who does not yet live in this way, if he truly longs for a holy manner of life, can approach frequently with great confidence: for by this he will obtain the greatest grace, and more efficiently attain the perfection he desires. Also, all else being equal, by celebrating Mass he helps others — both the living and the dead — more than by not celebrating Mass. Hence Chrysostom states: So let us return from that table as lions breathing fire, having become terrible to the devil.[236] Nevertheless, there are some good men who, although they have a zeal for God and yearn for spiritual progress, yet when something adverse occurs, are not only tempted, but are not easily able to escape from that temptation: although reason resists, sensuality battles the judgment of reason long and fiercely, and disturbs the spirit. I am of the opinion that it is advisable for such persons to refrain for a time, lest the imagination distract the mind during the celebration of the Mass, and the thought of the inflicted injury or adversity disturb their devotion. Meanwhile, they must earnestly beseech Christ for a more stable grace, sincere tranquility, and preparedness for the Sacrament, lest abstinence from the most divine Sacrament become habitual rather than a brief delay.

---

[235] Luke 10:42.   [236] E.N. St. John Chrysostom, Homily 46 on the Gospel of John.

ARTICLE XXXI
Regarding that which is said during the consecration of the Blood—the Mystery of Faith; and the necessity of having a certain and firm faith in this Sacrament.

The weapons of our warfare are not carnal, but mighty to God... destroying every height that exalts itself against the knowledge of God, and bringing into captivity every understanding unto the obedience of Christ.[237] It is by no means a light thing to consent to the Catholic faith, although it transcends natural reason. For it must be believed for the sake of God alone, and we recognize something as revealed by God based on miraculous works of which only God is capable. Since, we know through the Christian faith, confirmed by miracles of God's infinite power that Jesus is the Christ promised in the Law and truly described in the Gospels, we must believe firmly without ambiguity, examination, or question all the words and acts which are narrated about him in the Gospel and believed by the holy Church.

This manner of knowing is glorious to God and most meritorious for us. For it is glorious to a prince if his word is simply believed without the security of an oath, pledge, or surety. Indeed, it is disgraceful to him if people do not have implicit faith in his word. In fact, it is irksome to any man of sufficient and known goodness if his word is not believed. How much more will it displease the supreme King and Ruler of the entire universe if his word is not believed without the assurance of reason, which the Gentiles seek, or the certainty of signs, which the Jews seek, according to the Apostle: *For the Jews require signs, and the Greeks seek after wisdom.*[238] Further, this way of knowing by faith is meritorious for us. For assenting to something *per se* knowable, or necessarily demonstrated, or evidently proved, or manifest to the senses lacks merit, since it is not free, but is, as it were, coerced. But assent by faith based on the authority of the revealing divine word alone is completely free; hence, it is also meritorious, more so the more readily the intellect consents, and the more incomprehensible the thing believed is.

It is said that Hippocrates and Pythagoras gave this rule to their disciples: that they should not presume to question their teachings but hold the authority of the teacher as equal to reason itself. For this reason, the Prophet Isaiah said: *If you will not believe, you*

---

[237] 2 Cor. 10:4–5.   [238] 1 Cor. 1:22.

will not understand.[239] This accords with the words of Aristotle: It behooves the learner, he said, to believe.[240] Therefore, the authority of Christ—who said of himself, *I am your Teacher and Lord* and again, *Do not call yourselves teachers, for one is your Teacher, Christ*—is, therefore, the Christian's highest and most certain reason.[241] Nevertheless unless we knew that Jesus was the Christ promised in the Law based on the sufficient testimony of the Scriptures and the miracles possible only to God, then it would be frivolous to believe the contents of the Christian faith. For in such a case there would be no reason why we should believe Christ rather than someone else, such as Muhammad, or the like.

Moreover, as Hilary says, we owe God this most of all: that every sense, tongue, and our life speak of him; and just as we have received from God all that we have and all that we are, so also we ought to subject ourselves to him totally and obey him. Since, therefore, we have not only our affection, but also our understanding from God, we ought to subject our intellect to God no less than our will and affections, obeying the divine understanding (which we do by contentedly believing by faith alone the words of God which exceed human reason). For the divine law has two parts: testimonies and commandments. Testimonies concern the intellect, commandments the affection. And we are bound to fulfill the commandments, just as we are bound to believe the testimonies.

Wherefore, although the Sacrament of the Altar is a most wonderful mystery of faith, that is, the most obscure kind of article in the Christian faith, because Christ testifies to this truth we must most firmly believe out of reverence for authority alone, and consent to what the Church believes about this Sacrament without any over-curious scrutiny. For since Christ loved God the Father and the whole human race with the most ardent charity, it was most reasonable for him to institute this Sacrament as a sacrifice and peace offering. For the daily celebration of this Sacrament gives infinite glory, honor, and praise to God because the benefits of the divine goodness are unceasingly recalled, our sins are laid bare, and mercy is requested from God thereby. But this sacrifice is most salubrious and most fruitful for us also, as has already been made clear [in the previous Article]. For what Christ did and endured

---

[239] Is. 7:9 (according to LXX).
[240] E.N. Aristotle, *Sophistical Refutations*, II, 2, 165b3.
[241] John 13:13; Matt. 23:8, 10.

for us once on the altar of the Cross to the honor and glory of the Father,[242] this he does in a certain manner daily in this Sacrament or mystery of faith. Moreover, because Christ loved us with such ardent charity, it was fitting that he should leave us a suitable and efficacious memorial and pledge of his love before he departed this world and ascended to the Father. And he could not leave a more precious and salubrious memorial than his own Body and Blood under this most hidden Sacrament. Now there are many other beautiful considerations which one could introduce on this subject, but to avoid prolixity, let these suffice.

ARTICLE XXXII
Declaration on the eighth part of the Canon, namely:
Unde et memores, Domine, etc.

From the rising of the sun even to the going down, my name is great among the Gentiles, and in every place there is sacrifice, and there is offered to my name a clean oblation ... says the Lord of hosts.[243] With these words the Prophet Malachi prophesied beautifully about the sacrifice of the New Law, which is the Sacrament of the Altar. Now, this part of the Canon contains the execution of our Savior's command. For immediately before it was said: *as often as you do these things, you shall do them in remembrance of me.* So that the priest may show himself to be Christ's obedient servant, therefore, he says to God the Father:

UNDE, *wherefore,* that is, because Christ your Son so instituted, O DOMINE, *O Lord,* heavenly Father, NOS TUI SERVI, *we your servants,* that is, we who perform the priestly office, SED ET PLEBS TUA SANCTA, *and likewise your holy people,* that is, the Christian people standing around, MEMORES TAM BEATAE PASSIONIS, NECNON ET AB INFERIS RESURRECTIONIS, *calling to mind the blessed passion, together with his resurrection from the lower world*: for the soul of Christ was with the fathers in limbo even up to the hour of the Resurrection, as sung in the Psalm, *Because you will not leave my soul in hell, nor will you give your holy one to see corruption;*[244] SED ET IN CAELOS GLORIOSAE ASCENSIONIS, EJUSDEM CHRISTI, FILII TUI, DOMINI NOSTRI, OFFERIMUS PRAECLARAE MAJESTATI TUAE, *and also his glorious ascension into heaven, we offer*

---

[242] Heb. 7:27.   [243] Mal. 1:11.   [244] Ps. 15:10.

the same Christ, your Son, our Lord, unto your excellent Majesty, that is, unto your most excellent dignity, DE TUIS DONIS, *of your gifts,* that is, which you have given us, AC DATIS, *and presents,* that is, which we have offered to you; or, as Innocent said, *of your gifts* refers to the produce or crops of this earth, from which the bread that is converted into the Body of Christ is made, but *presents* refers to the fruits of the tree, from which the wine that is converted into the Blood of Christ is pressed; HOSTIAM ✠ PURAM, HOSTIAM ✠ SANCTAM, HOSTIAM ✠ IMMACULATAM, *a pure victim, a holy victim, a spotless victim,* that is, the Sacrament of the Body and Blood of Christ, which is a *pure victim,* for it is devoid of all stain, and a *holy victim,* because it is full of all grace and holiness, a *spotless victim,* that is, an undefiled and truly sanctifying offering, which was not the case in the sacrifices of the Old Law, which were not able to *make the comers thereunto perfect,* as the Apostle attests.[245] Indeed, the priest offering them was *unclean until the evening,* and always had to wash himself;[246] PANEM ✠ SANCTUM VITAE AETERNAE, ET CALICEM ✠ SALUTIS PERPETUAE, *the holy bread of eternal life, and the chalice of everlasting salvation.* These words were explained earlier. For before, the Body and Blood of Christ were designated under the one name of Victim. But because this Victim contains two things, namely, the Body and Blood of the Savior, therefore these two things are enunciated distinctly in what follows: *the holy bread of eternal life,* that is, we offer you the Body of Christ, which is the bread and the viaticum of the soul by which we merit eternal life, *and the chalice of everlasting salvation,* that is, the Blood of Christ, by the shedding of which eternal salvation or heavenly happiness has been restored, prepared, and given to us.

Moreover, note that the victim is now called *pure, holy,* and *spotless* in a different sense than at the beginning of the Canon where it was called *These holy unblemished sacrifices.* For something is holy in three ways, namely, by essence, as our sublime God; by formal participation, as intellectual creatures, which alone are the subjects of holiness and of grace; and by ordination or relationship to the divine, as an altar or vestments, which are called holy because they are set aside for divine worship. Now a fourth way might be added, inasmuch as sacraments are said to be holy because they are sanctifying. In other words, something can be called holy by reason of its effect, and because it contains

---

[245] Heb. 10:1b.   [246] Num. 19:7, 8, 10; Lev. 16:26.

sanctifying grace in some way, though not according to complete being. Further, something is said to be holy by representation, and also by state or office. In the third way, the victim is said to be holy and unblemished before consecration, because it is ordered towards the Body and Blood of Christ. But after the consecration it is holy and unblemished in the second way, for the Flesh and Blood of Christ are truly holy and pure because of the united soul and divinity. For although the flesh is not the immediate subject of grace but rather the soul is, the flesh is still a mediate subject to grace since it is subjected to the soul, which is the proximate subject of grace and holiness. Likewise, the victim before the consecration is called bread because it has the true nature of bread; but after the consecration it is called bread by similitude or effect, for it spiritually nourishes, increases, strengthens, and delights. Again, *eternal life* and *everlasting salvation* are the same thing.

Now, three works of Christ are commemorated here, namely, the Passion, the memory of which inflames charity; the Resurrection, which strengthens faith; and the Ascension, which invigorates hope. For what we believe has been accomplished in Christ as our head, we hope will be accomplished in us. When the priest says these words, he should briefly, but not superficially, nay earnestly recall the Passion of Christ, with heartfelt compassion; and the Resurrection and the Ascension with mental exultation, contemplating mentally how he rose again from the enclosure of the tomb, the soul returning to the body from the limbo of hell, and how at the Ascension the clouds bore him up beyond the sight of the disciples.[247]

In addition, five crosses are made at the aforesaid words because of Christ's five wounds, or because he suffered most violently in all five senses.

ARTICLE XXXIII
The explanation of the ninth part of the Canon, namely:
Supra quae propitio ac sereno vultu, etc.

There shall be a firmament on the earth on the tops of mountains, above Lebanon shall be the fruit thereof.[248] In addition to the other places in which the divine David clearly spoke of the sacrifice of the New Law, he most beautifully prophesied the Sacrament of the

---
[247] Acts 1:9.   [248] Ps. 71:16a.

Body and Blood of Christ in the seventy-first Psalm: *There shall be*, it says, *a firmament on the earth on the tops of mountains.* This he says of the Messiah king, the Christ, to whom everybody asserts that this Psalm refers. It begins: *Give to the king your judgment, O God.*[249] And as this Psalm progresses, the holy Prophet manifestly speaks of the twofold nature of Christ: the divine, where it states, *His name continues before the sun,* and *All kinds of the earth shall adore him*; the human, where it states, *He shall come down like rain upon the fleece.* Therefore, regarding this king or Christ he adds: *There shall be a firmament on the earth on the tops of mountains.*[250] Here the Hebrew reads, according to Nicholas of Lyra: *There will be an abundance of grain on the earth on the tops of mountains,* that is, of priests, who are called mountains on account of their excellence. But the Chaldean translation, which is regarded as authentic among the Jews, has: *There will be a cake of wheat upon the earth.* Jerome's translation is: *There will be memorable wheat.* David, therefore, saw clearly in the Spirit how during the time of the New Law Christ had to be offered daily by true priests under the species of wheat or wheaten bread.

We have said that there are three things in the Sacrament of the Altar: the sacrament only (*sacramentum tantum*), the reality and the sacrament (*res et sacramentum*), and the reality only (*res tantum*), which is sacramental grace. Hence, in this part of the Canon, the priest prays to obtain this grace and the effect of this sacrament from the Lord, saying:

SUPRA QUAE, *upon which*, that is, upon these offered gifts, namely, the Body and Blood of Christ, PROPITIO, *with favorable*, that is, with merciful, kindly, and gentle, AC SERENO, *and gracious*, that is, merciful, VULTU, *countenance*, or attention, RESPICERE DIGNERIS, *deign to look*. The priest prays this, not because God the Father could possibly deign to look with anger or contempt at the Sacrament of the Altar, the Body and Blood of his only Son, or be disdainful that they are offered by us because of our wickedness. Therefore, the priest prays in order that God the Father might look kindly upon the one offering, and this is explained by the words which follow: For it continues: ET ACCEPTA HABERE, *and accept them*, that is, deign to receive them, SICUTI ACCEPTA HABERE DIGNATUS ES MUNERA PUERI TUI JUSTI ABEL, *as you did deign to accept the gifts of your just servant Abel*, who is called a child

---

[249] Ps. 71:1a.   [250] Ps. 71:17a, 11a, 6a, 16a.

(*puer*) here because of the innocence of his life, and just because he offered the sacrifice of the best firstlings of the flock, as told in Genesis;[251] ET SACRIFICIUM PATRIARCHAE NOSTRI ABRAHAE, *and the sacrifice of our patriarch Abraham*, who, according to the Apostle, is the father not only of the Jews, but of all believers,[252] whose sacrifices pleased God, especially when he was entirely ready to sacrifice his only son;[253] ET, *and* that sacrifice QUOD TIBI OBTULIT SUMMUS SACERDOS TUUS MELCHISEDECH, *which the high priest Melchisedech offered unto you*, who is God's high priest, not in the strictest sense, but relative to that time—for Christ's priesthood is not only more worthy than the Levitical priesthood, but also than the priesthood of Melchisedech, because both of them were figures of Christ's priesthood. It is clear, therefore, that the priest of the New Law prays not that the sacrifice or the Sacrament of the Altar be pleasing to God in the way the sacrifices of these three men were pleasing, because those sacrifices did not contain grace, nor were they pleasing to God except by reason of the devotion and merits of those offering them; but the sacrifice of the New Law, namely, the Sacrament of the Body and Blood of Christ, contains the plenitude of grace, and is acceptable to God in itself; and its offering is fruitful not merely by reason of the merits of the person offering it, but because of the dignity of the offering itself. Therefore, the priest prays that his offering, that is, the Sacrament of the Altar, may be pleasing to God not as regards to the matter itself or the thing offered, which is holy in itself and pleasing to God, but as regards the person offering it, so that his action and devotion may please God in the same way the devotion of the ancient fathers pleased him, and so also that he may be found worthy to obtain the effect and grace of this Sacrament.

Now these three men are mentioned here in order to give honor to the Trinity. Further, these three are placed here in preference to others. First, because of the excellence of their sanctity; second, because they and their sacrifices so evidently prefigured Christ. For what did the *firstlings* of Abel signify but that Christ, who is the *firstborn among many brethren*, offered himself?[254] And just as Cain killed Abel, so the Synagogue killed Christ.[255] Further, Melchisedech, who was *without genealogy*—not because he had no origin, but because Scripture does not express it, although the Jews claim

---

[251] Gen. 4:4. [252] Rom. 4:11. [253] Gen. 22:10.
[254] Gen. 4:4; Rom. 8:29; Heb. 7:27. [255] Gen. 4:8.

that he was a son of Noah who in Genesis is called Shem,[256] and that he lived until the time of Isaac—this Melchisedech prefigured Christ. For according to the Apostle, he was *likened unto the Son of God*, whose [divine] generation no man is able to declare.[257] But his sacrifice also most clearly pre-signified the sacrifice of Christ, because he offered God bread and the wine as an act of thanksgiving for the victory granted to Abraham, wherein he defeated five kings, and rescued his grandson Lot from their hands.[258] Abraham, who was himself a priest, for by the law of nature, the firstborn—at least those whose father had no son after them, and, as a consequence were only-begotten—were priests, is also deservedly mentioned. First, because the promise of the coming of Christ was principally made to Abraham; and again because the sacrifice whereby he was ready to offer his most dear son is a figure of the sacrifice by which God gave us all his only-begotten Son.

And now is added at the end of this part: SANCTUM SACRIFICIUM, IMMACULATAM HOSTIAM, *a holy sacrifice, an unspotted victim*, which is a reference to the sacrifice of the New Law, which is called a sacrifice insofar as it is offered to God, and a victim insofar as by it God is propitiated. This can also be a reference to the sacrifice of these patriarchs, which is called holy and unspotted, inasmuch as it was a figure of the true sacrifice, which is formally unspotted and holy, namely, the Sacrament of the Altar. And these last words were added by blessed Pope Leo.

ARTICLE XXXIV
The meaning of the tenth part of the Canon, namely:
Supplices te rogamus, omnipotens Deus, etc.

Behold a man, the Orient is his name; and he shall build a temple to the Lord, and ... he shall be a priest upon his throne, and the counsel of peace shall be between them both.[259] The Prophet Zechariah penned these weighty words about Christ. Now the Chaldaic translation states it this way: *Behold a man, his name is Messiah.* For Christ, who bore witness about himself, saying, *I am the light of the world*, is rightly called the Orient.[260] He then built a temple to the Lord, that is, the holy Catholic Church. He is also a priest

---

[256] Gen. 5:31. [257] Heb. 7:3; cf. Is. 53:8a: *Who shall declare his generation?*
[258] Gen. 14:14–16, 18. [259] Zech. 6:12a, 13a. [260] John 8:12.

according to the order of Melchisedech,[261] and by his sacrifice, wherein he offered himself, he made a counsel of peace between those two peoples, that is, the Gentiles and the Jews: for Christ is the *chief cornerstone, who has made both one*, for the Church is collected from the Gentiles and the Jews, both agreeing in one religion and one faith.[262] Now this Church is called the Mystical Body of Christ; the priest prays for it in this part of the Canon, saying: SUPPLICES TE ROGAMUS, *humbly we beseech you*, etc.

Now the *Rationale* says that these words are so profound that the human intellect can scarcely grasp them. Nevertheless, they must still be explained. When the priest prays this prayer, he bows down, for the humbling of the body corresponds to an internal humbling of mind; he also bows down with crossed hands,[263] to show that he praises and wishes to gain grace by the virtue and merit of Christ's Passion and Cross. For the words of Pope Innocent should be carefully considered: The words of the Canon, he said, pertain to the consecration and to the impetration of sacramental grace, but the signs remind us of history, for by them the priest represents the events of Christ's Passion. Therefore, the priest must so humble himself in mind and body as if nailed to Christ, as with the most affectionate devotion and the most profound affection he says:

OMNIPOTENS DEUS, *O Almighty God*, that is, O eternal Father, who *can do all things*, to whom nothing is impossible, indeed no word is difficult,[264] SUPPLICES, *humbly*, that is, lovingly and humbly, TE ROGAMUS, *we beseech you*, that is, I, a priest (and the Christian people in his person), implore you, JUBE HAEC PERFERRI PER MANUS SANCTI ANGELI TUI, *command these to be carried by the hands of your holy angel*.

In the third part of his *Summa Theologiae* and his commentary on the fourth book of the *Sentences*,[265] St. Thomas says that the priest's intention in this prayer is not that the Body and Blood of Christ be actually carried by the hand of an angel to the sublime altar of God, but the Mystical Body (signified by the true Body of Christ) or the prayers and wishes of his people—these things he asks to be represented to God by the angel, so that the angel offering our prayers,

---

[261] Heb. 5:6, 10.   [262] Eph. 2:20b, 14a.
[263] E.N. In the Carthusian rite, the celebrant bows down at the *Supplices* with crossed hands, with the right over the left (*cancellatis manibus, ut quod sinistra sit inferior*). See Archdale King, *Liturgies of the Religious Orders*, 51.
[264] Wis. 11:24a; cf. Luke 1:37; Jer. 32:17, 27.
[265] *Summa Theologiae*, IIIa, q. 83, art. 4, at 9; Sent. IV, dist. 13, in exposit. textus.

wishes, and worship to God will carry back grace and forgiveness to us. But others think that this prayer can also be understood and expounded with regard to the Sacrament of the Altar. For everything in this part of the Canon is spiritual and demands a spiritual explanation; because an angel does not have bodily hands, nor does he carry anything bodily with him from the altar towards heaven, since by nature it does not move locally as does a body. And just as he does not carry the Body and Blood of Christ with him substantially before the sight of God, neither does he carry the Mystical Body, that is, the Christian people, of which Christ is the head, nor the prayers and wishes of the priest and people, since these are accidents which do not move from one place to another without their subject.[266]

Therefore, just as an angel is said to carry our prayers and wishes before the divine presence or the sublime altar of God—inasmuch as he mentions our goods before God, praying for us and asking for the effect of our prayer, as the angel in the Acts of the Apostles said to Cornelius: *Your prayers and your alms are ascended for a memorial in the sight of God*,[267] though nothing is hidden from God—so is the angel said to carry the Body and Blood of Christ to the sublime altar of God. It is not that he lifts it and carries it with him substantially, rather he places this great Sacrament before God on our behalf as the most efficacious means of receiving the desired grace and extinguishing the divine indignation or anger, and thus recommending and recalling our sacrifice before God, he procures for us the fruitful effects of this Sacrament. Thus it is to be understood in this sense: *command these*, that is, the Body and Blood of Christ, and also these our prayers and wishes, *to be carried*, that is, to be transported, not substantially, but representatively, by means of commemoration and prayers, *by the hands of your holy angel*, that is, by the service of the angel that is believed to participate in the celebration of the divine mysteries. Indeed, according to Ambrose, the heavenly host is present, and according to Bernard, an army of angels is present. How reverently ought we to be at this time! Or else: *by the hands of your holy angel*, that is, by Christ himself, who is the *angel of great counsel*;[268] and who, according to the Apostle, *makes intercession for us*, especially since John states: *We have an advocate with the Father, Jesus Christ the just, and he is the propitiation for our sins.*[269] For as Christ is the

---

[266] Col. 1:18. [267] Acts 10:4a, 31. [268] Is. 9:6 (LXX).
[269] Rom. 8:34b; 1 John 2:1b–2a.

giver and the gift in this Sacrament (for he gives himself to us), so also is he the offering and the offerer because through him our sacrifice is made acceptable to God the Father, inasmuch as our good works are founded upon his merit.

It continues: IN SUBLIME ALTARE TUUM, *to your altar on high*, that is, in that empyreal heaven wherein you specially dwell, hold court, govern, and hear our petitions in a special way, and when the holy angels arrive there, they offer our prayers and good works to you IN CONSPECTU DIVINAE MAJESTATIS TUAE, *in the sight of your divine majesty*, that is, before your face, so that you deign to notice them and do not turn your countenance from us. Moreover, by *your altar on high* some understand Christ; and this is not surprising given that according to Ambrose the material temple is a figure of Christ. The priest therefore prays that his offering be carried by the hands of an angel *to your altar on high*, that is, to Christ, so that he may offer it to the Father, interceding for us, showing the Father his side and his wounds. UT QUOTQUOT SUMPSERIMUS, *that, as many of us have received*, either sacramentally or spiritually, such a great sacrifice, indeed the SACROSANCTUM FILII TUI COR ✠ PUS ET SAN ✠ GUINEM, EX HAC PARTICIPATIONE ALTARIS, *the most sacred Body and Blood of your Son, by the partaking of this altar,*[270] that is, which takes place on this altar, OMNI BENE ✠ DICTIONE COELESTI, *with all heavenly blessing*, that is, every divine gift by which we reach heavenly things, ET GRATIA, *and grace*, that is, the supernatural quality which is the immediate and first formal principle of the entire spiritual life, by which the soul's very essence is made acceptable to God, REPLEAMUR, *we may be filled*, being made blessed and holy in mind and body, *failing in nothing*, but abounding *in every good work*, until we reach our happy end, PER EUNDEM CHRISTUM DOMINUM NOSTRUM, *by the same Christ our Lord.*[271] AMEN.

ARTICLE XXXV
On the eleventh part of the Canon, namely:
Memento etiam, Domine, etc.

It is therefore a holy and wholesome thought to pray for the dead, that they may be loosed from sins.[272] Those who have died in

---

[270] E.N. The order is as in the Dionysian text, which departs from the Roman Canon.   [271] James 1:4b; 2 Cor. 9:8b.   [272] 2 Macc. 12:46.

grace belong to the Mystical Body of Christ, and therefore it is reasonable to pray for them at Mass. Now that which was said above about the memory of the living [in Article XX] can be inserted and applied here in this article; because it has already been said once, it need not be repeated. But we ought fervently to pray for the dead. First, because they cannot help themselves, since they are not in a state of meriting or demeriting. Second, because when they enter into bliss, they will faithfully pray for those by whose suffrages they were helped. Thirdly, because they have a double punishment, namely, of loss and of sense, and both of these are greater than all the punishment of the present life. Thus the priest says:

MEMENTO ETIAM, DOMINE, FAMULORUM FAMULARUMQUE TUARUM, *remember also, O Lord, your servants and handmaids*, for whom I am especially obliged to pray, QUI NOS PRAECESSERUNT CUM SIGNO FIDEI, *who have gone before us with the sign of faith*, that is, with the works of charity, which are the sign of faith: for *faith without works is dead*.[273] For others, one need not pray.[274] Or else: *with the sign of faith*, that is, with the baptismal character, which is the sign impressed upon the soul of the baptized in Baptism that adheres indelibly to him, and by which we distinguish the faithful from the unfaithful. ET DORMIUNT IN SOMNO PACIS, *and sleep in the sleep of peace*, that is, they rest from the restlessness and labors of the present life, awaiting *the blessed hope of the coming of the glory of the great God*.[275] IPSIS DOMINE, *to these O Lord*, to those, namely, for whom we especially pray, ET OMNIBUS IN CHRISTO QUIESCENTIBUS, *and all who rest in Christ*, that is, who died in God's grace, LOCUM REFRIGERII, LUCIS, ET PACIS, *a place of refreshment, light, and peace*, that is, the heavenly paradise, UT INDULGEAS, *that you may grant*, that is, kindly concede, DEPRECAMUR, *we beseech*, PER EUNDEM CHRISTUM DOMINUM NOSTRUM, *through the same Christ our Lord*. AMEN.

---

[273] James 2:26b.
[274] E.N. Those who have died without the "sign of faith" have died in mortal sin and are in hell and are not helped by our suffrages. Those in heaven do not need our suffrages. Hence, when it comes to the dead, it is only necessary or profitable to pray for those in Purgatory.   [275] Titus 2:13.

ARTICLE XXXVI
On the last part of the Canon, namely:
Nobis quoque peccatoribus, etc.

For what is a man advantaged, if he gain the whole world, and lose himself, and cast away himself?[276] This being so, the priest should not be so solicitous in praying for others so that he forgets himself and those around him. Hence, praying for them he says: NOBIS QUOQUE PECCATORIBUS, FAMULUS TUIS, *to us sinners also, your servants.* And when he says this, he strikes his chest, representing the centurion and those who saw the marvelous things which occurred in the Passion, who *returned striking their breasts*;[277] or representing that Christ deigned to die for the ungodly; or it is to reprove his sins and those of the ministers gathered around him — indeed, according to Augustine, what else does it mean to beat one's breast except to declare the sin that lies within? DE MULTITUDINE MISERATIONUM TUARUM SPERANTIBUS, *who hope in the multitude of your mercies*: for we do not trust in our own merits, *nor in our own justifications do we present our prayers*;[278] PARTEM ALIQUAM ET SOCIETATEM DONARE DIGNERIS, *deign to grant some part and fellowship*: for in the Father's house there are many and diverse mansions,[279] that is, there is a difference of rewards according to our merits. For the blessed are not equal in the vision of God, which is the essential reward, nor are they equal in accidental rewards. Accordingly, the priest, reflecting on the smallness of his merits, humbly says: *deign to grant*, after the exile of this life, *some part*, even a small one, CUM SANCTIS TUIS, *with your Saints*, etc. The name John is mentioned here; According to some, this is John the Baptist, who was not mentioned earlier and is equal to the Apostles, or else John the Evangelist, whose name is repeated here because he was not only an Apostle, but also an Evangelist and a virgin. Further, Stephen is placed before the Apostles Matthias and Barnabas, either because he was a virgin (according to some), or because he was the first martyr. INTRA QUORUM, *into whose*, namely, the aforesaid Saints, CONSORTIUM, QUAESUMUS, ADMITTE NOS, *company, we beseech you to admit us*, giving us grace in the present and glory in the future, NON AESTIMATOR MERITI, *not weighing our merits*, that is, not doing to us according to our sins

---

[276] Luke 9:25. [277] Luke 23:47-48. [278] Dan. 9:18b. [279] Cf. John 14:2a.

or according to the imperfection of the good things which we do, SED VENIAE LARGITOR, *but granting us pardon*. For God rewards good more than it deserves and punishes evil less than it deserves, proving what is said: *His tender mercies are over all his works*.[280] PER CHRISTUM DOMINUM NOSTRUM, *through Christ our Lord*.

PER QUEM HAEC OMNIA, *By whom all these things*, namely, the bread, the wine, and the water, CREAS, *you do create*. For all things were created through the Son.[281] Or else: *you do create*, that is, you have created, giving them natural existence, and God also created the Body and Blood of Christ in this way. SANCTI✠FICAS, VIVI✠FICAS, BENE✠DICIS, *you sanctify, vivify, bless*. These words can be explained in two ways. First, by referring *these things* to the Sacrament of the Altar, into which the bread and wine have been converted. Therefore, seeing as the Body of Christ is holy and blessed, the fact that God the Father has converted *these things* into the Body and Blood of Christ means that he has sanctified, vivified, and blessed them. Secondly, they can be referred to various other things, so that the meaning is: *All these things you sanctify*, for you convert them into the Body and Blood of Christ, *you vivify*, that is, you work and confer spiritual life upon us through them, *you bless*, that is, through them you multiply the abundance of divine gifts in us. ET PRAESTAS NOBIS, *and bestow upon us*, so that we might sacramentally and spiritually consume them.

PER IP✠SUM ET CUM IP✠SO ET IN IP✠SO, *through him and with him, and in him*, etc. The meaning is: OMNIS HONOR, *all honor*, that is, all true ordered display of reverence, ET GLORIA, *and glory*, that is, widespread fame joined with praise and joy, EST TIBI DEO PATRI OMNIPOTENTI, IN UNITATE SPIRITUS SANCTI, *is unto to you, God the Father Almighty, in the unity of the Holy Spirit*, that is, together with the Holy Spirit who is consubstantial to you, *through him*, that is, through Christ your Son; for he has manifested his name among men, and taught the law of perfection by word and deed, and by following him the faithful honor you, God;[282] *and with him*, because the Son is not to be separated from the Father, but venerated together with him. For this reason, the Son himself said: *He that honors not the Son honors not the Father who has sent him*.[283] Now the honor shown to one Person is, at least implicitly, offered to the whole adorable Trinity. And *in him*, that is, all honor and glory is to you, the Father, and the Holy Spirit, or

---

[280] Ps. 144:9. [281] John 1:3. [282] Cf. John 17:6a; Acts 1:1b. [283] John 5:23b.

in the unity of the Holy Spirit, in your Son, because everyone who truly knows the Son of God glorifies and honors God the Father from the very fact of that knowledge, as it is written: *A wise son is the glory of his father.*[284] Some refer *through him and with him and in him* to the preceding words, namely, *you bless and bestow*, but this is less proper.

Finally, different reasons have been given as to why six crosses are made here. Three crosses are made when the words *sanctify, vivify, bless* are said, to designate that Christ was crucified at the third hour by the tongues of the priests, the Pharisees, and the people. And because the crucifixion lasted for three hours ending at the sixth hour, hence three crosses are made when it is said *through him, and with him, and in him.*

ARTICLE XXXVII
On the Lord's Prayer and its prologue.

We know that whatever we ask the Father in the name of the Son, he will give to us.[285] Gregory instituted that the Lord's Prayer be said in a loud voice immediately after the Canon, because of its efficacy, and the venerableness of its author, namely Christ, who taught it with his own mouth. Gregory also placed a certain prologue or preface before it, namely: PRAECEPTIS SALUTARIBUS MONITI, ET DIVINA INSTITUTIONE FORMATI, AUDEMUS DICERE, *instructed by your saving precepts, and formed by the divine instruction, we dare to say.* And its meaning is this: O Lord, *instructed*, that is, admonished or exhorted, *by your saving precepts*, that is, by Christ's saving commandments—for in the Gospel Christ often exhorts his disciples to pray;[286] *and formed by the divine instruction*, that is, taught by Christ's instruction, *we dare*, not out of pride, but from great filial confidence, *to say*:

PATER NOSTER QUI ES IN CAELIS, *our Father who art in heaven.*[287] Although this prayer is commonly addressed to the whole Trinity, which is one God and our Father by reason of creation and justification, nature and grace (for nature and grace come to us from the triune God), yet in the Mass it is specially directed

---

[284] Prov. 10:1. This reading departs from the Sixto-Clementine Vulgate, which reads, "a wise son makes the father glad."   [285] Cf. 1 John 5:15; John 16:23.
[286] Matt. 6:6; 26:41; Luke 18:1; etc.   [287] Matt. 6:9–13; Luke 11:2–4.

to the Father, as are the preceding prayers in the Canon, and the prayer that immediately follows it. Now this prayer is supremely perfect, according to Augustine in his book *On Praying to God, written to Proba*,[288] because it includes not only those things we should ask God for, but also puts them in the proper order of asking. For we must ask for those things which it is licit to desire, and it is fitting to ask first for those things which should be first and principally desired. Moreover, just as we are bound to love God first and foremost, so first of all ought we to pray for those things which pertain to the reverence of God. Therefore, the first part of the Lord's Prayer asks that honor may be paid to God by all men, when it says: SANCTIFICETUR NOMEN TUUM, *hallowed be thy name*, that is, be it regarded as holy by all men, and let your holiness be known by all men, so that all men may *serve you in holiness*. Second, we should ask for eternal happiness; and this we pray for when we say: ADVENIAT REGNUM TUUM, *thy kingdom come*, that is, let the number of the elect in heaven be completed, and *let the walls of the heavenly Jerusalem, which is our mother* and the Church triumphant, *be built*, so that we might be led towards and reach this kingdom.[289] This can also be understood as referring to the kingdom of the Church militant, which we also ask to reach heaven, that is, that its faithful may daily increase in perfection, number, and merit. But because no one reaches the kingdom of heaven unless he obeys God's commandments, thirdly, therefore, we should desire the grace to obey the divine precepts; and we pray for this by saying: FIAT VOLUNTAS TUA SICUT IN COELO ET IN TERRA, *thy will be done on earth as it is in heaven*, that is, as the holy angels obey you in heaven at your will, so may we obey you in all things on earth.

But because the soul needs the body in divine worship, therefore, we ask fourthly for the support of the body, that is, for all things which we need in this mortal life for the sustainment of the body, saying: PANEM NOSTRUM QUOTIDIANUM DA NOBIS HODIE, *give us this day our daily bread*. Nevertheless, priests, especially at Mass, should understand this particular part of the Lord's Prayer as referring to the heavenly bread, which is the Lord's Body. Hence in the Gospel according to Matthew it states: *Give us this day our supersubstantial* (or in Jerome's translation, "principal") *bread*,[290]

---

[288] E.N. Letter 130 to Proba, 11, 21, PL 33, 502.
[289] Cf. Ps. 50:20; Gal. 4:26.   [290] Matt. 6:11.

so that we might worthily receive this bread from your altar, O heavenly Father, so we might receive it with all reverence as if from your hand.

But because the impediments to these good things we have just asked for are three in number, namely, our own guilt, diabolical temptation, and the various punishments of the present life, which often engender sloth (*acedia*) in the soul, therefore we pray for the removal of these three evils in the three parts which follow, namely: ET DIMITTE NOBIS DEBITA NOSTRA, *and forgive us our debts*, etc. Now we pray that we not be led IN TENTATIONEM, *into temptation*, that is, to consent to temptation, but that we be given the power to efficaciously resist all temptations.

I omit an exposition of the Lord's prayer, since it may be found expounded fully in other books. Yet it is to be said at Mass with singular and supreme devotion, where Christ, its author, is so condescendingly and wonderfully and most truly present; and whoever says it in this way during Mass receives ineffable fruit.

This prayer, and also the following one, which expounds the last part of this prayer, are ordered to the devout and worthy perception of the Sacrament. But the prayer which follows, LIBERA NOS, QUAESUMUS, DOMINE, AB OMNIBUS MALIS, *deliver us, we beseech you, O Lord, from every evil*, etc., does not contain any difficulties in meaning. For the priest asks to be delivered by God's mercy from all evil and vice, past, present, and future. Then he requests peace from our Lord, through the intercession of the most worthy Virgin and of the Saints whom he names, UT OPE, *that through the assistance*, that is, through the help of your divine kindness, ADIUTI, ET A PECCATO SIMUS SEMPER LIBERI, *we may be aided, and be always delivered from sin*, not obeying the will of the devil, the flesh, or the world, ET OMNI PERTURBATIONE SECURE, *but safe from all disturbance*, both interior and exterior, and so that we do not fear the tribulations and disturbances which may raise up against us in the future or which exist presently more than right reason demands or is pleasing to God. Now the closer the priest approaches sacred communion, the more fearfully, reverently, and recollectedly must he conduct himself in his prayers, signs, and gestures, so that he may truly judge, that is, worthily discern, the Lord's Body from other foods and eat it.[291]

---

[291] E.N. Cf. 1 Cor. 11:29.

ARTICLE XXXVIII
From the Communion to the last part of the Mass.

I am the living bread which came down from heaven; if any man eat of this bread, he shall live forever.[292] After the preceding prayers, the *Agnus Dei* is said, by institution of Pope Sergius; and it is said three times against three vices, namely of the heart, of the mouth, and of deed, or else to the glory of the blessed Trinity. Now the host is divided because Christ also blessed and broke the bread.[293] But it is divided into three parts to designate the three states of the Mystical Body or the faithful people, namely the state of the Church triumphant, militant, and suffering in Purgatory. Also, according to some, the part which is put into the chalice signifies the Church triumphant, which is *intoxicated by the torrent of* the divine *pleasure*;[294] but according to others it is a figure of those who are afflicted in Purgatory, who are filled with the waters of tribulation.

Then the priest takes communion, which he must receive with great affection and the utmost reverence, not hurrying, but recalling most ardently the benefits of Christ, that is to say, his Incarnation, Passion, and love towards us, the great condescension and liberality with which he deigns to be with us and to be received by us in this way. Also, he should speak confidently to Christ, and intimately implore him for those things which he most ardently desires to obtain from him, both for himself as well as those dearest to him, imploring Christ that he might be made worthy to convert and be steadfast and always find strength in him. And it is safe to take not exceedingly little, but a relatively significant amount of wine after drinking the Blood, lest some of the species of the Sacrament adhere to some parts of the mouth.[295] And it is not proper to expectorate immediately after Communion, but to remain in custody and modesty in both mind and body in all things; and he should not be less solicitous to hold Christ gratefully than he had been before to receive him worthily. Hence, they who after communion and the end of Mass so promptly leave and become occupied in external things, unless necessity requires it, would appear to be very worthy of censure.

---

[292] John 6:51–52a.   [293] Matt. 26:26.   [294] Ps. 35:9b.
[295] E.N. This is a reference to the practice of washing one's mouth with unconsecrated wine after Communion, known as ablution. The practice persists in some Orthodox and Byzantine Rite Catholic Churches, and is known as *zapivka*.

ARTICLE XXXIX
On the last part of the Mass, namely, thanksgiving.

In all things give thanks to God through his Son, Jesus Christ.[296] Because the celebration of Mass is a divine and perfect work, it is fitting that as it begins with God so it ought to conclude in him; and therefore, the last part of the Mass is called thanksgiving. And the things that are said after Communion are ordered towards this very thing. For since God deserves thanks for every gift and favor, how much more for the gift of such a Sacrament? The greater and more worthy the benefit, the more greatly should God be given thanks. Verbal praise alone does not suffice, we also owe him affection and good works, since embracing the divine benefits with all the appetite of our mind, we praise and love the goodness of such a benefactor, and we take care to obey him in all things. To the extent we are daily more spiritually fattened by such food, we are perfected and made more godlike; and so every day we become more fit for the table of Christ, approaching with greater preparation and reverence, returning more devoutly, and in all things living our life worthy of God, to the glory of our Lord Jesus Christ who is, with the Father and the Holy Spirit, one God, sublime and blessed above everything. Amen.

HERE ENDS
THE EXPOSITION OF THE MASS

---

[296] 1 Thess. 5:18; Col. 3:17.

ON
FREQUENT
COMMUNION

INTRODUCTION
He who presides, let him preside with solicitude. Rom. 12:8.

SINCE THE PROPHET MICAH SAYS TO every man, *I will show you, O man,... what the Lord requires of you, verily... to walk solicitous with God;*[1] and the Apostle also says, *with fear and trembling work out your salvation,*[2] it follows that one who presides over others must be all the more solicitous and fearful before the most dreadful Judge as those over whom he presides are more numerous; and he is bound to lead those committed to him to a greater perfection of the virtues, the greater the dignity of the persons committed to him are, and the more the Creator and Lover of souls has done, the more hardships he endured, and the more precious the treasure he expended for their salvation. Additionally, these persons are rational creatures, adorned with the likeness of their Creator, and marked with the image of the supereminently glorious Trinity, for whose salvation the Creator of the universe, the Only-Begotten of the eternal Father and true God, became man and endured a most bitter and ignominious death, shedding his most precious Blood for them as the price of their redemption. In considering this, that most faithful religious superior, St. Bernard, exclaimed: If I had been standing under the Cross at the time of our Lord's Passion, and had collected the Blood dripping from our Lord's Body in a vessel, how carefully would I have carried and guarded that vessel! And behold, those very souls, for whose redemption that high and wise Merchant so copiously shed his Blood, have now been entrusted and committed to me.[3]

Now as your venerable Paternity,[4] my most excellent Father, has pondered and weighed these and like matters, you have asked my Littleness to respond to a certain question, a matter that is, if I am not mistaken, both intricate and fruitful, in such a way as to clarify

---

[1] Micah 6:8.   [2] Phil. 2:12.
[3] E.N. I was unable to trace this quote to any of the works of St. Bernard of Clairvaux. The notion of *Mercatur Christus*, Christ as a merchant (*mercator*) or a celestial bargainer (*negotiatore caelesti*) is certainly Augustinian. See, e.g., Augustine's Sermons 130.2, 233.3; his *Enarrationes in Psalmos*, 21.28, 30.3. This notion is also implicitly suggested in the *admirabile commercium*, the "wondrous exchange," of which we sing when we close out the Christmas Octave, and negatively in Judas, the *mercator pessimus* ("a terrible merchant"), of Holy Week.
[4] E.N. "Your Paternity" was a means of addressing a bishop, abbot, or prior.

doubts and quiet the conscience. Although you are the one better suited, with our Lord's help, to carry out this task, nevertheless, since I cannot possibly deny anything to your Kindness—nay, I dare not—I will commit all my strength to obey you.

ARTICLE ONE
A review of the subject this exposition addresses.

The letter your most dear Paternity sent to me contained among other things the following: "I have been deputed as a visitor to many monasteries of virgins and Sisters, and am troubled. For in these monasteries or congregations certain ancient practices flourish which I dare not fully approve, nor yet simply condemn: namely, these Sisters take communion very frequently, every Sunday in Advent or Lent to be exact, and in other seasons once every fortnight,[5] on all the major feast days of the Saints, that is, of the most holy Virgin, of St. John the Baptist, of the Apostles, of St. Michael, of St. Martin, and of their patron. And even if they receive the Eucharist during the week when a solemnity occurs on which it is their custom to commune, they still take communion the next Sunday if it is one on which they customarily receive communion."

As I mentioned, I do not disapprove of this custom, provided they approach with due preparation, devotion, and reverence. But every fruit has a worm that ruins it, and so does a laudably instituted action, once charity grows cold. Hence their confessors, who are conscientious men, lament that these Sisters are so passionate—indeed, even obstinate—to maintain their customs of taking communion, that no explanations can induce them to reduce the frequency of their communions. And yet some of them do not appear to be living such worthy lives that they can be assessed as having the due reverence to commune, nor do they obtain the fruits or achieve the progress as they ought to from such assiduous communion, since they remain obstinate and impudent. And, what is more serious, they refuse to acquiesce to their confessors when they decide that they should not be admitted to communion. Indeed, they prefer not to confess their faults if they know that it would

---

[5] E.N. *Quindena*, being a period of 15 days sometimes before a feast, spanning a feast, or after a feast. Here, Denis probably refers to the *Quindena Paschae*, that is, one week before and one week after Easter.

cause them to be suspended from communion, as has very often transpired. I have ever heard tell of one old woman who swallowed a piece of a sponge in order to suffocate herself out of impatience and anguish at being denied Holy Communion.

"Their confessors are afflicted by these perplexities. Now this custom of taking such frequent communion seems to have been introduced sometime in the past, because back then the nuns were fewer in number but greater in devotion. Hence I have been asked many times by their confessors to provide them a healthful remedy to apply in this case. In either event, a danger looms. For if the Sacrament is withheld from them at the customary times, the devout and fervent sisters are defrauded of their accustomed spiritual, salutary, and sweet food; it affords them a serious occasion for murmuring; and it will be well-nigh intolerable for them. On the other hand, if they are all admitted to Communion, the confessors' consciences are not satisfied, because they fear, or rather have no doubt, that many nuns will approach unworthily. But if they prohibit and exclude the more imperfect and negligent from communion, they immediately complain and say that they are confused, since they are among the more elderly, and they do not take it well—indeed, it is feared whether they will ever make a sincere and complete confession. What therefore is to be done about this business, I beg you to put briefly in writing for me."

ARTICLE TWO
Certain examples are offered by way of preface,
to clarify and respond to this subject.

The feminine sex is the sex of submission; so, by divine, natural, and positive law it is proper for women to be governed by, to be formed by, and to obey men. For this reason, the Apostle said: *Let the woman learn in silence, with all subjection. But I suffer not a woman to teach, nor to use authority over the man: but to be in silence.*[6] Hence Holy Orders, such as the priesthood, the diaconate, and the subdiaconate are not conferred on them, nor are they allowed to preach in public. Nevertheless, in the convents and congregations over which they preside, the abbesses, prioresses, and mothers can and ought to exposit and teach the Word of God to the sisters in a summary fashion, to reprove and correct them, albeit

---
[6] 1 Tim. 2:11–12.

as directed by their fathers, superiors, and confessors by whom, at certain established times, they are visited, guided, and (if need be) reproved and corrected. For women are by nature deficient, weak in reason, and greatly susceptible to their apprehensions and affections, which is to say to their passions. Consequently, it frequently happens that when something is denied or prohibited to them, they desire it more intensely. They are also prone by disposition to verbosity, levity, and laughter. Hence also whatever they are, they tend to be in excess. Those who by natural disposition or force of habit are angry or cruel, are very immoderately so, and they do not know how to subdue themselves well. Although this is the ordinary course of things, nevertheless by a special gift of God there are certain women who are inclined and suited by their natural disposition to honesty, probity, prudence, to true devotion and a religious way of life, especially with the help of God's grace and the infused virtues of the Holy Spirit. But laws and judgments are concerned with that which holds more commonly and in the plurality of cases.

It is clear from these things that all religious persons, but in particular female religious, must devote themselves to all subjection and humility, and freely and gratefully receive instruction, and by no means be pertinacious or obstinately attached to their own understanding. For, as the Apostle attests, the man was not seduced to sin, but the woman.[7] Moreover, although women religious ought promptly and diligently to attend to their mothers in matters that pertain to their regular observances, nevertheless in things that pertain to the sacraments, that is, to the use, reception, and exercise of the sacraments, they ought always and with all humility and with fear and reverence of God to obey their religious superiors and confessors, because with respect to these things their spiritual fathers—not their mothers—have jurisdiction, stewardship, and governance over them.

ARTICLE THREE
That every Christian is bound before God to be and to think in such a way and with such a purpose that he would rather die than offend God by mortal sin.

As the supreme Truth asserts in the Gospel, the first and greatest commandment is to love the Lord and true God with all one's heart,[8]

---

[7] Cf. 1 Tim. 2:14. [8] Matt. 22:37–38.

that is, incomparably more than oneself and all created things, because the most high and eternal God is the supreme, infinite, and incomparable good; indeed, he is pure goodness and infinitely perfect. In comparison with his lovableness, perfection, sweetness, and glory, each and all created things—even taken all together—fall infinitely short, as incomparably and incomprehensibly as a single grain of sand falls short of the magnitude of the highest and greatest heaven. True charity, therefore, so strongly unifies and conforms the rational creature's will with his most worthy Creator that it causes that rational creature to love and to desire, to regard and to value, to fear and to worship the Creator more than any creature—and also to grieve more deeply over any offense to his Creator and over the loss of his charity, grace, gracious indwelling, and presence than he does over any earthly damage or temporal inconvenience, or any bodily adversity, infirmity, or human confusion. And he who does not feel this in his heart, or does not so stand before God, or does not exhibit this in action and in habit, and at every opportune time, is not in a state of salvation, but in one of eternal damnation.

Hence it is clear that a sister so disposed that she would prefer knowingly to conceal some mortal sin in sacramental confession and to receive the Sacrament of the Eucharist without a complete and full confession than to be restrained, banished, and repelled from Holy Communion on account of that sin and to suffer human shame—it is clear, I say, that such a sister or brother is already by that act in a state of mortal sin and is worthy of perpetual condemnation, and within, in her soul, she is totally deformed, perverse, unjust, disordered, and bereft of divine love. Therefore, she is unworthy of the habit and name of religion; nor is she a bride of Christ, but an adulteress of the devil. This is true (as St. Augustine asserts) of every rational creature who is in mortal sin. Therefore, Albert adds that the penitent and contrite man is ready to perform all satisfaction and penance, and does not regard any temporal embarrassment, derision, rebuke, or discipline for his sins as sufficient, since by these he has grievously and in manifold ways offended his Creator and merited death and infernal shame.

Further, as St. Thomas writes, a murderer, robber, or thief sins mortally by not confessing his iniquity to a judge, even though he would be put to death for it. How enormous is the sin, therefore, of a religious person who hides his sin in sacramental Confession out of fear of human embarrassment or discipline, and moreover dares to approach the table of his Savior in such a state of blindness and with such a wretched heart to receive unworthily his Body and Blood, not being ashamed before the Most High, nor fearing the terrible words of the Apostle which threaten and affirm, *Whosoever shall eat this bread, or drink the chalice of the Lord unworthily, shall be guilty of the body and of the blood of the Lord?*[9]

Therefore, the religious person—indeed, every Christian—should always avoid with all diligence whatever is contrary to divine charity or salutary wisdom, and he should be more ashamed of the turpitude of his sin and the vices of his heart before the eyes of the most holy God than of just and charitable rebuke, correction, humiliation, and brief confusion before men; and he should rather be duly chastised for this manner of living before a few of his fellows than to wait for that terrible judgment when he shall be confounded and condemned before the whole world on the last day.

ARTICLE FOUR
On the foundation of religious living and a truly Christian life.

The following pertain to every Christian: to walk the narrow way of salvation;[10] to lead a life of penance; to crucify our own body with its vices and concupiscences;[11] to spend all the time conceded to us by God fruitfully; to conquer ourselves, that is, to extirpate the passions and vices; to obey our superiors, that is, to fulfill the precepts of God and of the Church; to acquiesce to our rulers; to order all our life to the honor of God; to make progress in divine love; to do to our neighbor as we wish reasonably to be done to ourselves;[12] to exhibit a clean heart before God and to serve him faithfully with a good conscience; to let no hate or love, disordered desire or fear of any creature to allow us to depart from the way of justice and truth; to endure adversities with equanimity; to humble ourselves in all things;[13] to follow in the footsteps of Christ; to persevere in these and similar virtuous acts to the end in holy fear of God and diligent custody of heart; and to strenuously and unceasingly resist temptations, for one is not crowned until he has fought the battle against the enemies of his salvation.[14]

---

[9] 1 Cor. 11:27. [10] Matt. 7:13–14. [11] Cf. Gal. 4:24.
[12] Matt. 7:12. [13] Ecclus. 3:20. [14] Cf. 2 Tim. 2:5.

Take heed: these things pertain to every one of the Christian faithful; this is very clear from the Gospel. Wherefore the most blessed Apostle Paul abundantly and fervently exhorts all the faithful regarding all these things in his epistles, saying: *I beseech you... in the Lord, that you walk worthy in the vocation to which you were called, with all humility and mildness, with patience, supporting one another in charity, careful to keep the unity of the Spirit in the bond of peace.*[15] *And be renewed in the spirit of your mind: And put on the new man, who according to God is created.*[16] *Let no evil speech proceed from your mouth; let all bitterness, and anger, and indignation, and clamor... be put away from you, ... and be kind one to another; merciful, forgiving one another, even as God has forgiven you in Christ.*[17] *Be... followers of God, as most dear children, and walk in love, as Christ also has loved us, and has delivered himself for us, an oblation and a sacrifice to God for an odor of sweetness.*[18] *Bless them that persecute you: bless, and curse not.*[19] Hence, our Savior and lawgiver, the Son of God, states in the Gospel: *Blessed are they that suffer persecution for justice's sake: for theirs is the kingdom of heaven. Blessed are you when they shall revile you, and persecute you, and speak all that is evil against you, untruly, for my sake: Be glad and rejoice, for your reward is very great in heaven.*[20] *Love your enemies: do good to them that hate you: and pray for them that persecute and calumniate you.*[21]

But perhaps one might be heard to say: it is heavy and difficult to fulfill these things. To which one might respond with the words of the Lord: *The kingdom of heaven suffers violence, and the violent bear it away.*[22] And again: *Enter in at the narrow gate: for wide is the gate, and broad is the way that leads to destruction, and many there are who go in thereat. How narrow is the gate, and strait is the way that leads to life: and few there are that find it!*[23] Moreover, although it is in a certain way laborious to fulfill these things, yet in comparison to the eternal and incomprehensible reward and the most glorious happiness which is given to elect and virtuous men in exchange for this brief and temporal labor and obedience, it is quite moderate, easy, and joyful. Similarly, all these things are easy to fulfil inasmuch as by them we avoid that infernal, intolerable, and perpetual damnation. For this reason,

---

[15] Eph. 4:1–3.   [16] Eph. 4:23–24.   [17] Eph. 4:29, 31–32.   [18] Eph. 5:1–2.
[19] Rom. 12:14.   [20] Matt. 5:10–12; cf. Luke 6:23.   [21] Matt. 5:44.
[22] Matt. 11:12.   [23] Matt. 7:13–14.

the Apostle says: *The sufferings of this time are not worthy to be compared with the glory to come, that shall be revealed in us;*[24] and again; *That which is at present momentary and light of our tribulation, works for us above measure exceedingly an eternal weight of glory.*[25] Additionally, although these things considered in and of themselves are difficult for man to fulfil, it is nevertheless made easy and pleasant by the help of God's grace and by the consolations and gifts of the Holy Spirit which are given to God's faithful servants. Hence, our Lord invites us and exhorts us: *Come to me, all you that labor, and are burdened, and I will refresh you. Take up my yoke upon you, and learn of me, because I am meek, and humble of heart: and you shall find rest to your souls. For my yoke is sweet and my burden light.*[26] It is also certain that all these things are made easy and joyful for us if the charity of God truly grows and makes progress in us.

Therefore, if we carefully consider what things, what kind of things, and how great of things the Saints and the elect of God did and endured to obtain that eternal and indescribable glory, we will regard as little and almost nothing all the obedience and labor which we offer to our God, especially if we consider with an enlightened mind how incomprehensible and immense is the dignity, holiness, excellence, and honorability of our Creator and Savior.

Furthermore, all these things that have been mentioned we are able to fulfill promptly with God's help if we forcefully strive with our heart to purge ourselves from self- and private love, which is the origin of all vices and crimes, so that we might love ourselves not in and of ourselves, but in God. This means to desire, love, and freely receive, practice, and endure all these things which are necessary or profitable to us in order to please the Lord God Almighty, and to make progress in his grace and his love, in true perfection, holiness, and everlasting glory. And what are these things except to humble oneself in all things, to receive joyfully reproofs and corrections, to practice works of penitence, to chastise one's own body, to submit and obey willingly—indeed to rejoice in subjection and abjection, to glory in humiliation of one's self and in facing adversity as if glorying in all riches? All this is to hate oneself in oneself in a good sense, and salubriously, spiritually, and wisely to love God. Hence, the Savior asserted: *He who hates his life in this world, keeps it unto life eternal.*[27] Finally, these things concern much more especially and

---

[24] Rom. 8:18.   [25] 2 Cor. 4:17.   [26] Matt. 11:28-30.   [27] John 12:25.

eminently those persons in a religious vocation, inasmuch as they are in a more perfect state and are bound to greater efforts than men in secular walks of life. Throughout all his life in this world, the Lord and Savior demonstrated by his deeds and taught by his words all these things from the beginning of his birth until his death on the wood of the Cross. Most correctly is it said, therefore, that this is the foundation of the religious life—indeed, also of the Christian way of life: to entirely extirpate self-love from one's heart, and to make progress in true charity.

Furthermore, the desire for riches, pleasures, and honors arises from private self-love. Therefore, the beginning of the religious life is to despise these things, to be content with simple food and clothing, and to humble oneself. Hence, as the holy man Climacus asserted: the avaricious man is a mockery of the Gospel; the proud man is an imitator of the devil; the ambitious man is a follower of that first wicked apostate, the devil, and teems with inexpressible sins; for, as the blessed Gregory writes, the faults which spring from that vicious and diabolic ambition cannot be numbered. In short, the lover of pleasures is a disciple of Epicurus, not of Christ.

Hence, by the solemn vow of poverty, a religious renounces opulence and property; by the vow of chastity, pleasure; by the vow of obedience, self-will, and arrogance, vanity, ambition, and a sense of self-aggrandizement. For this reason, just as they are obliged by reason of the vow of obedience to subject their own will to the will of their superior, so also ought they to subject the judgment of their own reason to the judgment of those who preside over them; indeed, religious persons are more bound to obey the precept of their superior than they are the dictates of their own conscience, as Alexander of Hales, who is called the *Irrefragable Doctor*, and master Bonaventure, the *Devoted Doctor*, teach. But he who acts against his vow not only sins mortally, but also much more enormously gravely than had he acted against his own judgment, as St. Thomas declares. And so, it is well known that although a religious person should be adorned with all the virtues, yet especially should he be with these three virtues that concern him: poverty, chastity, and obedience, because they are bound to them by a solemn vow.

ARTICLE FIVE

That all religious and spiritual persons are especially obliged to obedience.

The whole divine Scripture and the pages of both Testaments, and the rules and doctrines of all the Fathers most excellently praise holy obedience, especially in religious persons. This our Lord Jesus Christ, King of kings[28] and Prince of the universe—who (as the Apostle said) being in the form of God, that is, in the true nature of the Godhead, and true God, equal to God the Father emptied himself, becoming obedient to the Father even unto death[29]—most plainly and most particularly recommended, commanded, taught, and demonstrated to us by his example. Whence he also said, *I came down from heaven, not to do my own will, but the will of him who sent me;*[30] and again, *my meat is to do the will of him who sent me.*[31]

For what is more perverse, impious, and ungrateful than for a rational creature to be rebellious, disobedient, or resistant to the Creator or his representative? Were not our first parents irrecoverably thrown out of paradise and along with all their posterity rendered destitute of original justice and deprived of the kingdom of heaven?[32] Further, the highest angelic spirits were cast down and hurled out of heaven because of their prideful disobedience.[33] So also God told the Prophet Samuel when Saul, the first king of Israel, under the guise of piety and the divine worship had transgressed the precept of God: *I am repentant that I have made Saul king, for he has defied me.*[34] And since Saul desired to excuse himself before Samuel, saying, We have spared *the best of the sheep . . . that they might be sacrificed to the Lord your God,*[35] the holy Samuel immediately responded, *Does the Lord desire holocausts and victims, and not rather* that His voice *should be obeyed?*[36] And Samuel added the reason: *For obedience is better than sacrifices: and to hearken rather than to offer the fat of rams. Because it is like the sin of witchcraft* (that is, as the mortal sin of witchery, which is an act of superstition or a deed performed through the magical arts) *to rebel: and like the crime of idolatry, to refuse to obey.*[37] This authority, as asserted in the statutes of the Carthusian Order, is alone a sufficient

---

[28] Rev. 19:16. [29] Cf. Phil. 2:6–8. [30] John 6:38. [31] John 4:34.
[32] Gen. 3:1 et seq. [33] Cf. Is. 14:12–15. [34] 1 Kings 15:9–11. [35] 1 Kings 15:15.
[36] 1 Kings 15:22. [37] 1 Kings 15:22–23.

commendation of obedience and vituperation of disobedience. If this obedience is lacking, all the other things we do are not only deprived of a beatific and eternal reward, nay more, they also incur damnation. Heed this and fear it, O religious person: for if disobedience is such an enormous sin in a secular person who does not promise obedience, how much more is it in you, who have bound yourself to obedience by a solemn vow?

Additionally, just as it is sacrilege to plunder or steal a thing that has been consecrated and offered to God, much more serious than [the mere taking of] silver and gold or other simple substance, so is it sacrilegious theft to take back to one's self one's own will which, through a solemn vow, had been offered to God through the hands of his representative, and so to take it back from his representative and use it at one's own pleasure.

More, just as through obedience a man is greatly pleasing to God, so through disobedience he greatly displeases the supreme Judge. Is it not recited in the book of Joshua that that holy man Joshua, who was most obedient to God in all things,[38] obtained this from God: that at his request—nay, even at his command—the sun and moon stood still in the middle of the sky for the space of a day?[39] Behold how Almighty God exalts those who humble themselves willingly and promptly before God through true obedience.

Further, in the *Lives of the Fathers* it is related that two brothers were walking together, one of whom displayed great abstinence, the other great obedience, when they encountered a dead man. They invoked the Lord that he might raise him from the dead, and the dead man immediately rose from the dead. The brother who displayed great abstinence gloried in his heart, saying: "The merit of my abstinence raised this man from the dead." But God revealed that it was not on account of his abstinence, but because of the other brother's obedience that the miracle had been done. Thus also St. Maurus,[40] while yet an adolescent, obeying a command of his most blessed Abbot Benedict, was able to run across water without sinking. And a disciple of Abbot Paul by obeying his abbot bound up and led away a great dragon. And another good man obeying his abbot, threw his own son into a burning furnace, and that boy was not harmed in the fire. All these and

---

[38] Joshua 11:15.   [39] Joshua 10:12–14.
[40] E.N. St. Maurus (or Maur) was one of the first disciples of St. Benedict. He died in 584. For this particular incidence, see the *Dialogues* of Pope St. Gregory the Great, Book II, chapter 7.

many similar events the glorious and blessed God has done for the edification and consolation of the faithfully obedient, and for the confounding and weighty condemnation of disobedient, pertinacious, and rebellious men.

And thus, the holy and most excellent Fathers Jerome, Basil, Augustine, and others, whose words I have quoted in other of my small works and numerous sermons, admonished religious persons most fervently and seriously to holy obedience. These lessons, exhortations, and commands are founded upon what Christ stated in the Gospel: He who wishes to come after me, *let him deny himself, and take up his cross daily, and follow me.*[41] And he also stated to his vicars. *He who hears you, hears me; and he who despises you, despises me.*[42] The Apostle writes of this: *Let every soul be subject to higher powers: for there is no power but from God: and those that are, are ordained of God. Therefore, he who resists the power, resists the ordinance of God. And they who resist, purchase to themselves damnation.*[43] And again he says: *Obey your prelates and be subject to them. For they watch as being to render an account of your souls; that they may do this with joy, and not with grief.*[44]

ARTICLE SIX
From that which has already been stated, it is clear that a partial response has been made to the question asked.

In the same way that one who is conscious of mortal sin sins mortally if he presumes to celebrate Mass, so likewise he who takes Communion sins mortally if doing so while in a state of mortal sin. And since, as has already been said, a person in the religious life is obliged to obey his superior under the penalty of mortal sin and the moral desert of eternal punishment,[45] it is clear that he who approaches Holy Communion or forms the resolution to approach it with deliberation and full purpose against the advice, dictate, or will of his superior sins mortally. And this would be a totally unworthy participation in the most worthy and salutary Sacrament; indeed by consuming it he would fall into mortal sin, that especially great mortal sin of which the Apostle says: *Whosoever shall eat this bread, or drink the chalice of the Lord unworthily, shall be guilty of the Body*

---

[41] Luke 9:23.   [42] Luke 10:16a.   [43] Rom. 13:1–2.   [44] Heb. 13:17.
[45] L. *sub demerito*, under a demerit or moral desert of eternal punishment.

and of the Blood of the Lord.⁴⁶ And again: *He who eats and drinks unworthily, eats and drinks judgment to himself, not discerning the body of the Lord.*⁴⁷ Accordingly, the sin of him who has proposed to approach or who actually approaches [to partake in the Sacrament of the Eucharist] against the duty of obedience owed to the presiding authority is not a simple mortal sin, but an enormous one, as contrary to the vow of obedience and a violation of said vow.

Moreover, such a religious person is not only bound to obey his superior as the one placed over him and his spiritual father, but also as the spiritual judge and physician in the forum of conscience in regard to this issue of the sacramental food. Consequently, if against his [superior's] advice, judgment, or will he simply forms the resolution to approach or in fact approaches Holy Communion, he demonstrates that he is in mortal sin. He is like a man bodily sick who eats food and drinks against the advice of his physician who informs him that such consumption would lead to his death; such a one would kill himself, as St. Augustine puts it.

Therefore, such a person must submit humbly to his superior and confessor, and must commit himself to his discretion in all things pertaining to this matter; and he must lay himself open for total amendment, and he must also patiently accept the suspension or delay of Holy Communion, and feel compunction for and fully confess his sins, and make satisfaction for them as efficaciously as he can, completely trampling upon perverse and foolish, human and childish shame. And this will be for him truly honest, most salubrious, and most meritorious before God and all his Saints in the present and in the future. And unless such persons acquiesce to their confessor according to the manner just stated, they are not to be allowed to partake in the most high Sacrament. Accordingly, persons in the religious life should be frequently and wisely, timely and opportunely, fervently and abundantly instructed, admonished, advised, and warned regarding these things both in confession as well as outside confession.

Finally, all must be exhorted that they ought not to despise, nor temerariously judge, nor be scandalized by those they see suspended or deferred from taking Communion. Let them rather be edified by their obedience, and let them charitably pray for them. Indeed, this fully applies to every discrete and honest, charitable and pious Christian, that he may regard every neighbor of his with a kind and

---

⁴⁶ 1 Cor. 11:27.   ⁴⁷ 1 Cor. 11:29.

sympathetic mind, and comfort him with counsel and help, as may be opportune, for whatever cause or fault he is placed under discipline, corrected, humiliated, afflicted, looked down upon, or disconsolate. *For blessed are the merciful, for they shall receive mercy.*[48]

Hence the Apostle said this to the Romans: *Now we that are stronger, ought to bear the infirmities of the weak, and not to please ourselves. Let every one of you please his neighbor unto good, to edification.*[49] And also: *Therefore let us follow after the things that are of peace; and keep the things that are of edification one towards another.*[50] And also to the Galatians: *If we live in the Spirit, let us also walk in the Spirit. Let us not be made desirous of vain glory, provoking one another, envying on another;*[51] *and if a man be overtaken in any fault, you, who are spiritual, instruct such a one in the spirit of meekness, considering yourself, lest you also be tempted. Bear you one another's burdens; and so you shall fulfill the law of Christ.*[52] And elsewhere: *Let nothing be done through contention, neither by vain glory: but in humility, let each esteem others better than themselves;*[53] *and by charity... serve one another.*[54] *And do all things without murmurings... that you may be blameless, and sincere children of God.*[55] Therefore, *as the elect of God, holy, and beloved, put on the bowels of mercy, benignity, humility, modesty, patience: Bearing with one another, and forgiving one another, if any have a complaint against another;* [56] *let the peace of Christ rejoice in your hearts;*[57] *all whatsoever you do in word or in work, do all in the name of the Lord Jesus Christ, giving thanks to God and the Father by him.*[58]

ARTICLE SEVEN
A continuation of the response.

A cloister may be compared to a hospital in which there are many sick laboring under many diseases, who, because of the great diversity of their infirmities, need different medicines. So in a cloister there are many persons wounded with many and various spiritual diseases (that is, with a multiplicity of passions, faults, ignorance, and defects). Among these medicines are especially the seven Sacraments of the Church, of which the first is Baptism, which is a

---

[48] Matt. 5:7.   [49] Rom. 15:1-2.   [50] Rom. 14:19.   [51] Gal. 5:25-26.
[52] Gal. 6:1-2.   [53] Phil. 2:3.   [54] Cf. Gal. 5:13.   [55] Phil. 2:14-15a.
[56] Col. 3:12-13a.   [57] Col. 3:15a.   [58] Col. 3:17.

spiritual regeneration and a special medicine for original sin. Just as it is proper for the exterior physician to consider diligently which kinds of medicine are to be used for the bodily sin, so it is incumbent upon the spiritual physician, that is, the religious superior or confessor, to consider most vigilantly what spiritual remedies should be applied to the sheep of Christ committed and entrusted to him; and it is necessary that these sheep themselves acquiesce and obey their spiritual physicians, pastors, and confessors if they want to be cured and saved. Therefore, if at times their physicians judge that the Sacrament of the Eucharist ought to be denied and withdrawn from some for a time because of their unworthiness or indisposition, or so that in the meantime they might more fully prepare for it, neither they nor others ought to receive this as an evil, nor ought they to judge rashly, nor to interpret it in a negative manner, but, under the direction of him who presides over them, they ought, with sheep-like simplicity, to serve the Most High with reverence and fear.[59]

Further, as the common doctrine holds, virtues are a kind of mean between extreme vices, in the way that hope holds a middle ground between excessive presumption of the mercy of God and despair from an excessive and immoderate fear of the rigor of divine judgment. Accordingly, the ministers of Christ and persons in religious life must find themselves in a middle ground regarding the desire and reception of Holy Communion, so that the consideration of their own fault and weakness makes them fear to receive Holy Communion, but their inspection of the mercy of God and the charity of Christ and his benefits draws them to receive it.

Again, since he who partakes in communion outside a state of charity and grace of God sins mortally, and Solomon asserts: *There are just men and wise men, and their works are in the hand of God: and yet man knows not whether he be worthy of love, or hatred*,[60] it follows that a truly enlightened man does not desire to receive such a high Sacrament without great anxiety, because it is uncertain whether he is in a state of charity.

Moreover, no one ought to proceed to this Sacrament without a diligent examination of his conscience. Therefore, a religious person ought especially to probe his conscience as to whether he is truly obedient and ready to be obedient with his whole heart, preferring the judgment of his superior or confessor or judge to his own judgment. And if he does not find himself to be so disposed,

---

[59] Cf. Heb. 12:28b.   [60] Eccl. 9:1b.

by that very fact he is unworthy and ought to consider himself unworthy of this heavenly food and supersubstantial bread, and so he ought not approach the table of the highest King without the counsel of his confessor.

These things, most venerable and devout Father, occur to me at the present time regarding the question you proposed. Yet, a few years back I wrote a small work at the request of some persons that covers many things pertaining to this issue, especially the institution, dignity, and efficacy of this Sacrament, and also of the preparation for it, and of its effects, and of the frequency of celebrating Mass and taking Holy Communion, which I send together with this small tract,[61] recommending myself to the prayers of your Paternity and all those over whom you preside. To the praise and glory of the Almighty, who is above all things God, sublime and blessed. Amen.

END OF
THE SHORT TRACT
ON FREQUENT COMMUNION

---

[61] E.N. See *Dialogue on the Sacrament of the Altar and the Celebration of Mass.*

SIX SERMONS
on the Sacrament of the Eucharist

FIRST SERMON
*On the Sacrament of the Eucharist and
the three degrees of honoring it.*

MY FLESH IS TRUE FOOD. JOHN 6:56. OUR Lord and Savior, in whose right hand is a fiery law, gave this fiery law to men;[1] for this reason, the law of the Gospel is called the law of love. Are not all things that are handed down in the law of the Gospel blazing with the purest and most fervent love? Indeed, the beginning of the evangelical law is that Annunciation in which the holy archangel Gabriel announced to the most sacred and most highly favored Virgin that the incarnation of the eternal Word would take place through her, saying, *Behold you will conceive and bear a son.*[2] This was the proclamation of most excellent charity from which proceeded and emanated the means whereby the eternal Father sent and gave to men his only Son, uniting to him human nature, forming and outfitting him with the substance of human flesh from the most pure blood of the most blessed Virgin. Therefore, Scripture says: *For God so loved the world that he gave his only Son.*[3]

Therefore, because of the great charity with which he loved us, God the Father sent his Son in the likeness of human flesh.[4] Then, the incarnate Son of God, from the same ineffable charity and his incomprehensible condescension, deigned to be seen on earth and to live among men;[5] and he went about doing good and healing all those oppressed by the devil, copiously demonstrating the way of salvation by example and illustration. After this, celebrating the Last Supper with his disciples,[6] surpassing every measure of love, he instituted the superlatively wonderful Sacrament in which he offered and gave himself as food, and his blood as drink, showing himself to be both the Giver and the Gift. And a little later, he offered himself to the Father as an oblation and victim in an odor of sweetness,[7] to wash away the stain of all iniquity and all the stench and baseness of our transgressions. And so that the memory of all these things might remain perpetual and fervent, and cherished in our hearts, he instituted his Apostles to be priests at the same Supper, committing to them the celebration of such a great

---

[1] Deut. 33:2. [2] Luke 1:26, 31. [3] John 3:16. [4] Eph. 2:4; Rom. 8:3.
[5] Bar. 3:38. [6] Matt. 26:26-38; 1 Cor. 11:23-25. [7] Eph. 5:2.

mystery, the consecration of his Body and Blood, saying: *Do this in memory of me.*[8]

And so the Bride of the Word, the Church, desiring to repay so great a benefactor in whatever way she can, rightly, not only daily in her mystery and in the celebration of Mass, but also most specially once a year, on this excellent feast [of Corpus Christi], she performs the solemnities of so great a Sacrament. Recalling the charity, liberality, and goodness of her Savior, she gives thanks, she sings praises, and she reverently carries that most worthy Sacrament around in procession, leads it about with humble adoration, and follows it back to its place, which in time past was figured in the carrying about of the tabernacle of Moses and the ark of the covenant.[9]

Furthermore, just as there existed three orders of ministers for the conveyance [of the tabernacle] who carried out what had been committed to them, and the duties of which were distinct—some more mundane, some more spiritual—so in the procession of this Sacrament (which is rightly esteemed as the tabernacle of the supreme Deity, and is most truly called the Ark of the New Covenant, containing the superlatively sweet heavenly manna), some Christians offer to the Redeemer more corporal, some more celestial, and others a middling sort of service, public praise, and holocausts.

For there are three degrees among those who praise him. The first are those who honor Christ by exterior actions—by ringing bells, bearing burning candles, singing hymns, Psalms, and canticles, also cleaning the roads and streets and decorating them with branches of trees and the like—in order to venerate God in their own manner, and by such exterior means to summon forth an internal honoring. Thus, at the beginning of his conversion, Blessed Francis used to take a broom and run about sweeping physical churches in order to suggest that holiness befits the house of God, i.e., the hearts of the faithful, and that his ways are beautiful ways, and all his ways are ways of peace.[10]

The second grade, more sublime than the first, is that by which all men praise God within themselves, saying with the Psalmist: *I will praise you, Lord, with my whole heart,*[11] that is, with all my mind and the entirety of my affection. The soul of these persons is occupied with complete diligence and concentrated effort with the sense of the holy words and with the consideration of the majesty of him whom it praises, worships, and invokes; and the affection

---

[8] Luke 22:19.   [9] Num. 4:1–49.   [10] Ps. 92:5; Prov. 3:17.   [11] Ps. 110:1.

of these persons is ignited in a fire of love by meditations of this sort.[12] These men can say with the Apostle Paul: *I will sing with the spirit, and I will sing with understanding.*[13] They graciously experience what the holy man confesses: *My lips shall greatly rejoice when I shall sing to you;*[14] and similarly, *I have cried to him with my mouth, and I have exalted him with my tongue.*[15] As they sing out they undoubtedly experience the virtues of the Psalms, and taste how sweet the Lord is.[16] In fact, those who sing and pray like this are scarcely able to become fatigued. For they are constantly refreshed by the sweet flavor of the uncreated sweetness, by the immense goodness of the superlatively beautiful Godhead. Any spiritual acedia, or sluggish sleep, or vile or impious negligence flees from them whose souls are filled with an internal sweetness, a holy devotion, an ardor of divine love, as if with marrow and fatness.[17]

The third degree of the worship of God and of the ministers of Christ comprises those who have received the grace of contemplation, who have come to a deep heart,[18] and been set in the citadel of contemplation. The innermost recesses of these men's hearts are extended, affixed, and absorbed into the region of boundless light, and happily perceive how narrow and mean all creatures are with respect to, and in comparison with, the superexalted and boundless God. These men, the more clearly they contemplate the incomprehensible excellence of the Creator, the more they become profoundly aware of their own smallness, defectiveness, nay, even worthlessness and nothingness, become wholeheartedly disdainful [of themselves], and ever more vehemently humble themselves from the depths of their heart, saying with the Prophet: *My substance is as nothing before you,*[19] and *shall dust confess to you?*[20] Here they recognize themselves as altogether unequal and wholly unworthy to sing the praises of the superglorious God, exclaiming and proclaiming: *Who can stand before the sight of the Lord, of this holy God?*[21] For the pillars of heaven feel dread before his sight,[22] under whom they that bear up the world stoop.[23]

These men regard themselves as unable, and judge themselves unworthy, to sing God's praises. Sometimes this happens by the consideration of their own defects, being certain that praise in the mouth of the sinner is unseemly,[24] and because God says to the

---

[12] Ps. 38:4. [13] 1 Cor. 14:15. [14] Ps. 70:23. [15] Ps. 65:17.
[16] 1 Pet. 2:3. [17] Ps. 62:6. [18] Ps. 63:7. [19] Ps. 38:6.
[20] Ps. 29:10. [21] 1 Sam. 6:20. [22] Cf. Job 26:11. [23] Job 9:13.
[24] Ecclus. 15:9.

sinner: *Why do you declare my justices?*[25] Sometimes it happens by the consideration of their own insignificance and natural defectiveness. For man is the lowest species of all intellectual creatures, and the weakest intellectually. This is because, just as prime matter is in the order of things, so is the human intellect in the order of intellectual natures. Hence men are very weak, indeed, exceedingly weak and deeply prone to evil; and we most easily fall into error and prove ever unstable. To this we must add the baseness of our body, the corruption caused by our inclination to sin (*fomes peccati*), the instability of our mind, and the necessities of our flesh. Other times, this happens by the consideration of the infinite excellence of God, who is of such dignity, honorableness, holiness, and majesty, that even if one man were to offer up a veneration equal to that of the whole universe of creatures, still God would deserve infinitely more veneration. To the extent, therefore, that we venerate the Lord our God more perfectly, worship him with more devotion, and praise him more sublimely, the more clearly do we see and more humbly do we confess ourselves to be infinitely wanting, to be entirely useless, in offering him befitting praise, becoming worship, and due obedience; nay more, even the fact that we offer to him for a brief time whatever we are, whatever we are able to do, and whatever we possess, this too we confess to have received from him and have a duty to offer it all to him. Thus we recognize and feel the truth of the Savior's words: *When you shall have done all these things that are commanded you, say: We are unprofitable servants; we have done that which we ought to do.*[26] The divine and great Dionysius taught and described this saving wisdom, this salubrious practice, this contemplative, loving, flame-bearing practice in his book *Mystical Theology*.

Moreover, since each person is powerfully transformed into that with which he is united with a more fervent love and more complete affection, and to which his actions are completely conformed, the sincere lover, the fervent worshipper, while he is completely alienated from himself by the extirpation of self-love and fervently and unceasingly occupied with the Creator by the exercise of a contemplative life, he is rightly said to fail of himself, and no longer to live himself, but God in him.[27] And thus he is reduced to nothing, not in the sense of letting go of his natural existence or his proper substance, but because he no longer reflects on himself, no longer

---

[25] Ps. 49:16. [26] Luke 17:10. [27] Gal. 2:20.

seeks himself, nor anything ultimately in himself, or for himself, or because of himself, but all in God, to God, and because of God. Nor does he live according to the inclinations of his own nature, but according to the tenor of the divine law and the exigencies of supernal charity. And so intent is his contemplation and love, that he neither desires nor adverts to himself, nor, for a time, anything created. And therefore he is said to be liquified and dissolved by the ardor of seraphic love and to be plunged, sunk, submersed, and absorbed in the object of his contemplation, namely in the Source of all light and the Principle of all illumination, the most high, omnipotent God, as if in an ocean of infinite depth and an abyss of unbounded delights and eternal riches, and likewise to become one with him, to be and live as one, speaking here of a unity of most intimate and simplifying charity, not of a unity of substantial identity.

This is the language of mystical theology, which should be soundly and wisely understood; it is also founded in the canonical Scriptures and held up by the authority of the law of the Gospel, since the Truth says: *I pray, Father, that they who believe in me all may be one, as you, Father, in me, and I in you; that they also may be one in us;*[28] and again *Father keep them in your name whom you have given me; that they may be one, as we also are.*[29] This is also the manner of speaking of the Apostle: *I live, now not I, but Christ lives in me;*[30] and again: *He who is joined to God is one in spirit.*[31] Nevertheless, it does not seem very expedient for simple believers to occupy themselves much in speaking in this manner, inasmuch as it can easily be the occasion of hidden pride or vanity.

Therefore, it befits those who are learned in these things and in mystical theology, and who have experienced it in some way, to speak of these things cautiously and appropriately, and to clarify obscure expressions, lest readers and listeners be scandalized. For I have read these words in a sermon: "It is impossible for a man rightly dissolved, submerged, or annihilated in himself in this way, to be abandoned finally by God."[32] This proposition seems to have been stated incautiously: indeed, such a man having relapsed back into himself after that actual elevation had ceased, would still not be confirmed in grace—indeed, he might still sin mortally, as has

---

[28] John 17:20–23.   [29] John 17:11.   [30] Gal. 2:20.   [31] 1 Cor. 6:17.
[32] E.N. I have not discovered the reference to this anonymous sermon. It may arise from someone involved with the heretical Brethren of the Free Spirit. Denis appears to anticipate the dangers of, and the Church's future condemnation of, Quietism. He also rejects the notion of "once saved, always saved."

often happened, as Augustine said: I have seen cedars of Lebanon fall, of whose ruin I suspected no more than I would Jerome and Ambrose.[33] Certainly, King David, who from his childhood, when he was still shepherding flocks, was visited while in the pastures by the grace of theoretical contemplation and the mystical movements of burning love, and after prophetic illuminations, and after the most high heavenly contemplations, and after all the relishing of divine sweetness, after so many visions of mystical theology, loving excesses, transformations, and ardors, when he was already old and almost sixty years of age, fell into the most grievous crimes.[34] And it would not be impossible after such a fall and such an ungraceful and vile result to be finally abandoned by God.

Having briefly touched upon this, let us return to the diligent and affectionate consideration of the inexpressible charity, the kindliest condescension, the most munificent communications, and the highest liberality of our Lord and God who became incarnate for our sakes, who assumed all that was of us and from us, who used it for us, and who directed it for our profit. Certainly, since charity, as the divine Dionysius asserted,[35] is a unitive virtue, it follows that the Son of God loved us more viscerally and cherished us more fervently, the more closely he joined himself to us, the more condescendingly he attached himself to us, and the more abundantly he communicated and gave himself and his own possessions to us. Now what is so near, what is so intimately conjoined the one to another, as the eater to his food, the imbiber to his drink, or a patient to his medicine? And behold him whom the empyrean heaven cannot contain, whose divine nature the heaven of heavens are in no way able to circumscribe, enters our mouth in his assumed nature, under the modest sacramental form, so that thereby he might also enter more graciously into our hearts, and so heal the infirmities of our souls, and enlighten our understanding with his wisdom, and fill it with splendors, and enkindle the will with the ardors of divine love, and confirm and establish our memory in him—indeed, he converts, transforms, and enraptures us completely in himself, he possesses us always, and he leads us to the beatific enjoyment of himself. Alas, hard heart, vile, ingrateful heart which is not set aflame by such great charity, which so many great benefits do not

---

[33] E.N. This saying is commonly attributed to St. Augustine, but I have not been able to trace it to any authentic Augustinian source.
[34] 2 Sam. 11:1–26.   [35] *De Divin. Nom.*, c. 4.

soften and move to shame—indeed, which is not greatly humbled by the great condescension, even the humiliation of the most high Christ, which is not led by such great liberality towards generosity!

What shall we render to the Lord for all that he has rendered to us?[36] Let us incessantly give him heartfelt thanks; indeed, let us tirelessly and anxiously beseech him that he might make us grateful to him, so that in every situation—in prosperity and in adversity, but especially in adversity, in persecutions and scourges, in fraternal correction and paternal chastisements—we might render thanks back to him for his providence which surrounds us. And not only to him, but also to his representatives and to our neighbors, through whom in the present time he reproves, corrects, humbles, cleanses, heals, and indeed deigns to save us. Let us glory in these things, *as we do in all riches,*[37] for they are really more profitable for us than they are unprofitable. Are not these ineffably most salutary medicines, by which we are delivered and cured from vices and sins that are incomparably harmful to us, filled with the gifts of grace, preserved from the horrible and inestimably severe and afflictive sufferings of purgatory—indeed, even from the punishments of hell—and transferred by the shortest and most secure path to the prize of eternal happiness?

Let none of us be so obtuse and inexperienced, so blind and obdurate, that he considers himself to have been injured by reproofs and corrections, discipline and trials, but rather let him say in the depths of his heart: *I have sinned, and indeed I have offended, and I have not received what I have deserved.*[38] Let us regard ourselves as rude and negligent teachers and disciples in the school of virtue, who after so many days and months and (what is more shameful, indeed, more damnable), after so many years, have progressed so little in our vocation, so that we are still scarcely able to bear a word of rebuke or discipline with equanimity. Let us ponder what that venerable Judith said during that great time of tribulation: *Let us not avenge ourselves for these things which we suffer, but esteeming these very punishments to be less than our sins deserve, let us believe that these scourges of the Lord, with which like servants we are chastised, have happened for our amendment, and not for our destruction.*[39] Who are they who at hearing this goodly rebuke will thereafter speak out to contradict, to excuse, to ask for proof of what was said? If, as Thomas asserts in the second half of the second part of his *Summa*

---

[36] Cf. Ps. 115:12.   [37] Ps. 118:4.   [38] Job 33:27.   [39] Judith 8:26-27.

Theologiae,⁴⁰ those who refuse to confess before their judge the crimes for which they are to be put to death sin mortally, though the fear of death alleviates the fault somewhat, then what punishment, what condemnation imminently awaits those who either deny their faults before their superiors, or cover them up, or minimize them exceedingly? This is also against the teaching of Aristotle, who teaches in his *Ethics* that although one should never depart from the truth, yet in the telling or accusation of another's fault, we should err on the side of diminishing it, but in the accusation or narration of one's own fault, one should rather lean towards exaggeration.⁴¹

Therefore, in order that we may be rendered worthy to approach, reverently encounter, and salubriously receive this most worthy Sacrament of the Eucharist in accordance with the abilities of our smallness,⁴² let us cleanse ourselves from any filth of mind and body, and let us proceed prudently and tirelessly towards perfection through the path of regular discipline.⁴³ To the praise and glory of the Almighty, who is above all things, God sublime and blessed. Amen.

SECOND SERMON
On the institution and dignity of this Sacrament.

I am the bread of life. John 6:48. Our Lord Jesus Christ, on the night he was betrayed, took bread, and giving thanks, blessed and broke it, and gave it to his disciples and said: *Take and eat. This is my Body.*⁴⁴ Behold the abridged word that God made on earth.⁴⁵ Behold how simple is the narrative of a supernatural and most incomprehensible thing. Is it not a marvel the way the whole world was able to be persuaded to have faith in this Sacrament? One reads in Mark: *They went out to lay hold on him,* namely, Jesus, saying: *He is become mad.*⁴⁶ Further, as can be gathered from the other Evangelists, this occurred when Jesus preached in Judaea those things that are written in John about the Sacrament of his Body and Blood, where he says: *My Flesh is meat indeed, and my Blood is drink indeed; he who eats my Flesh, and drinks my Blood,* and so forth.⁴⁷ These words seemed to the carnal minded to be words of insanity and madness; and even

---

⁴⁰ *Summa Theologiae*, IIa IIae, q. 69, art. 1.   ⁴¹ E.N. *Nicomachean Ethics*, 1127b.
⁴² 2 Cor. 7:1.
⁴³ E.N. By "regular discipline," Denis means discipline according to the religious rule (*regula*).   ⁴⁴ 1 Cor. 11:23–24; Matt. 26:26.
⁴⁵ Is. 10:23; Rom. 9:28.   ⁴⁶ Mark 3:21.   ⁴⁷ John 6:56–57.

some of the Savior's disciples, scandalized by these words, turned back, saying: *This sentence is hard, and who is able to hear it?*[48]

Therefore, one of the wise men of this world, struck, puzzled, and put out by the marvels of this Sacrament—indeed, because he did not have the spirit of Christ, but only respected natural causes—said: I have traversed the world, and I have come upon various sects, and I have never found a sect so foolish as this sect of the Christians, because they devour with their teeth the God whom they worship.[49] You stated this, O most wicked and cursed Averroës, who were content with the natural law, and following Aristotle's doctrine you asserted that above the orbit of the moon there could be no evil—neither the evil of guilt nor the evil of punishment. Hence also you denied the existence of devils, whose existence is proved by so abundant and evident experience. Also, you contrived and purveyed the lie that there is one and the same intellect in all men, which is much more absurd and irrational than what the holy Christian people confess, namely, that there are three superlatively blessed uncreated Persons in one and the same essence.[50] Hence, God with a just judgment abandoned you, and allowed you to slide into the most irrational errors, so that you affirmed the souls of men to be mortal, like those of brute animals. You also followed the reprobate and invidious Cain who, at the beginning of this world, said to the most faithful Abel: There is neither providence nor judgment.[51] So also you denied that God's providence extends to things of this world and to human acts, and denied that men are judged for them. Thus, as far as you were able, you gave men free reign to follow their disordered desire. Finally, taking your stand on the natural law and the doctrine of the Peripatetics, you were not able to salvage those things which are abundantly and clearly open to the senses, for example, that one and the same delirious person can speak different languages at

---

[48] John 6:67, 61.
[49] E.N. An apocryphal statement attributed to Averroës (Craig Martin, *Subverting Aristotle* [Baltimore: Johns Hopkins University Press, 2014], 162), but that did not stop the opponents of the doctrine of transubstantiation—such as the Protestant Archbishop of Canterbury, John Tillotson (1630–1694), in his *A Discourse against Transubstantiation*, or Diderot (1713–1784) and d'Alembert (1717–1783) in their *Encyclopédie*, or David Hume (1711–1776) in his *The Natural History of Religion*—from citing it.
[50] E.N. See Ralph McInerny, *Aquinas Against the Averroists: On There Being Only One Intellect* (West Lafayette, LA: Purdue University Press, 1993).
[51] Denis the Carthusian, First Sermon on the Solemnity of Corpus Christi, *Opera Omnia* (Tournai: 1906), vol. 32, 126.

one and the same time, even those which he did not know or learn previously, nor was able to speak when his insanity had passed.

Therefore, I reject you along with your perfidies. We Christians, in whom alone is the saving wisdom, which flowed from heaven, which is confirmed in us, God bearing witness by various signs and portents and the distributions of the Holy Spirit,[52] who abandoned the Synagogue because it did not believe in Christ, and transferred the miracles which in times past he performed among the Israelite people to Christ's Church, in which he also ineffably performed more and greater miracles than he did before in the Synagogue. We Christians, I say, who alone have miracles in the true and most proper sense—namely, those possible only for Almighty God—most certainly believe all those things that the Scripture says and the Church holds of this most sacred Sacrament to be most true, namely, that Christ, the incarnate God, is the wisdom of the Father,[53] that he founded his Church and left it seven sacraments as medicinal vessels, in which and through which, as by sensible signs, our salvation is graciously and supernaturally effected. For that eternal Wisdom knew that man, constituted of soul and body, had to be connaturally guided, helped, and raised up by natural and sensible things to divine and spiritual ones.

Moreover, in this regard our faith is not a little strengthened by the fact that all that we believe has already been accomplished; we read how these things were so long and abundantly foretold in the books of the Prophets of the Synagogue. In the same books also we acknowledge that all that we believe of the Sacrament was prophesied, the holy Psalmist saying of Christ in the Psalm: *There shall be a firmament on the earth on the tops of mountains.*[54] In this place, others have this translation: *There will be grain*, and others: *There will be memorable wheat.* But the Chaldean translation, which is also considered authentic among the Hebrews, says: *There will be a cake of wheat on earth* (that is, in the Church militant, which is on pilgrimage on earth), *in the summit of the mountain*, that is, upon the heads of priests.

Finally, as he provided for and bestowed the Sacrament of Baptism upon man conceived in sin, and born with the inclination to sin (*fomes*), and therefore spiritually dead and a child of wrath,[55] by which sacrament he is spiritually reborn, and the Sacrament of Confirmation, by which he is spiritually strengthened and enlisted

---

[52] Heb. 2:3-4. [53] 1 Cor. 1:24. [54] Ps. 71:16a. [55] Cf. Eph. 2:3.

for the spiritual warfare; likewise to man so born and strengthened, he consecrated, bestowed, and left behind a Sacrament whereby he might be spiritually refreshed and grow till he acquires the proper and due stature and measure of spiritual consistency. And this is the Sacrament of the Eucharist, in which is contained not only (as in the other sacraments) Christ by grace and power and multiple effect, but also truly and substantially by essence. Indeed, as we see, in every order and genus of things that contains many things by participation and which are imperfect, there is one thing which is first by essence and perfect.[56] And since the sacraments of the New Law are many (namely seven), and they have among themselves an order of dignity in containing grace and working our salvation, one of them had not only to have grace participatively and contain grace imperfectly, but also to comprehend essentially the source of all grace, namely the incarnate Word, in whose assumed humanity grace is formally and completely included. But in the other sacraments grace is not contained nor present according to complete formal existence, since such grace adheres only to a rational and intellectual creature, which alone is the subject of holiness and grace.[57]

Now as to how grace is contained in the other sacraments, there are two established opinions. One of these is followed by Alexander of Hales, Bonaventure, William of Paris in his book on the sacraments, Scotus, and many others. Hence in his Commentary on the Fourth Book of the Sentences,[58] Bonaventure relates that the lord bishop of Paris, William, in the presence of master Alexander, in Paris in the convent of the Friars of the Order of St. Francis, approved the position of Alexander. Thomas, Albert, Giles [of Rome], Henry, and many others follow another opinion. And to be sure the first opinion is easier to understand and defend; yet the second is regarded as being more consonant with the writings of Saints Augustine, Bede, and the Fathers; for this reason, I agree with it more.

Furthermore, because Christ appears to us in this Sacrament as food, and food should be really conjoined to foodstuffs; therefore,

---

[56] E.N. Denis here refers to analogical predication. There are many analogates derived or related to the one analogon, the six other sacraments being analogates of the Sacrament of the Eucharist.

[57] E.N. Since, in contradistinction to the other Sacraments, the Eucharist is a person—the Incarnate Word—it strictly contains grace essentially, formally, and fully (*in sensu stricto*), whereas the other Sacraments, which are not persons but are things, contain grace only in a manner of speaking (*in sensu lato*).

[58] Bonaventure, *Commentarius in IV Libros Sententiarum*, III, d. 16, a. 1, q. 1, d. 40, a. 3, *Opera Omnia* (Quaracchi: 1885), vol. 3, 346, 895–96.

the Church rightly believes Christ to be really contained in this Sacrament. Now it was fitting for Christ to institute this Sacrament at the Last Supper, after which he was immediately handed over to die for us. For it had been foretold that he would be a new priest—perfect and true, and not imperfect and figurative, according to the order of Melchisedech,[59] and not according to the rite and order of Aaron—and also a new and perfect lawgiver; for once there is a transfer of priesthood it is necessary that there be a transfer of the law, as the Apostle argues and demonstrates in his epistle to the Hebrews.

Once the priesthood and the law were transferred, the sacraments and the sacrifice also had to change. All this Daniel summarily foretold and touched upon, saying: *In the middle of the week, the victim and the sacrifice will cease.*[60] For he speaks of weeks of years, each of which contains seven years, in the last of which Christ is killed, instituting the Sacrament of the Eucharist in the middle of the week and putting an end to the sacrifices of the Law. Indeed, if the last week is divided into two parts, each part contains three and a half years. Furthermore, Christ lived in mortal flesh thirty-three years and somewhat more from the day of his Nativity until the day of the holy *Parasceve*.[61] And so in the middle of that week, the sacrifice and offering of the Law ceased insofar as its obligatory nature was concerned.[62]

Moreover, because the Wisdom of the Father, the eternal Word, became incarnate for us and willed to immolate himself once (*semel*) on the Cross, he provided for our salvation in various ways thereafter. For him, it was not enough once (*semel*) to immolate himself for us on the Cross by suffering death, but in his infinite wisdom he devised, and in his immense clemency he ordained, and in his highest love he established, that this immolation be daily and perennially repeated in the mystery of the office of the Mass, by which he procured honor to God the Father, and help, grace, and salvation for the human race. A mind that is enlightened by God is compelled to say that this whole manner of proceeding was entirely appropriate,

---

[59] Heb. 7:11–12.
[60] Dan. 9:27.
[61] E.N. The day before the Passover Sabbath, that is, Good Friday.
[62] E.N. Denis is saying that Christ lived 33½ years, with a public ministry of 3½ years (that is, Daniel's "middle of a week," or one-half of 7 years). It was at the end of his 3½ years of public ministry that Christ replaced the Jewish temple sacrifice with his Sacrifice on the Cross and the implementation of the Eucharist and the sacrifice of the Mass.

and the more that mind is enlightened, the more clearly it discerns how reasonable, or rather how *beyond* reasonable, and most merciful, most wise, and most loving it is that every day we may freshly bring to mind the Lord's Passion, and assiduously recall the charity of God and his goodness and liberality towards us, and by remembering be enkindled, so that we may participate more abundantly in the merits of Christ, obtaining the effects of this Sacrament, as discussed below. Of the institution, we have sufficiently spoken.

Now, we must say as best we can something about the dignity of this Sacrament. Here we must consider that in this Sacrament there is something called the sacrament only (*sacramentum tantum*), that is, the exterior sacramental forms themselves, and something called the reality and the sacrament (*res et sacramentum*), namely the Body and Blood of Christ, and something called the reality only (*res tantum*), that is, ecclesiastical unity and the multiple graces of the Sacrament. Now neither the Soul of Christ nor his Divinity pertain to this Sacrament or to its essence directly and by virtue of the conversion, but only concomitantly. For the conversion of the bread terminates directly in the Body of the Lord, and the transubstantiation of the wine in his Blood; yet the Soul and the Divinity of the Savior are contained in both by concomitance; and so in this Sacrament the total and complete Christ is adored and received under both of its species.

If, therefore, we speak of this Sacrament with respect to that which is directly and by virtue of its conversion contained in it, its dignity is clearly exceedingly great, namely, the dignity of the Body of Christ, which is in itself exceedingly worthy, holy, and pure, completely free from all stain of sin, assumed from the most pure blood of the most holy Virgin, supernaturally formed in an instant by the Holy Spirit. Its dignity is augmented by the fact that it was joined with the soul of Christ, ineffably holy, preeminent, and glorious above all pure creatures, from the first instant of its formation, and was intrinsically informed and actuated by it. Moreover, it was most obedient to it in all things, in no way in conflict with it. Indeed, his Body was made inestimably more dignified and worthy by the fact that, along with his Soul, it was conjoined without intermediary, hypostatically connected, and inseparably united with the eternal Word from the beginning of its formation, and hypostasized (*substantificatum*, given concrete existence) by him in the personal and uncreated being of that same

Word. Indeed, as the Damascene attests in his third book,[63] the humanity of Christ is joined to the eternal Word as an immediate animated, conjoined, and proper instrument of that Word, as the body of every man is related to his soul as an immediate, proper, and conjoined instrument of that soul.

But if we speak of the Sacrament of the Eucharist with respect to all that is contained in it, whether directly or concomitantly, then of course its dignity is absolutely infinite, since the dignity of the person of the Word alone is of infinite dignity, and the humanity of Christ is dearer to God, and as a consequence is more worthy, than the entire rest of the universe. Hence, the divine Dionysius, in his book on the *Ecclesiastical Hierarchy*,[64] declares regarding the excellence of this Sacrament that all other sacraments are ordered to it, and that it is the completion and the consummation of the others, containing the fullness of all divine gifts, as you can find written about in many places.

In light of these truths, let us consider attentively, and contemplate with all the depth that we can muster, what impudence, what foolishness, what an enormity, and how damnable it is to stand before such a great Sacrament, its consecration, and its offering irreverently and without devotion, or to receive it unworthily, to celebrate, handle, or administer it to others with a stained conscience, when the Lord, speaking to Aaron, commanded the priests of the Old Testament who offered carnal sacrifices: *Whosoever of your seed has a blemish, he shall not offer bread to God.*[65] Hence St. Ambrose says in his prayer about the Sacrament which is said before Mass: With how great a contrition of heart and flowing of tears, with what chastity of body and purity of soul should that divine and heavenly Sacrifice be celebrated, O Lord, where your Flesh is in truth eaten, where your Blood in truth is drunk, wherein things lowest and highest are united, where the holy angels are present?[66]

Let us, therefore, approach such a great Sacrament with careful preparation; let us not become ungrateful after consuming the Sacrament, nay rather, let us each day have more devotion and greater thanks. To the praise and glory of Almighty God. Amen.

---

[63] E.N. The reference is to St. John of Damascus's *An Exposition of the Orthodox Faith.*   [64] *De Eccl. hier.*, c. 3.   [65] Lev. 21:17.

[66] E.N. This prayer, a series of seven prayers to be said before Mass each day of the week, is attributed to St. Ambrose, but is now thought generally to have been authored by John of Fécamp. It is found in most missals, including the Missale Romanum of Pius V, to be recited before Mass on Monday.

THIRD SERMON
On the fitting and due preparation for the celebration and consumption of this great Sacrament.

What society does light have with darkness? 2 Cor. 6:14. How much the incomprehensibly almighty God, essentially holy and just, hates and detests sin is shown by the terrible vengeance by which he inflicts eternal punishment for every mortal sin, no matter how small. Reason itself requires this. For we see that the more just and holy a person is, the more he abhors injustice and all vice. And since the glorious God is essentially holy and just, it is certain that he possesses infinite equity and holiness—indeed, that he *is* infinite holiness and justice; therefore, he immeasurably and infinitely detests and abhors all iniquity. Also, we find to be universally the case that the more perfect a person is in any virtue, the more vehemently he detests the vice that is contrary to that virtue. Now God is infinitely perfect in all wisdom and virtue; therefore, he ineffably hates all the iniquity, foolishness, and turpitude of mortal sin. For this reason, it is written in the book of Wisdom: *To God the wicked and his wickedness are hateful.*[67] The Psalmist agrees: *You hate all the workers of iniquity.*[68] And Jeremiah exclaims to the wicked: *The Lord could no longer bear because of the evil of your doings.*[69] As Moses proclaims, he thoroughly hates all injustice.[70]

What else is it to prepare oneself for holy communion, for the worthy celebration of Mass, other than to cleanse the mind, to guard and to preserve oneself from the stain of all sin? For he who presumes to take communion or celebrate Mass with mortal sin on his conscience, by that very fact sins mortally. It is not sufficient for someone to say, "I am not conscious of mortal sin," unless he has used due diligence to ascertain whether he is in such sin, sufficiently scrutinizing his conscience so far as able to see whether there is any mortal fault hidden in it. This is the general preparation required of every priest: to clear his conscience in this way before the celebration of Mass. Indeed, as St. Augustine asserts, in every sacrifice four things should be considered: who, what, to whom, and why; this also every priest should attend to before he celebrates Mass.

Therefore, O priest of Christ, first consider yourself, who you are, that is, how defective and weak you are in nature. To this

---
[67] Wis. 14:9.   [68] Ps. 5:7.   [69] Jer. 44:22.   [70] Deut. 25:16.

consideration pertain Job's words: *Man, born of a woman, living for a short time, is filled with many miseries; who comes forth like a flower, and is destroyed, and is as fleeting as a shadow, and never continues in the same state.*[71] Consider also how culpable you are in life, how you sin every day innumerable times, at least venially, by omission and commission, by the lack of custody of your interior and exterior senses, by an unrestrained tongue, by setting a bad example or scandal, by useless thoughts, by distractions, by engaging in frivolity, by negligence even in divine things, by immoderate use of food and drink, by disordered affections towards any created thing. In these and in many similar ways, pay heed to the fact that you are guilty and are sinning so many times every day that you are unable to count them or to notice each one—indeed you need to exhort and cry out to the Lord: *Who can understand sins? From my secret ones, cleanse me, O Lord.*[72] Moreover, if (God forbid) you committed grosser excesses, if you have been impatient in reprimands and corrections or admonishments, or indignant in some way against a superior, or have obeyed him less promptly, or have comported yourself towards him irreverently, striking or spitting upon Christ in his vicar; if in your dealings with your confrère or neighbor, you have been passionate, embittered, or angered by his imperfections or omissions, and played the fool by foolishly troubling yourself, seeing—you hypocrite—the mote in your brother's eye, but not minding the beam of confusion, the gall of bitterness, and the insincerity and pretense of the Pharisee in yourself;[73] or perverting the order of charity, you have not weighed your own iniquities and faults, but, deceived by foolish curiosity, you have observed, exaggerated, and turned over in your mind the defects of others; or you have scandalized the little ones by behaving turbulently, impetuously, or dishonestly: groan more painfully, weep more abundantly, accuse yourself more heartily, punish more sharply, spurn more vehemently, and be more guarded over these things; consider how little you have progressed in the Rule and how many good things you have omitted, and amend yourself efficaciously.

Second, ponder what you are doing, what you are offering, and what you are about to do during Mass, what you are about to sacrifice. Keep in view that as an official and minister of the Church you are about to offer to God the Father his only-begotten Son, you are about to consecrate, handle, and consume the Body and

---

[71] Job 14:1–2.   [72] Ps. 18:13.   [73] Matt. 7:3.

Blood of the Savior, and to pray for the whole Church, for yourself, and for all the living and the dead. Consider the truth and dignity of this Sacrament and Sacrifice as expressed in the preceding sermon; and so be greatly ashamed and afraid to touch with your iniquitous hands the Holy of Holies, to touch the most excellent and most unblemished Body of Christ, and to receive his most precious Blood with a foul mouth, to receive as guest the King of glory and the Lord of power in a polluted, filthy, and sordid soul. Take note how greatly the most blessed John the Baptist feared to touch his exterior even so slightly when baptizing him,[74] and how can you dare to receive him, already glorified, into your interior, to consecrate and to eat him, and to drink his most sacred Blood, though you are not cleansed nor properly prepared? How did you become so deaf that you are neither awakened nor terrified by that terrible voice, that fearful trumpet of the apostolic threat, *He who eats and drinks unworthily, is he not guilty of the body and blood of the Lord?*[75] Therefore, with all diligence and trembling, with all purity, reverence, and fervor, with the greatest care and compunction prepare, examine, confess, make satisfaction, and approach in the fullness of faith and zealous devotion. So begin, so pursue, so pray, so offer, so consecrate, and so distinctly pronounce each and every word with attention. Then, when the Mass is finished, give thanks with a fervent and most devout heart, and continue to be grateful; and be solicitous in all your manner of life lest you cause offense; be afraid and handle yourself in a humble and guarded way, lest you lose the grace you have received, lest you let slip from you the fruit obtained, and so in this way let your whole life be a continuous preparation for the celebration of Mass.

Third, take heed to whom you offer such a great Sacrifice — clearly to God the Father, the King of immense majesty, the Creator of all things; before whom the entire host of angels stands with trembling; upon whom the Cherubim and Seraphim hardly dare to look; in comparison to whom the entire world is as so much dust and sand — indeed, as nothing and worthless. And how will you dare to present yourself before him unprepared, unclean, distracted, and to offer him the sacred Victim irreverently, and to assist negligent and lukewarm? And so prepare yourself, present yourself, and carry out your whole priestly and monastic office in accord with what has been previously said.

---

[74] Matt. 3:14.   [75] 1 Cor. 11:27.

Fourth, attend to why you celebrate and why you ought to celebrate Mass. Namely, for the same reasons Christ offered himself on the Cross to God the Father, you also ought to be offering him to the Father upon the altar, that is, first and foremost for the whole Church, for the conversion of unbelievers, for the reformation of the faithful, for the salvation of all men, for whatever reasons occur or needs arise, for your relatives, those committed to your care, for your benefactors, for the faithful departed, and also for those you wish to pray for a particular reason, and for your own full and steady improvement in all areas. So that you are always ready to pray and offer Mass as best you can, endeavor also to present yourself unceasingly as pleasing to God, to cleave to him as a familiar, to embrace him lovingly within yourself, to contemplate him sincerely, and to love him more fervently every day. Consider the depth of the divine counsel, the disposition of the supereminently blessed Trinity, the decree of the most high God's eternal and infinite wisdom regarding the salvation and the means of redemption of the human race by the Incarnation and Passion of the only-begotten Son of the eternal Father. Admire, glorify, venerate, and praise such great charity, mercy, and liberality displayed towards us by the superglorious Trinity, and with all your heart return, enter, relax, rest, and sleep in the rest of God. Take delight, rejoice, and unceasingly occupy yourself in these things; imprint them indelibly upon your memory and constantly recall them.

Further, just as one in the religious life ought to be more spiritual, more perfect, and more circumspect in all things, so also you, O religious priest, ought to prepare yourself for the celebration of the divine mysteries more excellently than a secular priest. For them, it is a great thing to keep God's commandments, the canons and decrees of the Fathers, and also synodal statutes. Beyond these things, you must hold fast to the monastic vows and to the commandments of sacred religion; you are bound to the observances of the rule, you are obligated to strive for perfection. If therefore, you really desire to dispose yourself for the celebration of Mass, strive above all to do this: to observe diligently and blamelessly those matters which pertain to your Order and to which you are bound by profession, to maintain discretion in all things, immovably to remain and grow in profound humility, most honest patience, and glorious meekness, to attentively fulfill the canonical hours, and the more heartily you love the most sweet Virgin, the most excellent

Mother of Christ, to read her hours too with that much more devotion. Prefer nothing to holy obedience. Be terrified of causing scandal to anyone. This also solicitously intend: not to pass any moment of time of this uncertain and short time mercifully allowed you unfruitfully. Strive unceasingly to converse with God in the secret of your heart, which is to pray without ceasing.[76] Regard the time that has been allowed to you as a most precious gift; do not cease to invest, trade, and profit by it; that is, lay up your treasures in heaven.[77] With the great Elijah say often, think more often, and contemplate most often of all: The Lord lives, and I stand in his sight today.[78] And thus unceasingly aware that the eternal Judge is always present before you, watchful, and immediately at hand, always and everywhere maintain yourself in his presence purely and reverently, fearfully, fruitfully, and fervently.

Now, having laid this foundation and kept it, if you want to do something supererogatory, it is a great thing to dispose yourself for the celebration of Mass by higher exercises, by acts of virtue at the limit of excellence, by the imitation of heroic men. Indeed, one must begin from the purgative way and climb up from it to the illuminative way, and by it attain to the perfective way. For in each of the three virtues to which you have obligated yourself by solemn vow—indeed, in the other virtues also—there are three grades, as we have stated elsewhere in many places. If you take care and strenuously strive to make progress and to ascend, you will experience how by the observance of the rule, by the faithful fulfillment of the monastic professions, by daily solicitous progress, one may arrive at the citadel of contemplation, to the perfection of divine love, to mystical theology which is nothing other than the gift of wisdom according to its perfect degree, by which the purified and fervent mind stands in contact with the sun of uncreated Wisdom, that is, in the proximate disposition to actual supernal illumination, to an intense and strong internal enkindling, to a continual or at least frequent visitation, inundation, and enrichment by the Holy Spirit, having unceasingly before itself an immense expansive region, as it were, of uncreated light, into which it can enter and affix its gaze at will; and in this way one is transformed so powerfully towards the beloved, towards the super-beloved God, that without this enkindling, alteration, and kind of defection he is able scarcely to think, to talk, and to hear about it; and thus the

---

[76] 1 Thess. 5:17.   [77] Matt. 6:20.   [78] Cf. 1 Kings 17:1.

soul is frequently raised to rapture and ecstasy, often even unexpectedly and without its own cooperation, as if the spirit had been deprived of freedom, so that it is unable to resist or evade it. This happens in the most profound mercy of God, when the Spouse's grace anticipates and blinds such a mind, and the super-gracious and super-sweet Spouse, who begins to grasp, kiss, embrace, and draw into himself the enlightened and loving soul, suddenly in the immensity of his excellence in all perfection, amiability, beauty, graciousness, wisdom, and deliciousness, so overcomes and pleasantly overwhelms the soul that it entirely passes out of itself and is enraptured in him. Thus at last he is translated from the tumult of distractions to the delight and rest of silence, and there transpires, as it were, a half hour of silence in heaven,[79] on the throne of this spirit that has been brought out into the most serene day caused by the streaming of the Sun of understanding into the mind's bridal chamber. Then the best-beloved of the Lord shall dwell confidently, and he shall abide with him all the day long as it were in a bridal chamber.[80] And so he resides in the beauty of internal peace, in the relish of eternal peace that surpasses all understanding, and in profound rest.[81] In this way, by the aforementioned perfection, a man becomes as though a confidant and counselor of God.

Your profession binds you, O religious priest and brother, to desire this perfection, to pursue it, to obtain it as far as possible to you. Do not be satisfied with narrow boundaries. Do not say: I jump as far with a little stick as with a staff.[82] Do not be diffident, do not give up. In the way of God, not to make progress is to go backwards. You have the most apt means of attaining this; use them as you ought. You can do all things in him who is ready to strengthen you.[83] Do not be like the crab, going forward now, and a little later retreating through negligence, carelessness, talkativeness, distraction, and impatience. Woe to the dissolute of heart and the lukewarm who, remiss in sacred observances and inclined to petty consolations, approach divine things in a state of dry habit, and thus confess, thus celebrate Mass, and shortly after act as if they had neither confessed nor celebrated Mass.[84] These miserable and foolish religious inflict an insult upon Christ's sacraments; the more

---

[79] Cf. Rev. 8:1.   [80] Cf. Deut. 33:12.   [81] Cf. Is. 32:18; Phil. 4:7.
[82] L. *Tam remote salio cum bacillo sicut cum baculo.* An excuse for minimalism, for doing only what is minimally necessary in the spiritual life, forgetting that love demands supererogation.
[83] Phil. 4:13.   [84] Ecclus. 2:15.

frequently they partake of it, the more negligently they do so; and therefore they are not enriched, they are not spiritually fattened, indeed, they are rather rendered lazy, shallow, and garrulous, and immoderate in food and drink. But far be such behavior from us who are spiritual; and as diligently as good secular priests guard against mortal sins, so let us guard against venial evils; and let us confess and celebrate Mass all the more fearfully and fervently, all the more remorsefully and penitently the more frequently we do so; and let us pray unceasingly for the common good of the Church and the departed. To the praise and glory of the Almighty, who is above all things the sublime and blessed God. Amen.

FOURTH SERMON
On the grace, fruits, and effects of the Sacrament.

Whoever eats this bread will live forever. John 6:59. Our first parent transgressed God's precept in Paradise, and because as a result he was stripped of original justice and his posterity was also infected and condemned through him, the just and wise God decided to restore and save the human race, and to reconcile it to himself, in no other way than through a mediator whose merits would be more acceptable to him than, or at least as pleasing and acceptable as, the offense of the first parents and of all their posterity. Furthermore, the human race could not furnish such a mediator by itself, because it was already entirely dead to its root; nor could any mere creature have such merit, such acceptability and grace before God, so great a dignity and efficacy before him. Hence, the God of glory, merciful by nature, whose nature is pure and utterly infinite goodness, who remembers his mercy even when angry,[85] whose mercies are not shut up by his anger, when his creature entirely failed and human help fell short,[86] employed his divinity, devising and providing for an effective—indeed a most effective—remedy, by conceding, providing, and sending a mediator entirely suitable for men, and one certainly infinitely more powerful and worthy to reconcile, appease, redeem, and save than any other creature was to offend and ruin.[87]

---

[85] Hab. 3:2.   [86] Ps. 76:10.
[87] "Adam was a precarious mediator of supernatural life; Christ is its essential and unchangeable mediator." Joseph Wilhelm and Thomas B. Scannell, *A Manual of Catholic Theology* (London: Kegan Paul, Trench, Trübner & Co., 1901), vol. 2, 139.

And since such a mediator could not be a mere creature, the adorable Trinity arranged for one uncreated Person to assume human nature into his hypostatic (that is, personal) and uncreated being, and to hypostasize (*substantificare*) it in himself, so that in that in one uncreated and incarnate Person there would be two perfect natures and one hypostasis or suppositum, which, by reason of the assumed humanity, would suitably be able to earn merit, and so that, on the part of the assuming Word or united Godhead, there would be an infinite fittingness, dignity, and efficacy for merit. Indeed, this incarnate Person, according to his divine nature, was simply speaking (*simpliciter*) infinitely loved and acceptable to God the Father, and according to his assumed human nature as hypostatically joined to the eternal Word, was and is more dear and more acceptable to God the Father than the entire universe. For just as a greater good was communicated to him than to all the rest of creation,[88] namely, the uncreated hypostatic being of the Word, so also was the plenitude of grace, glory, and divine gifts as great as was able to be received by created nature; hence, the merit of Christ is indefectibly great—indeed, in a way, infinite. That merit is fully and integrally contained in the Sacrament of the Altar, in the way set forth in the second sermon, but partially or participatively in the other sacraments. For all the Church's sacraments obtain their entire virtue and grace from the virtue and merits of Christ's Passion—nay also of his most holy life in this world, but especially, from the Passion, in a consummative fashion. Hence, they are said to have flowed from the side of Christ as he hung asleep on the Cross. Accordingly, the merits of Christ are communicated in diverse ways by the ecclesiastical sacraments, and by the Sacrament of the Eucharist it is accomplished by means of restorative food and a refreshing and sober cup.

Now, just as there are two established opinions regarding the mode of existence of grace in the sacraments, as has been previously addressed, so are there two established opinions about the entity and the distinction of sacramental grace. One opinion is that sacramental grace is really distinguished from habitual or sanctifying grace, and also that the grace of one sacrament is different from the grace of another sacrament (which opinion Thomas, Albert, and others follow). The other opinion is that they differ only in reason and as regards their effects.

---

[88] John 10:29.

Moreover, since this Sacrament is served to us and conferred upon us in the mode of food and drink, hence whatever bodily food and drink naturally and usually do to the body, this Sacrament does proportionally in the soul. Therefore, in the way that food and drink delight the body's taste, repair and strengthen bodily strength and restore that which has been lost, preserve and continue life, preserve the radical moistures from corruption by natural heat,[89] supply the matter for necessary growth, increase interior heat, and externally cause a healthy color, so the Sacrament of the Body and Blood of Christ delights the heart's palate, increases, repairs, and preserves the power of the soul, recuperates lost devotion, conserves the life of grace in its vigor, maintains the flow of tears, the dew of heavenly showers, and the water of salutary wisdom, lest they be harmed, dried up, or quenched by the fire of concupiscence, the flames of cupidity, or the heat of self-love; it nourishes the increase of virtues, inflames charity, and confers such tranquility, exuberance, and happiness on the heart that it overflows, causing a good and cheerful disposition of body.

One could deliver a great and protracted sermon on this subject; but here I think it is sufficient to touch on a few things. Indeed, if we fully believe that the source of all grace, the Lord Jesus Christ himself, true God and man, is really contained in this Sacrament and from his incomprehensible and most ardent love towards us, both uncreated and infused, and from his most superlatively overflowing liberality and most gracious mercy, seeks to offer and generously communicate himself in this Sacrament, and also to perform in it such marvels for us, we cannot doubt but that he is most ready to pour out abundantly and very freely confer the gifts of his grace to those who receive this Sacrament, as far as he is able, that is, provided that those who take communion do not put up obstacles, but prepare themselves with all possible diligence, especially since the Lord and Savior so earnestly and lovingly—indeed, even with horrible warnings—invites us to this most sacred communion: *Unless you eat the Flesh of the Son of Man, and drink his Blood, you shall not have life in you.*[90]

If, therefore, you wish to be filled, refreshed, delighted, and to abound in and be fattened with the graces, fruits, and effects of so

---

[89] L. *humidum radicale*. A theory stemming from Aristotle and Galen proposed for explaining the fixed and essential components of the body and its growth and aging.   [90] John 6:54.

great a Sacrament, reflect most diligently on the depths of this great mystery, all the charity, mercy, and munificence of the only-begotten Son of God—indeed, of the whole superlatively worthy Trinity—towards you; and what, how much, and what kind of things the eternal Son of the Father did, assumed, and endured for your salvation; and that he deigns to visit you in this Sacrament. And so let your heart be enkindled by these considerations to return love to him most sincerely, to receive him reverently and fervently, to return thanks to him with all your heart, to honor him with all your strength, so that you may be unceasingly solicitous not to offend in any way his most benevolent countenance, not to dishonor his immense majesty in anything, not to drive away his gracious presence at any time or place from the guest-chamber of your heart. And briefly, to conclude many things in few words, since nothing can distance, impede, separate us from him except sin, be most solicitous to avoid fault, as far as human frailty allows. Indeed, mortal sin completely impedes the salutary effects of this Sacrament and involves the recipient in the gravest outrage and dreadful guilt. Yet venial sin, especially the grosser ones, and those things which happen through negligence, lack of self-custody, and carelessness, greatly hinder, diminish, and obstruct the salubrious and sweet fruits of this heavenly Sacrament.

If therefore you are always solicitous to avoid every fault, to remove every obstacle, to make yourself a clean receptacle, you will most certainly feel and experience the excellent and glorious effects of this Sacrament. Christ, the power and wisdom of God the Father, will befriend you and enter into your soul, into your understanding and affection, into the depths of your spirit with the effusion and the communication of his opulence. He will show to the eye of your mind the riches of his glory, as he promised the soul of St. Agnes, who said: He showed to me the incomparable treasures which he would give me if I would persevere with him.[91] The Sun of wisdom will come to you with the copiously flowing beam of heavenly enlightenment, he will illumine the eyes of your heart with luminous radiance so that you consider and understand the wonders of his law,[92] and have faith along with an understanding of the things to be believed and the understanding of a purified mind. Thus illuminated and spiritually led into God's sanctuary,[93] into the abyss of uncircumscribed light, surrounded by luminescence, you will

---

[91] E.N. See, e.g., Jacob de Voragine's *Golden Legend*.
[92] Ps. 118:18.   [93] Ps. 72:17.

observe the connection and order, the harmony, reasons, foundations, and underpinnings of your faith; and it will appear to you—and it is truly the case—that there is nothing more reasonable, nothing more certain, nothing more profound than the assertions of the Christian faith, when considered altogether. Oh how suddenly, by the arrival and bright flash of this visitation and enlightenment, will the clouds of passions, the gloom of inordinate affections, the disquiet of passions, doubts over the marvels of the faith, and the obscurities of error withdraw and flee from within you, and all things within you shall be serene, tranquil, and joyful! Now when Christ enters within you in this way, he will sup with you even before the meal,[94] he will serve himself to you on a plate, saying: *Eat, my friend, and drink, and be inebriated, my beloved*,[95] eat this bread of life and understanding,[96] taste and see how sweet am I.[97] There is no perishable food that so delights, comforts, fattens, and increases mortal flesh as the contemplation, relishing, and internal refreshment of wisdom, which is Christ himself, does the most faithful immortal soul.

Then, from so resplendent an intuition of the eternal Wisdom, your affection will immediately be enkindled by his love; and then truly you will be deifyingly and supernaturally changed into Christ, inasmuch as a predominating love (especially supernaturally infused) transforms the lover into the beloved. And since this uncreated Beloved is truly infinitely lovable, and at the same time immensely efficacious in drawing and enrapturing into himself, in altering and inflaming the apex of affectivity,[98] he in turn draws the lover's mind so strongly, so predominantly and graciously into himself, into the riches of his glory, into the ocean of delights of his bliss, that the apex of the mind is completely absorbed and immersed into that abyss of the Godhead, in the admiration, gazing-into, love, relish, and pleasure of which he falls away completely from himself, and the whole mind is so vehemently intent upon God, that all inferior sensitive powers are suspended, the harmony [of body and soul] is restricted as if by a kind of freezing,[99] the body is deprived of sense,

---

[94] Rev. 3:20.   [95] Songs 5:1.   [96] Ecclus. 15:3.   [97] Ps. 33:9.
[98] E.N. The *apex affectivae*, the peak or apex of affectivity, the summit of the human will, is where the most elevated affection of man—the affection towards God occurs—and hence the contemplative or mystical union occurs. Denis may have drawn this concept from his fellow mystic and theologian, the Carthusian Hugh of Balma (fl. thirteenth cent.).
[99] L. *harmonia*. The *harmonia* theory of the soul views the soul as the *harmonia* of the body. The soul is what harmonizes the various faculties of the body.

its members become stiff, the power of movement fails, and the flesh lies immobile as a log: and man does not then live an animal human life, but for a time only an intellectual or deiform life.

Much can be read about these things in books of certain holy persons, indeed, and of certain innocent and highly favored young women, who were led to such wonderful and divine perfections, not only for a time or rarely or for very short durations, but even very frequently and for long spans of time, and sometimes seven days a week or nearly every day, at every holy communion and celebration of Mass, especially at the elevation. But if anyone does not believe these things, it can be shown to him even in these days. Here and there devout maids and women, and perhaps some men, dwell and abide in the world and in the cloister in whom these and similar things take place and are seen, and to whom the almighty and eternal God shows his uncertain and hidden wisdom.[100] These persons, through such supernatural gifts of grace, are assuredly evident signs and sufficient proof of the truth of the Christian faith, especially to those who by experience or otherwise know how these things take place. Indeed, by supernatural anointings, enkindlings, mystical visions, transformations, illuminations, relishings, and raptures of this kind, the human mind is especially strengthened in faith, in the Catholic truth, and in ecclesiastical unity, in which by these experiences it is immovably established and superlatively clearly certified.

Indeed by these very things, the holy Doctors of the Church, the blessed Fathers Jerome, Augustine, Gregory, Ambrose, and innumerable other holy men and most enlightened men, were made so certain and steadfast in the truth of the faith; and these holy Doctors also in their books, to the praise and glory of the Creator, testified that these things happened to or were bestowed on them, and that they had experienced these and greater things. Indeed, in his Rule, the glorious Jerome admitted that he had frequently been absorbed, alienated, and asleep for entire weeks without interruption in raptures of this kind. The Church militant's sky was decked with innumerable such splendid stars; such witnesses we have to our faith. And today the number of believers is not greater than the number of qualified and most trustworthy witnesses, whose manner of living, faith, and doctrine were most abundantly approved and confirmed by most innumerable excellent miracles possible to God alone. These things escaped your notice, O reprobate and unhappy

---

[100] Ps. 50:8.

Averroës; and clearly, if you had ever, even if only once, partaken of the aforementioned effects and fruits of the most glorious Sacrament, you would not have spoken so blasphemously.

And so, in order to obtain these effects, we must strenuously prepare ourselves to taste the aforesaid fruits of the Sacrament; let us persist in being unceasingly fearful, circumspect, and fervent before the most High; let us detest with an infinite horror all dissimulation, duplicity, vanity, carnality, and diabolical ambition, which is the cause to innumerable sins; before the most high Judge let us be sincere and just in all things, wholly transformed into most sincere affection for the whole honest good, and inextinguishably enkindled with zeal for the divine honor and the common good. To the praise and glory of Almighty God.

FIFTH SERMON
On the impediments to celebrating Mass and communing; and especially whether it is licit for men in a State of passion or carrying bitterness in their heart to take communion or to celebrate Mass.

Priests that come to the Lord, let them be sanctified, lest he strike them. Exodus 19:22. It is manifest that the proper matter, form, and intention are required for the consecration of this Sacrament; but now I intend to speak of the impediments without the removal or avoidance of which it is not possible to celebrate Mass or take communion licitly. In the first place it is necessary for a man, having duly examined his conscience, not to be conscious of a mortal sin that has not been repented and confessed, although in some cases a purpose to confess at an opportune time may suffice. Hence, every mortal sin is an impediment to taking communion and celebrating Mass. Nevertheless, for special reasons some sins render a man particularly unworthy for the reception and celebration of this most high Sacrament. For as has been shown,[101] this Sacrament is chiefly the Sacrament of charity and unity, of peace and unanimity, from which flow the bowels of piety and the affections of sweetness. Hence, especially those things which are contrary to this virtue — namely, hatred, rancor, envy, dissension, division, confusion, discord, cruelty, and bitterness — impede the reception of this Sacrament. Moreover, since this is the Sacrament that is maximally spiritual,

---

[101] E.N. In the First and Fourth Sermons.

actual devotion is demanded for its celebration and reception; hence, vices of the flesh and those things which vehemently depress, implicate, and disturb the mind are known to impede one from it. As a figure of these things, in the Old Testament some members of the tribe of Levi and Aaron were prohibited from offering the legal sacrifices, among which were especially identified those suffering from hernia, which evidently refers to those with the weight of turpitude in their hearts.[102] Therefore it is highly incumbent upon priests—especially those who are in religious orders—to fulfil that which the Apostle said: *Be followers of God, like beloved children, and walk in love as Christ has also loved us;*[103] *be kind to each other, merciful, forgiving each even as God in Christ forgave you;*[104] and again, *I beseech you in the Lord that you may be found worthy to the vocation to which you are called, with all humility and meekness, with patience, supporting each other in charity, careful to serve the unity of the Spirit in the bond of peace.*[105] The Apostle wrote these and many similar things, not only for religious, but for all the faithful, also secular priests and married persons. They pertain to all Christians, as does the Apostle's exhortation here: *Do not be wise in your conceits, to no man rendering evil for evil, providing good things, not only in the sight of God, but also in the sight of all men; if it be possible, as much as is in you, have peace with all men.*[106] So also indeed does the Savior's command apply to every believer: *Love your enemies, and do good to those who hate you, and pray for those who persecute and calumniate you.*[107]

In fact, all the evangelical counsels, the three vows of the religious, and all their statutes are ordered to the perfect fulfillment of the precept of charity. But if secular priests are bound to these, what is one to think of religious priests who are so easily offended, angered, indignant, contentious, who go with loathing, rancor, and severity in their hearts, so that they do not desire to impart a sign of benevolence or kind word to their confrères, indeed who are not filled with the sweetness of charity, but rather with the sting of the gall of bitterness, and miserably afflict themselves, having their present and future dwelling in hell, unless they come to their senses and do suitable penance? And you who behave this way, know you not that there is no worse form of life than to dwell together bodily, but not in mind, without concord? Certainly, as the holy Fathers

---

[102] Lev. 21:20.
[103] Eph. 5:1–2.
[104] Eph. 4:32.
[105] Eph. 4:1–3.
[106] Rom. 12:16–18.
[107] Matt. 5:44.

attest, the man in religious life who does not zealously and habitually strive in the cloister to restrain and prevail over himself daily, to abandon his own inclinations, to overcome the impulses of his passions, to obey his superiors, and to deny and mortify whatever is contrary to charity is much worse than had he remained in the world, or even worse than worldly men. For as the Lord asserted, *to whomsoever much is given, much is required*;[108] and the prince of the Apostles teaches that it is better not to have known the way of justice, than to turn back after having known it.[109] Is such a person striving for perfection as his religious profession obliges him to?

Further, note that to feel the movements, pricks, and impulses of the passions is not immediately worthy of condemnation; to consent to them is. Yet to dwell on them and not to reject them sufficiently quickly and vigorously is not without fault; and unless reason resists, dissents, and prevails, it becomes mortal. But he who is struck by these emotions and stands strong in the fight, invoking the Lord, is not prohibited from taking communion or celebrating Mass. For some people by their natural dispositions are prone to such goads of passions, and they can approach the Sacrament as a source of salutary help, for the grace of quickly resisting and prevailing salubriously over them, in such a wise that by constant mediation and attentive reflection on our Lord's Passion they endeavor to sweeten the bitterness of their passions, to endure their adversities with equanimity, and to rejoice and give thanks in reproof and correction, in salubrious admonition and instruction.

Moreover, since celebrating Mass is such a privileged and noble work, especially honoring of the superlatively most excellent Trinity, excellently commemorative of the Passion of Christ and of the rest of his mysteries and benefits, and a most powerful aid to the whole Church—both the living and the dead—priests must be admonished not to cease from celebrating Mass daily unless some special obstacle arises. Indeed, they should so live their lives, so strive to make progress in this way, that they are as worthy as can be, inasmuch as human frailty allows, to celebrate Mass daily, practicing that which the arch-Apostle, St. Peter said: *Be all of one mind, having compassion on one another, being lovers of brotherhood, merciful, modest, humble.*[110] And also that which St. Paul teaches: *Put on therefore, as the elect of God, with bowels of mercy, benignity, humility, modesty, patience, supporting one another in charity, and*

---

[108] Luke 12:48.   [109] Cf. 2 Pet. 2:21.   [110] 1 Pet. 3:8.

forgiving one another, if any have a complaint against another.[111] And again: *If there be any consolation in Christ, if any comfort of charity, if any society of spirit, if any bowels of commiseration, fulfill my joy, that you may be of one mind, of one accord, agreeing in sentiment, nothing being done through contention, neither by vain glory, but in humility, let each esteem others better than themselves.*[112] *Do all things without murmurings that you may be blameless and sincere children of God.*[113]

Since these and like apostolic and evangelical examples are enjoined upon all Christians, let us consider how vile, detestable, and shameful, how repulsive and abominable it is for religious to fall short on these points, so that they are quarrelsome, contentious, and troublesome to each other, indignant, bitter, and partisan, not considering that which the holy Apostle James wrote: *If you have bitter zeal, and there be contentions in your hearts, glory not, and be not liars against the truth. For this is not wisdom descending from above, but earthly, sensual, devilish. For where envying and contention is, there is inconstancy, and every evil work. But the wisdom that is from above, first indeed is chaste, then peaceable, modest, easy to be persuaded, consenting to the good, full of mercy and good fruits.*[114] Oh how full of good counsel are these words! How sweet would be his life, even now, who lived up to them! And how far from these words are those unyielding brothers, self-minded men, children of their own senses, who are burdensome to themselves and others! Surely, he who is truly wise, is *sweet to his own soul.*[115] Yet *there is no understanding where bitterness abounds.*[116] Thus Moses said to the stiff-necked people: *Let there not be among you a root bringing forth gall and bitterness.*[117] And Paul said to all the faithful: *Follow peace with all men, and holiness: without which no man shall see God, looking diligently, lest any root of bitterness springing should hinder, and by it many be defiled.*[118] For, as Climacus says, one dog frequently casts the entire flock into confusion, and infects many sheep with one disease.

Therefore, *let us follow after the things that are of peace, and keep the things that are of edification one towards another.*[119] *Now may the God of patience and of comfort grant* to all of us to be of *one mind towards one another,* so that with *one mind, and with one mouth* we may *glorify God and the Father of our Lord Jesus Christ* in the Holy Spirit.[120] And let everyone of you *please his neighbor unto good, to*

---

[111] Col. 3:12–13; Eph. 4:2.   [112] Phil. 2:1–3.   [113] Phil. 2:14–15.
[114] James 3:14–17.   [115] Ecclus. 37:22.   [116] Ecclus. 21:15.   [117] Deut. 29:18.
[118] Heb. 12:14–15.   [119] Rom. 14:19.   [120] Rom. 15:5–6.

edification,[121] that we may be one in the Lord,[122] always peaceable and in harmony in him. *Blessed are the peaceful, for they shall be called the sons of God.*[123] But they who disturb and they who are unruly imitate their father, the devil, by whose envious hatred *death came into the world*: and they who excite dissension and scandal follow his example and *are on his side*.[124] And we know that *woe to that man by whom scandal comes*.[125] For as our lawgiver has testified, he that shall scandalize one of these little ones, *it were better for him that a millstone should be hanged about his neck, and that he should be drowned in the depth of the sea*.[126] If it is so damnable to scandalize but one little one, how much more damnable must it be to scandalize many in this manner, by impeding the advancement of others, by retarding their progress, by extinguishing their fervor, and by inducing them to slacken in good works.

Finally, may diabolical evil, detraction, whisperings, seeds of discord be infinitely far from us. And let us carefully avoid frivolity, dissoluteness, immoderate laughter, as poisons to spiritual progress. For he who is without fear, cannot be justified.[127] And *he who fears God, neglects nothing*.[128] Finally, in all that we do, let us place ourselves in the order of divine love, and let us unceasingly and wisely refer all our interior and exterior practices to the most fervent and sincere love of God and neighbor (but especially of God). To the praise and glory of the Almighty, who is above all things God sublime and blessed. Amen.

SIXTH SERMON
On frequently and devoutly partaking in the holy communion of the Eucharist.

He who eats this bread, shall live forever. John 6:59. Our Lord Jesus Christ, who is superlatively ardent, immense, and uncreated love according to his divinity, and according to his humanity is so full of holy, spiritual, and infused love that no mere creature can possess more than he: this sweetest only-begotten Son of the eternal Father himself, like a most ardent furnace filled with a fire of holy love, showed us his charity in manifold and copious ways, but especially in four ways.

---

[121] Rom. 15:2. [122] Cf. Gal. 3:28. [123] Matt. 5:9. [124] Wis. 2:24–25.
[125] Matt. 18:7. [126] Matt. 18:6. [127] Ecclus. 1:28. [128] Eccl. 7:19.

The first is that he joined our nature, true humanity, to his divine nature in a personal and proximate union, that is, in a unity of person, so that he, Jesus Christ, the Church's bridegroom, most beautiful in form among the sons of men,[129] in a most true sense became man,[130] while remaining unchangingly God. And he united our nature to himself and assumed it as his bride, in the womb of the most holy and most pure Virgin, whence on the day of his Nativity he emerged as a bridegroom from his bridal chamber, as a giant of twin natures,[131] exulting to run the way of this life and the present pilgrimage, until he offered himself on the altar of the Cross as an oblation and sacrifice to God the Father for the redemption and salvation of those whose nature he assumed.[132] And since love is a unitive power all the more perfectly and more closely uniting the lover with his beloved the more fervent and strong that love is, we recognize the most burning and most powerful love of the Son of God towards our nature and the human race, especially towards his elect, from the fact that he joined our nature to his divinity in a personal union—the most perfect and close union possible for creatures. Hence, we ought endlessly to rejoice in, most devoutly give thanks to, and most vehemently be inflamed towards Almighty God, who is the highest, pure, and infinite good, because the Lord God himself, the only Son of God the Father, became one of us, our brother, a sharer in our nature.

Second, he displayed his charity towards us by dwelling among men, as foretold by Zechariah: *Sing praise and rejoice, O daughter of Sion, for behold I come and will dwell in the midst of you.*[133] Hence also Baruch fore-announced: *He who made the stars, this is our God, afterwards he was seen upon the earth, and conversed with men.*[134] The holy evangelist John proclaimed that this had been fulfilled: *The Word*, he says, *became flesh, and dwelt among us, and we beheld his glory*, etc.[135] Oh how lovingly and sweetly, how fruitfully and salubriously, how holily and how exemplarily did he converse among men in all poverty, with most profound humility, with most steadfast patience, with most immovable meekness, and with the fullest charity!

Third, he showed us his most excellent charity at the Last Supper by instituting the most worthy Sacrament of his Body and Blood,[136] in which he bequeathed then and now also daily bestows

---

[129] Ps. 44:3.
[130] John 1:14.
[131] Cf. Ps. 18:6
[132] Eph. 5:2; Heb. 10:14–15.
[133] Zech. 2:10.
[134] Baruch 3:35-38.
[135] John 1:14.
[136] Matt. 26:26–28; 1 Cor. 11:23–25.

himself on us as a most salubrious food and drink for our souls. He gives himself to us in this Sacrament in such a way that he is both the giver and gift, the refresher and the food, the host and guest, and the life-giving bread, the heavenly manna, containing in himself every delight and sweet relish.[137] This is the supreme charity and highest liberality: wherein the giver bestows his very self.

Fourth, Jesus Christ showed us his most perfect love by offering himself to God the Father on the wood of the Cross for our sake, to reconcile us to the eternal Father and free us from all sin and infernal punishment, to obtain and merit for us charity, grace, and the gifts of the Holy Spirit in the present life, and thereafter salvation and eternal glory in the region of the Saints who enjoy the most superlatively glorious God without end. Certainly, as he himself proclaimed, *a greater love than this no man has, that he lay down his life for his friends.*[138] And it was not enough for him to offer himself once and for all to the most high Father out of the ineffable charity, kindness, and liberality of his most benign soul, but in addition he ordained and decreed that he should be offered daily for our salvation in the sacred and divine ceremony of the Mass, at which undoubtedly angels are present and attend with ineffable reverence. And not only does he invite and admonish us to receive this most excellent Sacrament, this angelic bread, this pledge of the most blissful refreshment to be provided in the heavenly paradise, nay, he even commands us to do it, in a most terrifying fashion speaking in the Gospel: *Except you eat the Flesh of the Son of Man, and drink his Blood, you shall have no life in you.*[139] Further, he promises the most exuberant fruit to those who devoutly eat this most salutary food, namely, the life of grace, the progress of virtues in this exile, and the life of glory and an eternally satisfying refreshment in the heavenly palace.

Regarding these things, one can ask whether it is permitted to devout laypersons to communicate daily or on alternate days each week. St. Thomas responds to this in the fourth book of his *Commentary on the Sentences.*[140] What happens in this Sacrament bears a likeness to what occurs in bodily nourishment. For when there is a continuous loss of natural humidness or radical moisture through the action of natural heat or physical exertion, the body must frequently consume nourishment to restore that which has been lost,

---

[137] Wis. 16:20.   [138] John 15:13.   [139] John 6:54.
[140] *Super Sent.*, lib. 4, d. 12, q. 3.

otherwise the continual loss leads to death. Correspondingly, our innate concupiscence and occupations with external matters leads to an ebbing of devotion and internal fervor; hence, the loss must be restored by the consumption of life-giving food. This response accords with the words of St. Ambrose, who asserts: This bread is "daily"; receive daily that which is useful daily for your salvation.[141]

Hence Thomas again affirms:[142] In this Sacrament two things are required on the part of the recipient. The first is desire for union with Christ, which love accomplishes. The second is reverence for the Sacrament, which belongs to the gift of fear. The first of these encourages daily or frequent celebration of Mass and communion; the second discourages one therefrom. Therefore, if one knows from certain experience that the fervor of charity and reverence towards the Sacrament grow in him as a result of the daily celebration of Mass and taking of communion, it is proper for such a person to celebrate Mass and to take communion daily. However, if he feels that daily communion will not increase these things within oneself, such a person ought to abstain sometimes, so that afterwards he might approach with greater reverence and fervor; indeed, he must also strive daily to acquire more fully the effects of this Sacrament. And as far as frequency is concerned, it is up to each person's judgment and discretion. Therefore, Augustine says: If one person says the Eucharist is not to be taken daily, but another affirms that it is to be received daily, let each one do that which he believes to be pious. And he proves this by the example of Zacchaeus and the Centurion, the first of whom welcomed Christ into his house rejoicing out of the fervor of charity, while the other out of reverence said: Lord I am not worthy that you should enter under my roof, etc.[143]

These counsels agree in every respect with the responses of Peter of Tarentaise, who was Supreme Pontiff, and Richard of Middleton in his writings on the fourth book of the *Sentences*, in the twelfth distinction.[144] The same are given in the *Summa Durandi*,[145] the

---

[141] Cf. Sermon 84, PL 39, 1908 (Augustine); *De Sacramentis*, V, 25, PL 16, 452 (Ambrose). [142] E.N. *Super Sent.*, lib. 4, d. 12, q. 3, a. 1, qc. 2, co.
[143] Luke 19:6; Matt. 8:8.
[144] E.N. Richard of Middleton (ca. 1249–ca. 1308) was a Franciscan scholastic philosopher and theologian.
[145] E.N. *Summa Durandi* is perhaps a reference to the *Summa Collectionum pro Confessionibus Audiendis* of the Franciscan Durand of Champagne (d. ca. 1307), but it also may be a reference to St. Durandus of Saint-Pourçain (ca. 1275–ca. 1332) and his famous commentary on the *Sentences*.

*Summa Confessorum,*¹⁴⁶ and in the *Summa Pisani.*¹⁴⁷ These authorities demonstrate the indiscretion of those who imprudently censure persons who are very devout and who burn with a singular affection for the daily reception of this most worthy Sacrament, in whom also the effects and signs of especial devotion are evidently observed. Moreover, in the early Church, when devotion was strong and the Blood of Christ was still warm in the hearts of the faithful, all Christians took communion daily. Whence also Pope Anacletus asserted: After the consecration is finished, all who do not want to be expelled from the ecclesiastical thresholds shall take communion; otherwise, they should be barred from entering the church. Hence Albert also said this: Between the attraction to celebrate Mass or to take communion caused by the fervor of charity and the inhibition arising from the fear of reverence, a temperate discretion charts a middle course.

But if the fervor of charity dominates in some persons, it is better to counsel them to approach daily. Yet it is also necessary to exercise care in this lest from the frequency of sacred communion they become less solicitous in preparing themselves daily with all their strength for the worthy reception of such a great Sacrament; indeed, they should unceasingly strive for greater purity of heart, recollection, fervor, and steadfastness in God.

Moreover, some extremely devout persons, whose pious and loving souls are often suddenly so graciously and powerfully seized and overtaken by the Holy Spirit that they are drawn away and estranged from themselves and enraptured into God, and are so strongly intent and suspended in him that they perceive nothing else except him and the things which are shown to them and which they see in spirit—such people, I say, can confidently and salubriously receive this Sacrament every day, and most heartily return thanks for such a gift to the Most High God, whom they embrace in themselves with all their hearts; the clear, face-to-face, and beatific vision and the most sweet, full, and eternal fruition of whom they so fervently desire, pant for, and sigh for that they swoon with love and are deprived for a time of bodily strength, senses, and motion. And since they are not yet able to behold and relish the heavenly Bridegroom clearly and sweetly within themselves, their principal consolation is to receive him in the Sacrament; and they

---

¹⁴⁶ E.N. The *Summa Confessorum* by the Dominican John of Freiburg (ca. 1250–1314).

¹⁴⁷ E.N. The *Summa Pisani* of the Dominican Bartholomew of San Concordio (ca. 1260–1347).

are wondrously comforted thereby because they are so closely united to the source of all grace and all the virtues.

Indeed, this very union or communion seems to be in a certain way more fruitful and salubrious than the vision and enjoyment of their Bridegroom Jesus Christ in the heavenly fatherland of the blessed—not because it is as perfect and delightful, but because it is greatly meritorious and obtains more abundant fruit and glory. This does not apply to the vision and enjoyment of the blessed, which is a reward, not a merit, but rather the end and recompense of all merit. Further, faith has the most important place in this Sacrament. And this communion is the figuration, beginning, and foretaste of that future blessed refreshment, that most delicious vision, that superlatively sweet enjoyment of the Saints in heaven. And the more we now receive Christ, God and man, with a purer mind, with a firmer faith, and with a more ardent affection, the more joyfully and felicitously shall we gaze upon his divinity, even the superlatively most glorious Trinity, in the heavenly paradise after the miserable exile of this life. But the carnal man does not grasp these things, nor does he taste the sweetness of this heavenly food; therefore, he sins gravely when he presumes to judge such spiritual and most devout persons, who are not to be judged according to the common and regular laws, since such persons are in a special way moved, directed, and inspired by the Holy Spirit. Such persons can say with a humble mind that which the Apostle said: *And I live, now not I; but Christ lives in me.*[148]

Bonaventure agrees with the above notions in his *Commentary* on the fourth book of the *Sentences*. If someone, he says, were always ready, it would always be useful to receive this Sacrament (that is, once daily), since having a clean receptacle, he could eat this food with special reverence and devotion and manifold fruits, as in the early Church. Therefore, the faithful in the early Church were allowed to receive daily. Afterwards, once charity grew cold, set times to communicate were established—not that it was illicit to receive more frequently, but so that people at least would.

Therefore, to communicate daily out of special devotion does not prejudice or derogate from these laws of the Church. Indeed, some priests, even priests in the religious life, are negligent and lazy, nay quite reprehensible and slothful in this regard, who abstain from the celebration of this great Sacrament, out of feigned humility or

---

[148] Gal. 2:20.

reverence, but really omit the celebration of Mass on just about any occasion or for any trivial excuse. If they really abstained out of virtue, they would not dare to behave so irreverently and lukewarmly in their other acts of divine worship. Further, such negligence and lukewarmness of heart are exceedingly unbefitting and unlawful for any religious, since the religious state is a state of perfection, or at least for acquiring perfection. For this reason, those in the religious life are strongly bound by their calling and profession to strive for spiritual progress and the fervor of charity, and to pray assiduously and to offer Mass for those who support them by alms.

Finally, although it may be commendable to abstain for a time from the celebration of Mass and communion out of humility and fear, yet it is much better out of fervent charity, with special devotion and zeal for the common good, to prepare oneself to celebrate Mass or take communion daily, because charity is more sublime a virtue than humility, and especially because this Sacrament is the Sacrament of all charity, liberality, and grace, and is medicine for the soul. And though it is equally good and meritorious for a priest, as far as he himself is concerned, to cease from the celebration of Mass out of humility, and to celebrate out of charity, yet as far as others are concerned, it is much more fruitful and salubrious to approach, because by approaching he provides manifold help to himself and to the whole Church, both the living and the dead, especially to those who are present, and those for whom he celebrates and prays.

I write and transmit this brief letter to you, most devoted handmaids of Christ, that is, to you, Mechtilde, who lie bedridden day and night in Noviomagus on account of the weakness of your body, fall asleep in unremitting raptures, and refresh yourself in Love, your body so asleep and inflexible that you appear as lifeless as wood or stone, and no part of you can be moved without moving your whole body.[149] And to you also, Christina, justly called Christina from 'Christ,' and who, like Christ, lately bore five wounds on your body, stigmata that are seen on you even to this day. And you also Catherine, who for a long time, even three years or more, took

---

[149] E.N. I have not been able to trace these three "devoted handmaids of Christ," and I assume, based upon Denis's words, that they were contemporaries of Denis and not the commonly known female canonized saints with those names. Noviomagus probably refers to Nijmegen (Netherlands), since Denis the Carthusian's priory was in Roermond, and Nijmegen is only 95 kilometers to the north.

no bodily nourishment except for a little cup of that liquid which remains after cheese is made from milk, and yet nevertheless you remained robust and ruddy, imbued with lively color, just like the other two just mentioned. I humbly recommend myself and my confrères to your most sincere prayers, and with all sincerity desire your unceasing progress, I, brother Denis, whose prayers, however meager, and whose ideas, which you have no need of, you have so frequently requested —

END

✳ ✳ ✳

For a monk cloistered for most of his life in a Charterhouse at Roermond, a city now in the Limburg province of the Netherlands—and a monk, moreover, bound by a strict discipline of silence—DENIS THE CARTHUSIAN (1402–1471) left a remarkably vivid and far-reaching legacy. Author of some 180 works arranged in forty-two volumes, he stands at the crossroads of the waning Middle Ages and the early Renaissance. Informally regarded as a saint and honored with the title *Doctor Ecstaticus*, Denis, clothed outwardly in the rough woolen habit of the Carthusians, adorned his mind with a richly multicolored intellectual inheritance.

He was above all a follower of Christ: an indefatigable commentator on Sacred Scripture (having written on every book of the Bible), a devoted student of the Fathers and Doctors of the Church, a disciple of St. Bruno, founder of his order, an heir to the mystical theology attributed to Dionysius the Areopagite, a loyal follower of St. Thomas Aquinas, a friend and correspondent of the great polymath Nicholas of Cusa, and a defender of the controversial Augustinian mystic and fellow Lowlander, Blessed John of Ruusbroec. For centuries, the study of his philosophically and theologically encyclopedic works was considered indispensable: *Qui Dionysium legit, nihil non legit*—"He who reads Denis leaves nothing unread."

That such a genius should now lie hidden beneath modernity's reductionist shadow and the scarcity of translators from Latin is a misfortune. It is to be hoped that recent English translations of his works—including this volume on the Eucharist and the Mass—may help remedy this eclipse and restore Denis the Carthusian to his rightful place in the Church's living memory.

www.ingramcontent.com/pod-product-compliance
Lightning Source LLC
Chambersburg PA
CBHW020351170426
43200CB00005B/131